The Phonology of Mono

Summer Institute of Linguistics and
The University of Texas at Arlington
Publications in Linguistics

Publication 140

Publications in Linguistics are published jointly by SIL International and the University of Texas at Arlington. The series is a venue for works covering a broad range of topics in linguistics, especially the analytical treatment of minority languages from all parts of the world. While most volumes are authored by members of SIL, suitable works by others will also form part of the series.

Series Editor

Donald A. Burquest
University of Texas at Arlington

Mary Ruth Wise
SIL International

Volume Editor

Rhonda Hartell-Jones

Production Staff

Bonnie Brown, Managing Editor
Margaret González, Compositor
Kirby O'Brien, Graphic Artist

The Phonology of Mono

Kenneth S. Olson

SIL International
and
The University of Texas at Arlington

© 2005 SIL International
Library of Congress Catalog No: 2005-926928
ISBN-13: 978-1-55671-160-2
ISBN-10: 1-55671-160-3
ISSN: 1040-0850

Printed in the United States of America

All rights reserved. No part of this publication may be reproduced, stored in a retrieval system, or transmitted in any form or by any means—electronic, mechanical, photocopy, record, or otherwise—without the express permission of SIL International. However, short passages, generally understood to be within the limits of fair use, may be quoted without written permission.

Copies of this and other publications of SIL International may be obtained from

International Academic Bookstore
SIL International
7500 W. Camp Wisdom Road
Dallas, TX 75236-5699
Voice: 972-708-7404
Fax: 972-708-7433
Email: academic_books@sil.org
Internet: http://www.ethnologue.com

This book is dedicated to the Mono people of the
Democratic Republic of the Congo

Contents

List of Figures ix
List of Tables xii
Preface xiii
Abbreviations xv

1 Introduction 1
   1.1 Demography and Geography 2
   1.2 Classification 4
   1.3 Ethnology and History 9
   1.4 The Sociolinguistic Situation 12
   1.5 Dialects 14
   1.6 Previous Research on Mono 15
   1.7 Remarks 16
   1.8 Salient Findings 17

2 Phonemes 21
   2.1 Consonants 23
   2.2 Vowels 34
   2.3 Distribution of Phonemes 38

3 Tone 43
   3.1 Lexical Tone 43
   3.2 Grammatical Tone 46
   3.3 Distribution of Tones 49

4 Labialization and Palatalization 53
- 4.1 Description 55
- 4.2 Suggested Interpretations 58
- 4.3 Distribution of Labialization and Palatalization 62

5 The Syllable 65
- 5.1 Syllable Types 66

6 Word Shapes 73
- 6.1 Nominal Word Shapes 74
- 6.2 Verbal Word Shapes 82
- 6.3 Adverbial Word Shapes 83
- 6.4 Grammatical Function Word Shapes 85

7 Morphology 87
- 7.1 Grammatical Categories 88
- 7.2 Phonological Processes Which Cross Morpheme or Word Boundaries 116
- 7.3 Summary 120

8 Acoustic Phonetics 121
- 8.1 Consonants 123
- 8.2 Vowels 145
- 8.3 Secondary Articulations 160
- 8.4 Summary and Further Research 163

Appendices 165
- A. Texts 165
- B. Wordlist 183
- C. Recordings 221
- D. Additional Examples 233

References 275

Author Index 285
Subject Index 287

List of Figures

Figure 1.1. The languages of northwestern DRC.. 3
Figure 1.2. The locations of the Mono people and their ancestors. . . 11
Figure 2.1. Consonant phonemes in Mono. 23
Figure 2.2. Articulation of a portion of the word àwĕtòrò 'activator in an animal trap' (Speaker A, cf. chapter 8). Frames are 30 ms apart. From Olson and Hajek (1999). 26
Figure 2.3. Vowel phonemes in Mono. 34
Figure 2.4. Reanalyzed Mono vowel system. 36
Figure 8.1. Waveform and spectrogram of the possible word aw̌a (Speaker K). 124
Figure 8.2. Waveform and spectrogram of the word áw̌árá 'fierceness' (Speaker K). 125
Figure 8.3. Waveform and spectrogram of the word jāw̌èlè 'catfish' (Speaker A). 125
Figure 8.4. Waveform and spectrogram of the word āwā 'road' (Speaker K). 126
Figure 8.5. Waveform and spectrogram of the word ⱳílí 'calf, shin'. Voicing precedes a word-initial labial flap (Speaker A). 126
Figure 8.6. Waveform and spectrogram of the word kɔ́-w̌à 'to send' (Speaker A). 127
Figure 8.7. Waveform of the possible word aba (Speaker K). . . . 129
Figure 8.8. Waveform of the possible word aɓa (Speaker K). . . . 129
Figure 8.9. Waveform of the possible word ada (Speaker K). . . . 130
Figure 8.10. Waveform of the possible word aɗa (Speaker K). . . . 130
Figure 8.11. Waveform and spectrogram of the possible word aba (Speaker K). Beginning and end of closure are indicated by the arrows.. 131
Figure 8.12. Waveform and spectrogram of the possible word aɓa (Speaker K). 131
Figure 8.13. Waveform of the word bá-àtí 'low' (Speaker K). 132
Figure 8.14. Waveform of the word kòɓà 'spirit' (Speaker K).. . . . 132
Figure 8.15. Close-up of waveform of the possible word aɓa (Speaker A). 133
Figure 8.16. Close-up of waveform of the possible word aɗa (Speaker A). 133
Figure 8.17. Close-up of waveform of the possible word aɓa (Speaker K). 133

Figure 8.18. Close-up of waveform of the possible word *aɗa* (Speaker K). 134
Figure 8.19. Close-up of waveform of the word *kòɓà* 'spirit' (Speaker K). 134
Figure 8.20. Close-up of waveform of the word *èɗè* 'who' (Speaker K). 134
Figure 8.21. Waveform of the word *kɔ́-ɓì* 'to hit' (Speaker K). . . . 135
Figure 8.22. Waveform and spectrogram of the word *kɔ́-gbɔ̀* 'to receive, to find' (Speaker K). 137
Figure 8.23. Waveform and spectrogram of the word *ágbá* 'dugout canoe' (Speaker K). 138
Figure 8.24. Waveform and spectrogram of the word *àbá* 'father' (Speaker K). 138
Figure 8.25. Waveform and spectrogram of the word *bàgá* 'cheek' (Speaker K). 139
Figure 8.26. Waveform and spectrogram of the word *kádá* 'oil' (Speaker K). 140
Figure 8.27. Waveform and spectrogram of the word *kpōkɔ̀* 'big hoe' (Speaker K). 141
Figure 8.28. Waveform and spectrogram of the possible word *amba* (Speaker K). 143
Figure 8.29. Plot of F_1 versus F_2 (Speaker K). 148
Figure 8.30. Plot of F_1 versus F_3 (Speaker K). 149
Figure 8.31. Plot of F_1 versus F_2' (Speaker K). 150
Figure 8.32. Plot of F_1 versus F_2 (Speaker K) with location of American English vowels [ɛ], [æ], and [ɑ] indicated. . 151
Figure 8.33. Spectrogram of Mono vowels spoken in isolation (Speaker K). 152
Figure 8.34. Waveform and spectrogram of the word *ōpōrō* 'egg' spoken with rapid and normal speaking rates (Speaker K). 154
Figure 8.35. Waveform and spectrogram of the word *ámbálá* 'bait' spoken with rapid and normal speaking rates (Speaker A). 154
Figure 8.36. Waveform and spectrogram of the word *mbàlà* 'elephant' spoken with rapid and normal speaking rates (Speaker K). 155
Figure 8.37. Waveform and spectrogram of the possible word *aba* (Speaker K). 157

List of Figures

Figure 8.38. Waveform and spectrogram of the possible word *ama* (Speaker K). 157
Figure 8.39. Waveform and spectrogram of the possible word *ana* (Speaker K). 158
Figure 8.40. Waveform and spectrogram of the word *bɔ̄lɔ̄* 'tobacco' (Speaker K). 159
Figure 8.41. Waveform and spectrogram of the word *kɔ̀nɔ́* 'hippo' (Speaker K). 159
Figure 8.42. Spectrogram of the word *kɔ́-gwà* 'pack, wrap up' spoken at a slow speaking rate (Speaker K). 161
Figure 8.43. Waveform, F_0 trace, and spectrogram of the phrase *ɔ́ gjáà gjà* 'it's difficult to stir' (Speaker K). 162
Figure 8.44. Waveform, F_0 trace, and spectrogram of the underlined portion of the phrase *èndʒē sɔ́ kɔ́-<u>kwáā-kwā</u> ngɔ́ngɔ́ nɔ̀ ásɔ́* 'they will be returning now' (Speaker K). 163

List of Tables

Table 1.1. Banda subclassification. 6
Table 1.2. Levels of intelligibility between Banda speech varieties . . 9
Table 2.1. Consonant-vowel combinations in Mono 40
Table 2.2. Vowel-vowel (CV_1CV_2) co-occurrences 41
Table 3.1. Consonant-tone co-occurrences 50
Table 6.1. Mono pronouns 80
Table 7.1. Mono phonological processes 120
Table 8.1. VOT values for labial, velar, and labial-velar stops
  (Speaker K) 141
Table 8.2. Closure duration of prenasalized stops in Mono
  (Speaker K) 144
Table 8.3. Formant averages. Units are Hertz; standard deviations
  are in parentheses (Speaker K) 147
Table 8.4. Bandwidth averages. Units are Hertz; standard deviations
  are in parentheses (Speaker K) 147
Table 8.5. Duration of vowels in CVLV sequences spoken at normal
  and rapid rates of speech. Standard deviations are
  given in parentheses (Speakers A and K) 153
Table 8.6. Comparison of the duration of long and short vowels
  in a word-initial syllable (Speaker K) 156
Table 8.7. Comparison of the values of F_1 and F_2 for the labialization
  in the token *kɔ́-gwà* 'pack, wrap up' spoken at a slow
  rate and the average values of F_1 and F_2 for *u* and *o*. . . 161
Table A.1. Frequency counts of consonants in texts. 180
Table A.2. Frequency counts of vowels in texts 181
Table A.3. Frequency counts of tones in texts. 181
D.1 Consonant-vowel co-occurrences 233
D.2 Vowel-vowel (CV_1CV_2) co-occurrence 250
D.3 Consonant-tone co-occurrences 252
D.4 Formant and bandwidth values for Mono vowels (Speaker K) . 256
D.5 Time location of vowel measurements 272

Preface

This book is a revision of my University of Chicago Ph.D. dissertation. Two of the appendices in the dissertation have been published elsewhere: *An Evaluation of Niger-Congo Classification* is available as Olson (2004), and *Cross-Linguistic Insights on the Labial Flap* has become two papers: Olson and Hajek (2003) and Olson and Hajek (2004).

A Mono proverb states, *úngú kpā dɔ̀ kùtí jē, ɔ́ déngɔ̀* 'Water runs by itself, and thus it curves and bends'. In other words, if you do something by yourself, you'll get off-track. Even though my name is on the title page of this book, many people were involved in making it a reality, and I would like to thank them. They are:

- my dissertation committee: John Goldsmith, Bill Darden, the late Karen Landahl, and the late Jim McCawley,
- the other faculty members at the University of Chicago, especially Salikoko Mufwene, Gene Gragg, Eric Hamp, and Rich Janda (now at Ohio State),
- my fellow students in the Department of Linguistics at the University of Chicago, especially Randy Eggert, Kati Gruber, Derrick Higgins, Joanna Lowenstein, Barbara Need, Elisa Steinberg, and Tami Wysocki,
- my former and present SIL colleagues in northwestern DRC: Richard and Trish Aze, Margaret Hill, Jim Fultz, Beat and Robyn Kunz, David and Sharon Morgan, JeDene Reeder, Ken Satterberg, Will and Judith Sawers, Brian and Barb Schrag, Harold and Ginny Smith, and Elaine Thomas,

- other linguists, including: Stephen C. Anderson, Patrick Bennett, Jutta Blühberger, Mary Bradshaw, Mike Cahill, Rod Casali, Nick Clements, France Cloarec-Heiss, Bruce Connell, Didier Demolin, Marcel Diki-Kidiri, Bill Gardner, the late Joseph Greenberg, Barbara Grimes, John Hajek, Robert Hedinger, Bonnie Henson, Beth Hume, Roger Kamanda, Mark Karan, Peter Ladefoged, Myles Leitch, Connie Kutsch Lojenga, Ian Maddieson, Steve Marlett, Rob McKee, Paul Newman, Doris Payne, Tom Payne, Rob Pensalfini, Geoffrey Pullum, Rich Rhodes, Jim Roberts, Doug Sampson, Keith Snider, Jürg Stalder, John Stewart, Rhonda Thwing, Dick Watson, and the late Kay Williamson,
- the expatriate workers in northwestern DRC from the Evangelical Covenant Church, the Evangelical Free Church, the Roman Catholic Church, and Mission Aviation Fellowship,
- the leadership of the Communauté Évangélique du Christ en Ubangi, the Communauté Évangélique en Ubangi et Mongala, and the Molegbe diocese of the Catholic Church,
- my language resource persons: Ama Geangozo Mbanza, Kilio Tembenekuzu, Mbakuwuse Tshangbaita, and Sangemale Tshebale Mandaba,
- my parents, Roger and Joan Olson, and
- the individuals and churches who have provided spiritual and financial support.

Research for this dissertation was funded by SIL International and a Century Fellowship from the University of Chicago. *SDG.*

Abbreviations

1PL.EXCL	first person plural exclusive	CONJ/conj.	conjunction
		COP	copula
1PL.INCL	first person plural inclusive	DEIC/deic.	deictic
		DET	determiner
1SG	first person singular	DISC	discourse marker
		DRC	Democratic Republic of the Congo
2PL	second person plural		
		EMPH	emphatic
2SG	second person singular	EXCL/excl.	exclamation
		F	falling tone
3PL	third person plural	FR	formal reduction
		FUT	future
3SG	third person singular	G	glide
		H	high tone
3SG.LOG	third person singular logophoric	IMP	imperative
		INAN	inanimate
ADJ/Adj./adj.	adjective	INF	infinitive
adj2	adjective following noun	Intr.	intransitive
		L	low tone; liquid
an	animate	LOC	locative
BEN	benefactive	LVS	leftword vowel spreading
C	consonant		
CERT	certainty	M	mid tone
CLEFT	cleft marker	MC	minimality condition
COND	conditional		

N/n.	noun	REP	repetitive
NEG	negation	S	sonorant
NF	non-future	SR	semantic restriction
O	obstruent	SRA	subminimal root augmentation
OB	obligations		
OLV	obstruent-liquid-vowel	SS	same subject
		SSP	sonority sequencing principle
PL/pl.	plural		
PM	phonological modification	STAT/stat.	stative
		SUBJ	subjunctive
P.N./p.n.	proper noun	TAM	tense, aspect, and mood
PREP/prep.	preposition		
QUEST/quest.	question	Trans.	transitive
RED	reduplicant	v.	verb
REFL	reflexive	V	vowel
REL	relative clause marker	Va	variation

1

Introduction

This book describes the phonology and morphology of the Bili dialect of Mono, a Banda language found in the northwestern corner of the Democratic Republic of the Congo (DRC, formerly Zaire).

The name *Mono* is used by the Mono people themselves (and by outsiders) to refer to the language they speak. The Mono people refer to themselves as the *à-mōnō* adding the *à-* prefix which marks plural on animate nouns. Some references, such as Tucker and Bryan (1956:33) and Kamanda (1998), list this as *à-mɔ̄nɔ̄*. This transcription may be due to the fact that the vowel *o* is nasalized following a nasal consonant, which can be perceived as a lowering of the vowel.

Outsiders refer to the Mono people as *les Mono* when speaking French or as *ba-Mono* when speaking Lingala (Bantu C), the local trade language. In the latter case, the speakers are simply employing the class 2 noun prefix *ba-*, which marks plural for persons in Lingala (Guthrie and Carrington 1988:14).

In many languages of the world, the term for the ethnic group is the same as the word for 'people' or 'human beings' (Payne 1997:13). In Mono however, this is not the case. The word for 'people' in Mono is *à-zū*, whereas the word *Mono* is not related.

The term *Mono* is also a derogatory term used by some people in the Central African Republic (CAR) to refer to the Congolese in general—e.g., *Les Monos ne sont que des voleurs* 'The Monos are nothing but thieves'. In fact, many people I have talked with in Central African Republic appear to be ignorant of the fact that Mono is a unique ethnic and linguistic group found in DRC.

There are several languages in the world with the name "Mono." The language which is the subject of the present study is given the code [MNH] in the *Ethnologue* (Grimes 2000). Other languages bearing the name Mono include an Adamawan language found in the North Province of Cameroon [MRU], a nearly extinct Uto-Aztecan language found in east central California [MON], and an Austronesian language found in the Solomon Islands [MTE].

The Mono people recognize that they are a part of a larger ethnolinguistic unit called Banda. The Banda languages are found predominantly in the eastern half of Central African Republic and in northwestern DRC. In addition, a small number are found in southwestern Sudan (cf. Cloarec-Heiss 1988).

1.1 Demography and Geography

Mono is spoken in five distinct regions of northwestern DRC. The Mono people identify these five regions as each having a distinct dialect: Bili, Bubanda, Mpaka, Galaba, and Kaga. The first two regions are in the Bosobolo Zone, whereas the last three are in the Libenge zone. These regions are stretched out like beads on a string in an arc starting just across the Ubangi River from Kouango, Central African Republic, and proceeding south and then west ending once again near the Ubangi River immediately to the south of Zongo (Fultz and Morgan 1986).

The first region is centered on the town of Bili, as shown in figure 1.1. Taking data from a 1984 census, Fultz and Morgan list the population for this region as 33,180. A map in Van Bulck and Hackett (1956) shows Kpagua (their "Pagwa") being spoken in the northeastern part of the Bili region, but Fultz and Morgan (1986:9) point out that all of these Kpagua villages have since adopted Mono, so that Kpagua is now *"une langue morte à cette côté de l'Ubangi"* 'a dead language on this side of the Ubangi'.

The Bili region is bordered by Gobu and Langbasi (Banda) to the northwest, Furu (West Central Sudanic, cf. Maes 1983) to the east, and an enclave of Ngombe speakers (Bantu C) to the south. The Furu region is not homogenous, as there are villages which speak other languages (e.g., Mbandja, Langbasi, Yakpa, Gbanziri, Kpala, and Ngombe) interspersed amongst the Furu villages.

1.1 Demography and Geography

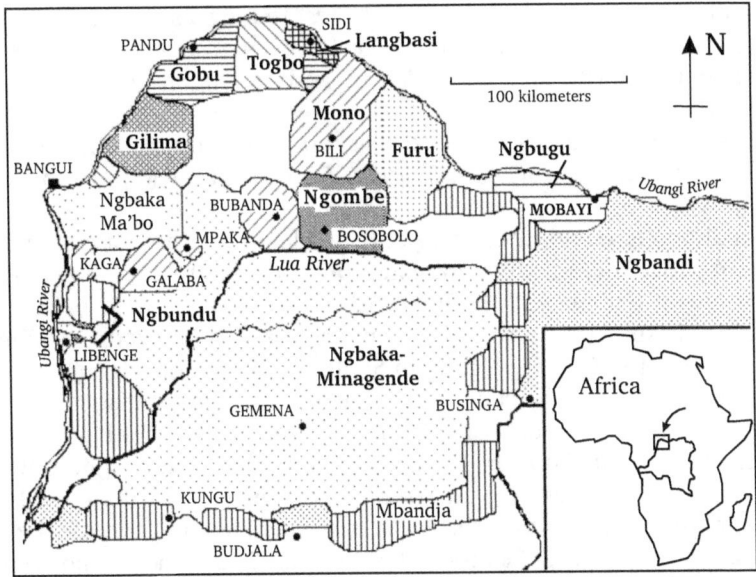

Figure 1.1. The languages of northwestern DRC. (Language names are bold. Town names are all caps.)

The Bubanda region is located to the southwest of the Bili region. The two regions are connected via a road which passes through the Ngombe region and also by a footpath which bypasses the Ngombe region. In fact, one of the easternmost villages in the Bubanda region, Modiri, actually speaks the Bili dialect. Fultz and Morgan list the population for this region as 11,962. The Bubanda region is bordered on the east by the Ngombe region, but there are a couple of Togbo villages on the border as well. On the west side, the Bubanda region is bordered by Ngbaka-Minagende.[1]

Further west past the Ngbaka-Minagende region is the Mpaka region. This region consists of only five or six villages. Fultz and Morgan do not distinguish it as a separate dialect (and thus do not give population data), but the people in this region consider their speech to be distinct from the other Mono dialects. It is bordered on the east by Ngbaka-Minagende. On the west, it is separated from the Galaba dialect region by four or five villages each of which speak either Ngbaka-Ma'bo or Gilima.

The Galaba region has a population of 13,540. It is bordered to the south by Ngbaka-Minagende and to the northwest by Ngbaka-Ma'bo.

---

[1]This group refers to themselves as "Ngbaka." However, some linguists use the label "Ngbaka-Minagende" in order to distinguish the group from other languages with the name "Ngbaka."

Finally, Kaga is the Mono dialect furthest to the west. It is found along the road between Zongo and Libenge and has 3,420 speakers. Kaga is bordered to the north by Ngbaka-Ma'bo and to the south by Ngbundu (Banda).

Thus the total number of Mono speakers according to Fultz and Morgan's data is 62,102 (Tucker and Bryan 1956:33 list the Mono population as 23,423).

In addition to Mono, several other Banda languages are found in northwestern DRC. These include Mbandja (approximately 200,000 speakers according to Grimes 2000), Gobu (12,283), Togbo (10,117), Langbasi (2,900), Yakpa (approx. 2,000, interspersed amongst the Furu), Ngbundu-North (6,572), Ngbundu-South (9,371), and Ngbugu (interspersed with Ngbandi west of Mobayi). (All population statistics are from Fultz and Morgan except where noted.) Two or three villages east of Pandu in the main Gobu region speak a language called Ngbulu which may belong to the Banda group, but survey needs to be done to clarify this. Cloarec-Heiss (1988) lists Kpala as a Banda language, but Fultz and Morgan note that it is in fact related to Ngbaka-Ma'bo. There is no present-day evidence that the Banda dialect Ngundu is spoken in DRC, contrary to what is listed in Grimes (2000).

The Bili dialect of Mono appears to be the dominant dialect. It has a larger population than all of the other Mono groups combined. In addition, it is the most prestigious of all the Mono dialects. All of the other groups hold a positive attitude toward the Bili dialect.

1.2 Classification

Linguistic researchers have consistently classified Mono as a part of the Banda language group (see, for example, Tisserant 1930:5 and Tucker and Bryan 1956:33), an ethnically homogenous yet linguistically diverse group with perhaps as many as fifty speech varieties (Cloarec-Heiss 1988). Banda is generally considered to be part of the Ubangi branch of Adamawa-Ubangi, itself a branch of Greenberg's (1970) Niger-Congo phylum.

The most widely accepted procedure for establishing the classification of a language family is to reconstruct proto forms and then describe the systematic changes resulting in the present-day forms by use of the comparative method. Classifications based on other evidence, such as typological features or cognate percentages, are less convincing.

1.2 Classification

1.2.1 Adamawa-Ubangi

Since Greenberg (1970), Adamawa-Ubangi has been considered to be a part of Niger-Congo. Greenberg offered as evidence for this affiliation resemblances in form and meaning (rather than correspondences in the accepted sense) between Adamawa-Ubangi and the rest of Niger-Congo, both in their noun class systems and in lexical items. This evidence is strong for the Adamawan languages but weak for most of the Ubangian languages. In fact, Boyd (1978) and Cloarec-Heiss (1995a) point out shared features between Ubangian languages and their Nilo-Saharan neighbors to the north and east. At present, it is generally thought that the Ubangian languages are genetically a part of Niger-Congo and acquired certain typological features from Nilo-Saharan as a result of language contact. The similarites between Nilo-Saharan and Banda led Cloarec-Heiss (1995a) to hypothesize that Proto-Banda was a pidgin with Central Sudanic as the substrate and Ubangian as the superstrate (i.e., the lexifier).

As far as the integrity of Adamawa-Ubangi is concerned, it is not clear that it forms a linguistic unit. Bennett and Sterk (1977), Bennett (1983), and Williamson (1989) point out that there is little evidence from lexicostatistics or shared innovations for an Adamawa-Ubangi node in the Niger-Congo tree. Instead, such evidence points more convincingly to a node consisting of both Adamawa-Ubangi and Gur, which Williamson calls "North Volta-Congo."

The integrity of Ubangi is also in question. Most of the classifications of the group have either incomplete data or have not specified clearly their criteria, or both. Bennett (1983) questions the inclusion of Gbaya within Ubangi and claims that there is more evidence for an Ubangi node which excludes Gbaya rather than including it. Once again, more research is necessary on this question.

1.2.2 Banda internal relationships

Table 1.1 presents a subclassification of Banda. Note that the node labels (e.g., "Central Core," "Mid-Southern") are not terms that the Banda people use to describe themselves, but were created by linguists for classificatory purposes. On the other hand, the name of the group as a whole, "Banda," and the names of the individual languages are used by the people in referring to themselves.[2]

---

[2]Grimes (2000) (1) does not list Buru in Sudan, (2) lists Buka, Mbre, Moruba, and Sabanga as occurring in Sudan, (3) lists Langbasi as "Langbashe," (4) does not list Mbandja in Central African Republic, and (5) lists Gbaga-North as "Gbaga-Nord." Cloarec-Heiss (1988) does not list Golo in Sudan.

Table 1.1. Banda subclassification

I. Central
   1. Central Core
      a. Banda-Bambari: Linda, Joto, Ndokpa, Ngapo, Gbende
      b. Banda-Banda: Banda-Banda, Bereya, Buru(+S), Gbaga-South, Gbambiya, Hai, Ka, Mbi, Ndi, Ngalabo, Ngola, Vidiri(+S), Gov̂oro(S), Wundu(S)
      c. Banda-Mbrès: Buka, Mbre, Moruba, Sabanga, Wada(+S)
      d. Banda-Ndélé: Ndélé, Junguru(+S), Tangbago(+S), Ngao, Ngbala, Kpaya(S)
      e. Mid-Southern: Bongo, Dukpu(+S), Yakpa(+C), Wasa(+S), Gobu (+C), Kpagua, Mono(C)
      f. Togbo-Vara: Togbo(+S, +C), Vara
   2. Banda-Yangere: Yangere
II. South Central: Langbasi(+C), Langba, Ngbugu(+C)
III. Southern: Mbandja
IV. Southwestern: Ngbundu(C)
V. West Central: Dakpa, Gbaga-North, Gbi, Vita, Wojo, Golo(S)

Note:
C/S – Languages found only in DRC or Sudan, respectively.
+C/+S – Languages in DRC or Sudan, respectively, as well as Central African Republic.
Unmarked languages occur only in Central African Republic.

The first attempt to subclassify Banda was done by Tisserant (1930:4–5). However, he does not provide data or evidence to support his classification. It appears that this classification is based purely on his impressions and not on a rigorous methodology. Tisserant himself admits that his classification is not to be taken as definitive.

Cloarec-Heiss (1978) studies eleven Banda dialects and sets up a classification based on phonological and lexical data. Her published data include an 80-item wordlist. Her phonological analysis consists of making an inventory of phonemes in each language and then classifying the languages according to three typological factors: (1) the presence or absence of individual sounds, (2) pertinent oppositions between sounds in various dialects, and (3) the syllable structure of certain lexical items. Her lexical comparison focuses on the percentage of cognates found in each pair of languages.

Cloarec-Heiss (1986) proposes a classification of forty-three Banda dialects (although she in fact analyzes only seventeen dialects), following the same phonological and lexical criteria used in her previous study, and makes a stronger attempt to differentiate dialects. Unfortunately, she does not discuss her data or analysis. She tentatively proposes two major groups—Central Banda and Peripheral Banda—based predominantly on native speaker sentiments (Cloarec-Heiss 2000). Central Banda is geographically central to the overall Banda region and consists of a group of languages which are phonologically, morphologically, and lexically homogenous. Nevertheless, six different subclasses of Central Banda do emerge. Peripheral Banda is made up of a more diverse group of languages which are geographically dispersed, mostly to the west and south of the Central Banda region. Cloarec-Heiss divides Peripheral Banda into five regions: West Central, South Central, Southern, Southwestern, and Western. Cloarec-Heiss (1988) offers a slight revision to her classification. She conflates Western with Central Banda, making Yangere a seventh subgroup of Central Banda.

In Olson (1996), I provide a comparative study of a 204-item wordlist in thirteen Banda dialects: Linda, Yangere, Ngao, Vara, Wojo, Dakpa, Langbasi, Mbandja, Mono-Bili, Mono-Bubanda, Mono-Galaba, Gobu, and Togbo. The data for the first eight languages are taken from Moñino (1988), while I include my own data for the last five languages. In my article I study several consonants, reconstructing Proto-Banda phonemes and sound laws to account for the present-day pronunciations. In addition, I examine the syllable structure which results from a reduplicative process in Banda, and provide cognate percentages for each pair of languages.

My analysis leads me to reject the Peripheral Banda node, since each grouping underneath the node is as distant phonologically and lexicostatistically from each other as from Central Banda. Thus, I elevate South Central, Southern, Southwestern, and West Central to the level of immediate constituents of the Banda node. In addition, I note that Yangere is more closely related to the Central Core than the other peripheral groups, and so I posit an intermediate node to account for that level of relatedness.

On the other hand, Cloarec-Heiss (2000) argues *for* the Peripheral Banda node, on the grounds that morphological rates of similarity between these speech varieties are high, in fact, higher than lexical rates of similarity. However, she bases this on rates of similarity rather than on a reconstructed morphology or definable shared morphological innovations. Further research is necessary to substantiate her claim.

The internal classification of the Central Core of Banda as shown in table 1.1 is from Cloarec-Heiss (1986, 1988). However, as mentioned before, she does not explicitly lay out her analysis, so it remains unclear exactly how she arrives at this internal classification. Also, in Olson

(1996) I do not make any claims regarding the internal classification of the Central Core.

Cloarec-Heiss (1978), Fultz and Morgan (1986), and Olson (1996) each provide lexicostatistical data comparing some of the Central Core languages. Unfortunately, none of these studies contain languages from all six subgroups. Olson (1996:275) compares languages within four of the subgroups: Banda-Bambari, Banda-Ndélé, Mid-Southern, and Togbo-Vara. For my data, the pairs of languages which are putatively part of the same subgroup consistently (with one exception) score higher than 90 percent. However, this is not exclusively so, so my results are inconclusive. A comprehensive lexicostatistical study informing the internal classification of the Central Core languages remains to be conducted.

It is also unclear whether the different subgroups within the Central Core consist of speech varieties which are indeed mutually unintelligible. In other words, can each node under Central Core be considered a separate language, or is it better to speak of the Central Core as being a single language with six major dialectal variants? One possible means of testing this is the Recorded Text Test (RTT, Casad 1974). In the RTT, texts are recorded in several related speech varieties. These texts are then played for speakers of the other speech varieties and the subjects are graded for their level of comprehension of each text. Of course, care must be taken to insure that the test is in fact measuring inherent intelligibility and not learned intelligibility.

In the mid-1990s, researchers with SIL and the Association Centrafricaine pour la Traduction de la Bible et l'Alphabetisation (ACATBA) in Central African Republic conducted language surveys in Linda (Blühberger 1996), Yakpa (Moehama 1994), Togbo (Buchanan 1996), Yangere (Moehama 1995), and Ngbugu (Kieschke 1993). The first four of these surveys conducted a "rapid appraisal" RTT, a simplified form of the test in which an evaluation of intelligibility is made by playing a text from a related speech variety for a group of people (rather than for individuals) who speak a language variety. The group is then evaluated as having one of three levels: (1) good intelligibility, (2) some intelligibility, or (3) no intelligibility. For the surveys conducted, the following scores were obtained:

1.3 Ethnology and History

Table 1.2. Levels of intelligibility between Banda speech varieties

	Linda	Mbre	Ndele	Mono	Togbo (CAR)	Togbo (DRC)	Vara	Ngbugu	Mbanza	Dakpa
Linda				2(+/−)				3(+)		
Yakpa		1−		1(−)				3		
Togbo (CAR)	1	2	1	1−		1	1	3		2
Yangere	1		1	1−	1	1−		3	3	3

In some cases, differences in levels of intelligibility were observed within a group. For example, in testing Linda speakers on Mono, some male speakers understood the text well, many speakers understood the general outline of the text, whereas young female speakers understood practically nothing in the text. In testing Yakpa speakers on Mono, a group from one village understood both Mono texts well, but groups in two other villages understood only the general outline of one text and nothing in the second text. In testing Linda speakers on Ngbugu, most members of the group understood nothing of the text, but a few men understood the general outline.

In general, speakers of Central Banda speech varieties had good intelligibility with other Central Banda speech varieties, whereas texts from the Peripheral Banda languages were usually not understood at all. This suggests that the Central Banda varieties are best understood as dialects of a single language. However, due to the tentative nature of the testing method, this must remain an open question until more accurate testing is performed.

1.3 Ethnology and History

The Mono people live in the border region between the tropical rain forest to the south and the savannah to the north. The year-round average high temperature is ninety degrees Fahrenheit with about sixty-five inches of rain per year. The rainy season lasts from around April to November, and the dry season from December to March each year.

The Mono people are predominantly agriculturalists. For subsistence, they raise manioc, corn, rice, plantains, sweet potatoes, palm nuts, peanuts, spinach, tomatoes, onions, pineapple, sugarcane, bananas, mangos, and papaya. As cash crops, they raise tobacco, cotton, and coffee. A tobacco processing plant and a cotton company are located in Bili. In addition, they raise small domesticated animals such as pigs, chicken, goats, and sheep. Large domestic animals such as cattle and horses do not survive long in the region due to the presence of tsetse flies. Hunting and fishing are common activities. The men hunt small game, but large game, such as elephants and buffalo, have for the most part been hunted out of the region. Fishing is common along the banks of the Ubangi River.

Many men practice trades, such as weaving, carpentry, blacksmithing, and tailoring, but for a given individual, this work complements rather than supplants farming.

The Mono people are traditionally animistic (Vergiat 1981). They believe in a supreme being who created the earth and humans and lives in the heavens. There are several other supernatural beings, each with a certain dominion, such as earth, water, or forest. The most noted of these is Toro, the *génie de la terre*, who is the principal character in many folk stories and legends. In his cunning way, he likes to trick people, which either works to his favor or backfires.

Sickness or misfortune may be caused by these supernatural beings, or they may be the result of a curse from another human. The remedy often consists of fetishes, offerings, and sacrifices, as prescribed by the local shaman. Individual clans are associated with a specific animal.

Around the time of puberty, the boys participate in a circumcision rite called *gaza*. There used to be a corresponding excision rite for girls, but this has been outlawed by the Congolese government.[3] The Mono people have a secret society called *Ngakoala*. Vergiat mentions *Maoro* and *Badagi* as additional secret societies found among the Banda people of Central African Republic. Eboué (1933) provides a 60-item wordlist of the secret Banda language Somalé in Central African Republic.

During the twentieth century Catholic and Protestant mission activity was successful among the Mono people, so today the majority call themselves Christian. As a result, the influence of the traditional religion has diminished but is by no means extinct. For example, the circumcision rites have for the most part died out in the Bili and Bubanda regions but are still practiced in the Mpaka and Galaba regions.

There are sparse sources available on the history of the Mono people, so a detailed historical account is not possible. When asked about their origins, the Mono people respond that they came from Sudan. However, if we accept the hypothesis that Banda is a part of the Niger-Congo family, then the following sketch of Mono history emerges.

---

[3]During the political chaos that ensued during the civil war in 1996–1997, this rite of excision was resurrected in some villages.

1.3 Ethnology and History

The Ubangian people, being of Niger-Congo stock, originated to the west of the present-day distribution. Newman (1995:141) places the Ubangian core near the source of the Sanaga River in Cameroon (see figure 1.2). This would have been their location at about 3000 B.C.

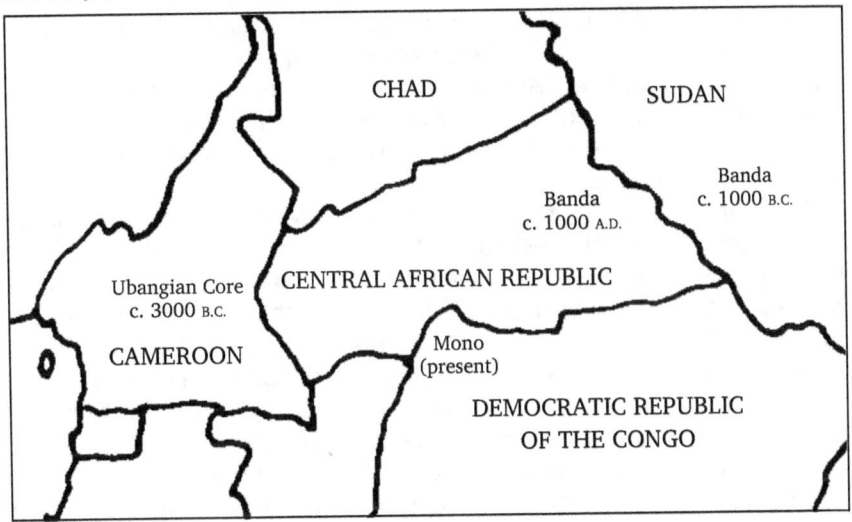

Figure 1.2. The locations of the Mono people and their ancestors.

Then, Ubangian expansion occurred in an easterly direction following the northern fringes of the tropical rainforest, which at the time covered at least the southern third of Central African Republic. At its peak, the Ubangian expansion may have reached to the White Nile, with the Banda family settling either in extreme eastern Central African Republic or in the Bahr-el-Ghazal province of Sudan. According to Bouquiaux and Thomas (1980), this migration took place around 1000 B.C.

However, once in southwestern Sudan, the Ubangian people, particularly the Banda, Ngbaka-Sere, and Ngbandi groups, had contact with the Central Sudanic people (Nilo-Saharan), whose languages originated in the region (Cordell 1983:37). Evidence of this contact is that the Banda group absorbed some Central Sudanic speakers (p. 38). The resulting conflict led to a slight western movement of the Ubangian groups, with the Banda people settling near the source of the Kotto River in eastern Central African Republic, while the Central Sudanic groups spread to the south and northwest of the Ubangian area. Bouquiaux and Thomas and Cordell both agree that this rearrangement was complete by around 1000 A.D.

At this point, the Banda people did not have a hierarchical system. According to Cordell (p. 38), they "were extremely decentralized, living in small groups of related males and their dependants. The clan was the only institution of broader scale." This decentralization made the Banda easy prey for the next contact they encountered—the Arab slave trade. It is not clear when the slave trade first impacted the Banda people. It was present in northern Africa by the fourteenth century and continued to grow until it reached its peak at the end of the nineteenth century. However, one piece of evidence—the susceptibility to diseases of Banda slaves in the mid-nineteenth century—suggests that the raiding reached their region more recently. Tisserant (1930) states that the majority of the Banda people were still residing near the source of the Kotto River in 1830. In fleeing the slave raids, some groups, such as the Yangere, moved west and settled in western Central African Republic. Others, such as the Ngbandi, Mbandja, and Mono moved southwest into the Democratic Republic of the Congo. Maes (1983) places the Ngbandi crossing of the Ubangi River at the end of the seventeenth century and the Mbandja crossing at the end of the eighteenth century. He also places the crossing of the Mono, Gobu, and Togbo groups at the end of the seventeenth century due to a Mbandja legend that they encountered Gobu speakers when they crossed, but the similarity of these languages to the other Central Core languages to the north would indicate that their crossing was probably much later, perhaps in the latter half of the nineteenth century.

Before we leave the topic of Mono history, I mention two residual items. First, Cordell (1983:56) points out that the Banda people acquired a poison oracle from the Azande, so there was likely contact between the two groups during the Azande expansion of 1750–1900. Second, Tisserant (1930:12) mentions that there was interbreeding between Mono and "a Sara group" about 120 years ago, but he does not elaborate this claim.

1.4 The Sociolinguistic Situation

In the Bili region, it is not uncommon for a Mono speaker to be multilingual, to different degrees, in several other languages. These languages include Lingala, French, other Banda languages in the region (Gobu, Togbo, and Langbasi), Ngbaka-Minagende, Ngbandi, and Sango.

Lingala (Bantu C), the trade language in the northern and western parts of the Democratic Republic of the Congo, is understood by many people, particularly those who have traveled in the region or received education elsewhere. Speaking the language is considered prestigious. It is used in contact situations with Bantu-speaking groups such as the Ngombe to the south, in governmental situations, and in primary school.

However, the Mono speakers are not homogenous with respect to fluency in Lingala. For example, male speakers have a higher level of proficiency in Lingala than female speakers. In addition, geographic location is a factor. Along major roads and in commercial centers, the level of Lingala is elevated, whereas in remote villages, the level of Lingala is reduced, both for men and women. The highest level of Lingala is to be found in Bili, the commercial and educational center of the region.

Fultz and Morgan (1986) performed a Lingala intelligibility test in the Mono-Bili village of Bida. They rated Lingala comprehension at 59 percent for men and 10 percent for women. The researchers rated on a percentage scale their impressions of a speaker's ability to understand a recorded Lingala text. We cannot place too much weight on the specific numbers in their results, but what we can deduce from the data is that the male Mono speakers in this village have a mediocre level of Lingala on average, whereas female Mono speakers have almost no comprehension of Lingala on average.

One unfortunate result of this testing method is that it does not give us a direct measure of the percentage of people who speak Lingala well versus those with less proficiency. However, if most women speak almost no Lingala, and many men speak it poorly, then we can estimate that the percentage of the population who speak it well is certainly less than 50 percent, and likely less than 30 percent.

French is spoken by some Mono people, particularly those with a high level of education, and carries a high level of prestige with it. It is officially the language of education in the schools from the third grade on, but in reality Lingala dominates in the classroom, particularly in the primary grades. I do not have statistics on the percentage of Mono speakers who know French, but it is certainly less than the percentage proficient in Lingala.

The Mono people have much contact with the Banda groups immediately to the north: the Gobu, Togbo, and Langbasi groups. They have a high level of comprehension of the three languages, with Gobu being the highest, Togbo second, and Langbasi third. This is at least partly due to the inherent intelligibility which results from the genetic relatedness of the languages. However, acquired intelligibility is likely a factor as well. As a general rule, if possible, people speak the language of the village they are in. For example, it is not unknown for a pastor to preach in the language of the local village people, regardless of his mother tongue.

Of the four languages, Mono appears to be the most dominant. Fultz and Morgan's intelligibility scores indicate that in general the speakers of the other languages understand Mono better than Mono speakers understand the other languages. Mono also has the largest population of any of these groups.

To a lesser degree, there is some bilingualism in Ngbaka-Minagende, the language of the largest ethnic group in northwestern DRC, and in Sango, the trade language spoken just across the border in Central African Republic.

Despite pressure from these other languages, particularly Lingala, Mono language use remains vigorous, and it does not appear that Mono is in danger of extinction in the near future. In fact, Fultz and Morgan (1986:9) observe an increase in the use of Mono in that several villages which used to speak Yapka, Togbo, or Kpagua now speak Mono. All in all, the attitude of Mono speakers towards their language is positive. Mono remains the language that children learn first at home, and Lingala is normally not learned until a child goes to school. Mono remains the language used in the local market. In all church services in the Mono region, the pastors preach in Mono. The only exception to this is in Bili where many non-Mono speakers reside. Even there, however, the pastor will switch into Mono during a sermon in order to explain a point more clearly to the Mono parishioners.

Code-switching is common in Mono, particularly in Bili. Lingala and (to a lesser degree) French words and expressions are commonly inserted into Mono sentences. This phenomenon is particularly prevalent among the youth, about which the older people say that they do not speak *Mono pur*. At this point in the evolution of the language, it is probably more appropriate to refer to this as code-switching rather than borrowing, but it is likely that many words from Lingala and French will eventually be integrated into the language. Also, code-switching is not limited to major grammatical categories, but occasionally occurs with grammatical function words as well. Two examples which are common include the French word *mais* 'but' and the Lingala word *te* 'not'.

1.5 Dialects

Dialectal variation is often reflected in geographical dispersion, and among the Mono people, this is indeed the case. One example of phonological variation occurs between the Bili and Bubanda dialects. Often (but not in all cases), a word containing *i* in the Bili dialect has a corresponding *i* in the

Bubanda dialect, e.g., kīndī̀ versus kīndī 'field', kɔ́-dì̄ versus kɔ́-dì 'to read', ī̀gī̀ versus īgī 'neck'. Occasionally, lexical items will be borrowed from a language which is in geographic proximity. For example, the Galaba dialect of Mono has borrowed the words tàmbè 'rock' and jākā 'dry season' from the nearby language Ngbaka-Ma'bo.

Sociological factors may cause dialectal variation within a given geographical region. In the Bili region, the most salient of these appears to be age. Many speakers of the Bili dialect differentiate between the speech of the older and younger generations, but this seems to be more of a gradient rather than polar opposition, with the youngest generation being influenced the most by the influx of Lingala. For example, my 35-year-old language resource person would occasionally go to the elderly people to find out the "real" Mono word for something, because he was accustomed to using a Lingala word instead. At the same time, he would bemoan the fact that the school children would mix Lingala with their Mono.

As mentioned before, the Bili dialect is the object of study in this book. But more precisely, the four language resource persons with whom I worked most closely were all male speakers in their 30s, residents of Bili, with at least a high school level of education. In addition, all had traveled or lived to some extent outside of the Mono region.

1.6 Previous Research on Mono

The Mono language has received some attention in the literature. Three previous studies of Mono phonology and morphology exist: an unpublished study by Kamanda (1985) which discusses the Bubanda dialect, and Olson and Schrag (2000) and Kamanda (1998) which both discuss the Bili dialect. Of these, Kamanda (1998) is the most detailed. In addition, Tisserant (1931) and Olson (1996) provide some lexical data for Mono. Several documents dealing with Mono cultural issues have been produced by Congolese students as bachelor theses. These include Yasikuzu (1987), Tabu (1989), and Ingozo (1990).

The present study contributes to our understanding of Mono in several ways: the study includes documentation which is not available in previous studies, including a significant number of lexical items and texts; it includes a discussion of typological issues which is absent from previous studies; it provides acoustic evidence to support the phonological analysis of Mono; and finally, it should be pointed out that the fieldwork and analysis for Kamanda (1998) and this study were performed independently of each other, an important point for descriptive studies. When two independent studies corroborate each other's data, we can raise our level of confidence that the data are indeed accurate. The few places where the data differ highlight items for future research.

The Banda language family as a whole has a limited but growing body of available literature. Grammars include Tisserant (1930) on Banda, Tingbo (1978) on Mbandja, and Cloarec-Heiss (1986) on Linda, with the latter being the most comprehensive. Phonologies include Cloarec-Heiss (1967, 1969) on Linda, Robbins (1984) on Mbandja, and Sampson (1985) on Tangbago, in addition to those mentioned above for Mono. Finally, documents which contain additional lexical information on Banda include Toqué (1906), Cotel (1907), Giraud (1908), Eboué (1918, 1933), Tisserant (1950), Santandrea (1965), Cloarec-Heiss (1978), and Moñino (1988).

1.7 Remarks

The purpose of this study is to document the present state of the phonology and morphology of Mono using structuralist phonology for the basic analysis with occasional use of notions from generative phonology. The study is synchronic in nature. My goal is to characterize accurately the language as it was spoken in the latter part of the twentieth century. At points in the study, I offer diachronic and comparative information, but I do so simply with the goal of informing the synchronic analysis. Having said this, I hope that the present study will contribute to comparative work, especially concerning questions of the place of Adamawa-Ubangi within Niger-Congo.

The data for this study were collected during two terms of field research. During the first term, from January 1994 until June 1995, I resided in the Mono village of Bili (see figure 1.1), working alongside my SIL colleagues Brian and Barbara Schrag. We were assisted in our work in Bili primarily by Rev. Sangemale Tshebale Mandaba and Mr. Mbakuwuse Tschangbaita, both mother-tongue speakers of Mono. During this first term, a language committee was established, consisting of governmental, educational, and ecclesiastical leaders in the Mono region. The researchers and the Mono language committee worked together to establish an orthography for the Mono language. A preliminary version was approved in 1994.

In the winter of 1998, we conducted additional linguistic research in Yaoundé, Cameroon. Unfortunately, civil unrest at the time prevented us from travelling to the Democratic Republic of the Congo. Instead, we arranged for two mother-tongue Mono speakers, Mr. Ama Geangozo Mbanza and Mr. Kilio Tembenekuzu, to travel from the Democratic Republic of the Congo to Yaoundé in order to assist us in the research.

The data that we collected consist of field notes and audio recordings of both elicited and natural speech. These data include wordlists, phrases, and texts of several genres. The texts include traditional proverbs, folktales, and songs. Literacy materials in Mono that have been published to date include a folktale book, a book on agriculture, two calendars including traditional Mono proverbs, and an alphabet chart. In collecting data in Yaoundé, we focused on filling in gaps from our data collected earlier in Bili. In addition, video recordings were made in Yaoundé in order to document more thoroughly the labial flap. This study relies predominantly on field notes, but acoustic analysis based on the recordings is presented to provide additional support for the transcribed data.

1.8 Salient Findings

In this section, I highlight briefly what I consider to be the salient aspects of Mono phonology.

Among the consonants, the labial flap w̌ is of interest due to its limited geographic distribution (central and southeastern Africa) and the fact that it has not received much attention in the literature. The default articulation of the labial flap in Mono is a voiced bilabial flap with egressive pulmonic air, unusual because the sound is most often described as labiodental cross-linguistically. I also note that a backing of the tongue co-occurs with the sound. There are four acoustic correlates for the sound: (1) a brief closure of less than 30 ms, (2) rising F_1 and F_2 transitions after release, (3) short duration of formant transitions after release, and (4) a slow, gradual drop in F_2 before the closure. The fact that the sound can be readily incorporated into the phonological system of a language provides additional evidence for the need of a phonological feature or phonetic parameter that distinguishes short from extra-short consonants.

The two implosives in Mono, ɓ and ɗ, are interesting because of their acoustic characteristics. The most salient acoustic correlate for Mono implosives concerns the signal amplitude during the closure period. Specifically, Mono implosives exhibit either an increase in signal amplitude during the latter part of oral closure or the maintenance of a large, level signal amplitude. In addition, a biphasic pattern indicative of laryngealization is observed in most tokens having a large, level amplitude.

The Mono vowel system lacks a front low vowel ɛ. This lacuna is attested in other African languages, but it is unusual in that it leads to a smaller inventory of front vowels than back vowels, contradicting a universal proposed by Crothers (1978). He claimed that the number of height distinctions in front vowels is greater than or equal to the number in back vowels. The Mono vowel system is also unusual in the fact that it has eight vowels.

Mono has three contrastive level tones—H, M, and L—as well as rising and falling tones that are analyzed as sequences of level tones. Tone has both a lexical and a grammatical function. Tonal morphemes identify several tense, aspect, and mood categories in the language. A tonal melody is attested on certain locative adverbs, and the *ga-* prefix on prepositions undergoes tonal polarity. Leftward tone spreading occurs with prothetic augmentation, mentioned below.

The two secondary articulations found in Mono, labialization and palatalization, are phonetically unusual in that they are perceived as being articulated like the mid vowels *o* and *e* rather than like high vowels. I provide acoustic evidence for this in chapter 8. As found in many African languages, these secondary articulations exhibit a delayed release with respect to the primary articulation. Palatalization occurs with more segments than labialization, and they can co-occur with the laryngeal consonants *h* and *ʔ*. The two secondary articulations present a challenge for a classical phonemic analysis in that there is not a unique solution, but rather several interpretations are possible.

Mono has a bisyllabic pattern, CV_1LV_1, in which the quality and tone of the two vowels is identical. The first V may be shortened or elided in rapid speech. I suggest in chapter 5 that the bisyllabic pattern has an underlying form of /CLV/ with an optional rule of echo vowel epenthesis (anaptyxis) creating the bisyllabic pattern.

Mono lexical words have a word minimality condition in that they must have at least two syllables. (Ideophonic adverbs can be an exception to this.) Many nominals in Mono have a V_1CV_1 word pattern, which I claim is the result of the prothetic subminimal root augmentation of an underlying /CV/ form. Interestingly, there is also a large number of words with the shape $V_1CV_1LV_1$, suggesting that both prothetic augmentation and echo vowel epenthesis apply to a /CLV/ underlying form. This overapplication of prothetic augmentation results in a non-surface-apparent opacity effect.

Leftward vowel spreading, discussed in chapters 6 and 7, involves the spreading of the features [high], [back], and [round] onto a preceding ə (or, in some cases, a), subject to certain implicational restrictions. Specifically, if

1.8 Salient Findings

it is possible for the feature [high] to spread, then the features [back] and [round] may only spread if [high] does. If [high] can spread but does not, then [back] and [round] do not spread.

Mono morphology is agglutinative and somewhat synthetic. It is predominantly prefixing, but reduplication and suprasegmental modification are also observed. There is a morphological distinction between animate and inanimate nouns, and a large number of nominals are derived from verbs. Also of note is the existence of cognate object constructions and morphologically-complex prepositions.

2

Phonemes

For identifying phonemes, I rely on data which can fit into the CV syllable pattern—the only unambiguous syllable pattern in Mono containing an onset. Tone contrasts will be presented in chapter 3. Syllables containing the secondary articulations of labialization and palatalization present a special problem of interpretation and will be discussed in chapter 4. The syllable patterns which occur in Mono, including ones which are ambiguous in their interpretation, will be discussed in chapter 5.

The main tool I use for demonstrating the distinctiveness of phonemes is the well-known methodology developed by the structuralists of identifying contrast in identical or analogous environments (e.g., Pike 1947).

In choosing lexical items for demonstrating contrast, I use the following criteria. First, I have used citation forms exclusively, with one addition: I also employ verb roots without the infinitive prefix as evidence for word-initial contrasts. Since the tonal property of the first syllable of verb roots varies depending on the tense, aspect, and mood of the verb, I present them here without tone markings. Second, I only employ multimorphemic forms as evidence for contrast when monomorphemic forms are not attested. Third, I have tried to avoid employing forms which exhibit phonological variation unless other forms are not attested. This includes unpredictable variation (for example kàlá ~ kèlá 'spoon') and variation due to optional phonological processes, such as leftward vowel spreading discussed in chapters 6 and 7.

Even when a contrast is established, researchers may not be convinced that a sound is integrated into the phonological system because of other factors. Sapir (1921:38) said, "All grammars leak." As a sound is added or lost in a language, it may go through a period where it is only marginally part of the system. Factors such as analogy, grammatical simplification, language contact, and sociolinguistic considerations can influence a sound's status (Goldsmith 1995). Diagnostics which inform us on this question include the following.

  1. *Distribution within the word.* If a sound can occur in both word-initial and word-medial position, this bolsters the claim that a sound is fully part of the phonological system of a language. In this chapter, I provide examples of onsets with only a single consonant; so in word-medial examples, the consonants are effectively in intervocalic position.

  2. *Co-occurrence of consonants and vowels.* If a consonant is attested before all of the vowels in the language, this is evidence that the consonant is a distinct phoneme, and not an allophone of another consonant. If, on the other hand, two consonant phones never occur before the same vowel, they would be considered to be in complementary distribution. Likewise, if a vowel can occur after all of the consonants in the language, this is evidence that the vowel is a distinct phoneme, and not an allophone of another vowel.

  3. *Distribution within grammatical categories.* In some languages, marginal phonemes only occur in certain sets of words, such as ideophones or plant and animal names. Criteria for identifying ideophones in Mono will be given in section 6.3. If a sound occurs in all major grammatical categories, this is further evidence that the sound is indeed part of the phonological system.

  4. *Frequency of occurrence.* If a sound is rare compared to other sounds in the language, this may call into question to what extent it is part of the phonological system. There are two ways of counting phonemes—frequency of occurrence within a text or frequency of occurrence within a lexicon. Trubetzkoy (1969:256) notes that the former is more appropriate for simple phoneme counts, whereas the latter is more appropriate for studying functional load. In this chapter, I will note when a phoneme is rare in discourse according to the frequency counts in tables A.1, A.2, and A.3 in appendix A. In addition, I will note if a phoneme is attested in less than a dozen items in the lexicon, given in appendix B. The lexicon contains about 2,000 lexical items.

  5. *Loanwords.* If a sound only occurs in words borrowed from another language, this calls into question its phonological status in the language. I make note of cases where a sound only occurs in loanwords.

Most of the data in this study are given in phonemic form. I present phonemic data in italics, e.g., *úngú* 'water'. Phonetic data, showing allophonic variation, is given in square brackets, e.g., [űŋgú] 'water'. In a

2.1 Consonants

few cases, I will discuss abstract analyses, akin to the Underlying Representations of generative phonology. In these cases, the data are presented between slash marks, e.g., /ngú/ 'water'.

The choice of presenting the data predominantly in phonemic form is to a certain extent a practical decision. On the one hand, a major goal of this study is to be as descriptive as possible. This leads me to keep abstract analyses to a minimum, although even a phonemic analysis is an abstraction to a certain degree. On the other hand, presenting the data with a narrow phonetic transcription would be cumbersome, especially in trying to present gradient behavior such as vowel nasalization.

2.1 Consonants

According to my analysis, Mono has thirty-three consonant phonemes, shown in figure 2.1. Three of these phonemes are given in parentheses, indicating that I consider them to be marginal in nature: ɗ, ɲ, and h. The implosive stops ɓ and ɗ are voiced and are produced with the ingressive glottalic airstream mechanism. All voiceless stops are unaspirated.

	labial	alveolar	palatal	velar	labial-velar	glottal
implosives	ɓ	(ɗ)				
vl. stops	p	t	tʃ	k	kp	ʔ
vd. stops	b	d	dʒ	g	gb	
prenas. stops	mb	nd	ndʒ	ng	ngb	
vl. fricatives	f	s	ʃ			(h)
vd. fricatives	v	z	ʒ			
nasals	m	n	(ɲ)			
flaps/trills	w̌	r				
laterals		l				
semi-vowels			j		w	

Figure 2.1. Consonant phonemes in Mono.

The pronunciation of each phoneme is the same as the identical symbol in the International Phonetic Alphabet, except where explicitly noted. Note that though some phonemes are shown as digraphs or trigraphs (e.g., kp and ndʒ), they are considered to be single phonemes. The choice of these particular representations is to avoid undue complexity in transcription. The phonetic detail of the phonemes will be discussed below.

Several typological observations concerning the Mono consonant system are worth noting. First, the implosive consonants follow the typological tendencies for such segments—they are voiced and they show a preference for fronted place of articulation, i.e., labial is preferred to coronal, and coronal is preferred to velar (Maddieson 1984:111). Second, Mono has a labial flap *ẘ* which is rare in the world's languages. (See Olson and Hajek 2003 for a discussion of the labial flap.)

Mono consonants share several traits with other Ubangian languages (Boyd 1989:199–201). First, the voiced/voiceless contrast is pertinent for both stops and fricatives. Second, there are prenasalized stops. Third, all consonants occur both word initially and word medially, with the exception of *ɗ*, which is not attested word initially in my corpus. This may be due to the fact that it is rare.

The consonant system presented here differs from the one presented in Kamanda (1998) in four respects. First, Kamanda considers prenasalized stops to be sequences of a nasal phoneme followed by a stop phoneme. His main reason for doing so is for the sake of economy (p. 148). By employing this analysis, he reduces the phoneme inventory by five phonemes. However, I have not followed that analysis mainly for distributional reasons. There are no unambiguous consonant clusters in Mono, and thus treating the prenasalized stops as N + C sequences would require introducing a CCV syllable pattern which is otherwise unwarranted in Mono. In many Bantu languages, such as Runyambo and Luganda (Hubbard 1995), prenasalized stops are analyzed as nasal + consonant sequences because of compensatory lengthening effects. It is important to highlight that such effects do not occur in Mono. I revisit this point in section 8.1.4.

A second way in which the consonant system presented here differs from that of Kamanda (1998) is that Kamanda classifies the labial-velar stops *kp* and *gb* as implosives. There are several reasons why I have not opted to do this. First, there are no corresponding labial-velar plosives in his system. Typologically, phonetically complex consonants, such as implosives, tend to imply the existence of their simpler counterparts (Burquest 2001:49). Second, implosive labial-velars are very rare. In fact, they do not occur in Maddieson's (1984) typological survey of phonetic sounds. Third, voiceless implosives are also very rare in the world's languages, which would discourage us from considering *kp* to be an implosive. On the other hand, labial-velar plosives are very common in African languages. Seeing no benefit typologically or analytically to classifying labial-velars as implosives, I have opted to classify them as plosives instead.

2.1 Consonants

Having said this, Ladefoged (1968) points out that labial-velars may have an ingressive aspect which may lead to an implosive-like percept. I discuss this in more detail in section 8.1.3.

A third way in which the consonant system presented here differs from that of Kamanda (1998) is that Kamanda groups palatal and velar consonants in a "dorsal" category. He is thus able to reduce the number of place of articulation columns by one, but he is then obliged to add an "affricate" manner of articulation row to his chart.

Fourth, Kamanda does not include a palatal nasal consonant ɲ in his inventory. Indeed, the phoneme is marginal in my own analysis. As we will see in chapter 4, it is possible to re-analyze the sound as a sequence of n + j in Mono.

2.1.1 Labial consonants

I group the bilabial and labiodental consonants into a labial category. Eight labial consonants are attested in Mono: ɓ, p, b, mb, f, v, m, and w̆. The fricatives f and v have a labiodental articulation, whereas the rest of the consonants in the category are bilabial. The labial flap is usually bilabial w̆, but it may alternatively be produced as a labiodental flap v̆. The choice of these symbols for transcribing the sound are based on the IPA's (1989:70) recommendation of indicating taps and flaps by use of the breve diacritic.

The implosive ɓ occurs in over twenty lexical items in my corpus. In terms of its occurrence in lexical items, it is not one of the more common phonemes in Mono. However, it does occur in certain morphemes which are common in discourse: ə̀ɓə̀ '2SG' and ɓá- 'at'. In many lexical items in my corpus, ɓ can be replaced by b, e.g., ngbāɓī ~ ngbābī 'bone'. More research is necessary to determine if this variation is limited to certain lexical items or if it can occur with any word containing the sound. This type of variation is also attested between ɗ and d, as discussed below.

Despite the fact that the labial flap w̆ is not widely attested in the world's languages, it is clearly a phoneme in Mono. It is attested in both word-initial and word-medial positions; it occurs before most vowels in Mono, including front, back, high, and low vowels; it occurs in nouns, verbs, and ideophones; and it is attested in over twenty-five words in my corpus. However, it is rare in my corpus of texts.

26   *Phonemes*

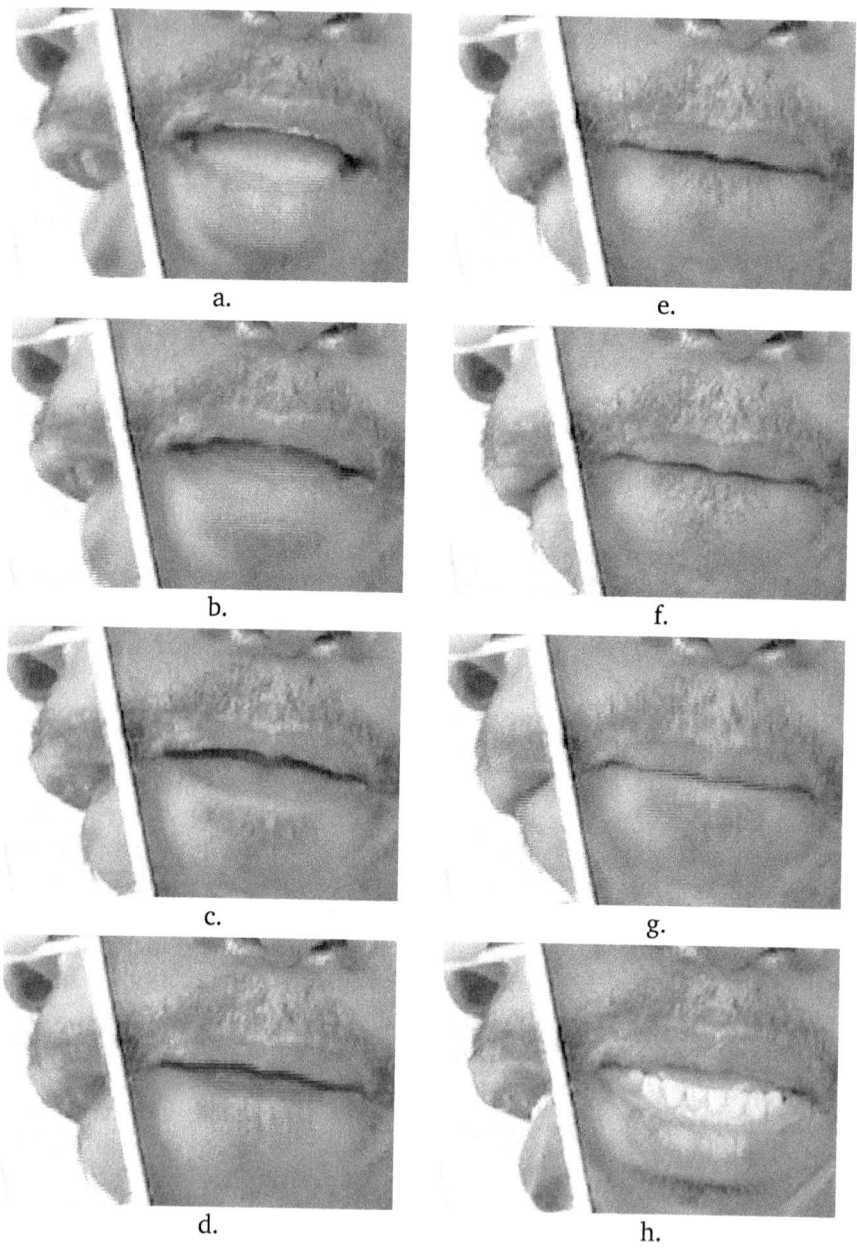

Figure 2.2. Articulation of a portion of the word àwĕtòrò 'activator in an animal trap' (Speaker A, cf. chapter 8). Frames are 30 ms apart. From Olson and Hajek (1999).

2.1 Consonants

There are two steps in the articulation of the labial flap w̌. In the first step, the lower lip retracts into the oral cavity to a position behind the upper teeth. At the same time, the upper lip descends to wrap over the upper teeth. In the second step, the lower lip moves forward quickly, flapping against the upper lip as it exits the oral cavity. It is voiced throughout the articulation. In addition, during the articulation of the sound, the tongue bunches in the back of the mouth, adding a velar component to the sound.

The video frames in figure 2.2 show eight steps in the articulation of a bilabial flap in Mono. The word is àw̌étòrò 'activator in an animal trap', produced by a thirty-year-old male speaker. The frames are in 30 ms intervals. Frame a shows the mouth during the articulation of the vowel [a]. Frames b through f show the first stage of the articulation of the flap during which the lower lip is slowly brought into the mouth. Also at the same time, the upper lip is brought down to cover the upper teeth. This stage takes about 120 ms. Frame g shows the beginning of the second stage of the articulation. The upper lip remains stationary as the lower lip begins its movement forward and makes contact with the upper lip. Frame h shows the lips immediately after the flap. Note that the lower lip has moved down exposing the lower teeth, while the upper lip has moved upward, but remains slightly tensed.

The data in (1) show sample contrasts between the labial consonants in Mono.

(1) a. Labial consonants before *a* in word-medial position

ɓ	ɓá-lɔ́	'at'
p	pa	'say'
b	bàdʒà	'rock'
mb	mbātā	'stool'
f	fa	'become'
v	va	'pour'
m	ma	'show'
w̌	w̌a	'send'

b. Labial consonants before *a* in word-medial position

ɓ	kòɓà	'illness'
p	àpá	'tsetse fly'
b	lóbà	'clothes'
mb	kàmbà	'knife'
f	àjī lèfà	'mid-wife'
v	gàvà	'panther'
m	gumà	'prepare'
w̌	kàw̌á	'gruel'

2.1.2 Alveolar consonants

Nine alveolar consonants are attested in Mono: ɗ, t, d, nd, s, z, n, r, and l. The phoneme r is pronounced as a trill [r]. It is often lengthened in discourse, as in the word [ə́rːə́] 'until'. The phoneme l is pronounced as [l], with no velarization.

The implosive ɗ is rare, only occurring in seven lexical items in my corpus.

(2) èɗè   'who'
    gàɗè   'what'
    káɗàwú   'hiccough'
    kɔ́ɗɔ̀   'monkey'
    kūɗā   'debt'
    tʃáɗɔ̀ngɔ́rɔ́   'voice'
    jɔ̄kɔ́ɗɔ̀   'toe'

However, two of these words, èɗè 'who' and gàɗè 'what', are common in discourse. In some lexical items, ɗ varies freely with its plosive counterpart, e.g., tʃáɗɔ̀ngɔ́rɔ́ ~ tʃádɔ̀ngɔ́rɔ́ 'voice'. Also, it is not attested in word-initial position. Because of these factors, I consider it to be a marginal phoneme.

The data in (3) show sample contrasts between the alveolar consonants in Mono.

(3) a. Alveolar consonants before *a* in word-initial position
       ɗ   —
       t   ta   'cut'
       d   da   'slap'
       nd   ndábà   'table'
       s   sa   'leak'
       z   za   'give, take'
       n   na   'go, come'
       r   ráwá   'yell'
       l   la   'lick'

2.1 Consonants

b. Alveolar consonants before *a* in word-medial position

ɗ	kūɗā	'debt'
t	kōtā	'large river, sea'
d	kádá	'oil, grease'
nd	màndà	'door'
s	gósá	'type of green vegetable'
z	mbāzā	'xylophone'
n	vànā	'four'
r	bāmàrā	'lion'
l	ámbálá	'bait'

2.1.3 Palatal consonants

I group alveopalatal and palatal consonants into a palatal category, which consists of seven consonants: tʃ, dʒ, ndʒ, ʃ, ʒ, ɲ, and j.

The phoneme ʒ is relatively rare, both in discourse and the lexicon. It occurs in thirteen words in my corpus.

(4)
ēʒē	'caterpillar'
īʒī	'tooth'
ngéʒì jāvūrū	'drizzle'
ōʒōrō	'fat'
tʃáàgūʒàrà	'shade, shelter'
ʒe	'grovel'
ʒerə̀	'descend'
ʒi	'belch'
ʒingbà	'grumble, roar'
ʒīwù	'embers'
ʒo	'wake up'
ʒu	'burn'
ʒūgwā	'forest spirit'

However, contrasts are readily attested, as shown below. In addition, it occurs in the major grammatical categories.

The phonemic status of ɲ is questionable for two reasons. First, it is rare both in discourse and the lexicon. It is attested in only five lexical items in my corpus.

(5) gàɲá   'branch'
    ngbáɲá   'echo'
    ɲáō   'cat' (loanword from Lingala, Van Everbroeck
                    n.d.:231)
    ɲa   'have patience'
    ɲi ~ ni   'rain'

Second, in at least one case, it can be replaced by an alveolar nasal, e.g., *ɲi ~ ni* 'rain'. In addition, *ɲ* can alternatively be analyzed as a sequence of *n* plus the secondary articulation *j* (discussed in chapter 4). On the other hand, it is attested in both word-initial and word-medial positions. I consider it to be a marginal phoneme.

The data in (6) show sample contrasts between the palatal consonants in Mono.

(6) a. Palatal consonants before *i* in word-initial position
       tʃ   tʃi   'shine'
       dʒ   dʒi   'sense'
       ndʒ   ndʒi   'be straight'
       ʃ   ʃi   'plant'
       ʒ   ʒi   'belch'
       ɲ   ɲi ~ ni   'rain'
       j   ji   'enter'

    b. Palatal consonants before *i* in word-medial position
       tʃ   tʃī   'song'
       dʒ   àkídʒì   'bead'
       ndʒ   ngbándʒì   'rust'
       ʃ   ngúʃī   'saliva'
       ʒ   īʒī   'tooth, tusk'
       ɲ   kɔ́-ɲì ~ kɔ́-nì   'to rain'
       j   àjī   'mother'

2.1.4 Velar and glottal consonants

Three velar and two glottal consonants are attested in Mono: *k, g, ng, ʔ,* and *h.* The prenasalized stop *ng* is pronounced [ŋg]. The phoneme *h* is pronounced with more friction than the *h* in English.

The phoneme *k* is the most commonly attested consonant in Mono discourse. This corresponds to Maddieson's (1997) observation that *k* is the most commonly attested consonant in most languages.

2.1 Consonants

There is much evidence to support the status of the glottal stop ʔ as a phoneme in Mono. First, it occurs in items from most grammatical categories.

(7) Sample words containing a glottal stop

    a. Nouns
       ïʔïrï   'name'
       káʔjá   'paddle'
       ɔ̀ʔɔ̀   'word'
       tàʔwá   'basin'

    b. Verbs
       ʔa   'suck'
       ʔe   'call'
       ʔurù   'blow'

    c. Pronouns
       āʔā   '1PL.EXCL'
       ēʔē   '2PL'

    d. Kinship terms
       āʔá   'aunt'
       àʔú   'uncle'

    e. Animal names
       jɔ̄ʔɔ́   'cricket'
       jáʔɔ̀ngɔ̀   'eel'

    f. Adverbs (both ideophones)
       vàʔè   'throw out'
       wǐʔí   'throw out'

Second, the glottal stop is not rare, either in the lexicon or in discourse.

Third, it is attested both in word-initial and word-medial positions. However, here a caveat must be noted. Its phonemic status in word-initial position is dubious, as is the case in many Ubangian languages (Boyd 1989:200). The cases of the glottal stop occurring in word-initial position in Mono are in cliticized pronouns (e.g., ʔā '1PL.EXCL', ʔē '2PL') and in inflected verbs (e.g., ʔa 'suck', ʔe 'call', ʔurù 'blow'). It does not contrast with its absence in this position, so one possible interpretation of the glottal stop in these cases is that it is epenthetic. There is evidence for and against this interpretation in the case of the pronouns. If the pronoun ʔā '1PL.EXCL' is the subject of a relative clause, the glottal stop is not attested.

(8) á   ʔā   → [aːꜜ],[1] not *[áʔā]
     REL 1PL.EXCL
     'that we (excl.)'

This implies that the lexical entry for the word '1PL.EXCL' is *ā* rather than *ʔā*. On the other hand, the glottal stop is obligatory in most other cases; for example *mɔ̄ bálà ʔē* 'I greet you (PL)' must be pronounced [mɔ̄ bálà ʔē], not *[mɔ̄ bálà ē]. In addition, evidence from verbal word patterns discussed in section 6.2 also suggests that the initial glottal stop is epenthetic. There, treating the glottal stop in inflected verbs as epenthetic fills in gaps within the set of attested word patterns.

The status of *h* as a phoneme in Mono is debatable. It is rare in both discourse and in the lexicon. It occurs in sixteen words in my corpus, most of which are ideophones, but it does occur in other grammatical categories as well, as shown in (9). I consider it to be a marginal phoneme.

(9) Words containing *h*
    a. Nouns
        éhérɔ́   'wax'
        hérélá   'gourd rattle, lock'
        hójá ò?ò 'whisper'
    b. Verbs
        herɔ̀ ōpōrō 'hatch'
    c. Adverbs (all ideophones)
        háàō   'empty-handed'
        hàgà   'hard, wide'
        hàò   'brightly'
        háò   'quickly, without reflecting'
        hàrá   'giant, high'
        héré   'sharp'
        hɔ̀rɔ̀gɔ̀   'hidden'
        hwìjà   'hot'
        kpàhà   'wide open'
        ngɔ̄hɔ́rɔ́   'narrow, hollow'
    d. Adjectives
        āhārā   'dry'
        táhárá   'light'

---

[1] The symbol [ꜜ] is the IPA tone letter for a high-falling tone.

2.1 Consonants

The data in (10) show sample contrasts for the velar and glottal consonants in Mono.

(10) a. Velar and glottal consonants before *a* in word-initial position
    ʔ   ʔa   'suck'
    k   ka   'be finished'
    g   ga   'be good'
    ng   nga   'bark'
    h   hàgà   'hard'

    b. Velar and glottal consonants before *a* in word-medial position
    ʔ   āʔá   'aunt'
    k   dakà   'borrow'
    g   bàgá   'cheek'
    ng   lēngā   'slit drum'
    h   kpàhà   'wide open'

2.1.5 Labial-velar consonants

Four labial-velar consonants are attested in Mono: *kp, gb, ngb,* and *w*. The phonetic pronunciations of the first three phonemes are [k͡p], [g͡b], and [ŋ͡g͡b], respectively. All four consonants are well attested, but *ngb* is rare in discourse.

The data in (11) show sample contrasts between all the labial-velar and labial consonants in Mono.

(11) a. Labial-velar and labial consonants before *a* in word-initial position
    kp   kpa   'flee'
    gb   gba   'moisten'
    ngb   ngba   'be many'
    w   wa   'cut'
    ɓ   ɓá-lɔ́   'at'
    p   pa   'say'
    b   bàdʒà   'rock'
    mb   mbātā   'stool'
    f   fa   'become'
    v   va   'pour'
    m   ma   'show'
    w̌   w̌a   'send'

b. Labial-velar and labial consonants before *a* in word-medial position

kp	ndʒòkpā	'ten'
gb	kógbà	'granary'
ngb	kéngbā	'alone'
w	bīwā	'nasal mucus'
ɓ	kòɓà	'illness'
p	àpá	'tsetse fly'
b	lóbà	'clothes'
mb	kàmbà	'knife'
f	àjī lèfà	'mid-wife'
v	gàvà	'panther'
m	gumà	'prepare'
w̌	kàw̌á	'gruel'

2.2 Vowels

According to my analysis, Mono has eight vowel phonemes: *i, e, ɨ, ə, a, u, o,* and *ɔ*. The pronunciation of each phoneme is the same as the corresponding symbol in the International Phonetic Alphabet. Long and nasal vowels exist, but these features are not contrastive phonemically. Olson and Schrag (2000) and Kamanda (1998) consider the system to be asymmetric, as shown in the chart in figure 2.3.

	front	central	back
high	i	ɨ	u
mid	e	ə	o
low		a	ɔ

Figure 2.3. Vowel phonemes in Mono.

In terms of Chomsky and Halle's (1968) distinctive features, Mono vowels can be categorized as shown in (12). These feature values will useful for describing the vowel spreading rules of Mono, which will be discussed in chapters 6 and 7.

2.2 Vowels

(12)

	i	e	ɨ	ə	a	u	o	ɔ
[high]	+	−	+	−	−	+	−	−
[low]	−	−	−	−	+	−	−	+
[back]	−	−	+	+	+	+	+	+
[round]	−	−	−	−	−	+	+	+

All other things being equal, vowel systems tend towards symmetry, so the system shown in figure 2.3 is unexpected. However, vowel systems which are symmetric except for the lack of the front low vowel ɛ are not uncommon in African languages. They have been attested in several language families.

(13) Languages which are symmetric except for a missing front low vowel ɛ[2]

   a. Banda: Langbasi, Ngbugu, Ngundu, Kpagua, Gubu, Gbi, Linda, and Yakpa (Cloarec-Heiss 1978)

   b. Adamawa: Karan (Hartell 1993)

   c. Gur: Lyele (Bassole 1982), Moba (Russell 1985)

   d. Grassfields Bantu: Ewondo and Metta (Hartell 1993), Moghamo (Stallcup 1978)

   e. Bantoid: Mambila (Perrin and Hill 1969)

   f. Central Sudanic: Sara-Mbay (Cloarec-Heiss 1995a:326)

Boyd (1989:202) notes that Adamawa-Ubangian languages typically have triangular seven- or nine-vowel systems, but if there is an asymmetry, it is usually manifested as the lack of ɛ. In Zing and Karang (both Adamawan), there has been a merger of e and ɛ. For Banda (which includes Mono), Boyd suggests that ɛ has shifted to a more central position.

A couple of typological observations are worth noting concerning the Mono vowel system. First, Crothers (1978) observes that eight-vowel systems are relatively rare in the world's languages, so the Mono system is not widely attested. Second, the Mono system appears to contradict a universal put forth by Crothers: "The number of height distinctions in front vowels is equal to or greater than the number in back vowels" (p. 122). According to the analysis of Olson and Schrag and Kamanda, Mono has three back vowels, but only two front vowels.

---

[2] Most of these references were pointed out to me by Roderic Casali (pers. comm.)

If *a* were reinterpreted as a low front vowel rather than a low central vowel, Mono would then have three front vowels, *i*, *e*, and *a*, two central vowels, *ɨ* and *ə*, and three back vowels, *u*, *o*, and *ɔ*. This analysis would result in a system which agrees with Crothers' universal concerning vowel height distinctions. It also results in a symmetric system if we followed Crothers in classifying vowels into *peripheral* (front, low, and back) and *interior* (central, but non-low) groupings. This reanalyzed vowel system is shown in figure 2.4.

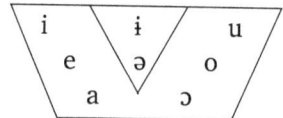

Figure 2.4. Reanalyzed Mono vowel system.

There is some phonetic justification for this reanalysis. In section 8.2.1, I note that the vowel *a* [a] in Mono is further forward in the vowel space than the corresponding vowel *a* of English, which is phonetically closer to [ɑ].

The mid central vowel *ə* is the most common vowel in Mono discourse, followed closely by *a*. Cross-linguistically, *a* is the most common vowel (Maddieson 1997), but in languages with central vowels, *ə* is often the most common. English and French offer familiar examples of this. In Mono, the frequency of *ə* may be due to the fact that it occurs in several words which are quite common in discourse, as shown in (14).

(14) Common words containing *ə*
    ə̄mə̄   '1SG'
    ə̀ɓə̀   '2SG'
    tʃə̀   '3SG'
    ə́   'same subject'
    kə́-   'INF'
    kə̀-də́   'be (equative)'
    nə̀   'DET'
    kə́-sə̀   'be (existential)'

The low central vowel *a* is optionally raised to [ʌ] when preceded or followed by a high vowel, as shown in (15). Phonetic evidence for this raising is given in section 8.2.1.

2.2 Vowels

(15) [tīmà] ~ [tīmʌ̀] 'tongue' [àmàzɪ̀] ~ [àmʌ̀zɪ̀] 'morning'
     [zúwā] ~ [zúwʌ̄] 'flour'³ [tʃáfù] ~ [tʃʌ́fù] 'odor'
     [bīʃà] ~ [bīʃʌ̀] 'two' [ŋg͡bābī] ~ [ŋg͡bʌ̄bī] 'bone'

Vowel nasalization is not contrastive in Mono. It occurs on vowels which follow nasal consonants. I also observed weak nasalization on word-initial vowels preceding a nasal or prenasalized consonant, e.g., [ə̃̀ndʒē] ~ [ɛ̃̀ndʒē] '3PL'.

According to my auditory impressions, nasalization is most pronounced on low back vowels and least pronounced on low non-back vowels. It is strongest on o and ɔ.

(16) [mõnõ] 'Mono'
     [mɔ̃] 'be tired'
     [kɔ̀nɔ̃́] 'hippopotamus'

On other vowels, nasalization occurs, but it is weaker.

(17) [kũmũ̀] 'head'
     [mĩ] 'bother'
     [ŋgómẽ] 'dew'
     [ɔ̃mɔ̃́] '1SG'
     [vànã̄] 'four'

This variation in the perceived strength of nasalization is likely due to the interaction of nasal formants with vowel formants. When there is significant overlap between these, the effect will be a greater perception of nasalization. Acoustic characteristics of vowel nasalization will be discussed in section 8.2.3.

Nasalization does not spread across a consonant.

(18) [dù mɔ́lɔ̄] 'play' (*[dù mɔ̃́lɔ̃̄])
     [mõtótòrò] '(proper name)' (*[mõtṍtõ̀rõ̀])

The data in (19) show sample contrasts between the vowels in Mono.

---

³A more common alternant is [zúwū].

(19) a. Contrasts between vowels following word-initial d
i	di	'be tangled'
e	de	'chop'
ɨ	dɨ	'count'
ə	də	'be (equative)'
a	da	'slap'
u	du	'tether'
o	do	'become a fool'
ɔ	dɔ	'stomp'

b. Contrasts between vowels following word-medial d
i	kómádīrɨ	'hawk'
e	àdēngɔ̀	'bend'
ɨ	ɨdɨ	'horn, antler'
ə	ɔ́dɔ̄	'and'
a	kádá	'oil, grease'
u	bùdú	'bottom'
o	gbàdò	'grub'
ɔ	ɔ̄dɔ̄	'laziness'

2.3 Distribution of Phonemes

2.3.1 Distribution in the syllable

Sampson (1985:140) and Cloarec-Heiss (1986:26) note co-occurrence restrictions between consonants and vowels in the Banda languages Tangbago and Linda, respectively, which are closely related to Mono. Specifically, two restrictions hold in those languages. First, the alveolar fricatives *s* and *z* do not occur before the front vowels *i* and *e*. Second, the palatal consonants *tʃ, dʒ, ndʒ, ʃ*, and *ʒ* do not occur before the central vowels *ɨ* and *ə*. These restrictions are shown in (20).

(20)
	i	e	ɨ	ə
s	−	−	+	+
z	−	−	+	+
tʃ	+	+	−	−
dʒ	+	+	−	−
ndʒ	+	+	−	−
ʃ	+	+	−	−
ʒ	+	+	−	−

2.3 Distribution of Phonemes

Olson and Schrag mention these same co-occurrence restrictions for Mono, but note that there are exceptions. Indeed, several exceptions exist in my corpus.

(21) səpè ~ sepè   'stay'
     ʃɨkù ~ ʃīkù   'scar'
     ʃɔ́tā ~ ʃétā   'intestine'
     tʃə̀ ~ èʃè   '3SG'
     tʃə́-   'towards'

In the Mono lexicon, exceptions to the general restriction are rare, but two of the forms, tʃə̀ '3SG' and tʃə́- 'towards' are quite common in Mono discourse. It appears then, that these restrictions are being relaxed in Mono. This may be partly due to pressure from the trade language, Lingala, spoken in the Mono region but not in the Tangbago and Linda regions. In Lingala, alveolar fricatives freely occur before front vowels, e.g., *sika* 'new', *sékó* 'always', *ko-zíka* 'to burn', *zéka* 'obstacle'.

Table 2.1 shows all the C+V combinations attested in Mono. A full set of sample words is given in table D.1 of appendix D. The first sign in each box is for word-initial syllables, the second sign is for non-initial syllables. A plus sign (+) indicates that the C+V combination is attested in my corpus. A minus sign (–) indicates that it is not attested. A minus sign with an asterisk (–*) indicates forms which are attested by Kamanda.

Some paradigms in the table are nearly complete, such as contrast before the vowel *a* in both word-initial and word-medial position. However, several C+V combinations are not attested in Mono (besides the cases in 20). The gaps involving the marginal phonemes can simply be attributed to the limited number of occurrences of these segments. On the other hand, certain categories are clearly dispreferred in Mono. These include a labial consonant followed by ɔ, a palatal consonant followed by ɔ, and velar and glottal consonants followed by ə.

Table 2.1. Consonant-vowel combinations in Mono

C \ V	i	e	ɨ	ə	a	u	o	ɔ
ɓ	+/+	–/–	–/–	+/+	+/+	–/+	–/+	–/–
p	+/+	+/+	+/+	–/–*	+/+	+/+	+/+	+/+
b	+/+	+/+	+/+	–/+	+/+	+/+	–/+	+/–
mb	+/+	+/+	+/+	+/+	+/+	+/+	–/+	–/–
f	–/–	+/+	–/–	+/–	+/+	+/+	+/+	–/–
v	+/+	+/+	+/+	–/–	+/+	+/+	+/+	–/–
m	+/+	+/+	+/+	+/+	+/+	+/+	+/+	+/+
w̌	+/+	+/+	+/+	–*/–	+/+	+/+	–/–	–/–
ɗ	–/–	–/+	–/–	–/–	–/+	–/–	–/–*	–/+
t	+/+	+/+	+/+	+/+	+/+	+/+	+/+	+/+
d	+/+	+/+	+/+	+/+	+/+	+/+	+/+	+/+
nd	+/+	+/+	+/+	+/+	+/+	+/+	+/+	+/+
s	–/–	+/+	–/–	+/+	+/+	+/+	+/+	+/+
z	–/–	–/–	+/+	+/+	+/+	+/+	+/+	–/+
n	+/+	+/+	+/+	+/+	+/+	–/+	–/+	+/+
r	+/+	–/+	–/+	+/+	+/+	+/+	+/+	–/+
l	+/+	+/+	+/+	+/+	+/+	+/+	+/+	+/+
tʃ	+/+	+/–	–/–	+/+	+/+	+/+	–/+	+/+
dʒ	+/+	+/+	–/–	–/–	+/+	–/+	+/+	–/+
ndʒ	+/+	+/+	–/–	–/–	+/+	–/+	+/+	+/–
ʃ	+/+	+/+	+/–	+/–	+/+	+/+	+/+	–/+
ʒ	+/+	+/+	–/–	–/–	–/–*	+/+	+/+	–/–
ɲ	+/+	–/–	–/–	–/–	+/+	–/–	–/–	–/–
j	+/+	+/+	–/–	–/–	–/+	+/+	+/+	+/+
ʔ	+/+	+/+	+/+	–/–	+/+	+/+	+/+	+/+
k	+/+	+/+	+/+	+/–	+/+	+/+	+/+	+/+
g	+/+	+/+	+/+	–/–	+/+	+/+	+/+	+/+
ng	+/+	+/+	+/+	–/–	+/+	+/+	+/+	+/+
h	–/–	+/+	–/–	–/–	+/+	–/–*	+/–	+/+
kp	+/+	+/+	+/+	+/–	+/+	+/+	+/+	+/+
gb	–/–	+/+	–/+	–*/–	+/+	–/+	+/+	+/+
ngb	+/+	+/+	+/+	+/+	+/+	+/+	+/+	+/+
w	–/–	+/+	–/–	–/–	+/+	+/+	+/+	–/–

2.3.2 Distribution in the word

Vowel harmony is attested in some Ubangian languages, especially of the Zande group, so it is worth examining if this phenomenon is evident in Mono. Table 2.2 lists the co-occurrence of vowels in CV_1CV_2 patterns. In most cases, the examples are taken from bisyllabic tautomorphemic words. Additional examples are from longer words, for example, CV_1CV_2CV or $CVCV_1CV_2$. Table D.2 in appendix D gives a complete list of the words used as evidence for these combinations. Plus signs in parentheses indicate forms which are either heteromorphemic or exhibit variation.

Most combinations of vowels are attested within Mono words, and so strict vowel harmony is not attested in Mono. However, it is also true that words containing both high and mid vowels are rare in the lexicon.

Table 2.2. Vowel-vowel (CV_1CV_2) co-occurrences

V_1 \ V_2	i	e	ɨ	ə	a	u	o	ɔ
i	+	−	+	(+)	+	+	(+)	+
e	+	+	−	+	+	+	+	+
ɨ	+	+	+	−	+	+	+	−
ə	+	+	(+)	+	+	(+)	+	+
a	+	+	+	+	+	+	+	(+)
u	+	+	+	+	+	+	+	+
o	−	+	−	+	+	+	+	+
ɔ	+	+	(+)	(+)	+	+	+	+

Consonant harmony is also attested in some Ubangian languages, for example, Ngbaka-Ma'bo (Thomas 1963). Such systems restrict the co-occurrence of consonants in C_1VC_2V patterns. However, I leave this topic for further research.

3

Tone

The majority of African languages have tonal systems, and Mono is no exception. Mono has three contrastive level tones: high (H, marked with an acute accent above the vowel), mid (M, marked with a macron above the vowel), and low (L, marked with a grave accent). Rising and falling contour tones also exist in the language, but I analyze them as sequences of level tones as discussed below.

Tone carries both lexical and grammatical function in Mono. In fact, tone bears such a significant functional load in the Banda languages that several speech surrogates have arisen. Sampson (1985:143) reports whistle talk in Tangbago. Arom and Cloarec-Heiss (1976) report the use of talking drums in Linda. In Mono, I have observed the use of xylophones for sending messages.

3.1 Lexical Tone

Lexical tone occurs on nouns, adjectives, adverbs, and grammatical function words, such as prepositions. In addition, there is some evidence that verbs have underlying lexical tone, a point which will be discussed in chapter 7. The items in (22) provide evidence of contrast between the three level tones in Mono and show at the same time the lexical function of tone.

(22) H vs. M [g͡bándà] 'net'   [àwó] 'lung'
              [g͡bāndà] 'hunting shelter' [àwō] 'wife'
     H vs. L [kúzū] 'semen'   [káʔjá] 'paddle'
              [kùzū] 'death'   [káʔjà] 'weaver bird'
     M vs. L [mārā] 'barren'
              [màrā] 'clan, fetish'

Mono also contains phonetic contour tones: falling (F, marked with a circumflex above the vowel) and rising (R, marked with a wedge above the vowel). I do not consider these to be contrastive, however, for the following reasons. First, the vowels which bear contour tones are always phonetically long, so minimal pairs with the level tones cannot be established. In tautomorphemic environments, phonetically long vowels always bear contour tones, and vowels with level tones are phonetically short. In heteromorphemic environments, if a morphological or syntactic process creates a situation where two identical vowels with identical tones are adjacent, an optional process applies to resolve the hiatus. For example, when the plural prefix à- is applied to a word beginning with à, an optional *l* is inserted, as in (23a). Also, if vowel hiatus (see section 7.2.2) creates an *a + a* sequence, the sequence is reduced to a short *a* in normal speech, as in (23b).

(23) a. à-àbá   → àlàbá   'fathers'
     b. mə̄ bálà ɓə̀ àtà → mə̄ bálà ɓàatà
                        → mə̄ bálà [ɓàtà]   'I greet you.'

(24) Tautomorphemic words containing contour tones
     bákjákjáà   'shallow'
     fōòtʃē   'fever'
     gbàdʒéè   'pineapple'
     háàō   'empty-handed'
     kàféè   'coffee' (borrowed from French)
     kòtóò   'how much/how many'
     kpə́ə̀ndòrò   'nudity'
     kpòó   'close together'
     lùú   'anew'
     mīndúù   'five'
     ngbáàkóró   'funeral'
     tóò   'clean'
     tʃáàngbēndè   'calf'
     tʃàálà   'hyrax'
     wáā   'very much'
     zɨ́ɨ̀   'smooth, flat'

3.1 Lexical Tone

Second, tautomorphemic contour tones are rare in the lexicon, and many of the occurrences are in plant and animal names, ideophones, and loanwords. All of the examples of tautomorphemic contour tones on phonetically long vowels in my corpus are shown in (24).

Note that contour tones occur in three words which are common in discourse: *mīndúù* 'five', *kòtóò* 'how much/how many', and *wáā* 'very much'.

Third, while minimal tone pairs are not found in my corpus due to the rarity of such examples in Mono, my language resource persons differentiate three types of falling tones in tautomorphemic environments, labeled HL, HM, and ML in (25).[1]

(25) HL   HM   ML
    [g͡bàdʒeːꜜ]   *[g͡bàdʒeːꜜ]   *[g͡bàdʒeːꜜ]   'pineapple'
    *[waːꜜ]   [waːꜜ]   *[waːꜜ]   'very much'
    *[foːꜜtʃē]   *[foːꜜtʃē]   [foːꜜtʃē]   'fever'

Finally, in at least one case, there is a minimal pair between two falling tones in a heteromorphemic environment. According to my analysis, one results from a HM combination, and one results from a HL combination, as shown in (26). The word *á* 'REL' is a relative clause marker. See section 2.1.4 for a discussion of the status of the glottal stop in this example.

(26) a. á ʔà [aːꜜ] 'that we (INCL)'
      b. á ʔā [aːꜜ] 'that we (EXCL)'

Thus, I interpret a contour tone to be a sequence of two distinct level tones. The question which arises is whether to consider the vowel associated with these tones to be a single vowel or a geminate. In tautomorphemic environments, there is evidence that it should be considered a single vowel. In the stative aspect and certainty mood, a single reduplicated vowel receives two tonal specifications. This will be discussed further in the next section. The independence of the number of tones and the number of vowels was observed as early as Pike and Pike (1947:82), who note this phenomenon in Mazateco. Mono and Mazateco differ in one major respect, however. In Mono, if two tones occur on a single vowel, the vowel is phonetically long, whereas in Mazateco, the length of the vowel remains nearly constant. In moraic theory, tautomorphemic contour tones in Mono are represented as in (27).

---

[1] The tone letters [ꜜ, ꜝ, ꜜ] (IPA 1999) indicate falling, high-falling, and low-falling tones, respectively.

(27)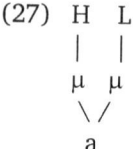

Heteromorphemic cases such as in (25a) clearly involve two distinct vowels. Those can be represented as in (28).

(28)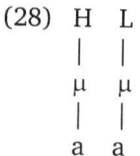

In both cases, I transcribe a contour tone as a sequence of two distinct level tones over adjacent identical vowels, for example, áà = [a:\]. I have done this for the sake of ease of transcription, but the reader should keep in mind that this represents the two different configurations in (27) and (28).

3.2 Grammatical Tone

Besides the lexical function, tone also has a grammatical function in Mono. Specifically, the change of tone on the first syllable of the verb (and in one case the subject pronoun) marks tense, aspect, and mood (TAM). A more detailed discussion of the TAM categories is given in section 7.2.

Verb morphology in Mono provides no evidence for lexical tone on verbs. Cloarec-Heiss (1986:319) notes that verbs in the related language Linda can be divided into two classes as to whether they bear a M or L tone for the consecutive aspect. However, in Mono, we have not observed this pattern. There is some evidence from derivational processes, however, that there is inherent tone on verb roots in Mono. This will be discussed in section 7.1.1.

3.2 Grammatical Tone

Non-future (NF)

The non-future tense indicates either the present or the past. It is marked by a H tone on the first syllable of the verb. All following syllables of the verb bear a L tone, as is the case in many tone languages.

(29) a. bākòŋɔ́ zá̱ āwā
　　　turtle take:NF road
　　　'The turtle left.'

　　b. ɔ́ tá̱rà ɓálàngú ɓá-ndɔ́ kɔ̀nɔ́
　　　SS descend:NF at-eye-water at-home hippo
　　　'He descended into the water to hippo's place.'

　　c. mɔ̄ ná̱ gà-lɔ́ kɨ̄ndɨ
　　　1SG go:NF to-in garden
　　　'I'm going to the fields.'

Future (FUT)

In the future tense, a H tone occurs on the final syllable of a subject pronoun preceding the verb, and a L tone occurs on the vowels in the verb. If the sentence does not have a subject pronoun in its non-future counterpart, the same subject pronoun ɔ́ is inserted for the future form as in (30).

(30) a. ɓɔ̱́ wù̱ mɔ̄ zə̀
　　　2SG:FUT see:FUT 1SG EMPH
　　　'You will see me!'

　　b. ò?ò nə̀ ɔ̱́ kà̱
　　　word DET SS end:FUT
　　　'The problem will be resolved.'

For ʔà '1PL.INCL', a rising tone results rather than the expected H tone.

(31) ʔàá̱ kò̱
　　　1PL.INCL:FUT fight.FUT
　　　'We will fight.'

A motivation for the existence of the rising tone in (31) is that it preserves contrast between the 1PL.INCL and 1PL.EXCL forms. If both pronouns followed the regular pattern of the paradigm by replacing the default tone with a H tone, then both would be realized as ʔá. The entire paradigm is shown in (32).

(32) citation form   subject form   future form
       āmā   mā   mɔ́   '1SG'
       ə́ɓə̀   ɓə̀   ɓɔ́   '2SG'
       èʃè   tʃə̀   tʃɔ́   '3SG'
       àzɔ́   ʔà   ʔàá   '1PL.INCL'
       āʔā   ʔā   ʔá   '1PL.EXCL'
       ē?ē   ʔē   ʔé   '2PL'
       èndʒē   èndʒē   èndʒé   '3PL'

Imperative (IMP)

The imperative mood (33a), as well as obligations (33b) and interdictions, is marked by a L tone on the first vowel of the verb.

(33) a. wu̱   sɔ́   nə̀   àdékē   ʔàá   kò...
         see:IMP   place   DET   that   1PL.INCL:FUT   fight:FUT
         'Know that we will fight...'

  b. ɔ́   lí   àdékē   ɓə̀   sə̱̀   də̀   kúwùsə́rə̀
      SS   be.necessary:NF   that   2SG   be:OB   with   wisdom
      'You need to have wisdom.'

Subjunctive (SUBJ)

Advice (34a) as well as actions which are dependent on the action of the previous clause (34b) are marked by a M tone on the first vowel of the verb.

(34) a. ʔà   nā   gà-ndɔ́   màgbà
         1PL.INCL   go:SUBJ   to-home   PN
         'Let's go to Magba's house.'

  b. zà   úŋgú   fə̄   mā   mā   ndʒō
      give:IMP   water   BEN   1SG   1SG   drink:SUBJ
      'Give me water (in order that) I drink.'

Stative (STAT)

In the stative aspect, the first syllable of the verb root is reduplicated and prefixed to the verb. The vowel of the reduplicant is lengthened (cf. 35b) and bears a HL pattern. The vowel of the verb root bears a L tone.

(35) a. ɔ́ ʃúù-ʃù
    SS RED:STAT-bitter:STAT
    'It is bitter.'

   b. café ʃú
      coffee bitter:NF
      'The coffee is bitter.'

Certainty (CERT)

In the certainty mood, the first syllable of the verb root is reduplicated and prefixed to the verb. The vowel of the reduplicant is lengthened, and bears a HM pattern. The first vowel of the verb root bears a M tone, and following vowels bear a L tone.

(36) ɔ́ zúū-zūrù
    SS RED:CERT-be.slippery:CERT
    'It is slippery.'

3.3 Distribution of Tones

3.3.1 Distribution in the syllable

In some languages, voiced obstruents are referred to as DEPRESSOR CONSONANTS. These are followed by a L tone, including in situations where one would expect a non-L tone. This could be looked at as the insertion of a L tone or the maintenance of a L tone in the position after a depressor consonant. Voiced sonorants and implosives rarely pattern with the voiced obstruents with respect to these effects (cf. Hyman 1975:228).

As mentioned in the previous section, the first syllable of a verb bears a H, M, or L tone in Mono, depending on the tense, aspect, and mood. Thus, we expect most, if not all C-tone combinations to be attested. This is indeed the case, as shown in table 3.1. This agrees with Boyd's (1995:15) observation that consonant-tone interaction is not attested in Ubangian.

The one combination which is not attested concerns the marginal consonant phoneme ɗ. A full set of sample words is given in appendix D.

Table 3.1. Consonant-tone co-occurrences

	H	M	L		H	M	L
ɓ	+	+	+	tʃ	+	+	+
p	+	+	+	dʒ	+	+	+
b	+	+	+	ndʒ	+	+	+
mb	+	+	+	ʃ	+	+	+
f	+	+	+	ʒ	+	+	+
v	+	+	+	ɲ	+	+	+
m	+	+	+	j	+	+	+
w̌	+	+	+	ʔ	+	+	+
ɗ	−	+	+	k	+	+	+
t	+	+	+	g	+	+	+
d	+	+	+	ng	+	+	+
nd	+	+	+	h	+	+	+
s	+	+	+	kp	+	+	+
z	+	+	+	gb	+	+	+
n	+	+	+	ngb	+	+	+
r	+	+	+	w	+	+	+
l	+	+	+				

3.3.2 Distribution in the word

Some languages have a limited number of tonal patterns in comparison to the total number of possible tonal combinations. One example concerns TONAL MELODIES. Verbs in Margi, for example, can have a H melody (*tsá* 'beat', *ndábyá* 'touch'), a L melody (*ghà* 'reach', *dzàʔù* 'pound'), or a LH melody (*hǔ* 'grow up', *pàzú* 'lay eggs'), but a HL melody is not attested (Kenstowicz 1994:312–313).

Certain locative adverbs in Mono have a tonal melody associated with them. Regardless of the underlying tones of the individual morphemes, tri-syllabic locative adverbs always have a HLH tonal pattern, as shown in (37).

3.3 Distribution of Tones

(37) a. tʃálàngú   'in the water'
       tʃá-àlà-ngú
       place-eye-water

    b. gásə̀ndá   'into the house'
       ga-ə́sə́-àndà
       to-place-house

Another process which can limit the number of possible tonal combinations is TONAL POLARITY, in which the tone of a morpheme is predictable given its environment. In Mono, the prepositional prefix *ga-* exhibits tonal polarity. If the following morpheme bears a H tone on the first syllable, then *ga-* bears a L tone (38a). If the following morpheme bears either a M tone or a L tone on the first syllable, then *ga-* bears a H tone (38b, c).

(38) a. gà-lə́   'to'
    b. gá-māngbá   'behind'
    c. gá-ndɨ̀rɨ̀   'to the side of'

Mono verbs have a limited number of tonal patterns marking TAM, as discussed in section 3.2. These could be interpreted as being examples of tonal melodies. In contrast to this, the other grammatical categories in Mono do not contain tonal melodies. Rather, all logically possible combinations of level tones for bisyllabic words ($3^2 = 9$) and nearly all possible combinations for trisyllabic words ($3^3 = 27$) are attested.

(39) Combinations of level tones in two-syllable words

HH	gósá	'type of green'
HM	zúwā	'flour'
HL	lóbà	'clothes'
MH	kākó	'leaf'
MM	lēngā	'slit drum'
ML	jāwò	'firewood'
LH	bùdú	'buttocks'
LM	zàjā	'anvil'
LL	gbàdò	'grub'

(40) Combinations of level tones in trisyllablic words

HHH	píngɨ̋wɨ́	'suddenly'
HHM	pélézū	'bat'
HHL	tə́kə́kà	'pain'
HMH	pákūlú	'parrot'
HMM	kómbēlē	'butterfly'
HML	ndíbɨ̄dà	'heel'
HLH	káɗàwú	'hiccough'
HLM	ɓámbàtʃā	'tomorrow'
HLL	gbákòtò	'latrine'
MHM	dʒī-ngíndɨ̄	'bladder'
MHL	gbā-lóbà	'rag'
MHH	—	
MMH	gbāngbālé	'baldness'
MMM	bātīmā	'rope'
MML	ngbāngēwò	'type of cat'
MLH	gūgàtɨ́	'prostitute'
MLM	bākòngō	'tortoise'
MLL	gbā-kòtò	'anthill'
LHH	kàlábí	'head pad'
LHM	àdə́-kē	'that'
LHL	dʒèngétè	'pepper'
LMH	àbūtʃɔ́ ~ būtʃɔ́	'night'
LMM	àgbɨ̄vɨ̄	'pimple'
LML	màkātò	'boundary, frontier'
LLH	bìrùlú	'porcupine'
LLM	kàmàjū	'dung beetle'
LLL	bàngànà	'zebra'

Not all possible combinations are attested for quadrisyllabic words, but this is likely due to the rarity of such words in Mono, and the large number of logically possible combinations ($3^4 = 81$). Some sample words with four distinct tones are given in (41).

(41) Sample combinations of level tones in quadrisyllabic words

HLHM	móròpágō	'traveler'
HLMM	ndógòlēyā	'day before yesterday'
LLLH	àdʒùkùmá	'ghost, ogre'
LHMH	àlédʒōzó	'hail'
LHLH	ndùɓúrùɓú	'blunt'

4
Labialization and Palatalization

Mono syllables may have one of two secondary articulations: labialization or palatalization. All three of these terms have been used in different ways in the literature. Thus, before discussing the realization of these phenomena in Mono, a few definitions are in order.

Ladefoged and Maddieson (1996:354) define a SECONDARY ARTICULATION as "an articulation of a lesser degree of stricture accompanying a primary articulation of a higher degree." In most cases, the secondary articulation is an approximant, but fricatives have also been interpreted as such. The difference in stricture between primary and secondary articulations distinguishes this type of phenomenon from doubly-articulated segments (Catford 1977 refers to these as "co-ordinate co-articulation"), such as [k͡p], where the two articulations have the same degree of stricture.

The timing of a secondary articulation with respect to a primary one has been a topic of consideration as well. Pike points out that there are two cases attested:

> At the time the stop closure is made, an additional modification may be added at the lips (labialization), or at the front of the mouth (palatalization). This articulation may be released either simultaneously with the release of the stop closure or there may be a delayed release. (1947:32)

In other words, in the first case the secondary and primary articulations are pronounced simultaneously. In the second case (which is the case in Mono), the secondary articulation lags behind the primary one so that it is heard as an off-glide in relation to the primary articulation. Ladefoged and Maddieson (1996:355) point out that the distinction between these two cases can be difficult to make, because of the fact that the start and end of an approximant are difficult to demarcate acoustically. However, there are instances where the distinction between the two types of secondary articulation is contrastive. For example, in Russian there is a contrast between *s'est'* [sʲestʲ] 'sit down', in which palatalization occurs simultaneously with *s*, and *syest'* [sʲjestʲ] 'eat up', in which a palatal glide follows the *s* in a consonant-glide cluster. Note that the *s* is palatalized as a result of the following glide. However, if there is a syllable boundary between a consonant and an ensuing palatal glide, then the consonant is not palatalized. For example, *ot'éc* [atʲets] 'father' versus *otjéxat'* [atjexatʲ] 'to go away riding' (Bill Darden, pers. comm.).

The terms LABIALIZATION and PALATALIZATION have been used to refer to both phonetic and phonological phenomena. In the phonetic usage, they describe certain types of secondary articulations, as discussed above. Labialization refers to the addition of a lip rounding gesture (Ladefoged and Maddieson note that in most cases, there is an accompanying raising of the back of the tongue as well), and palatalization refers to the addition of a high front tongue position, i.e., [i]. For example, Russian contrasts the presence and absence of palatalization on certain segments: [krɔf] 'roof' versus [krɔfʲ] 'blood' (Ladefoged 1982:210). Pohnpeian contrasts the presence or absence of labialization on certain segments: [kap] 'bundle', [kapʷ] 'new' (Ladefoged and Maddieson 1996:360).

The other use of the terms concerns phonological alternations in which the primary articulation itself is modified. For example, English *s* is said to be "palatalized" when it becomes ʃ, such as in the change from *press* to *pressure*. Also, the phoneme *k* is said to be "palatalized" in English when it precedes a front vowel, as in [k̟ʰij] 'key' versus [kʰɑɹ] 'car'.

When I use the terms labialization, palatalization, and secondary articulation in discussing Mono, I am referring specifically to the presence of lip rounding or front tongue position in addition to a primary articulation, and to the fact that these secondary articulations are realized as off-glides from the primary articulation.

4.1 Description

The presence of labialization in Mono is not surprising, since as Ladefoged and Maddieson (1996:356) note, it is the most widely attested secondary articulation in the world's languages.

Labialization and palatalization in Mono are most often heard as the phonetically short mid-vowels [o̞] and [e̞], respectively, but they may also be heard as [u̞] and [i̞]. The fact that they are most often realized in the mid range of the vowel space as opposed to the high range is of typological interest, since cross-linguistically they are most often considered to correspond to high vowels rather than mid ones. Leftward vowel spreading, which is discussed in detail in sections 6.1 and 7.2.1, provides additional evidence that these secondary articulations are mid rather than high in the vowel space. In one example of this process in (42), the quality of the vowel of a verb root is spread to the schwa of an infinitive prefix.

(42) kə́-jù → kṳ́-jù   'to ask'

When the root begins with a syllable containing a secondary articulation, it is the quality of the secondary articulation, rather than the vowel, which spreads.

(43) kə́-gjà → ké̱-gjà   'to stir'

In this case, the vowel of the prefix becomes *e*. If palatalization in Mono were fundamentally high in the vowel space, we would expect the vowel of the prefix to become *i*, yielding **kí-gjà*.

In this study, labialization and palatalization are written as *w* and *j*, respectively. They are in complementary distribution with the labial and palatal semi-vowel phonemes by the fact that they occur following a consonant, rather than in syllable-initial position. Both contrast with their absence: *āgā* 'horn' versus *āgwā* 'buffalo', and *ángá* 'another' versus *ángjá* 'bamboo'.

Contrary to Kamanda's (1998) transcription, labialization and palatalization do not bear tone in Mono. In cases where a verb containing a secondary articulation bears a HM or HL tonal pattern, the first tone is not heard on the secondary articulation but rather is heard on the vowel.

(44) a. èndʒē sə́   kə́-kwá̱ā-kwā
         3PL   be   INF-RED-return:CERT
         'They will return.'

b. ɔ́   gjáà-gjà
   SS   RED-stir:STAT
   'It is difficult.'

Evidence for this analysis comes from the tonal patterns in the certainty mood, discussed in section 3.2. In this mood, the first syllable of the verb root is reduplicated and the reduplicant is then prefixed to the root. The reduplicant takes a HM tone pattern, the first vowel of the root bears a M tone, and remaining vowels in the root bear a L tone, as in (45).

(45) ɔ́   zúū-zūrù
      SS   RED:CERT-be.slippery:CERT
      'It is slippery.'

Consider (44a) above. If labialization bore tone in this example, we would expect it to take the M tone and the vowel *a* in the root to take a L tone, as in (46).

(46) *èndʒē sɔ́   kɔ́-kóā-kōà
       3PL   be   INF-RED-return:CERT
      'They will return.'

However, this is not what we find. Instead, the M tone skips the secondary articulation and lodges on the *a* instead. In other words, the secondary articulation is transparent to the tone patterns, and so it is best to interpret it as not bearing tone.

The two secondary articulations have a limited distribution in the syllable. Both are attested following the velar and glottal consonants: *k, g, ng, ʔ,* and *h*. In addition, the palatal off-glide is attested following *l* in two lexical items, *wūljā* 'giraffe' and *ngbàljāljā* 'November', and following *m* in one lexical item, *kɔ́-mjà* 'to shake'. Also, the marginal phoneme *ɲ* could be interpreted as the sequence *n + j*, as mentioned in section 2.1.3, but there is more evidence for the phonemic status of *ɲ* than for *lj* or *mj*. It occurs in more lexical items, and it is found in both word-initial and word-medial position. Nevertheless, its interpretation as a phoneme is tentative.

Two observations concerning the distribution of labialization and palatalization are worth noting. First, Ladefoged and Maddieson (1996:356) note that cross-linguistically labialization most commonly co-occurs with velar obstruents. This generalization holds for Mono as well. On the other hand, Ladefoged and Maddieson note that of all the secondary articulations, it is labialization which usually co-occurs with the largest number of

4.1 Description

different types of segments (p. 356). In Mono, we see that palatalization lays claim to this, since it co-occurs with *l* and *m* (and *n* depending on how *ɲ* is interpreted) in addition to the velar and glottal consonants.

Within a morpheme, the off-glides are nearly always followed by the vowel *a*. The only exceptions to this are either in ideophones (*ngjērā* 'sound of a bell' and *hwɨ̀jà* 'hot') or body parts (*àkjó* 'hoof'). The secondary articulations do not immediately follow labial-velar consonants, and they do not combine with each other in the same syllable. The examples in my corpus are listed in (47).

(47) Secondary articulations attested in my corpus of Mono
    a. kw
        àkwà   'work'
        ákwárá   'chick-peas'
        àkwàrà   'arrowhead'
        kɔ́-kwà   'to return'
        zɨ àkwándɔ́ ngwàrə̀   'eat first of new crops'

    b. kj
        kjākjā   'small'
        àkjó   'hoof'

    c. gw
        zūgwā ~ ʒūgwā   'a type of forest spirit'
        kɔ́-gwà   'to pack, wrap up'
        kògwà   'box'

    d. gj
        àgjà   'animal'
        kɔ́-gjà   'to stir'
        màgjà   'sickle'

    e. ngw
        ángwá   'difficulty'
        àngwà   'seed (grain)'
        gbàngwà   'a type of large leaf'
        ngwàrə̀   'seed (general)'
        àjīkōngwá   'insect'
        ngwángwà   'gizzard'

    f. ngj
        ángjá   'material inside bamboo'
        ngjērā   'sound of a bell'

    g. hw
        hwɨ̀jà   'hot'

h. hj
———

i. ʔw

    tàʔwá   'basin'
    ʔwàrà   'until morning'

j. ʔj

    áʔjárá   'small (PL)'
    káʔjà   'weaver bird'
    káʔjá   'paddle'
    kōʔjà   'fruit bat'
    ʔjárá   'flayed'

k. lj

    wūljā   'giraffe'
    ngbàljāljā   'November'

l. mj

    kə́-mjà   'to shake'

4.2 Suggested Interpretations

Chao (1934) notes that there are cases where a classical phonemic analysis does not lead to a unique solution. For example, Ladefoged and Maddieson (1996:357) point out that for the Australian language Arrernte, analyses have varied as to whether labialization should be considered a property of the consonant system or the vowel system.

For many African languages, Mono included, both labialization and palatalization present such a problem of interpretation. In these languages the only unambiguous syllable pattern is CV (and V in word-initial position), and a classical phonemic analysis would require that the syllables containing labialization and palatalization, CwV and CjV, be interpreted in such a way as to fit into the available unambiguous syllable patterns. Alternatively, an additional syllable pattern (CCV or CVV) could be posited, but there must be clear motivation for doing so. Bendor-Samuel outlines the basic problem:

> Are these features to be regarded as consonants or vowels? If they are consonants, do they form a consonant cluster with the preceding consonant (to give a CCV pattern), or are they to be analysed as part of a single complex consonant (CV)? If they are vowels, do they form a sequence of two vowels with the following vowel (to

4.2 Suggested Interpretations

give a CVV pattern), or form part of a complex vowel nucleus? (1962:86)

All of these possible solutions, as well as two additional ones, have been suggested for the Banda languages. The first solution is to posit additional consonant phonemes, corresponding to the possible consonant-glide combinations: ʔw, ʔj, kw, kj, gw, gj, ngw, ngj, hw, hj, lj, and mj. This solution accounts for the limited distribution of the sounds with respect to the preceding consonants. In addition, no new syllable patterns need to be posited. There are a couple of disadvantages to this solution, however. First, it requires the addition of twelve consonant phonemes to the inventory, all of which are poorly attested in my corpus. (Note, however, that Hockett 1958:110 considers economy to be the "least useful and most vague" of the basic principles for evaluating phonemic analyses.) Second, it does not account for the co-occurrence restrictions between the off-glides and the following vowel.

A second solution is suggested by Sampson (1985) for the Banda language Tangbago. He posits two additional vowel phonemes, the diphthongs $^w a$ and $^j a$, where the secondary articulations are interpreted as on-glides to the vowel a. This solution accounts for the tautomorphemic distributional restriction of the secondary articulations before a. In addition, there is an economy of phonemes in that only two additional ones are needed.

However, there are a couple of disadvantages to this solution. First, it does not account for the co-occurrence restrictions between the secondary articulations and the preceding consonants. These must be stipulated separately. Second, it does not account for the data resulting from subminimal root augmentation, a process which prevents monosyllabic nouns, which is discussed in section 6.1. For example, the word gjà 'animal' occurs in Mbandja, but the reduplicated forms, *àgjà and *gjàgjà, do not. In Langbasi, the entire syllable is reduplicated resulting in the form gjàgjà. In Mono, only the vowel is reduplicated in this set of nouns. For example: àdà 'leg', úngú 'water', īpī 'dance', etc. If labialization or palatalization were the initial part of a phonemic diphthong, we would expect the diphthong to reduplicate in its entirety, yielding jàgjà in Mono. Instead, only a reduplicates, giving àgjà. This suggests that the jà sequence is analyzable, and is thus not a single phoneme.

A third solution is posited by Cloarec-Heiss (1969) for the Banda language Linda. She adds an additional syllable pattern CVV to the inventory by virtue of the fact that several vowel sequences are attested in Linda, ia, *io, ao, oa*,[1] and that there are tones on each vowel in the sequence. She considers labialization and palatalization to be vocalic, filling the first V slot in a CVV syllable. This is supported by the fact that in certain cases, the secondary articulations bear tone in Linda.

In Mono, there are three arguments for this analysis. First, there are a handful of words which could be considered to contain CVV syllable patterns: *bòā* 'priest', *hàò* 'brightly (ideophone)', *mbíù* 'very white (ideophone)', *ɲáō* 'cat' (a loanword from Lingala), *háàō* 'empty-handed (ideophone)', *háò* 'quickly (ideophone)', and *téāʃó* 'small'. Second, vowels having contour tones are phonetically long and could be considered to be a sequence of two vowels. Third, there is a case where a labial consonant off-glide is formed in a heteromorphemic environment. A *u* becomes *w* preceding a vowel with the same tone.

(48) a. mɔ̄   gú   jé   [mɔ̄ gwí]
     1SG return:NF EMPH
     'I returned.'

    b. sóngbā àgjà nɜ̀ fú jé   [sóngbā àgjà nɜ̀ fwí]
      flesh animal DET rot:NF EMPH
      'The meat rotted.'

However, the evidence for a CVV pattern is weakened by certain factors. First, the words which contain this syllable pattern are small in number and are mostly ideophones and loanwords. Second, such words could be interpreted as containing a CV syllable followed by a V syllable (CV.V), and as such would fit into the present inventory of unambiguous syllable patterns, although this interpretation would require positing additional word patterns. In fact, each word has an alternate pronunciation in which the two-vowel sequence may be split up by a semi-vowel. For example, *bòā* may also be pronounced [bòwā]. Third, the case of labialization in (48) results in a glide which is high in the vowel space rather than mid, i.e., [u̯] rather than [o̯]. Fourth, the case in (48) creates a glide-vowel sequence which does not adhere to the normal co-occurrence restriction associated with the secondary articulations. Thus, we cannot confidently posit a CVV pattern for Mono. In addition, phonetic reasons discourage us from following this solution for Mono: the fact that the secondary articulations are phonetically short and do not bear tone dissuades us from giving them a vocalic interpretation.

---

[1] Diki-Kidiri and Cloarec-Heiss (1985) mention the following vowel sequences in Linda: *iu, iɔ, ia, əu, oa, ae*.

4.2 Suggested Interpretations

A fourth solution is suggested by Robbins (1984) for the Banda language Mbandja. She suggests that labialization and palatalization (as well as prenasalization) should be considered prosodies, in the Firthian sense of the word, presumably as features of the syllable (but unfortunately she does not clarify this). Firthian prosodic analysis allows for an element to be considered prosodic, even if it fills only a single segmental slot, if it can be demonstrated that the element functions in some way on a higher prosodic level (Robins 1970). However, in Mono, I have found no evidence to demonstrate conclusively that labialization or palatalization function at a higher prosodic level.

A fifth solution is put forth by Olson and Schrag (2000). In that study we posit an additional syllable pattern CGV (G = glide) for Mono. This type of analysis was first suggested by Pike (1947) and reiterated in Bendor-Samuel (1962).

> If only two types of sequences of consonants occur at the beginning of utterances, and one of these consists of labialized stops and the other of palatalized stops in each of which the off glide to [w] and [y] is quite clearly delayed until after the release of the stop itself, it seems best to consider that the contrasting pattern causes a separation of these items into sequences of two separate phonemes. (Pike 1947:135)

In Olson and Schrag we claim the solution is motivated by virtue of the Sonority Sequencing Principle (SSP, see, e.g., Blevins 1995), which observes that onsets rise in sonority as one approaches the nucleus, and codas fall in sonority as one moves away from the nucleus.

The most common syllable pattern in African languages is a consonant followed by a vowel (CV). In addition, many African languages have CGV syllable or CLV (L = liquid) patterns. In these cases, a co-occurrence restriction typically requires the initial consonant to be lower in sonority than the following sonorant (i.e., adhering to the SSP). In most cases, Mono included, this initial consonant is an obstruent.

In his rendition of phonemics, K. L. Pike assumes that sounds in a given language are subdivided into two major groups: consonants and vowels. In the positing of unambiguous syllable patterns, then, the researcher is forced to label the elements within a syllable as either C or V. This ignores the cross-linguistic tendency for languages to have syllable patterns which obey the SSP, such as OSV (O = obstruent, S = sonorant). Subsequent work in the structuralist framework relaxed this restriction. Jacobson allowed for the inclusion of canonical syllable patterns of the OSV type in a phonemic analysis. E. V. Pike (1954) argued that it is necessary to take into account "rank of stricture" (somewhat analogous to the SSP) in the analysis of consonant clusters. In Olson and Schrag we suggest that

OSV syllables should be considered unambiguous in cases where other possible interpretations are exhausted.²

There are at least two problems with the Olson and Schrag account. First, it accounts for neither the co-occurrence restrictions between the secondary articulations and the preceding consonants nor the co-occurrence restrictions between the secondary articulations and the following vowel. As Bendor-Samuel (1962:87) points out, these restrictions must be stated in addition to accepting the additional syllable pattern.

Second, while this account essentially treats the secondary articulations as the two semi-vowel phonemes *w* and *j* occurring in a unique position in the syllable, it should be remembered that there is a clear phonetic difference between the secondary articulations and the regular articulations of the semi-vowels. As pointed out above, the secondary articulations are more mid than high in the height dimension (i.e., [o̯] and [e̯]), whereas the semi-vowels *w* and *j* are high.

For the analysis in this study, I will assume the interpretation of labialization and palatalization argued for by Olson and Schrag (2000). However, in the spirit of Chao's basic observation, I admit that this choice is not clear-cut:

> [G]iven the sounds of a language, there are usually more than one possible way of reducing them to a system of phonemes, and...these different systems or solutions are not simply correct or incorrect, but may be regarded only as being good or bad for various purposes. (Chao 1934:363)

4.3 Distribution of Labialization and Palatalization

There are cases in the world's languages where both labialization and palatalization occur in the same syllable. Ladefoged (1982:211) gives evidence from Twi (Niger-Congo, Ghana). Both secondary articulations occur in the name of the language, resulting in the semi-vowel [ɥ]. The name Twi, then, is pronounced [tɥi]. In my corpus of data, there are no cases of labialization and palatalization occurring in the same syllable.

There are three cases in my corpus of more than one syllable in a single word containing a secondary articulation.

---

²One interesting investigation, beyond the scope of this study, would be a typological study to determine if there are any implicational universals regarding OSV syllable patterns. Specifically, if a language has OLV patterns, will it necessarily also have OGV syllables?

4.3 Distribution of Labialization and Palatalization

(49) a. kjākjā 'small'
 b. ngwángwà 'gizzard'
 c. ngbàljāljā 'November'

In all three words, the two syllables containing the secondary articulation are identical (except for the tones in 49b). Also, in (49a), the word may be a case of reduplication. There are no attested cases in my corpus in which both labialization and palatalization occur in the same word. If further research reveals this gap to be a general phenomenon in the language, that would be evidence that a secondary articulation has the entire word as its domain, which would lend support to Robbins' (1984) analysis of the phenomena as prosodies. Further research on Mono is required concerning this issue.

5

The Syllable

There has been much discussion in the literature on how best to define the syllable. Phonetic definitions, mostly revolving around the notion of "chest pulse" (e.g., Pike 1947; Stetson 1951, cited in Ladefoged and Maddieson 1996) have proved elusive. Rather, most linguists in both structuralist and generative frameworks assume that the syllable is a phonological unit within which segments are distributed (cf. Ladefoged and Maddieson, pp. 281–282).

According to Pike (1947), classical phonemics assumes both phonetic and phonological syllables, although with respect to his analytical procedure, it is the phonological syllable which is crucial. In a given language, certain sequences of segments can unambiguously be interpreted as belonging to a given syllable type. For example, consider a hypothetical language which, in deference to Pike (p. 68), I will call Kalaba. The words [ma], [bo], [su], and [sa] in Kalaba (p. 61) each unambiguously consist of a single CV syllable. If this is the only unambiguous syllable pattern in the language, then other syllables in the language should be interpreted in such a way as to fit into this syllable type.

Some individual segments could be interpreted as being either a consonant or a vowel. Suppose Kalaba contains the word [ia]. The high front segment [i] could conceivably be interpreted as either a vowel, in which case the word would be transcribed phonemically as *ia*, or as a semi-vowel, in which case the word would be transcribed phonemically as *ja*. Only the latter case fits into the unambiguous CV pattern, and so *ja* is the preferred interpretation.

In some cases a sound could be interpreted as a single segment or a sequence of segments. Suppose Kalaba contains the word [tʃa]. The alveopalatal affricate [tʃ] could be interpreted as a sequence of two segments, [t] followed by [ʃ], in which case the word would be transcribed phonemically as *tʃa*, or it could be interpreted as a single segment, [č], in which case the word could be transcribed phonemically as *ča*. Only the latter case fits into the unambiguous CV syllable pattern, so [tʃ] is interpreted as a single segment rather than a sequence of segments in Kalaba.

The syllable thus plays the following role in phonemic analysis:

- Language is assumed to have an abstract phonological unit called the syllable.
- Based on our understanding of cross-linguistic behavior, certain sequences of segments are assumed to comprise unambiguous syllable patterns in a given language.
- Sequences of segments which are cross-linguistically assumed to comprise ambiguous syllable patterns are interpreted in such a way that they fit into the unambiguous syllable patterns attested in a given language.

One issue which has not received much attention in the literature is whether or not to take into consideration marginal data in putting forth an analysis of syllable structure. That is, syllable patterns may (1) be rare, (2) only occur in loanwords or ideophones, or (3) have only a limited distribution within the word. I take these criteria into account in considering whether or not to include a given syllable pattern in the inventory of Mono syllable types.

5.1 Syllable Types

In Mono, there are two unambiguous syllable patterns: CV and V. The CV syllable type is generally considered to be a typological universal (Burquest 2001:150),[1] perhaps because of the perceptual salience of the release portion of a consonant (Ohala and Kawasaki 1984), so its presence in Mono is to be expected. The V syllable type has a limited distribution, only occurring unambiguously in word-initial position in Mono. However, word-initial onsetless syllables are cross-linguistically very common

---

[1] See Breen and Pensalfini (1999) for a possible counter-example to this claim in the Australian language Arrernte.

5.1 Syllable Types

(Burquest 2001:154), so its presence in Mono is also unproblematic. There are no cases of syllable-final consonants in Mono.

Several ambiguous syllable types occur in Mono. These include CGV (G = glide, or semi-vowel), CV_1V_2 (where $V_1 \neq V_2$), CV:, and CLV (L = liquid).

The first ambiguous syllable type is CGV. This pattern was discussed in detail in chapter 4 with respect to labialization and palatalization. Distributional restrictions limit the segments which precede and follow the semi-vowel in these syllables. Velar and glottal consonants (k, g, ng, ʔ, and h) may precede both semi-vowels (w and j), and in rare cases m, n, and l precede j. With a few exceptions discussed in chapter 4, the semi-vowels in this position always precede the vowel a. The fact that the semi-vowels co-occur mostly with stop consonants and the low vowel a is not surprising. These phonemes represent the extremes of the sonority hierarchy. As Goldsmith (1990:111) points out, "[L]anguages may...require that the differences in sonority between adjacent segments be greater than a certain amount." If a language allows only a radically reduced set of three-segment syllables, it seems reasonable to expect that the initial and final segments should be limited to those found at the extremes of the sonority hierarchy. One possible explanation for the lack of labial and coronal stops in the onset of such syllables is suggested by Blevin's (1995:211) sonority hierarchy (for English) in which t has a higher sonority than k.[2] On the other end of the scale, the lack of the low ɔ in the nucleus may be explained by the fact that ɔ is usually considered to have an open-mid aperture in phonetic descriptions, even though it patterns as a low vowel in Mono.

The presence of the CGV syllable type is not unusual. In many languages of the world, the only case of consonant clusters involves CG sequences (Kenstowicz 1994:42; Bendor-Samuel 1962),[3] and Boyd (1995:15) notes that this is true in Ubangian. In many of the languages where this is the case, it is clearly advantageous to add this syllable type to the inventory of syllable types in the language. As mentioned in chapter 4, Pike (1947) allows for this possibility. Burquest (2001:159) cites the case of Senoufo where this is clearly the preferred solution. Based on these reasons, and the discussion in chapter 4, I have added CGV to the inventory of syllable patterns in Mono.

---

[2] Having said this, it appears, however, that Blevins has misread the figure in Ladefoged (1982) from which she obtains this hierarchy. In the original chart (figure 10.1, p. 222), t and k have equal sonority.

[3] According to Clements' (1990) Sonority Dispersion Principle, OLV is the most optimal three-member initial cluster, suggesting that it would be the first three-member cluster to appear in a language. Empirical evidence suggests, however, that OGV is the first to appear.

The second ambiguous syllable type is CV_1V_2. A small number of words in Mono contain two non-identical vowels in hiatus, for example, bòā 'priest' (a complete list was given in chapter 4). These vowels could be analyzed as belonging either to the same syllable (CVV) or to separate syllables (CV.V). The first option would require the addition of a CVV syllable type to the Mono inventory. Both options would require increasing the inventory of word shapes. However, these words are limited in number and are found mostly in ideophones and loanwords. Because of their marginal nature, I do not incorporate them into the present analysis. This pattern was discussed in more detail in chapter 4.

Syllables containing phonetically long vowels (CV:) are attested in Mono, for example, mīndúù 'five'. These syllables always occur in conjunction with contour tones, which are analyzed as sequences of non-identical level tones. (See section 3.1 for a discussion of optional exceptions to this.) In chapter 3, I gave evidence for considering length to be non-contrastive in Mono. As a result, I interpret CV: syllables as variants of CV syllables and thus an additional syllable pattern does not need to be posited for Mono to account for them.

Finally, the syllable type CLV (L = liquid) is an optional variant of the two-syllable combination CV_1LV_1, in which the two vowels are identical in quality and in tone. In careful speech, CV_1LV_1 is produced, but in casual speech the first vowel is shortened or it is completely elided. For example, the word ámbálá 'bait' is also pronounced ámbḁlá or ámblá. Words exhibiting this phenomenon include nouns (e.g., gàfūrū 'mortar'), verbs (e.g., kɔ́-mbɜ̀rɜ̀ 'to cut'), and adjectives (e.g., áʔjárá 'small (PL)'). Obstruents and semi-vowels are attested in the first position of the pattern, but liquids and nasals are not. (The word màlūlū 'cold weather' is attested, but it is not clear that the first u can be elided in this case.) Example (50) shows the consonants which can occur in this pattern. Note that the final vowel is ə or i, if the preceding vowel is e or i, respectively.

(50) Sample words with CV_1LV_1 pattern
    a. Labial

b	—	
p	pélézū	'bat'
	ōpōrō	'egg'
b	ábálá	'hello'
	jābùrù	'goat'
mb	ámbálá	'bait'
	mbìrìlù	'pale color'

5.1 Syllable Types

		f	fūrūtʃā	'soap'
		v	jāvūrū	'rain'
		m	—	
		w̌	ángbɔ́ būw̌ìlɨ̀	'type of banana'
			áw̌árá	'fierceness'
	b.	Alveolar		
		ɗ	—	
		t	àtàrà	'age-mate'
		d	àkɨ́dàlà	'dusk'
			bādōrō	'sweet potato'
		nd	àndòrò	'witchcraft'
		s	kpàsùrù	'slipperiness'
		z	kɔ́-zɨ̀-rə̀	'food'
		n	—	
		l	màlūlū	'cold weather'
		r	—	
	c.	Palatal		
		tʃ	tʃētʃērə̄	'insect'
		dʒ	ùdʒùrù	'waterfalls'
		ndʒ	ndʒàràpándà	'ladder, scaffolding'
		ʃ	íʃírɨ́	'shadow'
		ʒ	ōʒōrō	'fat'
		ɲ	—	
		j	jālāwū	'grinding stone'
			éjérɔ́	'yellow'
	d.	Velar		
		k	dɔ́kɔ́lɔ́ngbā	'scorpion'
			òkòrò	'chest, torso'
		g	bágàrà	'cow'
		ng	ángàlà	'ladder'
			àngàrà	'single person'
	e.	Labial-velar		
		kp	àkpàlà óʃó	'platform'
			kpàràkà	'July'
		gb	tʃágbòlò	'smallness'
			àgbárá	'comb'

		ngb	kpīngbīlī	'plank'
			úngbúrú	'old'
		w	kə́-wù-rə̀	'vision'
f.	Glottal			
		ʔ	éʔélé	'grudge holding'
			īʔīrī	'name'
		h	āhārā	'dry'
g.	With labialization or palatalization			
		kw	àkwàrà	'arrowhead'
		ʔj	áʔjárá	'small (PL)'

If CV_1LV_1 comprises the entire word, then elision of the first vowel is not attested. For example, *dōrō* 'partridge' is attested, but **dro* is ill-formed. This is due to a word minimality condition preventing monosyllabic lexical words, which is discussed in chapter 6.

The presence of the CV_1LV_1 pattern may have a diachronic explanation. It is conceivable that Mono had at one time an unambiguous CLV pattern which was subsequently expanded to CV_1LV_1. This would explain the large number of words which exhibit this pattern. Future comparative work is needed to support this hypothesis.

To account for these patterns in a synchronic analysis, we could posit a /CLV/ underlying form and introduce a rule of VOWEL EPENTHESIS to break up the CL sequence. This rule can be formalized as in (51).

(51) Vowel epenthesis
$\emptyset \rightarrow V_1 \, / \, C\_\_LV_1$

In section 6.1, we will see that the interaction of vowel epenthesis with the word minimality condition lends additional support to this type of analysis.

This type of syllable patterning is not unique to Mono. Welmers (1973:26ff.) notes that the orthography of Ewe recognizes CLV syllable shapes, for example, *flé* 'buy' and *àgblè* 'farm', but that tonal evidence indicates there may be a vowel between the C and L. For example, in *tàfˊlàtsé* 'excuse me', there is a high tone at the release of the *f* which is distinct from the preceding and following tones. He suggests that the tone bearing segment be interpreted as *i* before unrounded vowels and *u* before rounded vowels, yielding *tàfīlàtsé* in the above example. Like Mono, the quality of the vowel between C and L is predictable from the following vowel.

5.1 Syllable Types

Goldsmith (1990:134) points out a mirror image case in Selayarese in which a phonological word ends in *l*, *r*, or *s* underlyingly. Here, a vowel is epenthesized word-finally which is a copy of the preceding vowel. Thus, /katal/ 'itch' becomes *katala*, and /noʔnos/ 'shake liquid' becomes *noʔnoso*. The fact that the final vowel is predictable from the preceding vowel is evidence that it is indeed epenthetic. Additional evidence for this is that these words bear stress on the antepenultimate syllable, rather than on the penultimate syllable, which is the normal case in the language.

6

Word Shapes

Some authors, such as Hockett (1958:284ff), refer to word shapes as CA-NONICAL FORMS. The shape of a word is dependent on at least three parameters: (1) whether it is a lexical word or a grammatical function word, (2) the specific grammatical category of the word, and (3) whether a word is spoken in isolation or produced in the context of a sentence. I will take all three of these parameters into consideration in discussing word shapes.

LEXICAL WORDS are also referred to as content words or contentives. These include words within the major grammatical categories of a language, usually taken to be nouns, verbs, adjectives, and adverbs. They comprise an open class of words. GRAMMATICAL FUNCTION WORDS are also referred to as grammatical words, function words, or functors. They comprise closed classes of words, including conjunctions, prepositions, and pronouns.[1] This distinction is important with respect to at least one typological observation. McCarthy and Prince (1995) note that in a large number of the world's languages, lexical words must be at least bimoraic or disyllabic, depending on the language. Following Goldsmith (1995), I will refer to this as a MINIMALITY CONDITION (MC).[2] MCs do not appear to be limited to a specific language family or geographic region. Kenstowicz (1994:640ff.) discusses examples from a diverse group of languages,

---

[1]Hockett (1958:264) includes substitutes (e.g., N → pronouns, V → 'do', Adv → 'so'), markers, inflectional affixes, and derivational affixes in the class of functors. Since not all of these morphemes constitute words, he avoids the term "word."

[2]McCarthy and Prince claim that word minimality is derivable from two other notions: the Prosodic Hierarchy and Foot Binarity. Thus there is no "Minimal Word Constraint" in their model.

including English, Yidin^y, Arabic, Japanese, Lardil, Estonian, and Choctaw. Hockett (1958:284) makes similar observations for Fijian. As we will see, this phenomenon is also operative in Mono. Also, Hockett (1958) points out that shorter words are more common than longer words, taking the MC into account.

The attested word shapes may vary depending on the grammatical category of the word. I will examine each major grammatical category in Mono separately. The MC is most evident in words spoken in isolation, also referred to as CITATION FORMS. The restriction may be lifted when words are spoken in certain contexts within a sentence.

Due to their rarity, I do not discuss word shapes that involve labialization or palatalization. A comprehensive list of these words in my corpus is given in section 4.1 (example 6).

6.1 Nominal Word Shapes

Nominal words include nouns, adjectives, and pronouns, all of which show similar behavior with respect to word shapes.

Nouns

The word shapes in (52) are attested for nouns spoken in isolation in Mono.

(52)   Attested word shapes of Mono nouns
      VCV   àbá   'father'
      CVCV   lōsú   'pot'
      VCVCV   òfōrò   'grass'
      CVCVCV   bākòngɔ́   'tortoise'
      VCVCVCV   àlédʒōzɔ́   'hail'
      CVCVCVCV   málègbāngā 'ladle'

As noted in chapter 5, onsetless syllables are only found unambiguously in word-initial position. The shorter forms (VCV, CVCV, VCVCV) are much more frequent than the longer forms, both in the lexicon and in texts, which is consistent with Hockett's (1958:284–285) observations for Fijian and English.

Noun compounding is a very common process in Mono. Many nouns in my corpus which have two or more syllables are compounds, and it is likely that additional nouns listed in appendix B as monomorphemic will

6.1 Nominal Word Shapes

turn out to be multimorphemic given further research. This would provide additional evidence that most Mono nouns are of the shorter forms mentioned above.

Mono lacks monosyllabic nouns, that is, ones with a V or CV word pattern. It thus appears that there is a MC in Mono preventing nouns of less than two syllables.[3] Hockett (1958:288–289) suggests that a similar MC in Fijian is due to the limited inventory of Cs and Vs in that language. However, that explanation is not possible for Mono, which has a robust inventory of both Cs and Vs.

The evidence in (53) lends additional support for a MC on Mono nouns. First, Mono contains a rather large number of nouns with a V_1CV_1 word pattern in which both Vs are identical in quality and in tone in careful speech.[4]

(53) Sample V_1CV_1 nouns in Mono
    a. ɔ̄ʒī ~ ɨ̄ʒī ~ īʒī   'tooth'
    b. ədɨ ~ ɨdɨ   'horn'
    c. ɔ́ngú ~ íngú ~ úngú   'water'
    d. əbè ~   èbè   'liver'
    e. ərə   'thing'
    f. əgò ~   ɔ̀gò   'hunger'
    g. àmà   'mouth'
    h. àlɔ̀ ~   ɔ̀lɔ̀   'sun'

The value of the first vowel in each word is predictable given the value of the second vowel, as discussed below. Since Mono lacks surface monosyllabic nouns, we can posit an abstract underlying form which does not include the initial vowel of the word.

A process of SUBMINIMAL ROOT AUGMENTATION (SRA) then inserts a vowel at the beginning of the word. If the root vowel is [+low], then a is inserted. If the root vowel is [–low], then the inserted vowel is ə. The rest of the forms in (53) can be derived by the assimilation of the qualities of the root vowel to the inserted vowel, a process which I refer to as LEFTWARD VOWEL SPREADING. In terms of distinctive features, the inserted vowel in the second column of (53) acquires its value of the feature [high] from the root vowel. Then, the inserted vowels in the third column

---

[3] There are two nouns, which could be considered to be bimoraic: bòā 'priest' and ɲáō 'cat' (loan from Lingala), but in section 3.2 I argued that these forms are marginal to the phonological system.

[4] Cloarec-Heiss (1978:21) notes that this group of nouns contains a large proportion of words for body parts, elements, and instruments. However, this cannot be construed as a semantic class, as nouns from many other semantic domains are attested here as well.

acquire their values of the features [round] and [back] from the root vowel (in addition to the feature [high]). Interestingly, there is an implicational relationship here. The features [round] and [back] only assimilate if the feature [high] has assimilated. As a result the forms *ēʒī 'tooth' and *óngú 'water' are not attested. Thus, the forms in (53) can be derived from those in (54) via SRA and leftward vowel spreading. This analysis accounts for the large number of V_1CV_1 nouns in Mono, as well as the distributional gap in our inventory of nominal word shapes in (52).

(54) Underlying forms of sample V_1CV_1 nouns in Mono
/ʒī/   'tooth'
/dɨ̀/   'horn'
/ngú/   'water'
/bè/   'liver'
/rə̀/   'thing'
/gò/   'hunger'
/mà/   'mouth'
/lə̀/   'sun'

A question which arises is whether subminimal root augmentation should be thought of as simple vowel epenthesis or as reduplication. Most of the features of the inserted vowel can be attributed to the optional process of leftward vowel spreading. However, the agreement of the feature [low] in the inserted vowel with the root is obligatory. In addition, this agreement ignores an intervening secondary articulation (e.g., àkwà 'work'), but as we will see in chapter 7, secondary articulations normally do participate in leftward vowel spreading. As a result, I suggest that the inserted vowel should be thought of as a reduplicated V, bearing the specification of the feature [low] of the root, and underspecified for other place features. Then, leftward vowel spreading can be formalized as in (55), with the restriction that if (55) or (56) apply, then (55) must also apply if it can.

(55) Leftward vowel spreading (feature geometric formalism)

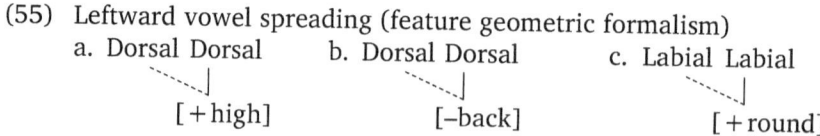

    a. Dorsal Dorsal   b. Dorsal Dorsal   c. Labial Labial
           [+high]   [−back]   [+round]

Leftward vowel spreading also occurs across morpheme and clitic boundaries. This will be discussed in section 7.2.1.

6.1 Nominal Word Shapes

In the related language Langbasi (Moñino 1988), the corresponding subminimal root augmentation process is clearly reduplicative. Roots cognate with those discussed above for Mono undergo reduplication to satisfy the MC.

(56) Subminimal root augmentation in Langbasi
    ʒīʒī   'tooth'
    dùdù   'horn'
    ngúngú 'water'
    ʁə̀ʁə̀   'thing'
    gògò   'hunger'
    màmà   'mouth'
    lòlò   'sun'

Kamanda (1998:257–258) lists eleven nominals in Mono which he considers to have a CV word shape. If true, this would be evidence against the MC for nouns. However, none of these forms is solid evidence for a nominal CV word shape, and in fact some of his examples support the MC analysis. Two of the words he lists, bə̀ '2SG' and jē '3SG' are pronouns given in their clitic form rather than their citation form. Their citation forms are ə̀bə̀ and ēʃē, respectively, which obey the MC. Three of the words, sə́ 'existence', tə́ 'body', and ndə́ 'place' (his glosses), are given in their prepositional form. When used as nouns, they are expanded to two syllables via SRA, yielding ə́sə́, ə́tə́, and ə́ndə́. Three of the words, ʔí 'far', kpì 'different', fà 'above half', are part of a category which Kamanda calls "quasi-nominal." These forms are traditionally interpreted as adverbs rather than nouns. Two of the words, ndʒá 'pointed' and ndō 'short', are adjectives which are bisyllabic in their citation form (ándʒá and ōndō). Finally, one word pá 'above', is in fact a preposition.

In the related language Linda, Cloarec-Heiss (1986:126) considers the first vowel of V_1CV_1 words to be a derivational prefix. However, I argue against interpreting it as a prefix in Mono for the following reasons. First, not all of the forms are derived from other grammatical categories. For example, the word ò?ò 'word' is not derived from a verb. Second, considering the first vowel a prefix does not explain why the process only occurs with monosyllabic verb roots. The purely phonological account explains the cases in which the process occurs. I say more on this in section 7.1.1.

A second factor which lends support to the notion of an MC on Mono nouns is that there are cases where the unaugmented forms in (54) actually surface in the context of a sentence or phrase. For example, in a noun phrase where a V_1CV_1 noun follows an adjective, the noun optionally surfaces as CV.

(57) ádʒá   ʔò
      true   word
      'That's right.'

In verbs where the object has been grammaticalized, the object surfaces as CV.

(58) a. kə́-pà   ʔò
         INF-say   word
         'to speak'

    b.   kə́-wù   sə́
         INF-see   place
         'to understand'

Third, when underlyingly monosyllabic nouns are compounded, the resulting word is bisyllablic. The minimality condition is satisfied, and as a result SRA does not apply. For example, /mà/ 'mouth' + /ndà/ 'house' → màndà 'door' (*àmààndà). In words with a VCV pattern where the two vowels are distinct, this reduction is not observed in compounding, for example, /àjī/ 'person' + /bó/ 'flesh' → àjībó 'relative'.

One additional comment regarding SRA is in order. There is one case where SRA appears to overapply. Nouns which contain a CV_1LV_1 pattern usually have the word shape $V_1CV_1LV_1$ rather than CV_1LV_1. Thus, the word for 'bridge' is àgbàrà, not *gbàrà. Since the form *gbàrà is bisyllabic, it should satisfy the word minimality condition. However, the trisyllabic form is the one that is attested rather than the bisyllabic form. We can account for this pattern by appealing to a suggestion made in chapter 5 that the underlying form of such words is /CLV/. Thus the underlying form of àgbàrà would be /gbrà/. In a rule-based account, the ordering of SRA before vowel epenthesis (example (51) in chapter 5) would lead to the correct output form in (59).

(59) UR   /gbrà/
      SRA   àgbrà
      V-epenthesis   àgbàrà
      SR   [àgbàrà]

6.1 Nominal Word Shapes

Descriptive adjectives

Descriptive adjectives in Mono pattern like nouns with respect to word shapes. Criteria for defining this category will be discussed in section 7.1.1. Adjectives spoken in isolation have the same word shapes as nouns.

(60) Word shapes of Mono adjectives
VCV ɔ́tʃɔ́ 'good'
CVCV tāfò 'new'
VCVCV égérɔ́ 'big'
CVCVCV dʒākātā 'true'
     kpàhúrú 'large, massive' (Kamanda 1998:683)

VCVCVCV —
CVCVCVCV kpòròkòtò 'black'

The adjective *kjākjā* 'small' is attested. This could be considered a case of reduplication, but since it is always realized as bisyllabic, it cannot lend support to a CV word pattern for adjectives.

There are a large percentage of adjectives which are of the V_1CV_1 shape.

(61) Sample V_1CV_1 adjectives in Mono
ɔ́kpí ~ íkpí ~ íkpí 'tart'
ɔ̄lɨ ~ ɨ̄lɨ   'heavy' (Kamanda 1998:671)
ɔ̄bū ~ ɨ̄bū ~ ūbū 'black'
ɔ́kpé ~   ékpé 'bad'

ɔ̄ndō ~   ōndō 'short'
ádʒá   'true'
átʃɔ́ ~   ɔ́tʃɔ́ 'good'

Many of these derive from the same base as a verbal form. For example, *ūfū* 'smelly' and *kɔ́-fù* 'to be smelly, to rot' come from the same root /fū/. This phenomenon will be discussed in detail in section 7.1.1.

Other nouns

Kinship terms, body parts, and plant and animal names are subcategories of nouns which often exhibit novel phonological behavior. With respect to word shapes, the only group which appears to have unique behavior are the kinship terms. While all of the word shapes in (52) are attested for kinship terms, well over half of the kinship terms begin with a vowel, most with the vowel *a*. Despite this, only three kinship terms, *ájá* 'brother', *ìngì* 'younger sibling', and *ɔ́gbɔ́* 'older sibling' exhibit a V_1CV_1 word pattern, statistically much less than found among other Mono nouns.

Pronouns

Strictly speaking, pronouns are not a subcategory of the major grammatical category of nouns. Rather, they are usually considered to be a type of grammatical function word. However, pronouns in Mono exhibit similarities in behavior to nouns with respect to word shapes, and so they will be discussed here.

Table 6.1 shows the forms of the pronouns in citation form, in subject position of a clause, in object position in a clause, and in an associative noun phrase.

Table 6.1. Mono pronouns

	citation form	subject	object	associative
1SG	ə̄mə̄	mə̄	mə̄	mə̄
2SG	ə̀ɓə̀	ɓə̀	ɓə̀	zə̀
3SG.AN	èʃè	tʃə̀	ʃè	jē
3SG.INAN		ɔ́ or ɔ́tə́nə̀	tə́nə̀ or nə̀	nə̀
1PL.EXCL	ā?ā	?ā	?ā	?ā
1PL.INCL	àzɔ́	?à	àzɔ́	?à/àzɔ́
2PL	ē?ē	?ē	?ē	?ē
3PL	èndʒē	èndʒē	èndʒē	èndʒē

The citation form of each pronoun is an augmented version of the object pronoun form, following the rules of SRA discussed above. Since *àzɔ́* '1PL.INCL' and *èndʒē* '3PL' are already bisyllabic in their reduced form, augmentation of these forms does not take place.

The reduced forms of the Mono pronouns are the default forms used in Mono discourse, in contrast to nouns where the augmented form is the default. The citation form of the pronouns is employed in a limited set of constructions in addition to isolation. These include predicate nominal constructions, both proper inclusion (62a) and equative (62b) clauses, cleft sentences (62c), and appositional noun phrases (62d) and (62e).

6.1 Nominal Word Shapes

(62) Constructions in which the citation form of pronouns is employed

a. ə̀ɓə̀   kə̀dɔ́   mōnō
   2SG   COP   Mono
   'You are a Mono.'

b. èʃè   dɔ́-dɔ́   àbá   mə̄   nēnē
   3SG   RED-COP father 1SG NEG
   'He is not my father.'

c. ə̄mə̄   dá   sə̄   kɔ́-ɓì   ītʃī
   1SG   CLEFT be   INF-hit song
   'I'm the one that sang the song.'

d. àzɔ́   də̀   mə̄   ʔà   sɔ́   də̀   ʔò
   1PL.INCL with 1SG 1PL.INCL be   with word
   'You and me, we have a problem.'

e. ə̄mə̄   mɔ́   sə̀   ɓá-lɔ́   gūsū
   1SG   1SG:FUT be:FUT at-in   bush
   'And me, I'll be in the bush.'

One question which arises is whether the glottal stop in the words āʔā '1PL.EXCL', ēʔē '2PL' and òʔò 'word' is epenthetic. As we will see in the next section, there is some evidence that a root-initial glottal stop in Mono verbs is epenthetic, and perhaps such an analysis is appropriate for these nominal forms as well. The advantage to such an analysis would be the existence of an underlying /V/ word shape for nouns, which is otherwise unattested. I discussed the advantages and disadvantages of this in section 2.1.4. Note, however, that the number of lexical items at issue here is limited to three.

There is one additional form in Mono which appears to undergo SRA. This concerns the interrogative pronoun èdè 'who'. This word is formally similar to the interrogative pronoun gàdè 'what'. One possible analysis of this latter word is that it contains the prefix gà- 'towards', although the meaning of the prefix is bleached, and the root /dè/. If this is the case, then the form meaning 'who' could be considered to consist of the same root having undergone SRA.

6.2 Verbal Word Shapes

Verbs in Mono take the infinitive prefix kə- (H tone on prefix, L tone on vowels of the root) when spoken in isolation. Consequently, all of the attested verbal word patterns begin with a consonant.

(63) Word shapes of Mono verbs
    CVCV   kə́-ʔì   'to attach, bind'
                  kə́-gù   'to return'
    CVCVCV   kə́-ʔòmà   'to boil over'
                  kə́-dàkà   'to borrow'
    CVCVCVCV kə́-pàgàtà   'to forbid'

Note, however, that there is no contrast between the presence or absence of ʔ in the initial position of the root. It is conceivable that roots beginning with ʔ could be interpreted as having an initial vowel, and that ʔ is epenthesized by rule. Such an interpretation would give us both C-initial and V-initial verb root patterns, more in line with the pattern for nouns. However, I have found no independent evidence that the glottal stop in these positions is inserted.

Because of the presence of the infinitive prefix, verbal citation forms are at a minimum bisyllabic. As a result, the MC is met for verbs and thus SRA does not apply.

As with nouns, the shorter verbal word shapes are the most widely attested. The majority of Mono verb roots consist of (a) a single syllable, or (b) two syllables in which the second syllable contains a liquid followed by a vowel identical to the vowel in the first syllable.

(64) Mono bisyllabic CV_1LV_1 verb roots
    gerə   'grow'
    kərə   'quarrel'
    bɨlɨ   'incite'
    fara   'deceive'
    gɔrɔ   'drive away, chase'
    guru   'fade'
    ndʒoro   'suck'
    mbərə   'do'

When both tones of the verb root are low, the first vowel is optionally shortened or elided. Thus, kə́-mbə̀rə̀ ~ kə́-mbə̰̀rə̀ ~ kə́-mbrə̀ 'to do'. However, in forms where the two vowels have different tones, the reduction is not possible. For example, mbárə̀ 'do.NF' cannot be reduced.

6.3 Adverbial Word Shapes

Documenting the word shapes of Mono adverbs is problematic, for a couple of reasons. First, as Payne (1997:69) points out, the category "adverb" is often treated as a "catch-all" category, including words which cannot easily be categorized as nouns, verbs, or adjectives. Often the category adverb includes words referring to manner, time, and location. Second, Mono contains a large number of IDEOPHONES[5] (Welmers 1973, Childs 1994, Elders 2000), most of which fit grammatically into the class of adverbs. Ideophones are noted for having exceptional phonological behavior, and thus are not good evidence for the general patternings of the language. A brief excursus on their behavior is in order. This excursus is based predominantly on Childs (1994).

The ideophone is a form of sound symbolism found in a large number of African languages, as well as other parts of the world. It involves a nonarbitrary mating of sound and meaning. The term can be traced to Doke (1935) who defined the ideophone as "A vivid representation of an idea in sound. A word, often onomatopoetic, which describes a predicate, qualificative or adverb in respect to manner, colour, smell, action, state, or intensity" (p. 118).

Ideophones can express several different types of notions. The most well-known examples are onomatopoetic terms in which a word imitates a sound in nature, but this can be metaphorically extended to the other human senses (sight, smell, taste, and touch), for which the term "synesthesia" can be employed. Ideophones can express lengthening or repetition of an action or state ("iconic lengthening"). In addition, phonesthemes are generally considered to be ideophonic as well.

Doke considered the ideophone to be a grammatical category in Bantu, distinct from nouns, verbs, etc. However, Childs notes that they ordinarily make up a subset of one or two already established classes in a given language. It is usually more accurate to refer to ideophonic nouns, ideophonic verbs, etc. In the majority of cases, ideophones function syntactically as adverbs.

Several features are used to identify ideophones, but there is no single feature which is criterial. As a result, Childs states, "It is thus best to think of

---

[5]Ideophones are sometimes referred to as "expressives" (see, e.g., Diffloth 1994). In the Africanist literature, however, the term "ideophone" is more current.

ideophones as a prototype category with a core of good members. The full set of ideophones also contains less optimal members radiating outward from this core type and becoming less and less ideophone-like" (p. 181).

Ideophones often have unusual phonological features, such as overly short or long duration, segments which are not a part of the regular phonemic inventory, and sequences of segments which violate phonotactic constraints. They may have unusual morphological features, most notably the repetition of a word. Syntactically, they are often set apart from the rest of the sentence. Pragmatically, they are often only found in declarative sentences and certain types of discourse.

Several of these features may be found in Mono ideophones. This includes aberrant syllable patterns; for example the word hàò 'brightly' has a CVV syllable pattern. There are unusual co-occurrence patterns; for example, the word hwìjà 'hot' contains a high vowel following a secondary articulation. There are unusual phonemes; for example, Mono ideophones have a disproportionately large number of occurrences of the labial flap, as in the word wěgē 'hot'. There are unusual tonal patterns, such as the rising contour tone in the word kpǒò 'near'. Finally, ideophones are often repeated, as in the expression in (65). The entire word is repeated rather than just the first syllable, which is the case for verb reduplication (see chapter 7).

(65) ɔ̀lɔ̀ tɔ́   wěgē-wěgē
     sun pound:NF   RED-hot
     'It is hot.'

This having been said, the word shapes in (66) are attested for Mono adverbs.

(66) Word shapes of Mono adverbs
     CV   ndʒē   'also'
               kpí   'different'
               gbō   'sound of a drum (ideophone)'
     CVV   hàò   'brightly (ideophone)'
     CVVV   hááō   'empty-handed (ideophone)'
     VCV   àtà   'thus'
     CVCV   kātʃā   'quickly'
               hàgà   'hard (ideophone)'
               kpàhà   'wide open (ideophone)'
     VCVCV   —
     CVCVCV   píngíwǐ   'suddenly (ideophone)'

In my corpus of data, adverbs beginning with a vowel are dispreferred. However, Kamanda (1998) includes several vowel-initial adverbs in his wordlist, shown in (67). More research is needed to resolve this discrepancy.

(67) àdà-ɔ̀lɔ̀ 'east'
 àdɨ̀là ~ dɨ̀là 'evening'
 àgbù 'onomatopoeia, imitation of the noise of the fall of a heavy object'
 àgbúrú ~ gbúrú 'of one bound'
 àkɨ́dà ~ àkɨ́dàlà ~ kɨ́dàlà 'evening'
 àlà-fó 'standing'
 àmà-zɨ̀ 'morning'
 àngbángì ~ ngbángì 'brusquely'
 àrà 'energetically'
 àtà 'in this way'
 àtà-kē 'in this way'
 éárá-éárá 'in small pieces'
 ìndìrì 'near to, next to'
 òàrà 'all'
 ɔ̄kɔ̄ 'reluctantly'
 ɔ̀lɔ̀-gàɗè ~ ɓá-ɔ̀lɔ̀-gàɗè 'when'
 ūcū 'before, in front of, early'
 úkúrú 'middle, between'

It is not clear that the word minimality condition observed in nouns and verbs holds for adverbs. Several adverbs with CV word shapes are attested in my corpus, as shown in (66). More research is necessary on this point.

6.4 Grammatical Function Word Shapes

As expected, Mono function words are not subject to the MC found in the major grammatical categories. Word shapes that are attested are given in (68).

(68) Grammatical function word shapes
V	ɔ́	'same subject pronoun'
	à	'question marker'
CV	nə̀	'DET'
	dá	'CLEFT'
	nɔ́	'of'
VCV	ɔ́də̄	'and'
	ásɔ́	'this'
CVCV	ɓàtà	'since, like'
VCVCV	àdé-kē	'that'

7

Morphology

Morphological typology has been a topic of discussion in linguistics since at least the early part of the nineteenth century.[1] Comrie (1989:46ff.) offered a revision of traditional typology, in which he categorizes languages along two continua—the index of synthesis and the index of fusion.

The INDEX OF SYNTHESIS classifies languages according to the number of morphemes a word can contain. Languages in which a word typically contains only one morpheme are termed ISOLATING, whereas languages in which a word typically contains several morphemes are termed POLYSYNTHETIC. In Mono, most words are monomorphemic, and most multimorphemic words contain only two morphemes. For example, in the first text in appendix A, the first ten sentences have fifty-one monomorphemic words, eighteen bimorphemic words, and two trimorphemic words. As a result, Mono is more isolating than it is polysynthetic. Since there is some morphology, but not enough to express a whole proposition in a single verb, Mono can be characterized as "somewhat synthetic." Mono verbs may have up to four morphemes, but this is quite rare. For example, the verb in (69) contains four morphemes, the root *na* 'go', the conditional marker *kə̀-*, the prefixal reduplicant *na* marking negation, and a high tone marking non-future.

(69) tʃə̀ kə̀-ná-ná   nēnē...
     3SG COND-RED-go:NF NEG
     'If he/she doesn't go...'

---

[1] A large portion of the data in this chapter was collected and compiled by Barbara Schrag, and I wish to extend my thanks to her for contributing it to this volume.

The INDEX OF FUSION classifies languages according to whether morphemes contain a single component of meaning or multiple components. Languages in which a given grammatical morpheme typically has a single component of meaning are termed AGGLUTINATIVE, whereas languages in which a given grammatical morpheme may subsume multiple meanings are termed FUSIONAL. On this continuum, Mono is closer to the agglutinative end, since the grammatical morphemes of Mono usually have single components of meaning.

Another typological parameter worth considering is the type of morphological processes most common in the language (Payne 1997:30). These can be prefixation, suffixation, infixation, stem modification, reduplication, or suprasegmental modification. Mono is predominantly a prefixing language, but reduplication and suprasegmental modification are also attested. The lack of suffixes in Mono is typologically unusual.

Morphology in Mono is manifested on nouns, verbs, prepositions, and a handful of particles. Nominal morphology consists of a plural prefix on animate nouns. Verbal morphology consists of (1) prefixes marking the infinitive, condition, and repetition, (2) reduplication marking negation and some tense, aspect, and mood categories, and (3) tonal morphemes which mark tense, aspect, and mood. Prepositional morphology consists of prefixes which mark precision in location.

Some phonological processes in Mono (such as vowel hiatus and glide formation) become evident only when we look across morpheme or word boundaries. Other processes which are known to apply within a morpheme are also applicable across morpheme or word boundaries.

7.1 Grammatical Categories

My primary purpose in examining the morphology of Mono is to inform the phonology, and for this purpose the structural properties of the grammatical classes are more fruitful than the distributional properties. For those interested, a treatment of the syntax of Mono can be found in Kamanda (1998). In addition, Cloarec-Heiss's (1986) analysis of the related language Linda is also beneficial for understanding Mono syntax.

7.1 Grammatical Categories

7.1.1 Nominal morphology

Animate versus inanimate nouns

One of the prototypical characteristics of Niger-Congo languages is a robust noun class system, such as the one found in Bantu. In the Ubangian languages, however, the only subgroup that shows a clear relationship to the Niger-Congo noun class system is Mba. The rest of Ubangian has what Greenberg (1970:12) calls "uncertain survivals of the Niger-Congo system of affixes." The evidence for this is so weak, however, that Boyd (1989:205) has stated that "there is little evidence of the prior existence of noun class systems" in Ubangian. As we will see, the one noun class found in Mono appears to have its source in a more general process and is likely not traceable to the Niger-Congo noun class system.

Nouns in Mono may be classified into two subgroups, based on whether or not they accept the plural prefix à-. Nouns which accept the plural prefix include those which refer to animals and those which represent people, including kinship terms. These I will refer to as ANIMATE nouns. Examples are given in (70). Since the combination of plural morpheme + root is always at least bisyllabic, subminimal root augmentation does not apply on plural animate nouns (cf. 70d–e). Some proper names take the plural prefix as well (70f–g).

(70) Sample animate nouns

a.	gbòlò	'child'	àgbòlò	'children'
b.	bākòngɔ̄	'turtle'	àbākòngɔ̄	'turtles'
c.	éjà	'firstborn'	àéjà	'firstborns' (Kamanda 1998:323)
d.	ūzū	'person'	àzū	'people'
e.	ēʒē	'caterpillar'	àʒē	'caterpillars'
f.	bìlī	'Bili (town name)'	àbìlī	'Bili-ites'
g.	mōnō	'Mono person'	àmōnō	'Mono people'

INANIMATE nouns do not take the plural prefix. This category includes those words which are considered prototypical nouns (Givón 1984:51), such as 'rock', 'tree', 'mountain', and 'house'. It also includes plant names and body parts, as in (71).

(71) Sample inanimate nouns

    a. bàdʒà   'rock'   bàdʒà   'rocks'
    b. ɔ̄jɔ̄   'tree'   ɔ̄jɔ̄   'trees'
    c. kàgà   'mountain'   kàgà   'mountains'
    d. àndà   'house'   àndà   'houses'
    e. ngímá   'palm nut'   ngímá   'palm nuts'
    f. kānə́   'hand'   kānə́   'hands'

If an animate noun has the vowel *a* in word-initial position, then the plural prefix may optionally take the form *àl-*. All the cases in my corpus of this behavior are with kinship terms (72).

(72) Sample animate nouns which take *à-* ~ *àl-* 'PL'

    a. àbá   'father'   ààbá ~ àlàbá   'fathers'
    b. àʔú   'uncle'   ààʔú ~ àlàʔú   'uncles'
    c. ájá   'brother'   àájá ~ àlájá   'brothers'
    d. átà   'grandparent/   àátà ~ àlátà   'grandparents/
               grandchild'   grandchildren'

The phonetically long vowel with a level tone which results from the concatenation of the plural prefix to the forms in (72a) and (72b) is not attested tautomorphemically and thus appears to be dispreferred by the grammar. The insertion of the *l* in such cases serves to break up this structure into more acceptable syllable patterns. The *l* is also inserted to break up a rising tone in (72c) and (72d), a structure which is rare in tautomorphemic environments and thus also dispreferred.[2]

Certain noun modifiers may also take the plural prefix. Descriptive adjectives take the prefix when they modify animate nouns. For example, in the noun phrase *à-gbōrō à-gjà* 'large animals', the adjective takes the plural prefix in modifying the animate noun, but in the noun phrase *ōgbōrō jāfī* 'large cups', the same adjective is in its default form since the noun is inanimate. Cloarec-Heiss (1986:50) notes that in Linda, an ordinal

---

[2]A similar allomorph occurs in the related language Linda. Cloarec-Heiss (1986:209) suggests that the *l* is inserted in order to avoid confusion between the plural prefix and the initial vowel *a* of the stem, which she considers a non-productive prefix. Thus, the use of *àl-* would prevent the creation of a long vowel as in the words *ààbá* 'fathers' and *ààʔú* 'uncles' in (72a–b). This explanation seems motivated, but Kamanda (1998:332) points out that there are cases in Linda where the *àlà-* prefix (the form in Linda) occurs with words in which the initial vowel of the stem is not *a*, e.g., *òwō* 'spouse' versus *àlàwō* 'spouses'. Tisserant (1930:27) on the other hand considers the use of *àlà-* to be a sign of respect.

7.1 Grammatical Categories

number may also take a plural prefix, as in (73). This is likely the case in Mono as well, but I could not verify this with my corpus of data.

(73) Ordinal number with plural prefix in Linda
  à-bīʃì   nə̀   kpé
  PL-two   DET   flee:NF
  'The second ones fled.'

Besides the plural prefix à-, there are several lexical means for marking plural. First, different verbs forms may be employed depending on whether a certain argument is singular or plural. For example, the verb *za* 'give' is employed if the direct object is singular whereas the verb *ko* 'give' is employed if the direct object is plural.

(74) Lexical marking of plural in verbs: *ko* versus *za* 'take'
  a. vōtɔ̀   kɔ́-kò   bīʃà   ɔ́   sɔ́pè   bàlē
     three INF-give(PL) two   SS remain one
     'Three minus two equals one.'

  b. mīndúù kɔ́-zà   ɓàlē ɔ́   sɔ́pè   vànā
     five   INF-give(SG) one   SS remain four
     'Five minus one equals four.'

Second, certain adjectives are lexically marked for plural. For example, the adjective *égérɔ́* 'big' is singular and the adjective *ōgbōrō* 'big' is plural, as in (75).

(75) Lexical marking of plural in adjectives: *égérɔ́* versus *ōgbōrō* 'big'
  a. ásɔ́   kə̀dɔ́   égérɔ́   jāʃí
     this   COP   big(SG)   cup
     'That is a big cup.'

  b. ásɔ́   kə̀dɔ́   ōgbōrō   jāʃí
     this   COP   big(PL)   cup
     'Those are big cups.'

Third, plural can be indicated by use of quantifiers, either numeral or non-numeral, as in (76).

(76) Lexical marking of plural in quantifiers
    a. Ken só də̀ jāʃí bīʃà
        PN   be with cup two
        'Ken has two cups.'

    b. Ken só də̀ jāʃí ndʒòró
        PN   be with cup many
        'Ken has many cups.'

Before leaving the topic of the plural in Mono, one additional observation needs to be made. In Mono, there is a large number of lexical items which begin with the vowel à-, but do not carry the semantic notion of plural. These include some animate nouns, inanimate nouns, and adverbs. In the case of the adverbs, the initial à- is optional.

(77) Sample words beginning with the vowel à-
    a. Animate nouns
        àgjà   'animal'
        àtʃó   'louse'
        àbá   'father' (kinship term)

    b. Inanimate nouns
        àlúgù   'mushroom'
        àkwà   'work'
        àkjó   'hoof' (body part)

    c. Adverbs
        àngbángì ~ ngbángì   'brusquely, abruptly'
        àbūtʃɔ́ ~ būtʃɔ́   'night' (time word)
        àkɨ́dàlà ~ kɨ́dàlà   'evening' (time word)

    d. Other
        àndʒòró ~ ndʒòró   'many'
        àbálādúwū   'June'
        àngándʒá   'August'

In at least one case, the word containing this initial à can be analyzed. The word àgārāwò 'match' is made up of an initial à, gara 'scratch', and òwò 'fire'.

Kamanda (1998:328ff.) suggests that this initial à is a remnant of an earlier plural prefix. He offers comparative data from several other

7.1 Grammatical Categories

Ubangian languages to support this claim. In Mbandja (Tingbo 1978:68–69), the category of "animate" is broader than in Mono, including plant names and heavenly bodies. Thus, the plural forms in (78) are attested.

(78) Sample Mbandja plurals

Singular		Plural		Mono form (inanimate)	
lúgù	'mushroom'	àlúgù	'mushrooms'	àlúgù	'mushroom(s)'
mbílípìlì	'star'	àmbílípìlì	'stars'	àngérépè	'star(s)'

In Ngbugbu, the plural prefix applies to both animate and inanimate nouns (79). Note that the plural forms for the animate nouns are analogous to the forms for Mono (in either the singular or plural).

(79) Sample Ngbugbu plurals

Singular		Plural		Mono form	
gìà	'animal'	àgìà	'animals'	àgjà	'animal(s)'
tʃɔ̄	'louse'	àtʃɔ̄	'lice'	àtʃó	'louse/lice'
gɔ̄	'village'	àgɔ̄	'villages'	ōgō	'village(s)'

In Ngbandi (Toronzoni 1989:209–210, cited by Kamanda), the plural prefix *á-* can occur on almost any noun, with the exception of terms regarding liquids and some vague concepts.

(80) Sample Ngbandi plurals

Singular		Plural		Mono form	
kùà	'work'	ákùà	'works'	àkwà	'work(s)'
bâ	'father'	ábâ	'fathers'	àbá	'father'

Thus, according to Kamanda's hypothesis, the proto-language containing the above speech varieties had a plural prefix which was generalized to include most if not all nouns. Then, in Banda (including Mono), the prefix ceased to apply to inanimate forms, leaving traces of its presence in certain present-day inanimate nouns. Given this hypothesis, one question that remains is the presence of the initial *à* in some adverbs, such as in (77c).

Compound nouns

Compounding is a common and productive process in Mono (cf. Kamanda 1998:304ff.). Words and particles in normal grammatical constructions can become fused together to create new words, examples of which will be shown below. Cloarec-Heiss (1986:140) notes that the degree to which a construction can be considered a compound correlates with the frequency of use of a construction.[3] This appears to be the case in Mono.

There are different parameters on which we can judge the degree of compounding (cf. Cloarec-Heiss 1986:133ff.). First is the notion of SEMANTIC RESTRICTION (SR). In a compounded form, the sense of the word is often limited compared to the original grammatical construction. For example, the compound *būlà* 'blindness' is more restricted semantically than the construction it comes from: *ūbū àlà* 'black eye'. Semantic restriction can occur without a reduction in the form of the construction. For example, the noun phrase *ɔ́ɾɔ́rɔ́ kàkó* 'lit., dry leaf' has the restricted meaning 'notebook, book', but no formal reduction is attested *ʔɔ́rɔ́kàkó*.

Second is the notion of FORMAL REDUCTION (FR). A compound may be reduced in structure from the original form. The associative noun phrase *élé ɔ́jɔ́* 'fruit (seed + tree)' may be reduced to *léjɔ́*, in which the first vowel of each noun is deleted. The loss of the first vowel in this case is not unexpected, since both of these nouns are of the word form V_1CV_1. As we saw in section 6.1, such nouns can be interpreted as having an underlying form /CV_1/, with the process of subminimal root augmentation inserting the initial vowel in the word. Since the compound is already bisyllabic, the motivation for SRA is lost, hence yielding *léjɔ́*.

Third is the degree of VARIATION (Va). The formal reduction may be obligatory, optional, or unattested. The word for 'door' in Mono is *màndà* which comes from *àmà* 'mouth' and *àndà* 'house'. I have not attested the associative noun phrase *àmà àndà*, so this appears to be a case in which the reduction is obligatory. In the case of 'fruit' discussed above, both *léjɔ́* and *élé ɔ́jɔ́* are attested, so the reduction is optional. A case in which formal reduction is unattested is the word *ɔ́kɔ́ àmà* 'lip (skin + mouth)'. Here, semantic restriction has occurred, but formal reduction has not, i.e., *kɔ́mà.

Finally, a compound may exhibit irregular PHONOLOGICAL MODIFICATION (PM). For example, the word *jāwò* 'firewood' comes from the combination *ɔ́jɔ́* 'tree' and *òwò* 'fire'. Given the phonological structure of the base words, we would expect the compound to have the form *jɔ̄wò, but this is unattested. Rather, the ɔ of /jɔ̄/ has changed to *a* in the compound.

---

[3]In fact, Cloarec-Heiss claims that the degree of compounding is a *function* of the frequency of use of the construction, but it is not certain that the causality is in this direction.

7.1 Grammatical Categories

Examples of compound nouns in Mono are given in (81). The most common type of compound results from the fusion of the elements in an associative noun phrase, in which the first element is the head (81a). Also common is the combination of an adjective and noun (81b). However, the elements which make up a compound noun are not limited to those found in a noun phrase, as seen in (81d, e). The result of these compounds is nevertheless a nominal word.

(81) Sample compound nouns in Mono

    a. N + N (Associative noun phrase)

ràdà 'shoe'	< ə̀rə̀ 'thing' + àdà 'foot'	(SR,FR,-,PM)
ròg̀ò 'food'	< ə̀rə̀ 'thing' + ògò 'hunger'	(SR,FR,-,PM)
jāwò 'firewood'	< ɔ́jɔ̄ 'tree' + òwò 'fire'	(SR,FR,-,PM)
ndə́dà 'footprint'	< ə́ndə́ 'mark' + àdà 'foot'	(-,FR,-,-)
ngwàrə̀ 'seed (for planting)'	< àngwà 'grain' + ə̀rə̀ 'thing'	(SR,FR,-,-)
ʃīkù 'scar'	< íʃírí 'image' + ùkù 'wound'	(-,FR,-,PM)
ndàwò 'forge'	< àndà 'house' + òwò 'fire'	(SR,FR,-,-)
màndà 'door'	< àmà 'mouth' + àndà 'house'	(SR,FR,-,-)
sùkūmù 'hair (of head)'	< ùsù 'hair' + kūmù 'head'	(-,FR,-,-)
àgjàngú 'fish' (also àgjà tʃálàngú)	< àgjà 'animal' + úngú 'water'	(SR,FR,Va,-)
gōrūjū ~ ōgōrō ūjū 'anus' (also, gūrūjū)	< ōgōrō 'hole' + ūjū 'excrement'	(SR,FR,Va,PM)
léjɔ̄ ~ élé ɔ́jɔ̄ 'fruit'	< élé 'seed' + ɔ́jɔ̄ 'tree'	(-,FR,Va,-)
ɔ́kɔ́ àmà 'lip'	< 'skin' + 'mouth'	(SR,-,-,-)
úngú òwò 'coffee, kerosene'	< 'water' + 'heat'	(SR,-,-,-)
ògò úngú 'thirst'	< 'desire' + 'water'	(-,-,-,-)

    b. Adjective + Noun

būlà 'blindness'	< ūbū 'black' + àlà 'eye'	(SR,FR,-,-)
gbádà 'lame'	< ágbá 'useless' + àdà 'foot'	(SR,FR,-,-)
ɔ́ʔɔ́rɔ́ kàkó 'book'	< 'dry' + 'leaf'	(SR,-,-,-)
íkp̂ ndímò 'sour orange'	< 'sour' + 'orange'	(-,-,-,-)

    c. Number + Noun

bàlēlà 'one-eyed'	< bàlē 'one' + àlà 'eye'	(SR,FR,-,-)

    d. Noun + Verb

làʔɔ́rɔ̀ ~ lɔ̀ʔɔ́rɔ̀ 'lesson'	< àlà 'eye' + ʔɔrɔ 'dry'[4]	(SR,FR,-,PM)
úngú kə́ndʒò tə́nə̀ 'drinking water'	< 'water' + 'drink' + 'it'	(-,-,-,-)

---

[4]In Togbo, the word for 'lesson' is lɔ̀kɔ́rɔ̀, which can be analyzed as ɔ̀lɔ̀ 'eyes' + kɔrɔ 'open'.

e. PREP + PREP/V/N

tʃátʃū ~ tʃʌ́tʃū 'face'	< tʃá 'place' + ūtʃū 'in front of'	(SR,FR,-,PM)
tʃáfù ~ tʃʌ́fù 'smell'	< tʃá 'place' + fu 'smell bad'	(SR,FR,-,PM)
tʃábàgá 'jaw bone'	< tʃá 'place' + bàgá 'cheek'	(SR,-,-,-)
tʃə́lə́mà 'palate'	< tʃə́-lə́ 'in' + àmà 'mouth'	(SR,FR,-,-)

f. N + N + N

ndə́mà?ò 'account, report'   < ə́ndə́ 'mark' + àmà 'mouth' + ò?ò 'word'

g. N + ?

élé ōwō ~ éléwō 'rice'	< élé 'fruit, grain' + ōwō '?'	(SR,FR,Va,-)
kā́nə́ gèlè 'left hand'	< 'hand' + 'left'	(-,-,-,-)
ngūzù 'pregnancy'	< úngú 'water' + zu 'give birth'	(SR,FR,-,-)
jámē 'my brother'	< ájá 'brother' + mə̄ 'my'	(-,FR,Va,PM)

h. V + PREP

gbètʃə́lə́ 'hope'   < gbe 'think' + tʃə́lə́ 'in'   (SR,-,-,-)

One additional construction needs to be examined before leaving the topic of noun compounding. In Mono, there are a large number of AGENTIVE NOUNS (Cloarec-Heiss 1986:134, refers to them as "noms d'agent"), consisting of àjī 'person, owner' plus a noun or infinitive verb (82). The form àjī is a truncation of àjēngɔ̀ 'person, owner'.[5] In some cases, there is variation between the two, for example, àjī àkwà ~ àjēngɔ̀ àkwà 'servant, employee'.

(82) Sample agentive nouns
àjōgō	'inhabitant' < àjī 'person' + ōgō 'village'
àjī āngbā ~ àjēngɔ̀ āngbā	'thief'
àjī kā́nə́	'thumb'
àjī bī-tū	'deaf person'
àjī à-gènè	'host'
àjī à-jāʃē bīʃà	'polygamist'
àjī kú-wù-sə́-?ò	'wise person'
àjī kə́-ndʒò kɨ̄ndɨ̄	'farmer'

---

[5]Cloarec-Heiss (1986:135) states that in Linda the agentive form comes from the word èjī 'mother'. There is indeed formal identity between the two words in Linda (and in Mono as well), but the source in Mono of the agentive form is clearly àjēngɔ̀ 'person, owner', based on examples such as àjī àkwà ~ àjēngɔ̀ àkwà 'servant, employee' where there is variation between the two, as well as native speaker intuitions about the source.

This process is reminiscent of an agentive construction in English in which the morpheme "man" or "person" is suffixed to a noun (e.g., milkman, postman, congressman, chairperson).

Agentive nouns in Mono share some properties with compounds. First, they are of the same form as the associative noun phrase, with the head being the first element. Second, there is formal reduction, since àjēngɔ̀ becomes àjī. Third, there can be semantic restriction, for example, àjī kānɔ́ 'thumb (lit., person of hand)'. Fourth, there is phonological modification in that the *e* of àjēngɔ̀ becomes *i* in àjī.

It is not clear whether àjī should be considered a separate word or whether the compound has truly become fused. It is a bound morpheme which must occur with a following element, whereas àjēngɔ̀ is a free morpheme. However, when the following element begins with a vowel, vowel hiatus results which is typically not resolved (that is, one of the vowels is not deleted), contrary to the normal case with most compounds.

Kamanda (1998:319) hypothesizes that this is a case of grammaticalization in process. What began as an associative noun phrase has undergone compounding. Now àjī is in the process of becoming a derivational agentive prefix, but does not yet exhibit all the properties of a true prefix.

Derivation

Mono has several derivational processes. Boyd (1995:11) claims that derivation in the Ubangian languages essentially creates nominals from verbs (he specifically discusses Gbaya, Banda, Ngbandi, and Sango). Both Cloarec-Heiss (1986:116, 121) and Kamanda (1998:281) interpret the data in this way as well. I will treat derivation in the same way, but there is some evidence (which I will discuss) that some cases of derivation could be interpreted as progressing in the opposite direction, that is, from a nominal to a verb.

The first derivational process to be discussed is the creation of a nominal from a verb with no affixation, but with the process of subminimal root augmentation applying if its structural description is met. In Mono, a large number of mostly stative and intransitive verbs can become either a noun or a descriptive adjective. Since nominals must be bisyllabic, subminimal root augmentation applies to monosyllabic forms, as shown in (83). Note that SRA also applies to verbs of the form CV_1LV_1.

(83) Nominals derived from stative or intransitive verbs
    a. High tones

íkpí 'tart'	< kpi 'be tart'	(Adj < Stat V)
úndú 'sweet'	< ndu 'be sweet'	(Adj < Stat V)
ɔ́ʔɔ́rɔ́ 'dry'	< ʔɔrɔ 'dry'	(Adj < Intr V)
égérə́ 'big (SG)'	< gerə 'grow'	(Adj < Intr V)
ébé 'big, fat'	< be 'swell, become fat'	(Adj < Intr V)
ódóró 'ripe, red'	< doro 'ripen' (Kamanda 1998:659)	(Adj < Intr V)
ə́sə́ 'place'	< sə 'be (existential)'	(N < Stat V)
áná 'trip'	< na 'come, go'	(N < Intr V)
élé 'fruit'	< le 'bear fruit'	(N < Intr V)
ɔ́mɔ́ 'laughter'	< mɔ 'laugh'	(N < Intr V)

    b. Mid tones

ūfū 'rotten'	< fu 'be rotten'	(Adj < Stat V)
īkī 'sharp'	< ki 'be sharp'	(Adj < Stat V)
ūʃū 'bitter'	< ʃu 'be bitter'	(Adj < Stat V)
ɔ̄tʃɔ̄ 'delicious'	< tʃɔ 'be tasty'	(Adj < Stat V)
ɔ̄mɔ̄ 'soft'	< mɔ 'be tired' (cf. ká-mɔ̀ ɔ́mɔ́ 'to laugh')	(Adj < Stat V)
īmī 'thick'	< mi 'grow, be thick'	(Adj < Intr V)
ōgbōrō 'big (PL)'	< gboro 'grow'	(Adj < Intr V)
ōdō 'foolishness'	< do 'be foolish'	(N < Intr V)
ōlō 'day'	< lo 'lie down' (cf. kálò ōlō 'sleep')	(N < Intr V)
ūzū 'person'	< zu 'give birth'	(N < Trans V)

    c. Low tones

òwò 'fire'	< wo 'be hot' (cf. fōwò 'heat')	(N < Stat V)

This process is best thought of as deverbalization rather than nominalization since the resulting form is either a noun or a descriptive adjective, whereas the underived form is always a verb.

Cloarec-Heiss (1986:126) and Kamanda (1998:281) both consider the reduplicated vowel to be a prefix.[6] I question this interpretation for the following reason. The epenthetic vowel only occurs with forms which can

---

[6] Kamanda considers this an instance of a more general process of reduplication in Mono in which the first syllable of a nominal is reduplicated indicating intensity, for example, dàmbá 'tail' → dàdàmbá 'tail (intensive)' (p. 285). However, the items at issue do not bear any notion of intensity, and their form can be explained without any reference to other morphological processes in Mono.

7.1 Grammatical Categories

be analyzed as underlyingly monosyllabic, for example, *ūfū* < /fū/ 'rotten', *ɔ́ʔrɔ́* < /ʔrɔ́/ 'dry'. Longer words do not undergo SRA though they can have a nominal form, for example, *zìtì* 'cold, peaceful' < *zìtì* 'cool off'. If the form is indeed a prefix, we would expect the reduplication to apply to all such forms. The prefix interpretation does not explain why it is only the monosyllabic underlying forms which undergo the process. The attested pattern follows directly from a purely phonological explanation involving SRA.

Note that the resulting forms bear one of the three level tones in Mono. The tone which occurs on a given item is unpredictable. This could be interpreted in at least two ways. First, this could indicate that verbs do have an underlying tone, as suggested by Cloarec-Heiss (1972:86) for Linda. However, not all verbs are attested in a nominalized form. For those which are not, there is no means of identifying the underlying tone. Second, the tone could be considered a part of the underlying form of the nominal, in which case the derivation would proceed from the nominal to the verb. The disadvantage of this interpretation is that, for Ubangian, linguists typically analyze this type of derivation as proceeding from verbs to nouns.

In Ubangian, it is common for some verbs to take a direct object which is the nominalized form of the verb (Boyd 1995:13). Levin (1993:95) refers to this as a COGNATE OBJECT CONSTRUCTION. Cognate objects appear to be widespread, occurring in languages as diverse as Igbo (Nigeria, Benue-Congo; John Goldsmith, pers. comm.) and English (Levin 1993 and references therein). Several cognate objects are attested in Mono, shown in (84).

(84) na áná   'travel'   (< 'go' + 'trip')
     lo ōlō   'sleep'   (< 'lie down, sleep' +
                                          'slumber, day')
     wo òwò   'have a fever'   (< 'be hot' + 'fire')
     kpa ákpá   'run (for exercise)' (< 'flee' + '?')

The second derivational process to be considered also concerns the nominalization of a verb. This process involves a prefix with the same segmental shape as the infinitive prefix, *kə-*. The resulting tonal pattern is either high-low or high-mid, depending on the lexical item (85). One such verb with a stative conjugation is also attested in my corpus (85c).

(85) Nominalized verbs (kɔ́-) (cf. Kamanda 1998:295–303; Cloarec-Heiss 1986:123)

    a. High-low melody
        kɔ́-nà 'going'   < na 'go'
        kɔ́-zɨ̀rə̀ 'food'   < zɨ ərə 'eat (something)'
        kɔ́-jìndɔ́rə̀ 'kindness'   < ji ndɔ́ ərə 'like, love (something)'
        kɔ́-wùsə́rə̀ 'knowledge' < wu sɔ́ ərə 'know (something)'
        kɔ́-wùrə̀ 'vision'   < wu ərə 'see (something)'
        kɔ́-dòngà 'honor'   < dòngà 'honor'

    b. High-mid melody
        kɔ́-gā 'beauty'   < ga 'be good, be beautiful'
        kɔ́-ndʒā 'vomiting'   < ndʒa 'vomit'
        kɔ́-wū 'breath'   < wu 'breathe'
        kɔ́-zō gàràngà 'bread'   < zo gàràngà 'bake manioc'
        kú-zū 'semen'   < zu 'give birth' (cf. kùzū 'death')

    c. High-fall melody
        kɔ́-ngáàngà 'acidity'   < nga 'be bitter'

Tisserant (1930:159) refers to these nominalized verbs as "infinitives." However, this does not explain the tonal patterns found in (85b, c) which do not follow the infinitive high-low tone melody.[7]

In my corpus, both types of derivation are attested for one verb form, as shown in (86). Note that áná 'journey' has high tones, whereas the tone on the root of the nominalized verb kɔ́-nà 'going' is low.

(86)   Verb   SRA   Nominalized verb
      kɔ́-nà 'come, go'   áná 'journey'   kɔ́-nà 'going'

Finally, a brief note of a couple of patterns in Mono morphemes which may be vestiges of historical morphological processes. First, as mentioned in section 6.2, there are a large number of Mono verbs which have the form CV_1rV_1, for example *suru* 'tear', *kɔrɔ* 'open', *para* 'choose', *mbərə* 'do', and *ndʒoro* 'suck'. This may be a vestige of an ancient derivational process in Ubangian. Kamanda (1998:502) notes that Ngbandi and Ngbaka-Minagende both presently have a *-rV* derivational suffix. In Mono, there is semantic relation between a few verbs of the form CV and

---

[7]In the related language Mbandja (Tingbo 1978:77), infinitives and nominalized verbs are distinct in form. For example, the infinitive of the root *ti* 'fall' is *tá-tì* whereas the nominalized form of the verb is *kī-tí*.

7.1 Grammatical Categories

those of the form CV₁rV₁, for example, *su* 'uproot' versus *suru* 'tear', and *ʒe* 'grovel' versus *ʒerə* 'descend'.

Second, there are a number of animate nouns in Mono which begin with *jā-*, for example, *jābùrù* 'goat', *jākóró* 'snake', *jānū* 'bird', *jārə̀* 'livestock', *jāvóró* 'dog', *jāwèlè* 'catfish', *jākōʃē* 'male', *jāʃē* 'female', *jāngá* 'friend', and *jāwāzà* 'old woman'. Cloarec-Heiss (1986:121) considers this to be an unproductive prefix in Linda meaning 'domesticated animal'. The words which include this form in Mono, however, are broader in semantic scope than this. In any case, it is clear that this form is not productive in Mono.

7.1.2 Verbal morphology

Mono verbs can be modified by the addition of one of several prefixes, by reduplication of the first syllable of the verb, and by changes in the tone on the verb (and the preceding pronoun). Most constructions require a combination of these modifications, and so I will discuss the constructions in turn. But first, a few preliminaries.

The prefixes that modify a verb are shown in (87). I consider these to be prefixes because there are no attested intervening words between these forms and the verb roots. There can, however, be an intervening reduplicant of the verb root.

(87) Mono verbal prefixes
    a. kɔ́-   'infinitive'
    b. kɔ̀-   'conditional'
    c. kpá-   'repetitive'

In the infinitive form, the prefix always bears a H tone, and all of the syllables of the root bear L tones (88a–b). The infinitive form of a compound verb includes the tones of the second element of the compound (88c). The forms of the conditional and repetitive will be discussed below.

(88) Sample infinitive verbs
    a. kɔ́-nà   'to go'
    b. kɔ́-zì-rə̀   'to eat'
    c. kɔ́-jì-ndɔ́-nə̀   'to want'

I also analyze verbal reduplication as a case of prefixation. That is to say, a reduplicant is prefixed to the verbal root, rather than suffixed.

There are two arguments for this interpretation. First, prefixation is the most common morphological process in Mono, and so we would expect that to be the first choice for an interpretation. Second, the reduplicant is a copy of the first syllable of the base, rather than of the entire base.

One use of reduplication in Mono is to mark negation. This involves the combination of a reduplicated verb and the particle *nēnē* in clause-final position, as in (89). (Example (89b) is taken from Kamanda 1998:16.) Reduplication is used in several other constructions as well, as discussed later in this section.

(89) Reduplication in Mono
    a. mā   mbɔ́-mbɔ́rɔ̀   tɔ́nɔ̀   nēnē
       1SG   RED-do:NF   it   NEG
      'I didn't do it.'

    b. èndʒē   ká-kákàrà...   nēnē
       3PL   RED-uproot   NEG
      'They didn't uproot....'

Modifications in the tonal patterns on Mono verbs indicate different tense, aspect, and mood (TAM) characteristics. These tonal patterns may affect not just the verb, but also a preceding subject pronoun. This is evidence that subject pronouns may be considered clitics in Mono, since they are grammatically part of the subject but phonologically dependent on the verb. All three level tones are attested on the first syllable of a verb root, several tonal patterns are attested on reduplicants (H, HM, and HL), and a H tone may replace the regular tone on a subject pronoun. Note that regardless of the tense, aspect, or mood under consideration, the second and third syllables of a verb root always bear a L tone.

Teasing out the exact semantic nuances in a TAM system is a difficult task, and there has been some discussion in the literature on the precise nature of the system in Mono and related languages. Several analyses have been proposed for Banda (see, e.g., Cloarec-Heiss 1986, 1995b; Olson and Schrag 2000; Kamanda 1998), but more research needs to be conducted in order to clarify this issue. In this study, my main goal is to document clearly the formal properties of Mono phonology and morphology, so semantics has not been the main focus of my research. In the discussion that follows, not too much weight should be put on the labels of each TAM category. Clarifying the meanings of each category will require further research.

7.1 Grammatical Categories

Non-future tense (NF)

The non-future tense (either present or past) is identified by a H tone on the first syllable of the verb root. A preceding subject pronoun retains its lexical tone. A temporal adverb can specify the time frame. Example (90a) is in the present, whereas examples (90b–c) are in the past.

(90) a. ʔā jí.ndɔ́ kɔ́-dʒì ndɔ́mà.tòrò ngɔ́ngɔ́ nɔ̀ ásɔ́kē
       1PL.EXCL want:NF INF-hear story   time DET this
       'We want to hear a folk story now.'

   b. ɔ̀lɔ̄ bàlē bākòngɔ̄ **ná** ɓá-ndɔ́ mbàlà
       day one tortoise go:NF at-home elephant
       'One day, tortoise went to elephant's place.'

   c. èndʒē **kó** límā jāmbùrù
       3PL take(PL):NF long.ago stones
       'Long ago they took stones.'

Future tense (FUT)

The future tense is indicated by a H tone on the clitic subject pronoun[8] preceding the verb, and a L tone on first syllable of the verb root (91). When the subject of a clause is a noun, then the same subject pronoun ɔ́ is inserted between the noun and the verb (91c). The HL tone melody can be broken up by an intervening morpheme (91d).

(91) a. **ɓɔ́** **wù** mā̄ ɓámbàtʃā
       2SG:FUT see:FUT 1SG tomorrow
       'You will see me tomorrow.'

   b. **mɔ́** zùrù tʃɔ́lɔ́ zɔ̀ kɔ̀rɔ̀ná
       1SG:FUT stomp:FUT inside 2SG broken
       'I will crush you.'

   c. jésù **ɔ́** kwà tɔ́-jē gà-pá lɔ̀ʃɔ̀
       Jesus SS return:FUT REFL-3SG on-top soil
       'Jesus will return to earth.'

---

[8] It is manifested as a rising tone on the 1PL.INCL pronoun.

d. ʔàá   kpá-zì   ángá   nə̀   zə̀
   1PL.INCL:FUT REP-eat:FUT another DET EMPH
   'We will eat again later.'

There has been some discussion in the literature concerning the precise distinction between what I am calling the non-future and the future tenses. Boyd (1989:206) notes that many Adamawa-Ubangi languages have a basic distinction between perfective aspect (the situation is looked at from the outside, without distinguishing its internal structure) and imperfective aspect (the situation is looked at from the inside, and is concerned with the internal structure; cf. Comrie 1976:4). For Linda, Cloarec-Heiss (1986:310ff.) considers this distinction to be one of completed *(accompli)* aspect (the process or state is considered to be acquired or certain) versus incompleted *(inaccompli)* aspect (the process or state is considered to be uncertain or in the process of succeeding; cf. Boyd 1995:22). This is the distinction that Kamanda chooses in describing Mono. However, Cloarec-Heiss (1995b:85) changes her mind and considers the distinction in Linda to be one of real mode (the process or state is considered to be existing) and virtual mode (the process or state is considered possible or desirable; cf. Boyd 1995:22). The data in my corpus point toward a distinction of non-future versus future, but a more detailed study is necessary to clarify this.

Progressive aspect

The progressive aspect is indicated by the verb *kə́-sə̀* 'to be' inflected for tense, followed by the infinitive form of the main verb.

(92) a. mə̄   sə́   kə́-bì   ītʃī
        1SG be:NF INF-hit song
        'I am (was) singing.'

   b. mə́   sə̀   kə́-bì   ītʃī
      1SG:FUT be:NF INF-hit song
      'I will be singing.'

   c. mə̄   sə́-sə́   kə́-nà   gálàngú   nēnē
      1SG RED-be:NF INF-go   to.water NEG
      'I'm not going to the water.'

7.1 Grammatical Categories

Repetitive aspect (REP)

The repetitive aspect is indicated by the invariable prefix *kpá-* before the verb stem. The verb stem may be inflected for various TAM.

(93) a. mə̄ kpá-sú ángá nə̀
  1SG REP-draw:NF other DET
  'I drew (water) again.'

  b. kpá-pà ángá nə̀
  REP-say:IMP other DET
  'Repeat. (lit., say again)'

  c. mə̄ kpá-sə́ kə́-jù àjī mə̄ àdə́kē tʃə̀ pàrà údú
  1SG REP-be INF-ask mother 1SG that 3SG look.for rest

  ə̀rə̀ nə̀ fə̄ mə̄
  thing DET BEN 1SG
  'I was again asking my mother to look for some leftovers for me.'

Stative aspect (STAT)

The stative aspect (cf. Payne 1997:240) is marked by reduplication of the first syllable of the verb. The reduplicant bears a HL falling tone while the first syllable of the verb root bears a L tone.

(94) a. ə́ ʃúù-ʃù
  it RED:STAT-bitter:STAT
  'It is bitter.'

  b. ə́ gjáà-gjà
  it RED:STAT-stir.with.difficulty:STAT
  'It is difficult to stir.'

  c. kpàtà zúù-zùrù
  mud RED:STAT-be.slippery:STAT
  'The mud was slippery.'

Conditional mood (COND)

The conditional mood is indicated by the invariable prefix kə̀- plus the verb stem. In my corpus, the verb stem is marked as non-future. The second clause in the construction is often marked as future.

(95) a. 6ə̀   kə̀-mbə́rə̀   àtà   gbòlò   nə́ mā,   mə́   jì ndə́   zə̀
        2SG COND-do:NF thus child   of 1SG   1SG:FUT like:FUT 2SG

         wáā
         much
      'If you do this, my child, I will love you a lot.'

   b. 6ə̀   kə̀-ná-ná   nēnē ə́tə́   nə̀   kə̀-də́   ò?ò
      2SG COND-RED-come:NF   NEG   being DET COP   problem

         nə́ zə̀   bàlē
         of 2SG one
      'If you do not come, the problem will be yours alone.'

Imperative mood (IMP)

The imperative mood is indicated by the absence of a subject and the occurrence of a L tone on the first syllable of the verb stem. In the negative form, a H tone occurs on both the verb root and the reduplicant.

(96) a. kò   màngé   nə̀
        take(PL):IMP   corn   DET
        'Take the corn.'

   b. nà   də̀   ə́tʃə́   nə̀
      go:IMP with   good   DET
      'Good-bye (lit., go well).'

   c. zí-zí   sə́ngbā àgjà   nēnē
      RED-eat   meat   animal NEG
      'Don't eat meat.'

7.1 Grammatical Categories

Obligation/interdiction mood (OB)

Obligations and interdictions are indicated by a L tone on the first syllable of the verb root. This is the same form as the imperative, but the subject is present. In addition, this form usually appears in a subordinate clause.

(97) a. ɔ́ lí àdə́kē ɓə̀ sə̀ də̀ kúwùsə́rə̀ gà-pá nə̀
       ss suffice:NF that 2SG be:OB with wisdom on-top DET
       'You need to have wisdom as well.'

    b. mə̄ sɔ́ kə́-jì ndɔ́ nə̀ àdə́kē àjūngō mə̄ də̀ à-jāʃē
       1SG be:NF INF-like DET that PL-sibling 1SG with PL-woman

       èndʒē lì gàlɔ́ nə̀ gázə̀ nēnē
       3PL enter:OB inside DET there NEG
       'I didn't want my sisters to go in there.'

    c. mə̄ kpá-sɔ́ kə́-jù àjī mə̄ àdə́kē tʃə̀
       1SG REP-be:NF INF-ask mother 1SG that 3SG

       pàrà údú ərə̀ nə̀ fə̄ mə̄
       look.for:OB rest thing DET BEN 1SG
       'I was again asking my mother to look for some leftovers for me.'

    d. ɔ́ lí àdə́kē mə̄ ʔì tə́-mə̄
       it suffice:NF that 1SG tie:OB REFL-1SG
       'I need to go to the bathroom.'

Subjunctive mood (SUBJ)

The subjunctive mood is indicated by a M tone on the first syllable of the verb root. It is often used to connote the idea of correctness or advice, and it is conveyed in an English translation by use of the auxiliary 'should' (98). In addition, it is employed in a reason-result structure (99).

(98) a. ɔ́ sɔ́ kɔ́pà àdə́kē ʔà nā gàndɔ́ ènē
       ss be:NF INF-say that 1PL.INCL come:SUBJ to 3SG.LOG
       'He is saying that we should go to him.'

b. ájá,   nà   gámə́ ə́ fā̱   lòsù zə̀ jé
   brother come:IMP here SS change:SUBJ heart 2SG EMPH
   'Brother, come here. You should really change your heart.'

c. jésù sə́   də̀   ògò   àzə́   àdə́kē ʔà   nā̱
   Jesus be:NF with hunger 1PL.INCL that 1PL.INCL come:SUBJ

   gà-ndə́   ènē
   to-home 3SG.LOG
   'Jesus has a desire for us that we should come to him.'

(99) a. ò?ò nə̀ kó   mə̄ wáá á   mə̄ nā̱   kə́-jù
        word DET bother 1SG much CONJ 1SG come:SUBJ INF-ask

        ɓə̀ ásə̄
        2SG this
        'Those words hurt me a lot, so (that is why) I came to talk to you about it.'

   b. ə́   zá   fə̄ ʃè tʃə̀ nḏʒō̱
      SS take:NF BEN 3SG 3SG drink:SUBJ
      'I got him (water) so that he could drink.'

   c. ə́ sə́   kōló nə̀ àtà á   ʔā̱   sə̱̄
      SS be:NF only DET thus CONJ 1PL.EXCL be:SUBJ

      kə́-lò   tʃákùdú nə̀
      INF-lie.down under   DET
      'It (the house) was like that, so we were sleeping under it.'

Certainty mood (CERT)

One additional TAM form is a HM falling tone on a reduplicant followed by a M tone on the verb root. The precise meaning of this form remains to be determined, but it is glossed 'certainty' in the examples in (100).

(100) a. ká̱ā-kā̱   àdékē... ə́ sə́ ɓàtà ə́tʃə́ ə̀rə̀
         RED:CERT-leave:CERT that...   it be like good thing
         'Be aware that...this is a good thing.'

b. èndʒē sɔ́ kɔ́-<u>kwáā-kwā</u>   ngɔ́ngɔ́ nə̀ ásɔ́
   3PL   be INF-RED:CERT-return:CERT time DET this
   'They will indeed be returning now.'

7.1.3 The copula and 'to be'

The copula *kɔ́-də̀* and the verb *kɔ́-sə̀* 'to be' both have irregular properties which I will discuss briefly here. The copula is used to express equation (the entity of the subject and the predicate nominal are the same), proper inclusion (the entity of the subject is in the class of items indicated by the predicate nominal), and possession such as "The book is John's." The form of the copula is *kə̀-dɔ́* in the positive and *dɔ́-dɔ́* in the negative. Occasionally the positive form is shortened to *dɔ́* or left out entirely. If a pronoun occurs in subject position, it is in its citation form.

(101) a. Proper inclusion
      ə̀bə̀ <u>kə̀dɔ́</u> mōnō
      2SG COP   Mono
      'You are a Mono person.'

   b. Equative
      èʃè <u>dɔ́-dɔ́</u> àbá   mə̄ nə̄nē
      3SG RED-COP   father 1SG NEG
      'He is not my father.'

   c. Possession
      jāvóró nə̀   ásɔ́ <u>kə̀dɔ́</u> tʃə̀ nɔ́ zə̀   à
      dog   DET this COP   3SG of 2SG QUEST
      'Is this your dog?'

The verb *kɔ́-sə̀* 'to be' is employed in existential clauses, possessive clauses (such as "Sally has nineteen cats"), predicate adjectives, and predicate locatives. It is also used as an auxiliary in a progressive construction, as discussed above. It can be marked for TAM. In some constructions, it has an irregular negative form *gu*.

Existentials

Examples of the existential use of *kɔ́-sə̀* are given in (102). In the negative non-future, the irregular form *gu* is employed. In the negative future, either *sə* or *gu* may be employed.

(102) Existential
    a. ngátɔ̀ sɔ́ zə̀
       chicken be:NF EMPH
       'There is a chicken.'

    b. ngátɔ̀ gú-gú nēnē
       chicken RED:NF-be(NEG):NF NEG
       'There is no chicken.'

    c. *ngátɔ̀ sɔ́-sɔ́ nēnē
       chicken RED:NF-be:NF NEG
       (unattested)

    d. ngátɔ̀ ɔ́ sə̀ zə̀
       chicken SS be:FUT EMPH
       'There will be a chicken.'

    e. ngátɔ̀ ɔ́ gù nēnē
       chicken SS be(NEG):FUT NEG
       'There will not be a chicken.'

    f. ngátɔ̀ ɔ́ sə̀ nēnē
       chicken SS be:FUT NEG
       'There will not be a chicken.'

There is a plural form kɔ́-lə̀, which is only used by the older generation and is thus disappearing. The younger generation employs kɔ́-sə̀ for both singular and plural. The negated form is not changed.

(103) a. à-ngátɔ̀ sɔ́ zə̀
       PL-chicken be:NF EMPH
       'There are chickens.'

    b. à-ngátɔ̀ lɔ́ zə̀
       PL-chicken be(PL):NF EMPH
       'There are chickens.'

    c. à-ngátɔ̀ gú-gú nēnē
       PL-chicken RED:NF-be(NEG):NF NEG
       'There are no chickens.'

7.1 Grammatical Categories

A quantity may be specified in the noun phrase, or it may occur after the verb.

(104) a. à-ngátɔ̀ bīʃà sɔ́ zɔ̀
PL-chicken two be:NF EMPH
'There are two chickens.'

b. à-ngátɔ̀ sɔ́ bīʃà
PL-chicken be:NF two
'There are two chickens.'

Possessive clauses

In a possessive clause, the verb is followed by a prepositional phrase with the preposition 'with'. In the negative form, *sə* is reduplicated. The form *gu* is not attested.

(105) a. ɔ́ sɔ́ dɔ̀ ɔ́gbɔ́ nɔ̀
SS be:NF with hardness DET
'It is hard.'

b. ɔ́ sɔ́-sɔ́ dɔ̀ ɔ́gbɔ́ nɔ̀ nēnē
SS RED:NF-be:NF with hardness DET NEG
'It is not hard.'

c. *ɔ́ gú-gú dɔ̀ ɔ́gbɔ́ nɔ̀ nēnē
SS RED:NF-be(NEG):NF with hardness DET NEG
(unattested)

Predicate adjective

In an adjectival clause, the verb is followed by an adjective. In the negative form, *sə* is reduplicated. The form *gu* is not attested.

(106) a. ɔ́ sɔ́ téāʃó
SS be:NF small
'It is small.'

b. ɔ́ sɔ́-sɔ́ téāʃó nēnē
SS RED:NF-be:NF small NEG
'It is not small.'

c. *ə́ gú-gú   téāʃó nēnē
   SS RED:NF-be(NEG):NF small NEG
   (unattested)

Predicate locatives

In a locative clause, the verb is followed by a prepositional phrase. Either *sə* or *gu* may be employed in the negative, but there is no reduplication.

(107) a. tʃə̀ sə́   ɓá-ndə́   mə̄
       3SG be:NF at-home 1SG
       'He/she is at my place.'

   b. tʃə̀ sə́   ɓá-ndə́   mə̄   nēnē
      3SG be:NF at-home 1SG NEG
      'He/she is not at my place.'

   c. tʃə̀ gú   ɓá-ndə́   mə̄   nēnē
      3SG be(NEG):NF at-home 1SG NEG
      'He/she is not at my place.'

   d. tʃə́ sə̀   ɓá-ndə́   mə̄   ɓámbàtʃá
      3SG:FUT be:FUT at-home 1SG tomorrow
      'He/she will be at my place tomorrow.'

   e. tʃə́ sə̀   ɓá-ndə́   mə̄   ɓámbàtʃá nēnē
      3SG:FUT be:FUT at-home 1SG tomorrow NEG
      'He/she will not be at my place tomorrow.'

   f. tʃə́ gù   ɓá-ndə́   mə̄   ɓámbàtʃá nēnē
      3SG:FUT be(NEG):FUT at-home 1SG tomorrow NEG
      'He/she will not be at my place tomorrow.'

Motion verbs express a locative goal in a similar manner, but they are reduplicated in the negative.

(108) a. tʃə̀ ná   ɓá-ndə́   mə̄
       3SG come:NF at-home 1SG
       'He/she came to my place.'

7.1 Grammatical Categories

b. tʃə́ ná-ná ɓá-ndɔ́ mə̄ nēnē
3SG RED:NF-come:NF at-home 1SG NEG
'He/she did not come to my place.'

7.1.4 Prepositional morphology

Most prepositions and locative adverbs in Mono are morphologically complex. There is a closed set of prefixes which may attach to a base element to make the meaning of the base more precise (cf. Cloarec-Heiss 1986:272; Kamanda 1998:522). The prefixes are:

- ɓá- 'at'. This prefix implies no movement with respect to a designated location.
- gà- ~ gá- 'to'. This prefix indicates movement towards a designated location. The value of the tone depends on the following tone. If the following syllable bears a high tone, then the tone on ga- is low. If the following syllable bears a low or mid tone, then the tone on ga- is high. Cases of tonal polarity are common in two-tone systems, but cases in three-tone systems have not been discussed much in the literature. Our language resource persons noted that in most cases either tone could appear in a given context. However, in actual speech, the tonal polarity phenomenon was observed.
- kpɔ́- 'just in'. This prefix indicates a precise place or time.
- tʃɔ́-, tʃá- 'at/place'. The meaning of these forms is unclear. Our language resource persons indicated that these two forms have slightly different meanings, but they could not specify the difference.

Teasing out the exact meaning of the prefixes is difficult, so more research is needed to fine tune the definitions given above. These prefixes may attach to several different types of bases. First, they may attach to prepositions, as in (109), to create a complex preposition. More than one prefix may be attached to a given base (109e). In addition, the base may appear in isolation (109f), but the prefix may not.

(109) a. bākòŋgɔ̄ ná ɓá-ndɔ́ mbàlà
turtle go:NF at-home elephant
'The turtle went to the elephant's home.'

b. mā sɔ́ kɔ́-nà gà-lɔ́ kɪ̄ndɪ̄
   1SG be INF-go to-in field
   'I'm going to the field.'

c. zà tʃàdʒà nɔ́ zə̀ gá-ūtʃū ndábà
   take:IMP pencil of 2SG to-in.front.of table
   'Put your pencil in front of the table.'

d. ùndù jē ró pá àgjà tʃɔ́-lɔ́ gūsū kɔ́kɔ́ jé
   size 3SG pass:NF over animal in-in bush all   EMPH
   'His size surpasses all the animals in the bush.'

e. Kendigia sɔ́ kɔ́-dè jāwò ɓá-tʃá-kùdú ājā àndà
   PN be INF-chop firewood at-at-hole small house
   'Kendigia is chopping firewood in the straw hut.'

f. mɔ́ pà lɔ́ āgā
   1SG:FUT speak:FUT in horn
   'I will speak on the two-way radio.'

Second, the prefixes may be attached to a variety of forms to create a locative adverb, as in (110).

(110) a. nà gá-mā
   come:IMP to-1SG
   'Come here.'

b. mā sɔ́ kɔ́-nà ɓá-ʔé
   1SG be INF-go at-there
   'I'm going over there(somewhere).'

c. ʔà wūtà gà-úʃú
   1PL.INCL exit:SUBJ to-outside
   'Let's go outside.'

There is a subset of these locative adverbs which has an obligatory HLH tonal pattern. This pattern replaces whatever underlying tones are normally associated with the individual morphemes.

7.1 Grammatical Categories

(111) a. lì   gá-sə̀-ndá
         enter:IMP   to-place-house
         'Enter.'

   b. ángá à-bākòngɔ̄ sɔ́ ndʒē ɓá-là-ngú
       other PL-turtle   be also at-eye-water
       'Other tortoises live in the water.'

   c. tʃə̀ sɔ́ kɔ́-pà ʔò fɔ̄ à-zū tʃá-là-kpɨ́ də̀ lēngā
       3SG be INF-speak words BEN PL-person place-eye-? with drum
       'He is speaking to the village people with a talking drum.'

7.1.5 Other morphology

There are certain grammatical function words which are morphologically complex. First, the locative question words in (112) include one of the prefixes mentioned in the previous section.

(112) a. ɓə̀ sɔ́ kɔ́-nà gá-tà
         2SG be INF-go to-on:QUEST
         'Where are you going?'

   b. kafe nɔ́ jē sɔ́ ɓá-tà
       coffee of 3SG be at-on:QUEST
       'Where is his/her coffee?'

Second, the demonstrative ásɔ́ 'this' can take the suffixes -kē or -mə̀ to mark degree of distance, for example, ásɔ́-kē ~ ásé-kē 'this' or ásɔ́-mə̀ 'that'. The meaning can be temporal or locative depending on the context. Similarly, the manner adverb àtà 'in this manner' can take these two suffixes, for example, àtà-kē 'like this' and àtà-mə̀ 'like that'.

Finally, the reflexive marker tɔ́- is prefixed to a pronoun to give the forms in (113).

(113) tɔ́-mā   'myself'
      tɔ́-zə̀   'yourself'
      té-jē   'himself/herself'
      tá-ʔā   'ourselves (EXCL)'
      tá-àzɔ́   'ourselves (INCL)'
      té-ʔē   'yourselves'
      té-èndʒē   'themselves'

7.2 Phonological Processes Which Cross Morpheme or Word Boundaries

In this section, I discuss phonological alternations which can occur across morpheme or word boundaries. These include leftward vowel spreading, vowel hiatus resolution, glide formation, and raising of *a*.

7.2.1 Leftward vowel spreading

Leftward vowel spreading (LVS) was introduced in section 6.1, where it was shown to occur in monomorphemic environments in which ə or a is inserted as a result of subminimal root augmentation (SRA). LVS is also attested across morphological and clitic boundaries. If a morpheme with a schwa ə as the nucleus of the final syllable is followed by a morpheme with a non-low vowel in the initial syllable, the schwa optionally takes on the quality of the following vowel. The morpheme following the schwa must begin with a consonant, and this consonant cannot be a glottal stop (the case of glottal stop will be considered in the next section). In the case of a high vowel, the schwa may alternatively become ɨ. If the schwa is followed by a morpheme with ɔ as the nucleus of the first syllable, then the schwa becomes o. For example, consider the case where the infinitive prefix *kə-* is attached to a verb, as in (114).

(114) kə́vì ~ kívì ~ kɨ́vì   'to dance'
      kə́kɨ̀ ~ kɨ́kɨ̀   'to cry'
      kə́ʒù ~ kɨ́ʒù ~ kúʒù   'to burn'
      kə́dè ~ kédè   'to chop'
      kə́sə̀   'to be' (no alternation)
      kə́dʒɔ̀ ~ kódʒɔ̀   'to cultivate'
      kə́nà   'to go' (no alternation)
      kə́tɔ̀ ~ kótɔ̀   'to forge'

These alternations result directly from the LVS rule given in (55) in section 6.1. Note that there is no assimilation of the feature [low].

In verbs which begin with a sequence of a semi-vowel followed by an *a*, or which contain a secondary articulation in the first syllable, it is the quality of the semi-vowel or secondary articulation which is spread, rather than the quality of the nuclear vowel.

7.2 Phonological Processes Which Cross Morpheme or Word Boundaries

(115) kə́wa ~ kówà   'to cut'   (cf. kə́wù ~ kúwù 'to see')
kə́jà tə́ ~ kéjà tə́   'to rest'   (cf. kə́jù ~ kújù 'to ask')
kə́kwà ~ kókwà   'to return'
kə́gja ~ kégjà   'to stir'

These patterns were not evident in section 6.1, because SRA inserted an *a* before [+low] vowels (cf. *āwā* 'road', *ájá* 'brother', *àkwà* 'work', *àgjà* 'animal').

So far, we have seen examples of LVS applying in augmented monomorphemic words and between a prefix and a root. LVS may also occur between a root and a suffix, for example, *àdə́-kē* → *àdé-kē* 'this'. But it is not limited to applying across morpheme boundaries within a word. The process is attested across word boundaries. For example, it is attested between a clitic pronoun and a verb, as in (116).

(116) a. ə́   lì...   → i̱ lì ~ i̱ lì
    SS   be.necessary:FUT
    'It is necessary...'

b. ɓə́   rò   ɓátà   → ɓó̱ rò ɓátà
    2SG:FUT pass:FUT   where
    'Where are you going?'

It is also attested between prepositions and nouns.

(117) a. fə̀   ʃè   → fe̱ ʃè
    BEN   3SG
    'for him/her'

b. tʃə́lə́   ūtū   → tʃə́lú̱ ūtū ~ tʃúlú̱ ūtū
    in-in   ear
    'in the ear'

Finally, LVS is attested in non-augmented monomorphemic environments. Several lexical items have a schwa which alternates with *e*.

(118) a. kpə́kē ~ kpékē   'a week ago'
      b. səpè ~ sepè   'stay'
      c. nə̄nē ~ nēnē   'NEG'

There are additional monomorphemic items in my corpus which have the environment for the application of LVS, but it is not clear if the process applies in these cases. Further field research is necessary to verify that the process applies to these forms. Examples are given in (119).

(119)   Attested form   Predicted alternation
   a.   kpə̄līndūvū   kpɨ̄līndūvū ~ kpīlīndūvū   'kidney'
   b.   ngbə̄lēkō   ngbēlēkō   'iron'
   c.   tə̀ràlē   ——   'directly'
   c.   kpɔ́ə̀ndòrò   kpóòndòrò   'naked'
   d.   lə̀tɔ̀rɔ̀   lòtɔ̀rɔ̀   'toad'

LVS shares some features with both lexical and postlexical rules. It is similar to a lexical rule in that it is structure preserving. The forms which are created are all phonemes in the language. It is similar to a postlexical rule in several ways. It may occur across word boundaries, it is optional, and it does not appear to have lexical exceptions.

7.2.2 Hiatus resolution

Certain phonological alternations may occur in Mono when two vowels are brought into hiatus. I refer to this process as hiatus resolution. If a word-final schwa ə is followed by a V-initial syllable, the schwa optionally takes on the quality of the following vowel, creating a long vowel. This process differs from leftward vowel spreading in that it occurs with low vowels as well as non-low vowels.

(120) ɔ́   sə́   àtà   → [ɔ́ sá̰ àtà]
      ss   be   thus
      'That's right.'

If the tones of the two syllables are identical, then the schwa may assimilate or be elided.

(121) mə̄ bálà ɓə̀ àtà   → [mə̄ bálà ɓà̰ːtà] ~ [mə̄ bálà ɓà̰tà]
      1SG greet 2SG also
      'I greet you in return.'

7.2 Phonological Processes Which Cross Morpheme or Word Boundaries

Interestingly, this same pattern occurs if there is an intervening glottal stop, but not if another consonant intervenes. Example (122) shows two such cases.

(122) a. ʔā ná də̀ tə́-ʔā → [ʔā ná də̀ tá̠-ʔā]
    1PL.EXCL go:NF with REFL-1PL.EXCL
    'We (EXCL) went ourselves'

b. fə̄ ʔā → [fá̠ʔā]
    BEN 1SG.EXCL
    'for us'

Hiatus resolution is not always structure preserving, as it may create a long vowel with a level tone, as in (121). It applies across word boundaries, is optional, and it has no lexical exceptions.

7.2.3 Glide formation

There are cases in which glides are optionally formed from vowels due to heteromorphemic environments. Most cases in my corpus involve the particle *jé* 'EMPH' which reduces to *í* in casual speech (123a). If the vowel preceding *jé* is *u*, then it is the *u* which shortens yielding *wí* (123b). In addition, glide formation occurs before other particles as well (123c).

(123) a. fūrūtʃā ká jé → [fūrūtʃā ká_í_]
    soap be.finished EMPH
    'The soap is gone.'

b. mə̄ gú jē → [mə̄ gwí]
    1SG return:NF EMPH
    'I've returned.'

c. ɓə̀ tó ɓátà á gù ā → [ɓə̀ tó ɓátà á gwàā]
    2SG come where REL return QUEST
    'Where are you coming from?'

Glide formation is not structure preserving, since it violates the phonotactic constraints of secondary articulations as in (123b). It applies across word boundaries and is optional. It may be limited to certain lexical items, but more research is necessary on that point.

7.2.4 Raising of *a*

The raising of *a* to *ʌ* discussed in chapter 2 may apply across morpheme or word boundaries. An example is given in (124).

(124) mə̄ kpá-lú ángá nə̀ → [mə̄ kpʌ́-lú ʌ́ŋgʌ́ nə̀]
 1sg REP-planted other DET
 'I planted more again.'

It is not structure preserving, as it creates an allophone of a phoneme. It is optional and it does not have lexical exceptions.

7.3 Summary

As a summary, table 7.1 lists the phonological processes which I have posited for Mono and indicates if they are structure preserving, if they apply across word boundaries, if they are optional, and if they have lexical exceptions.

Table 7.1. Mono phonological processes

	Structure preserving	Across word boundaries	Optional	Exceptions
a. V-nasalization	N	N?	Y	N
b. Raising *a*	N	Y	Y	N
c. V-epenthesis	Y	N	N	N
d. V-shortening	N	N	Y	N
e. Subminimal root augmentation	?	N	N	N
f. Leftward vowel Spreading	Y	Y	Y	N
g. Hiatus resolution	N	Y	Y	N
h. Glide formation	N	Y	Y	Y?

8

Acoustic Phonetics

While phonological analysis is sufficient for identifying contrastive segments in Mono, there are at least two potential problems with it. First, impressionistic phonetic transcription is a methodology subject to human error. Linguistic researchers struggle with the difficult task of identifying unfamiliar contrasts, many of which may escape their hearing during the initial stages of fieldwork. And they must overcome the bias of their own mother tongue's phonological system, which colors the way they hear the sounds they are transcribing. Studying the acoustic phonetic details of sounds offers a check on the accuracy of phonetic transcription.

Second, the identification of phonological categories in Mono and the subsequent assignment of certain symbols to those categories may give the false impression of identity with similar sounds in other languages. Simply put, just because researchers describing two different languages use the same symbol for a particular phoneme does not necessarily mean that the two sounds are in fact pronounced the same. This issue is crucial for those who study linguistic typology. By giving more detailed acoustic data for specific sounds, I hope to give readers a clearer picture of what I mean by my phonetic transcription.

The data for this chapter were obtained during two recording sessions. The first set of recordings was made in Bili on September 26, 1994 using a Marantz PMD 420 analog tape recorder and a Shure dynamic microphone. The subject, Speaker M, was an adult male native speaker of Mono, about 35 years old. We recorded the 204-item wordlist found in Olson (1996) as well as forty-seven phrases, listed in appendix C. The subject read from a page, and each item was recorded once. These data were digitized at 10,000 Hz using Kay Elemetric's Computerized Speech Lab at the University of Chicago Language Laboratories and Archives.

The second set of recordings was made by Brian and Barbara Schrag at the SIL recording studio in Yaoundé, Cameroon, on March 16–18, 1998. Mike Fox was the recording engineer. The recordings were made with a Nakamichi 550 analog tape recorder and an AKG D330DT microphone. The two subjects, Speakers A and K, were both adult male native speakers of Mono, about 30 years old. The recordings included real and possible (i.e., nonsense) words spoken in isolation, sample phrases, and a folk story. The subjects told the story in their own words, and then read the story from a script. All tokens were spoken at normal rate. Some of the sample phrases were spoken at a fast and a slow rate as well. A complete list of tokens is given in appendix C. In addition, they recorded Speaker K producing a 2,000-item wordlist, included in appendix B.

A digital audio tape (DAT) copy was made at the University of Chicago Language Laboratories and Archives at a sampling rate of 48,000 Hz and then converted to WAV files using SoundDesigner II, version 2.8. The files were then downsampled for analysis to 11,025 Hz using Cool Edit 2000.[1]

Analysis of the tokens was done primarily using Kay Elemetric's Computerized Speech Lab. Additional analysis was done using SIL's Speech Analyzer, version 1.06a. Each figure in this chapter indicates which of the two programs was used for a given analysis.

In this chapter I discuss the acoustic properties of consonants, including labial flaps, implosives, labial-velar stops, and prenasalized stops, and the acoustic properties of vowels, including the formant values of the vowels, duration, and nasalization. Preliminary evidence that secondary articulations are closer to mid vowels than high vowels is provided, and I discuss phonetic evidence that secondary articulations do not bear tone. Finally, I summarize the findings and discuss items for future research. Except where noted, the findings of this chapter are valid for all of the subjects.

---

[1] One reason for downsampling is that SIL's Speech Analyzer program can only read WAV files which are sampled at a rate which is an integer multiple of 11,025 Hz. In cases where higher accuracy was needed (e.g., studying the possible high frequency energy of implosives), I examined the tokens sampled at 48,000 Hz using CSL.

8.1 Consonants

8.1.1 Labial flap

Because the labial flap is rare in the world's languages, there has been little acoustic research carried out on the sound. Three previous works discuss the acoustic properties of the sound: Ladefoged (1968) for Margi, Thelwall (1980) for Ndogo, and Demolin and Teston (1996, reiterating Demolin 1992) for Mangbetu. Of these, Demolin and Teston go into the greatest detail. The present work represents the first study of the acoustics of the labial flap in Mono.

The labial flap can be identified by virtue of a combination of four acoustic correlates: (1) a short closure duration, (2) ascending transitions for F_1, F_2, and F_3 immediately after release, (3) a short duration of the formant transitions immediately after release, and (4) a slow, gradual drop in F_2 before the closure.

Concerning the first correlate, Catford (1977:130) notes that taps and flaps typically have an oral closure duration of 10–30 ms. This duration distinguishes taps and flaps from stops, which typically have a closure duration of at least 50–60 ms. According to my measurements, the average closure duration of the labial flap in Mono is 23 ms (SD = 5.0, $n=15$). Ladefoged notes that the contact is less than 30 ms in Margi, and Demolin and Teston note an average length of contact of 14 ms. This contact is denoted by a brief interruption of the formant structure and a decrease in signal amplitude during the closure period. These properties are evident during the time period indicated by the arrows in figure 8.1, which shows a spectrogram of the possible word *aw̌a*.

Note, however, that the closure of the labial flap is not always complete, and so this acoustic property is not always visible. Sixty percent of the tokens I examined exhibit an obvious closure. Consider the spectrogram of the word *áw̌árá* 'fierceness' in figure 8.2. The general movement of the formant transitions is essentially identical to those of figure 8.1 during the onset and release of the flap. However, there is no clear break in the formant structure nor a drop in signal amplitude. In this case, other acoustic correlates must be present to identify the flap, which we will turn to now.

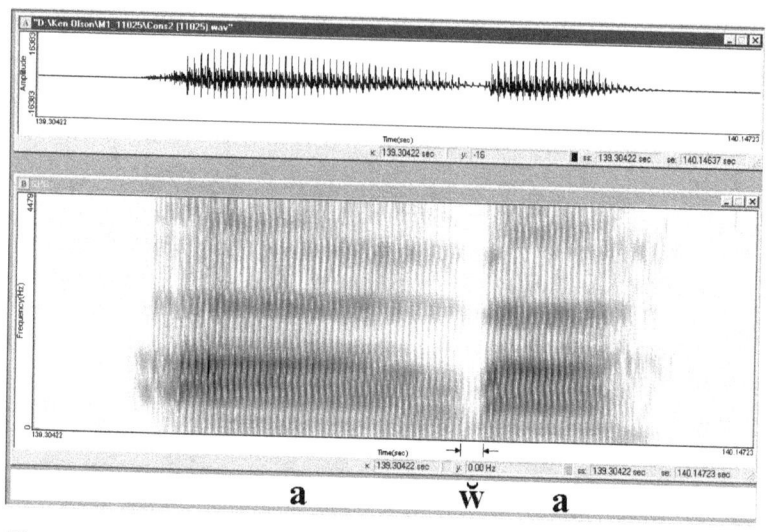

Figure 8.1. Waveform and spectrogram of the possible word *awǎ* (Speaker K).

The second acoustic correlate of the labial flap is the rise of the first three formant frequencies—F_1, F_2, and F_3—during the transition into the following vowel. These rising transitions are typical of labial articulations in general (Lieberman and Blumstein 1988:225). Thus, this property can be employed to distinguish labial flaps from alveolar taps and flaps. In some cases, F_3 appears to be flat with an abrupt transition. Figure 8.1 shows an example of this case. However, figure 8.3 shows a spectrogram of the word *jāwèlè* 'catfish' in which the rise in the transition of F_3 is visible.

Third, during the articulation of the labial flap, the transition of the formants into the following vowel is very brief, as noted by Thelwall (1980:81). This transition has an average of 19 ms (SD = 4.8, n = 25) in Mono. This is slightly shorter than for stop consonants, which typically have a formant transition duration of 20–40 ms (Lieberman and Blumstein 1988:224). This property is particularly useful for distinguishing the flap from semi-vowels, which must have a formant transition duration of at least 40 ms (p. 226). Figure 8.4 shows a spectrogram of the word *āwā* 'road'. The duration of the formant transitions at the release of the *w*, about 40 ms, are indicated by the arrows. Even when the closure of the labial flap is not evident, such as in figure 8.2, this rapid formant transition of the labial flap is still present, and so still distinguishes the flap from a semi-vowel.

8.1 Consonants

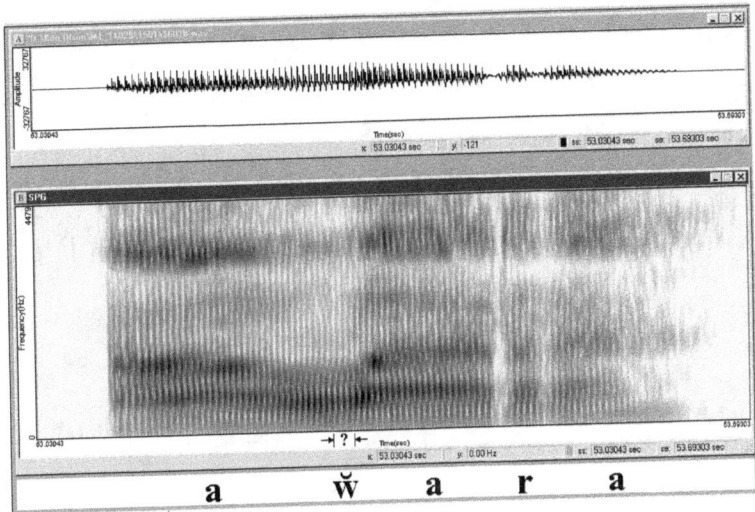

Figure 8.2. Waveform and spectrogram of the word *áw̌árá* 'fierceness' (Speaker K).

A sound can also be distinguished from other sounds by the lack of certain acoustic properties. During the production of a labial flap, there is no aperiodic noise such as is characteristic of fricatives, nor is there a burst such as is characteristic of stops.

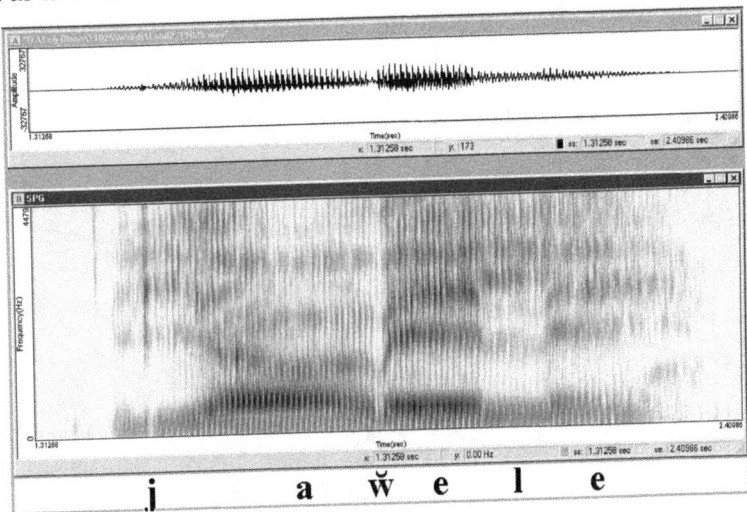

Figure 8.3. Waveform and spectrogram of the word *jāw̌èlè* 'catfish' (Speaker A).

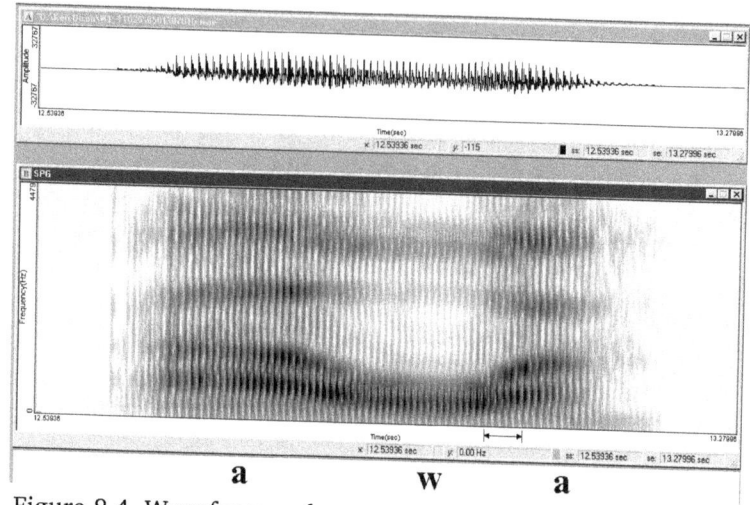

Figure 8.4. Waveform and spectrogram of the word *āwā* 'road' (Speaker K).

When a labial flap occurs in word-initial position, it is preceded by a short period of voicing. This indicates that the onset of the sound may be important in its perception. Figure 8.5 shows a spectrogram of the word *w̌ílí* 'calf, shin'. The period of voicing preceding the labial flap is indicated by the arrows. F_2 is visible during this period, dropping from a value of about 1140 Hz to 780 Hz immediately before closure.

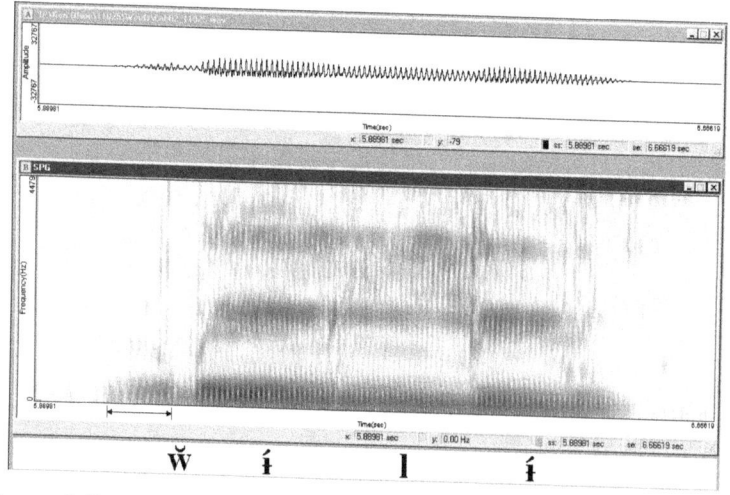

Figure 8.5. Waveform and spectrogram of the word *w̌ílí* 'calf, shin'. Voicing precedes a word-initial labial flap (Speaker A).

8.1 Consonants

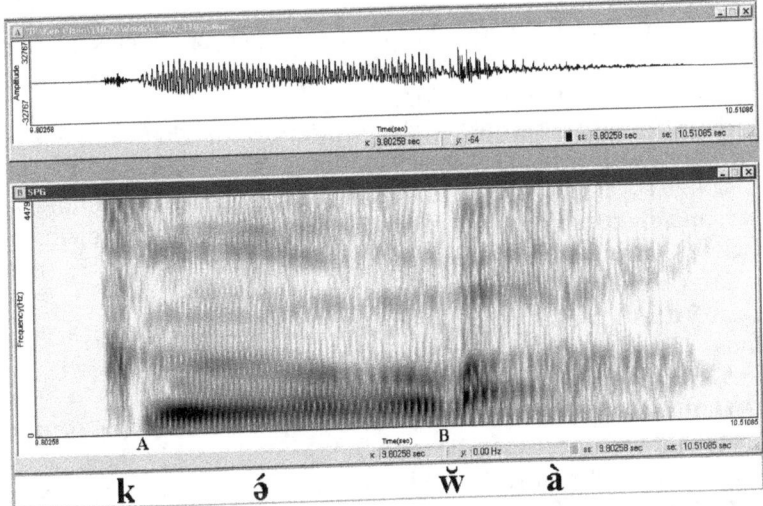

Figure 8.6. Waveform and spectrogram of the word *kɔ́-w̌à* 'to send' (Speaker A).

In many tokens, a gradual drop of F_2 is observed preceding the labial flap. For example, figure 8.6 shows a spectrogram of the word *kɔ́-w̌à* 'to send'. At the beginning of the vowel *ə* (point A), F_2 has a value of 1400 Hz. There is a gradual decrease in the value of F_2 until just before the closure of the flap (point B), F_2 has dropped to a value of 900 Hz. This drop in F_2 correlates both with the slow constriction of the lips preceding the flap as well as the backing of the tongue observed by one of my language resource persons. See Lieberman and Blumstein (p. 48) and de Jong and Obeng (2000) for further discussion on this point.

8.1.2 Implosives

As discussed in chapter 2, Mono has two implosive consonants ɓ and ɗ, which are optionally realized as their plosive counterparts, *b* and *d*, respectively. Lindau (1984) points out phonetic differences between the implosives found in several Niger-Congo languages on one hand (Degema and three Eastern Ijo languages), and the Chadic language Hausa, on the other. The Niger-Congo languages she studied exhibit certain regular acoustic patterns. First, the signal amplitude of the implosives either increases gradually during the oral closure period or it is level and sizeable throughout the closure, whereas plosives exhibit a gradual decrease in signal amplitude during closure. Second, the implosive sound waves include high frequency energy during the first part of the closure. She interprets this as a period of laryngealization (i.e., creaky voice), which is then followed by modal phonation.

In Hausa, there is considerable variation in the production of implosives. One of Lindau's subjects produced implosives like those of the Niger-Congo speakers, five subjects produced a voiceless beginning of the closure, and eight subjects produced implosives with aperiodic vibrations throughout the closure. Ladefoged and Maddieson (1996:85) refer to these latter sounds as "creaky voiced implosives."

Lindau's characterization of laryngealization as aperiodic vocal cord vibrations resulting in high frequency spectral energy is peculiar. Ladefoged and Maddieson (1996) consider laryngealization to be periodic and note two possible articulations. The parts of the vocal cords near the arytenoid cartilages may be held tightly so that only the ligamental parts vibrate, or alternatively the ligamental and arytenoid parts vibrate separately and out of phase with each other. This second articulation leads to an apparent doubling of the glottal pulse rate. Ladefoged (1968:16) notes that laryngealization sometimes but not always occurs in implosive consonants.

I examined twenty-five tokens of Mono implosives to determine if there was evidence for either high frequency energy or a biphasic pattern. Among these, fifteen exhibited a rising signal amplitude during the period of closure, whereas ten exhibited a large, level signal amplitude. There was some evidence for the type of laryngealization described by Ladefoged and Maddieson, as discussed below. In addition, a small number of tokens exhibited voicelessness during part of the period of closure. I will discuss these points in turn.

First, I consider the signal amplitude during the period of closure of Mono implosives. Speaker K produced the possible words *aba*, *aɓa*, *ada*, and *aɗa*, shown in figures 8.7–8.10. (In addition, spectrograms of *aba* and *aɓa* are given in figures 8.11 and 8.12, respectively.) Here, we see the same general amplitude patterns as those observed by Lindau. For the tokens with plosive consonants, *aba* and *ada*, there is a gradual decrease in signal amplitude from the beginning to the end of the closure. For the tokens with implosive consonants, *aɓa* and *aɗa*, there is a gradual increase in signal amplitude. Note that this augmentation in signal amplitude does not begin at the start of closure, but rather begins about one third of the way into the closure. This augmentation of signal amplitude is evident in the spectrogram as well. In figure 8.12, we can see the presence of formant bands during the second half of the closure period for F_1, F_2, F_3, and F_4.

8.1 Consonants

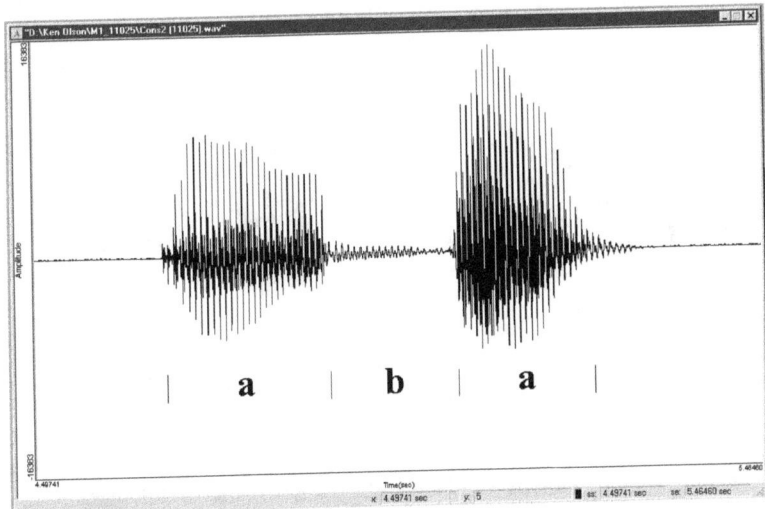

Figure 8.7. Waveform of the possible word *aba* (Speaker K).

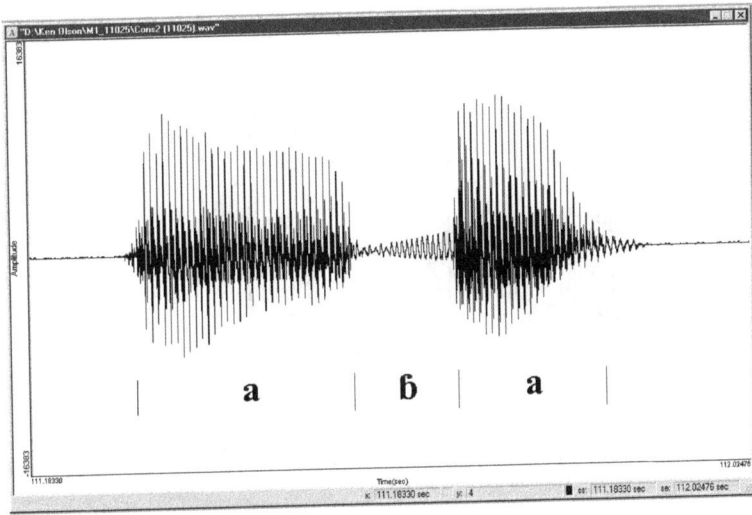

Figure 8.8. Waveform of the possible word *aɓa* (Speaker K).

130

Acoustic Phonetics

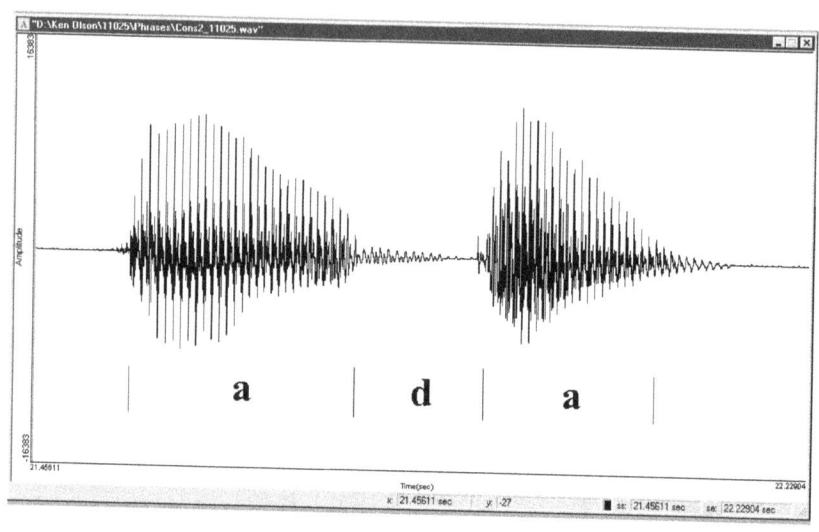

Figure 8.9. Waveform of the possible word *ada* (Speaker K).

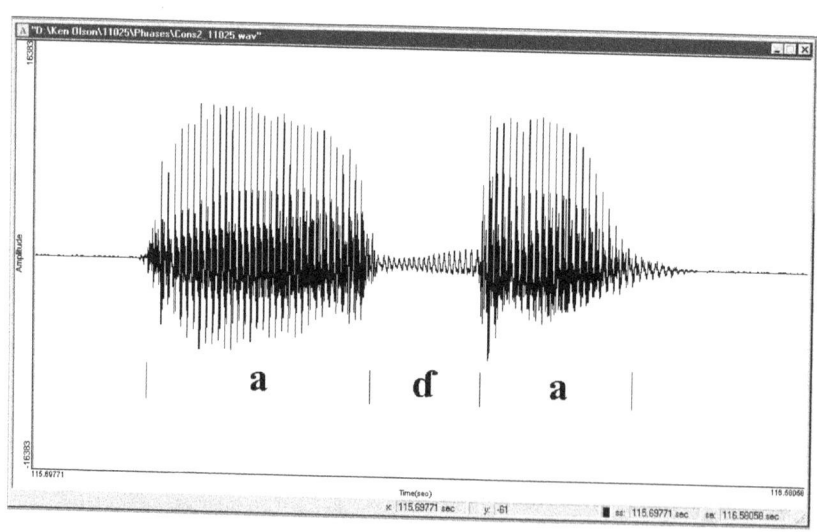

Figure 8.10. Waveform of the possible word *aɗa* (Speaker K).

8.1 Consonants

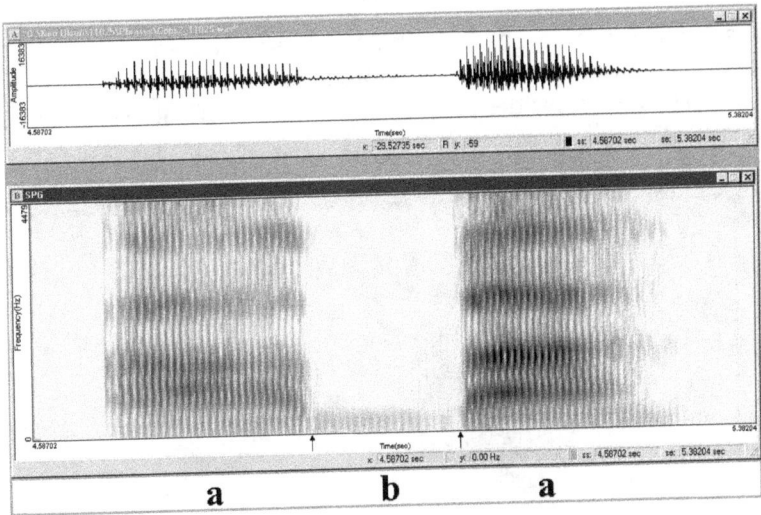

Figure 8.11. Waveform and spectrogram of the possible word *aba* (Speaker K). Beginning and end of closure are indicated by the arrows.

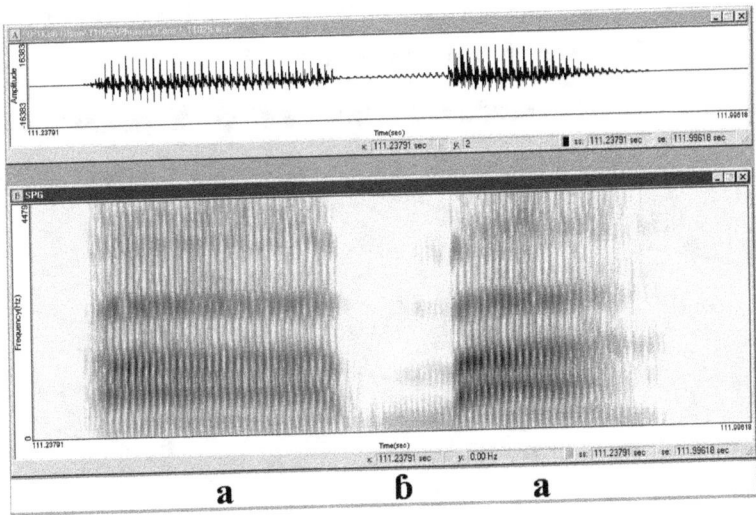

Figure 8.12. Waveform and spectrogram of the possible word *aɓa* (Speaker K).

This increase in signal amplitude is also attested in word-initial implosives. Figure 8.13 shows the word ɓá-àtɨ́ 'low'. Here, there is an increase in signal amplitude from the beginning of the utterance until the release of the implosive.

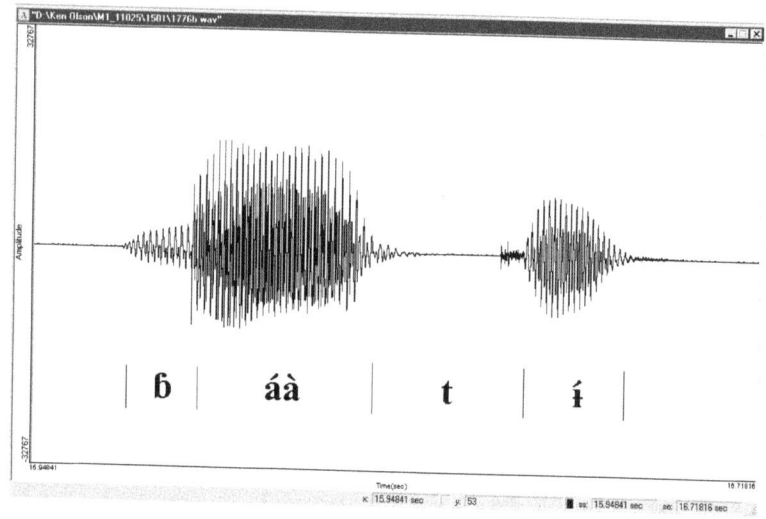

Figure 8.13. Waveform of the word ɓá-àtɨ́ 'low' (Speaker K).

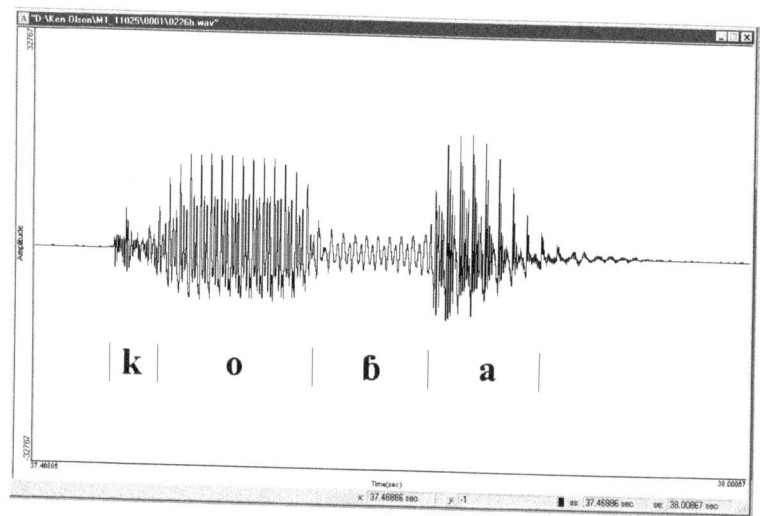

Figure 8.14. Waveform of the word kòɓà 'spirit' (Speaker K).

8.1 Consonants

In possible words and in words where the implosive is in initial position, the increase in signal amplitude is a consistent pattern. In other tokens, however, a second pattern is sometimes attested. Consider the waveform of the word kòɓà 'spirit' shown in figure 8.14. Here, the entire closure period of the implosive is characterized by a relatively large, level amplitude rather than an increase in signal amplitude from the start to end of closure. This alternative amplitude property was also observed by Lindau for the Niger-Congo languages in her study.

The second property of implosives that I examine is the phonation type, specifically whether there is evidence for laryngealization. Figures 8.15–8.18 are close-up views of the closure period of the signal for the possible words aɓa and aɗa uttered by both Speakers A and K. In Speaker A's tokens, there is a small amount of noise incorporated into the initial pitch periods of closure, but it is of a much smaller magnitude than that found by Lindau. In Speakers K's tokens, this aperiodic noise is absent. There is no clear evidence for significant high frequency energy in the Mono tokens.

Figure 8.15. Close-up of waveform of the possible word aɓa (Speaker A).

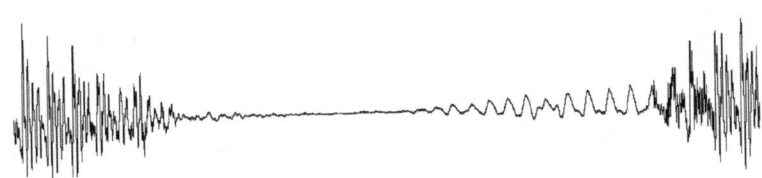

Figure 8.16. Close-up of waveform of the possible word aɗa (Speaker A).

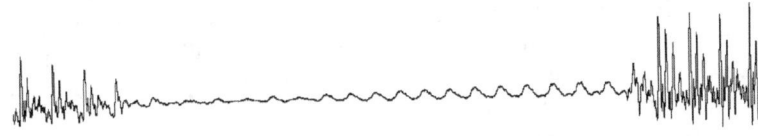

Figure 8.17. Close-up of waveform of the possible word aɓa (Speaker K).

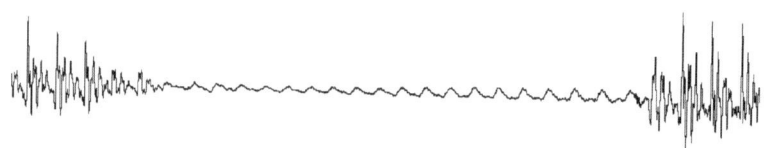

Figure 8.18. Close-up of waveform of the possible word *aɗa* (Speaker K).

Figures 8.19 and 8.20 show close-up views of the closure period for the words *kòɓà* 'spirit' and *èɗè* 'who'. Both of these tokens exhibit a large, level signal amplitude during closure rather than a rising amplitude. Here we see that in addition to the main pulses occurring at the period of the fundamental frequency, there are also intermittent smaller pulses of about half to two-thirds the amplitude of the main pulses. This is similar to the biphasic pattern which Ladefoged and Maddieson claim corresponds to laryngealization (cf. their figure 3.3, 1996:54).

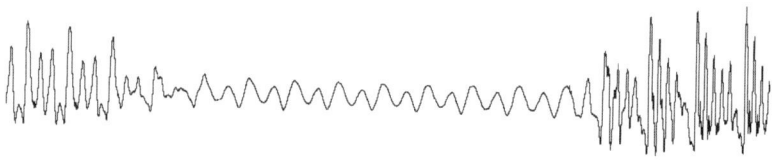

Figure 8.19. Close-up of waveform of the word *kòɓà* 'spirit' (Speaker K).

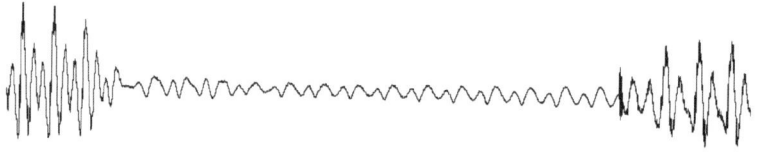

Figure 8.20. Close-up of waveform of the word *èɗè* 'who' (Speaker K).

In the tokens I examined, then, I found two distinct patterns. First, two-thirds of the implosives exhibited a rising amplitude during the second half of the period of closure. In these tokens, the voicing was nearly always modal. Second, one-third of the implosives exhibited a large, level amplitude during the period of closure. In these tokens, a biphasic pattern indicative of laryngealization was usually evident.

The third acoustic property of Mono implosives to be discussed is voicelessness. A small percentage of the implosives in my data show voicelessness during the period of closure. Figure 8.21 shows a waveform of the word *kɔ́-ɓì* 'to hit'. Here, voicing tapers off at the beginning of the closure

8.1 Consonants

to the extent that it ceases in the middle of closure. Then, this is followed by a period of increase in signal amplitude before the release of the implosive. This is similar to the production of some of the Hausa speakers recorded by Lindau.

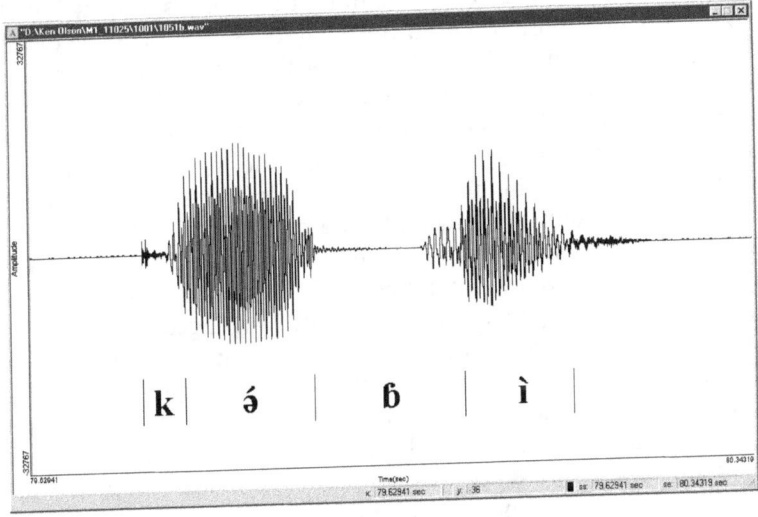

Figure 8.21. Waveform of the word kɔ́-ɓì 'to hit' (Speaker K).

In summary, the most salient acoustic correlate to Mono implosives concerns the signal amplitude during the closure period. Specifically, Mono implosives exhibit either an increase in signal amplitude during the latter part of oral closure or the maintenance of a large, level signal amplitude. In addition, a biphasic pattern indicative of laryngealization is observed in most of the tokens having a large, level amplitude, and a small number of tokens exhibit voicelessness during the initial part of the closure period.

8.1.3 Labial-velars

There are several articulatory gestures which may be manifest in labial-velar stops and may distinguish them from other types of stops. I will examine the acoustic evidence for these in Mono. First, in some languages labial-velar stops employ a complex airstream mechanism. Second, in many languages there is evidence that the labial and velar gestures are staggered, with the velar gesture slightly in advance of the labial one.

Third, it has been claimed that the voice onset time (VOT) of labial-velar segments is shorter than for labial and velar segments.

First, I address the issue of airstream mechanism. As pointed out in chapter 2, Kamanda (1998) classifies labial-velar stops as implosives in Mono. I offered typological evidence in that chapter as to why that characterization is not appropriate. In this chapter, I offer acoustic evidence for their classification as plain stops rather than implosive stops.

Ladefoged (1968) studied the airstream mechanism of labial-velar stops in thirty-three African languages. He found that the majority of the languages (twenty-three) had both pulmonic egressive and velaric ingressive airstreams. The dorsum slides back in the articulation of the sound, and as a result air flows into the oral cavity at both ends. The velaric ingressive airstream gives an auditory impression of suction at release, which could give the impression of an implosive sound.

In addition, Ladefoged found that eight languages had labial-velar stops which involved three airstream mechanisms: a pulmonic egressive mechanism followed by a brief glottalic ingressive mechanism, and overlaid by a velaric ingressive mechanism. These stops were partly voiced. Thus, in some languages, labial-velar stops do have an implosive element. It is worth examining the acoustic properties of labial-velars in Mono to establish if there is evidence of an implosive aspect to these sounds.

Figure 8.22 shows a waveform of the word *ká-gbɔ̀* 'to receive, to find'. If we look at the period of closure, we see that the amplitude is level through the first half of closure, and then there is a gradual drop in amplitude toward the end of the closure. As we saw in the last section, the main characteristic of an implosive is a gradual increase in the signal amplitude during the latter half to two-thirds of closure. Thus, the labial-velar stops do not exhibit the primary acoustic property which characterizes implosive stops in Mono.

The labial-velar stops in Ladefoged (1968) which had a glottalic ingressive component to their airstream mechanism exhibited a brief increase in signal amplitude just before release (cf. Ladefoged's plate 3a). In figure 8.22, this pre-release increase is not attested, nor is it attested in the other tokens examined. Thus, Mono labial-velar stops cannot be considered implosive based on this acoustic property.

8.1 Consonants

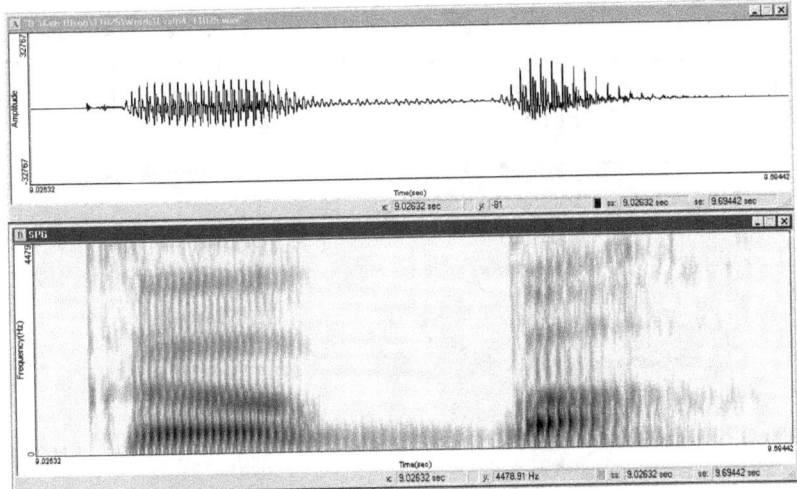

Figure 8.22. Waveform and spectrogram of the word *kɔ́-gbɔ̀* 'to receive, to find' (Speaker K).

The popping sound occasionally heard in Mono labial-velar stops, then, is likely attributable to velaric suction. Mono labial-velars appear to pattern like the majority of labial-velars in Ladefoged's study, that is, they have both pulmonic egressive and velaric ingressive airstreams, but no glottalic ingressive airstream.

The second issue concerning labial-velar stops is whether the two articulations are produced simultaneously, or whether they are staggered. My auditory impressions of the sound in Mono indicate that the velar closure begins prior to the labial closure, and that the velar release occurs prior to the labial release. Maddieson (1993, cited in Ladefoged and Maddieson 1996) provides evidence for this from electromagnetic articulography for Ewe. Connell (1994) points out that several researchers have provided acoustic evidence for this staggering by showing that the formant transitions at the release of the labial-velars correspond to those at the release of labial stops. Specifically, the values of F_1, F_2, and F_3 all rise on release. Figures 8.23, 8.24, and 8.25 show spectrograms of the words *ágbá* 'dugout canoe', *àbá* 'father', and *bàgá* 'cheek', respectively. Note that the formant transitions at the release of the labial-velar and labial stops all rise, whereas F_2 of the velar stop has a noticeable drop in value after release. One significant difference between the labial-velar and labial stops is that the F_2 transition of the labial-velar stop (figure 8.23) shows a rise from a value of 1000 Hz to 1400 Hz in about 23 ms, whereas the F_2 transition for the labial stop (figure 8.24) appears to have an abrupt transition.

Connell (1994) claims that the labial-velar F_2 transition is steeper and more prominent than the labial F_2 transition. While I could not verify this claim, we can see from comparing figures 8.23 and 8.24 that the F_2 transition plays a prominent role in distinguishing the two sounds.

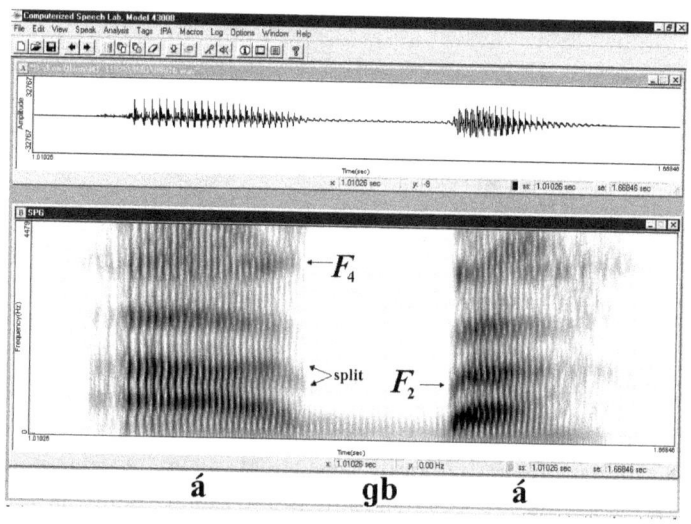

Figure 8.23. Waveform and spectrogram of the word *ágbá* 'dugout canoe' (Speaker K).

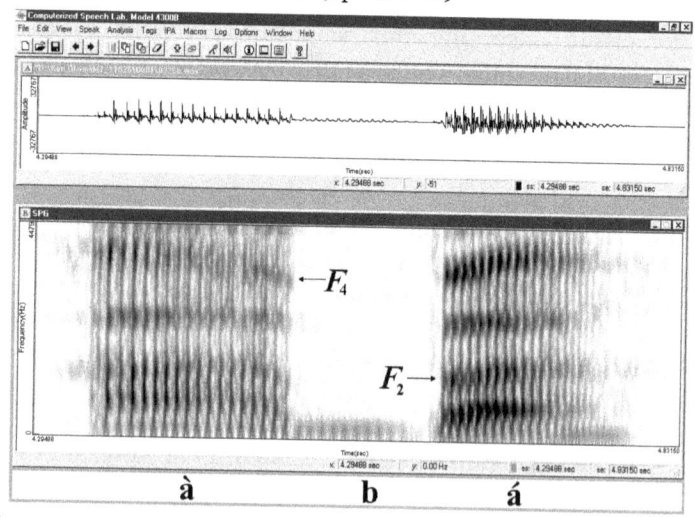

Figure 8.24. Waveform and spectrogram of the word *àbá* 'father' (Speaker K).

8.1 Consonants

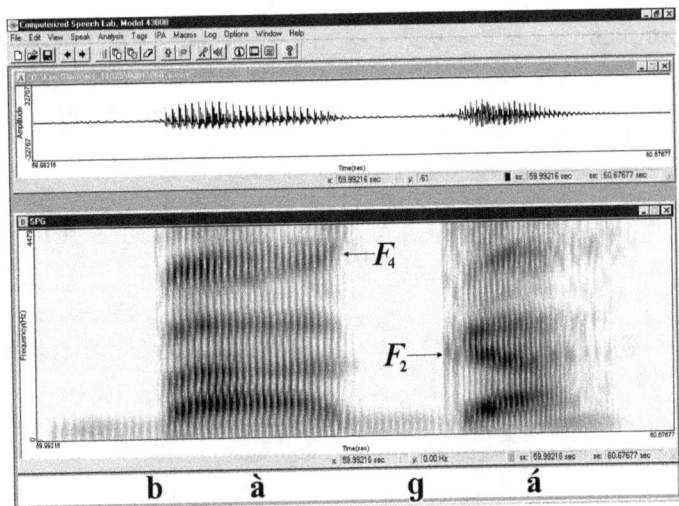

Figure 8.25. Waveform and spectrogram of the word *bàgá* 'cheek' (Speaker K).

Given the auditory impressions mentioned above, we also expect that the transitions into the closure of a labial-velar stop should correspond to those of a plain velar stop. There is some indication that this is the case.

The F_2 transition into the labial-velar stop shares the characteristics of the labial and velar stops. The F_2 transition into the labial stop drops in value, whereas the F_2 transition into the velar stop remains level. The F_2 transition for the labial-velar stop exhibits a split just before closure, with one part dropping as in the labial stop and the other part remaining level as in the velar stop.

The F_4 transition into the labial-velar stop is similar to the velar one. The F_4 transition into the labial stop drops in value, and the F_4 transition into the velar stop and the labial-velar stop rises.

The third issue is the question of voice onset time (VOT) for labial-velar stops. Both Maddieson (1993, for Ewe) and Connell (1994, for Ibibio) note that the VOT of labial-velar stops is shorter than that of labials or velars. For Ibibio, the VOT of labial-velar stops is actually negative. A preliminary investigation indicates that this pattern is found in Mono as well. I examined six tokens each of word-initial *k*, *p*, and *kp* from Speaker K. I measured the interval from the release burst to the onset of voicing. For *k* and *p*, the release burst precedes the onset of voicing, and so by convention VOT is positive. For *kp*, the onset of voicing precedes the release burst, and so VOT is negative.

An example of a positive VOT in which the release burst precedes the onset of voicing is in figure 8.26, which shows a spectrogram of the word *kádá* 'oil'. The period from the release burst to the onset of voicing is indicated by the arrows.

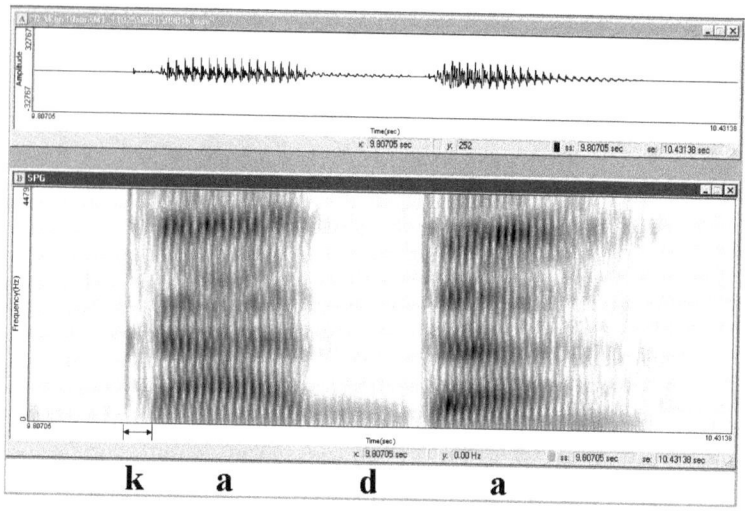

Figure 8.26. Waveform and spectrogram of the word *kádá* 'oil' (Speaker K).

An example of a negative VOT in which the onset of voicing precedes the release burst is in figure 8.27, which shows a spectrogram of the word *kpōkɔ* 'big hoe'. The period from the onset of voicing to the release burst is indicated by the arrows. The average values of VOT and the standard deviations are given in table 8.1.

The VOT of the labial-velar stop is negative in all but one of the tokens. Note that the standard deviation of the labial-velar VOTs is larger than that for the other stops. Connell also noted that there was a greater variation in VOT for labial-velar stops than other stops in Ibibio.[2]

---

[2]Connell implies that a negative value of VOT for *kp* is evidence of a glottalic ingressive component to its articulation. However, pharyngeal pressure measurements would be necessary to substantiate this.

8.1 Consonants

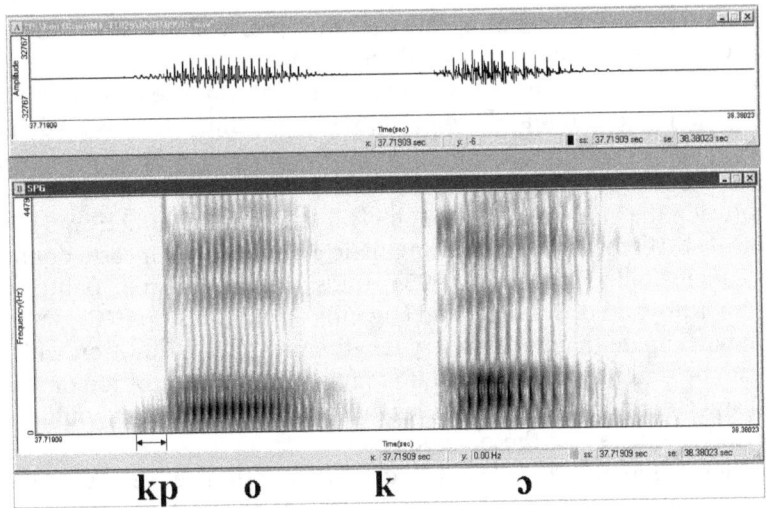

Figure 8.27. Waveform and spectrogram of the word *kpōkɔ̀* 'big hoe' (Speaker K).

Table 8.1. VOT values for labial, velar, and labial-velar stops (Speaker K)

Wd-initial stop	VOT (ms)	SD (ms)
k	27.6	1.5
p	10.2	2.6
kp	-10.0	9.5

In summary, then, we see that labial-velar stops in Mono have the following characteristics. The primary acoustic correlate of implosive consonants is not present; the formant transitions at the release of the stop are similar to those of labial stops with a noticeable variation in F_2; the F_2 into closure splits, showing similarity with both labial and velar articulations; F_4 rises in a way similar to a velar stop; and the voice onset time of voiceless labial-velar stops in word-initial position is shorter than that of labial or velar stops, and in most cases is negative.

8.1.4 Timing of prenasalized stops

In chapter 2, I argued that prenasalized stops in Mono should be considered single segments rather than sequences of a nasal plus an obstruent.

My argument was a phonological one—that prenasalized stops have the same distributional properties as single segments.

One question that arises is whether phonetic evidence can bolster this claim. Ladefoged and Maddieson (1986) suggest that "there is no demonstrated phonetic difference in timing between nasal + stop sequences and prenasalized stops" (cited in Maddieson 1989:57), and as a result deciding between the analyses is a phonological rather than phonetic question.

However, there is some cross-linguistic evidence which casts doubt on this conclusion. Hubbard (1995) finds that in three Bantu languages—Runyambo, Sukuma, and Luganda—nasal + stop (NC) elements which participate in compensatory lengthening have a duration which is at least one and a half times, and up to four times, the duration of singleton N and C elements. She concludes that prenasalized stops should be interpreted as clusters in these languages.

Further, Hubbard argues that there is a correlation between the phonological representation and phonetic durational effects. She proposes that the mora is both an abstract and a surface timing unit. The implication of this is that the presence of a mora to account for compensatory lengthening results in a reflex at the phonetic level, including an increase in the duration of the following NC compared with regular Ns and Cs.

One could infer from this that in languages without compensatory lengthening, or other processes which involve the presence of a second mora in a syllable, NC sequences should *not* be lengthened with respect to singleton Ns and Cs. There is some evidence to suggest that this is the case. For example, Maddieson (1989) finds that prenasalized stops in Fijian have the same closure duration characteristics as plain stops and liquids.[3]

With these observations in mind, I examined the closure duration of prenasalized stops in Mono to determine if there is a noticeable increase in duration in comparison to plain stops. Mono is actually a better test case than Fijian for such a study. In Mono, as in Fijian, prenasalized stops unambiguously pattern as single segments.[4] But Mono has a three-way contrast between voiceless, voiced, and prenasalized stops, whereas Fijian only has a contrast between plain voiceless stops and prenasalized stops. In Fijian, prenasalized stops could be interpreted phonologically as plain voiced stops, but in Mono such an interpretation is impossible.

---

[3]Maddieson measured closure duration in his study. On the other hand, Hubbard measured individual segments following Peterson and Lehiste's (1960) criteria for demarcation.

[4]Also, there are no nasal + stop sequences across morpheme or word boundaries.

8.1 Consonants

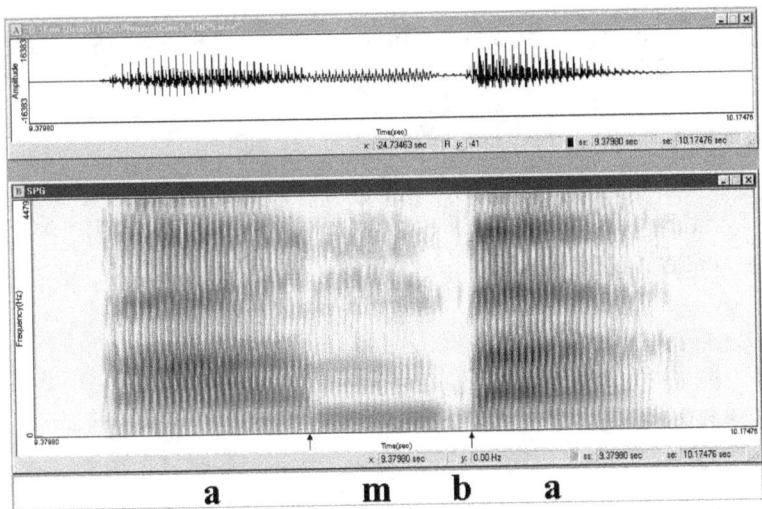

Figure 8.28. Waveform and spectrogram of the possible word *amba* (Speaker K).

I identified the start and end of closure via the following criteria. For plain stops, the beginning of closure was marked where vertical striations disappeared from across frequency range and only low-frequency striations remained visible. For prenasalized stops, the beginning of closure was marked where there was a significant drop in the strength of the formants and there was a clear change from the oral resonance values to the nasal resonance values. The end of closure was identified by the spike representing the stop burst. In all cases, the closure start- and end-points were readily identifiable. For example, the beginning and end of closure is indicated by the arrows in figures 8.11 and 8.28.

Table 8.2 shows closure duration measurements for twelve plain voiced stops and twelve prenasalized stops with the same places of articulation for each set. The tokens used were possible words of the segmental frame *aCa*, where C is the stop being measured.

Table 8.2. Closure duration of prenasalized stops in Mono (Speaker K) Tokens taken from *cons2.wav*. Time is in seconds.

Plain stops		Prenasalized stops	
aba2a	0.152	amba2a	0.177
aba2b	0.174	amba2b	0.204
aba2c	0.150	amba2c	0.175
ada2a	0.129	anda2a	0.141
ada2b	0.128	anda2b	0.135
ada2c	0.117	anda2c	0.123
aga2a	0.139	anga2a	0.157
aga2b	0.143	anga2b	0.135
aga2c	0.138	anga2c	0.133
agba2a	0.171	angba2a	0.176
agba2b	0.152	angba2b	0.187
agba2c	0.166	angba2c	0.169
Mean	0.147		0.159
SD	0.0172		0.0246

As can be seen, there is a small increase in the duration of the closure for prenasalized stops in comparison to plain voiced stops, an increase of about 8 percent on average. However, a one-tailed t-test (Woods, Fletcher, and Hughes 1986) found that this increase was not significant ($t = 1.38, p < .1$).

Thus, the insignificant increase in closure duration for prenasalized stops in Mono should not be characterized as comparable to the durational effects found in the Bantu languages studied by Hubbard. Rather, the behavior of prenasalized stops in Mono is more akin to that found by Maddieson for the phonologically simple Fijian prenasalized stops. If there is indeed a mapping between phonology and phonetics such as is proposed by Hubbard, then this is evidence that Mono NC sequences should be interpreted as single segments rather than N + C clusters.

8.2 Vowels

8.2.1 Vowel space

In this section, I examine the acoustic properties of the Mono vowel space. Since even within its own language family the Mono vowel system is typologically rare due to the lack of a front lower mid vowel ε, it is important to document its acoustic characteristics in more detail.

Since Peterson and Barney (1952), vowels have typically been plotted according to their first two formants (or resonances), F_1 and F_2. Others have modified this basic classification for a variety of reasons. Ladefoged (1982) suggests charting F_1 vs. $F_2 - F_1$ because "There is a better correlation between the degree of backness and the distance between the first two formants" (p. 179). Liljencrants and Lindblom (1972) and Fant (1973) suggest plotting F_1 vs. F_2', where F_2' is a weighted average of F_2 and F_3, according to (125).

$$(125)\ F_2' = F_2 + .5\,(F_3 - F_2)\,\frac{(F_2 - F_1)}{(F_3 - F_1)}$$

The advantage of employing F_2' is that it takes "into account a gradual increase in the importance of the third formant as F_2 is raised in frequency" (Fant 1973:52). My goal here is exposition of the data, and so in this section, I will plot F_1 versus F_2 and F_1 versus F_3 in order to present the data in the least processed form. In addition, I will plot of F_1 versus F_2' for reasons which will become apparent later in this section.

I chose ten tokens of each vowel from Speaker K for measurement by employing the following criteria. First, I attempted to identify vowels in comparable contexts. Ladefoged (1997) suggests choosing two sets of vowels, one following a coronal stop and one following a labial stop. As far as possible, I chose vowels in the initial syllable of a word following these two sets of stops. However, in some cases these were not attested in my corpus. Second, I avoided vowels which may have been affected by the context. These included (1) vowels adjacent to a nasal consonant (e.g., mõnõ 'Mono'), which are subject to nasalization in Mono, (2) the first vowel in a bisyllabic CV_1LV_1 pattern within a word (e.g., õndōrō 'mist'), which is subject to shortening or deletion, and (3) vowels which are subject to the optional process of leftward vowel spreading (e.g., úngú ~ ɨngú ~ ə́ngú 'water'), which calls into question the actual vowel quality being measured. The low vowel *a* can optionally be raised to [ʌ] as a result of a nearby high vowel (e.g., [bīʃà] ~ [bīʃʌ̀] 'two').

This case will be analyzed separately from cases where the vowel *a* is not raised. The full set of tokens used are given in table D.3 found in appendix D.

Unfortunately, there is at present no precise algorithm which can unequivocally determine the best position for measuring formant frequencies. In this study I followed the following criteria. First, I visually inspected a wide-band spectrogram of each token to verify that there was a steady state period for the vowel. I then calculated the midpoint of the steady state based on measurements of the start and end points. The window of analysis was then centered on this midpoint. I took three measurements of each formant frequency: (1) by visual inspection on a wide-band spectrogram (BW = 215.33 Hz, 75 points), (2) by drawing parabolas over an FFT plot, and (3) by employing LPC analysis. In addition, bandwidth measurements of each resonance were documented using LPC analysis. The parameters for the FFT and LPC analyses are given in (126). Tables 8.3 and 8.4 show the average values for the first three formants and bandwidths, respectively for each vowel.

(126) LPC and FFT parameters

    a. LPC
      Frame length: 20 ms
      Filter order: 12
      Pre-emphasis: 0.900
      Analysis method: autocorrelation
      Window weighting: blackman

    b. FFT
      Frame length: 512 points (46.44 ms) and 256 points (23.22 ms)
      Pre-emphasis: 0.000
      Window weighting: blackman
      Smoothing level: none

8.2 Vowels

Table 8.3. Formant averages. Units are Hertz; standard deviations are in parentheses (Speaker K)

	F_1		F_2		F_3	
i	272	(28.4)	1940	(32.0)	2845	(90.7)
e	345	(24.5)	1920	(74.8)	2687	(66.4)
ɨ	270	(18.7)	1565	(181.7)	2222	(91.1)
ə	367	(50.1)	1410	(88.9)	2375	(51.23)
a	682	(47.4)	1292	(126.5)	2335	(106.8)
u	270	(35.0)	897	(55.3)	2302	(77.0)
o	385	(37.4)	897	(79.4)	2494	(78.9)
ɔ	547	(23.6)	965	(66.3)	2407	(153.7)
ʌ	552	(58.6)	1372	(83.3)	2397	(145.1)

Table 8.4. Bandwidth averages. Units are Hertz; standard deviations are in parentheses (Speaker K)

	BW_1		BW_2		BW_3	
i	9.7	(1.9)	53.5	(23.4)	61.8	(20.1)
e	23.5	(7.2)	56.6	(16.7)	103.5	(22.7)
ɨ	30.9	(13.5)	136.1	(44.5)	88.33	(54.3)
ə	40.1	(8.1)	83.0	(26.1)	91.3	(43.7)
a	53.0	(19.7)	94.1	(36.6)	94.0	(20.2)
u	39.3	(15.0)	80.8	(47.0)	104.6	(62.6)
o	72.3	(43.8)	85.1	(29.7)	93.2	(49.1)
ɔ	92.6	(29.0)	114.0	(74.9)	98.7	(25.0)
ʌ	57.8	(18.8)	85.6	(45.9)	139.2	(71.8)

Figure 8.29 shows a plot of F_1 versus F_2 created using the Plot Formants Hypercard program from the UCLA Phonetics Lab. A vowel symbol is given for each individual token.

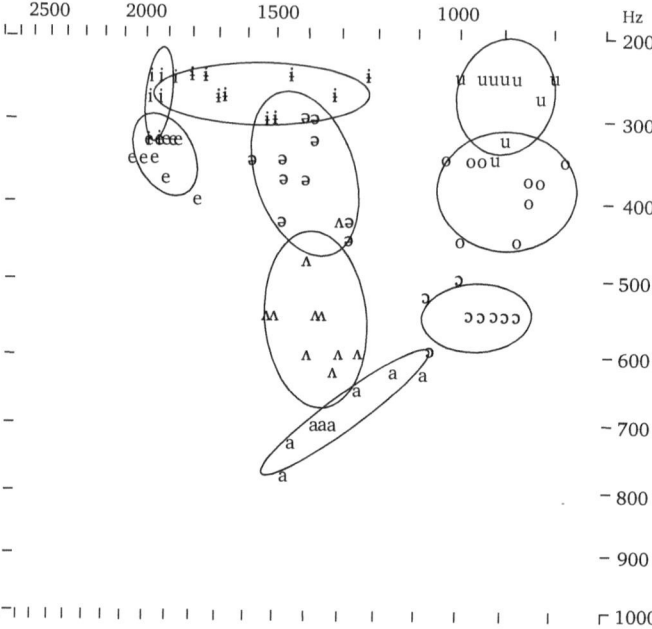

Figure 8.29 Plot of F_1 versus F_2 (Speaker K).

The axes are marked in Hertz, but scaled on the Bark scale, which reflects the ear's sensitivity to differences in pitch (cf. Ladefoged 1996:80). The equation for calculating bark units from Hertz (Zwicker and Terhardt 1980) is in (127).

(127) B = 13 arctan (0.76 f) + 3.5 arctan (f/7.5)^2

        B – critical band value in Bark
        f – frequency in kHz, arctan in radians

The ellipses are centered on the mean for each vowel and have radii of two standard deviations "along the first two principal components of the distribution" (Maddieson and Anderson 1994). There is reasonable separation between the vowels indicating that the values of F_1 and F_2 are sufficient acoustic properties for distinguishing the vowels. However, some overlap exists between *i* and *e*, *i* and *ɨ*, *i* and *ə*, and *u* and *o*, which indicates that other factors may assist in distinguishing these pairs of vowels.

Concerning *i* and *e*, there is a large difference in bandwidth between the F_1 values of the two vowels, which may be an additional cue for distinguishing

8.2 Vowels

the sounds. The vowel *i* has a mean bandwidth of 9.7 Hz (SD = 1.9), whereas the vowel *e* has a mean bandwidth of 23.5 Hz (SD = 7.2).

Concerning *i* and *ɨ*, there is a difference in the value of F_3 between the two vowels, as is evident from the plot of F_1 versus F_3 shown in figure 8.30. Since F_2' takes into account the influence of F_3, a plot of F_1 versus F_2' also shows this separation between *i* and *ɨ*, as seen in figure 8.31. Concerning *ɨ* and *ə*, and *u* and *o*, I found no parameter resulting in an absolute separation between the two respective values in each pair.

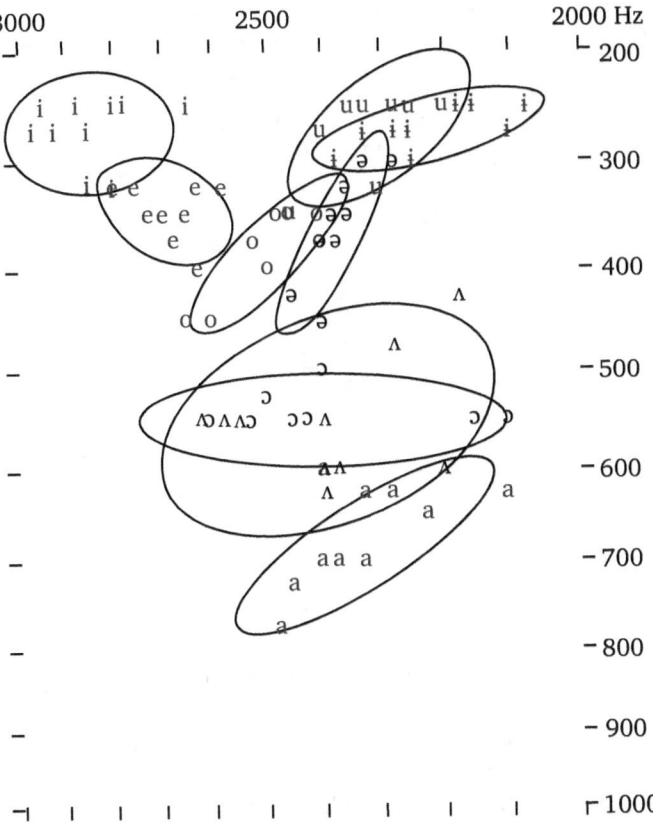

Figure 8.30. Plot of F_1 versus F_3 (Speaker K).

A couple of points should be noted with regard to these results. First, in general terms, the vowels are evenly distributed throughout the vowel space, in line with Crothers' (1978:125) observation that "[T]he vowel phonemes of a language tend to disperse evenly in the available phonetic space." However, there is one gap in the region where we would expect the vowel [ɛ]. In other words, the lack of [ɛ] is not just phonological, but it is indeed a phonetic phenomenon in Mono. The average American English values of F_1 and F_2 for male speakers are 550 Hz and 1770 Hz, respectively (Ladefoged 1982:176). At this point in the chart in figure 8.29, there is a noticeable gap in the data. This figure is repeated in figure 8.32 with the position of [ɛ] indicated. This occurs halfway between the regions where *e* and *a* are attested.

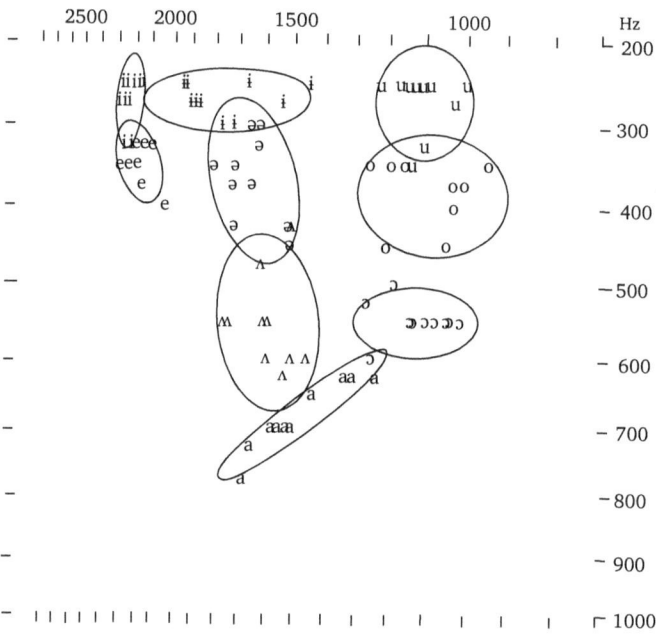

Figure 8.31. Plot of F_1 versus F_2' (Speaker K).

Second, the value of F_2 for the Mono vowel /a/ provides evidence that that is the correct symbol to use in transcribing the sound. The mean value of F_2 is 1292 Hz, which is higher than the value of F_2 in the vowel [ɑ] of a typical male American English speaker (~1100 Hz), but lower than the value of F_2 in the vowel [æ] of a typical American English speaker (~1660 Hz, Ladefoged 1982:176).

Of course, these observations are based on the assumption that the vowel space of the Mono speaker correlates with the average vowel space of a male speaker of American English. Unfortunately, as of yet, a foolproof method of normalizing such data has yet to be developed.

8.2 Vowels

Ladefoged (1982:195–196) admits that "[P]honeticians do not really know how to compare acoustic data on the sounds of one individual with those of another." He suggests two possible approximations: (1) use the average value of F_4 as an approximation of an individual's head size, or (2) assume that "each set of vowels is representative of the complete range of a speaker's vowel qualities."

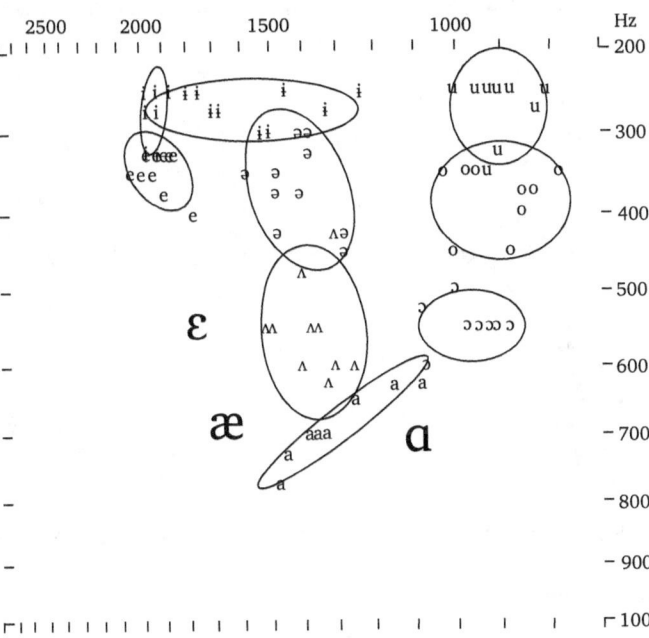

Figure 8.32. Plot of F_1 versus F_2 (Speaker K) with location of American English vowels [ɛ], [æ], and [ɑ] indicated.

In the case at hand, the average F_1 and F_2 values for i and u are approximately the same for American English and Mono, as shown in (128), so the assumption that the vowel space is the same is a reasonable approximation.

(128)
	English		Mono (Speaker K)	
	F_1	F_2	F_1	F_2
i	280	2250	272.5	1940
u	310	870	270	897.5

Finally, note that there is separation between /a/ and its allophonic variant [ʌ]. This provides acoustic support for the raising process exemplified in (15) of section 2.2.

For comparison, figure 8.33 shows each Mono vowel spoken in isolation.

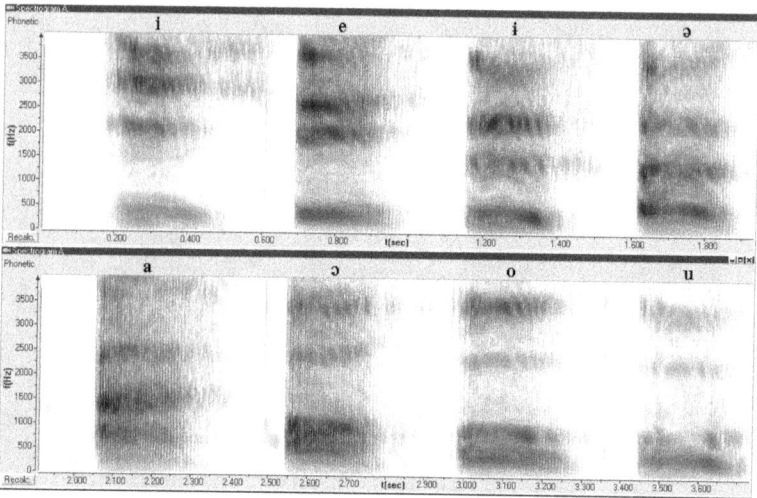

Figure 8.33. Spectrogram of Mono vowels spoken in isolation (Speaker K).

8.2.2 Vowel duration

There are two aspects of vowel duration which were introduced previously in this study. First, in chapter 5, I noted that in words containing a CV_1LV_1 sequence (L = liquid), the first vowel may optionally be shortened or even elided. In this section, I will provide acoustic evidence for this optional rule and show that speaker rate is one environment in which the process applies. Second, in chapter 2, I noted that vowels with contour tones are phonetically longer than other vowels. In this section, I will provide some tentative acoustic evidence for this phenomenon.

First, let us examine the instance of a shortened or elided vowel in a CV_1LV_1 sequence. One circumstance in which this occurs is in the case of rapid speech. I measured the duration of both vowels in fifteen words containing CV_1LV_1 sequences spoken at both normal and rapid rates by Speakers A and K. The first vowel was measured from the burst of a previous stop or the end of aperiodic noise of a previous fricative to the start of *l* or *r*. The second vowel was measured from the end of *l* or *r* to the point

8.2 Vowels

where the F_2 of the vowel was no longer clearly visible. The results are given in table 8.5.

Table 8.5. Duration of vowels in CVLV sequences spoken at normal and rapid rates of speech. Standard deviations are given in parentheses (Speakers A and K)

	Normal	Rapid	Decrease
Speaker A			
C$\underline{V}_1$LV$_1$	146 (31.7)	56.8 (26.0)	62%
CV$_1$L$\underline{V}_1$	132 (26.4)	87.6 (25.7)	34%
Speaker K			
C$\underline{V}_1$LV$_1$	205 (37.8)	46.4 (17.8)	77%
CV$_1$L$\underline{V}_1$	122 (25.8)	74.9 (29.5)	39%

The duration of each vowel in each word was significantly shorter in rapid speech than in normal speech. However, the shortening was consistently far more pronounced for the first vowel of each sequence than the second. The first vowel was reduced by 60–80 percent of its value in normal speech, whereas the second vowel was decreased by 30–40 percent of its value in normal speech.

Figure 8.34 shows an example of this shortening process. The figure contains two tokens of the word ōpōrō 'egg', the first produced with a rapid speaking rate and the second at a normal rate. In rapid speech, both vowels in the CoLo sequence are shorter than in normal speech, but the duration of the first *o*, indicated by the arrows, has been reduced in duration to a far greater extent than the second *o*.

In some cases, the first vowel is completely elided in rapid speech. Figure 8.35 shows two tokens of the word ámbálá 'bait'. The first token was produced with rapid speech, whereas the second one was produced with normal speech. In rapid speech, the first *a* in the CaLa sequence has been completely elided, yielding [ámblá]. In normal speech, the first *a* is visible.

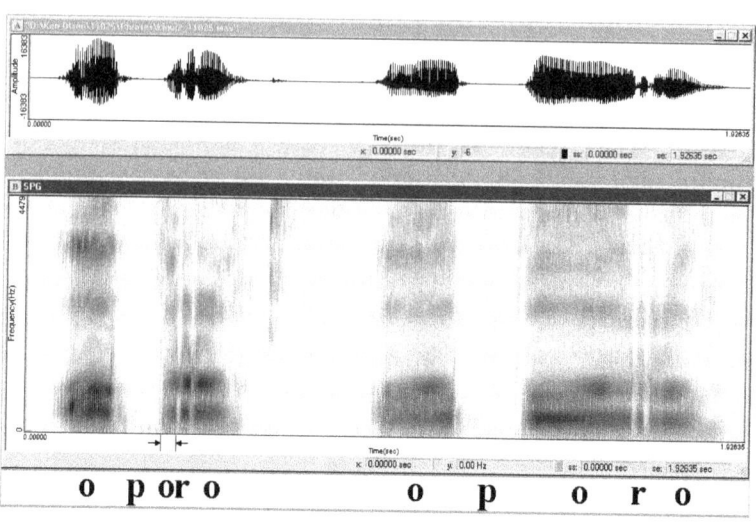

Figure 8.34. Waveform and spectrogram of the word *ōpōrō* 'egg' spoken with rapid and normal speaking rates (Speaker K).

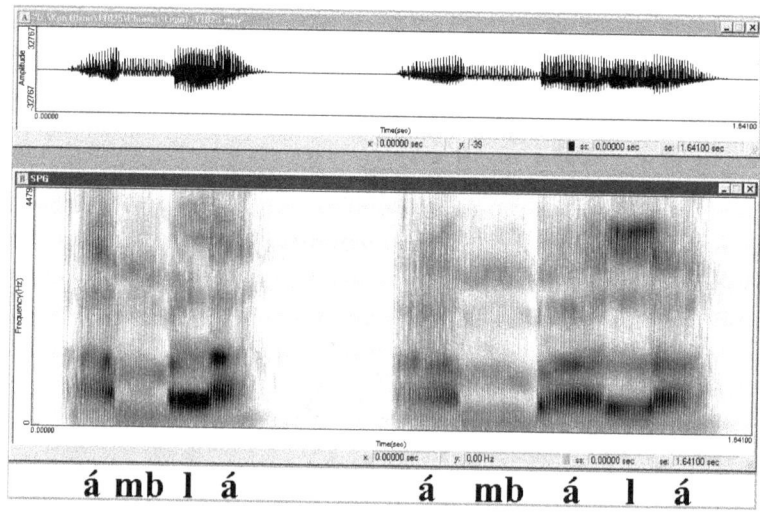

Figure 8.35. Waveform and spectrogram of the word *ámbálá* 'bait' spoken with rapid and normal speaking rates (Speaker A).

Words with only two syllables should not exhibit this elision, in order to satisfy the word minimality condition discussed in chapter 6. Indeed, if we look at figure 8.36, we see that this is the case. The figure presents two

8.2 Vowels

tokens of the word *mbàlà* 'elephant'. In the first token, produced with rapid speech, we see that both vowels, rather than just the first, are shortened. There is also a significant shortening of the intervening consonant *l* as well.

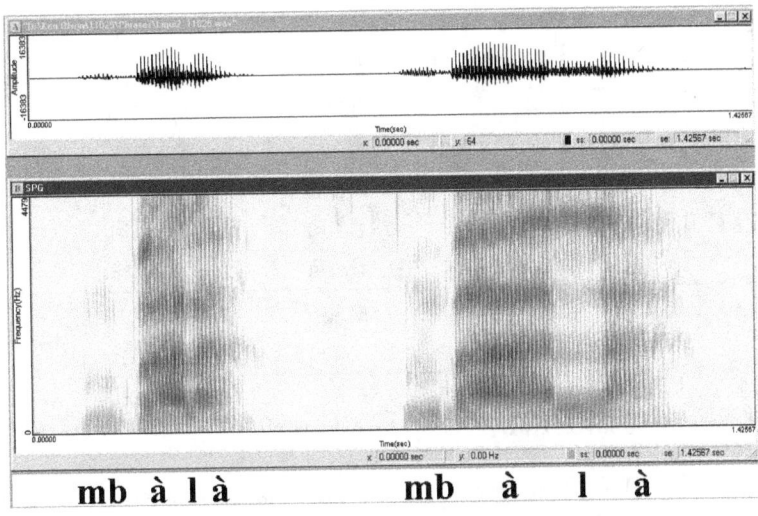

Figure 8.36. Waveform and spectrogram of the word *mbàlà* 'elephant' spoken with rapid and normal speaking rates (Speaker K).

Thus, rapid speech appears to be one condition for the occurrence of vowel shortening or elision of the first V in a CV_1LV_1 sequence. This does not exclude the possibility that other factors may also produce this shortening. Further studies are needed to consider other possible causes.

In chapter 2, I noted that vowels with a contour tone are longer than those with level tones. To test this, I compared two-syllable words containing a contour tone on the first syllable against two-syllable words containing a level tone on the first syllable. I measured the duration of the first vowel in these tokens. Measurement criteria were taken from Peterson and Lehiste (1960). The results are shown in table 8.6. The average duration of a vowel with a contour tone was about 15 percent greater than the average duration of a vowel with a level tone. A one-tailed *t*-test indicated that the difference was significant ($t = 1.955, p < .025$).

Table 8.6. Comparison of the duration of long and short vowels in a word-initial syllable (Speaker K)

Token	Duration of long V (ms)	Token	Duration of short V (ms)
ɓáàtɨ́	191	ɓápá	140
ɓáàtɨ́	158	tʃátʃū	200
tʃáàtʃí	192	tʃátʃū	177
tʃáàtʃí	202	tʃáfù	160
tʃàálà	218	tʃáfù	162
tʃàálà	240	tʃádà	190
		tʃádà	196
Mean	200	Mean	175
SD	25.5	SD	20.4

8.2.3 Vowel nasalization

In chapter 2, I claim that vowels adjacent to a nasal consonant may be nasalized. In this section, I provide acoustic evidence for this claim. The following results are based on examination of fifteen tokens containing nasal consonants.

The first step in determining the nasalization of vowels is to identify acoustic correlates of such nasalization. Lieberman and Blumstein (1988:223) note:

> [T]he primary acoustic cue for vowel nasalization is a reduction in the spectral prominence of the first formant. This is accomplished by either broadening the F_1 peak (making it wider in bandwidth) or creating an additional spectral peak nearby.

Compare figure 8.37 (*aba*) with figure 8.38 (*ama*). In figure 8.37, there is good separation between F_1 and F_2, both before and after the stop, so that the two formants are distinguishable from each other. In figure 8.38, however, the separation between the two formants is not clear, especially before the nasal consonant. This is likely due to the presence of a nasal formant at the same general frequency (this nasal formant is visible in the nasal consonant). The same loss of separation between F_1 and F_2 can be seen in the possible word *ana* in figure 8.39. In addition, the formant structure of the vowels in figures 8.38 and 8.39 (adjacent to a nasal consonant) is less well defined than that found in figure 8.37 (adjacent to an oral consonant).

8.2 Vowels

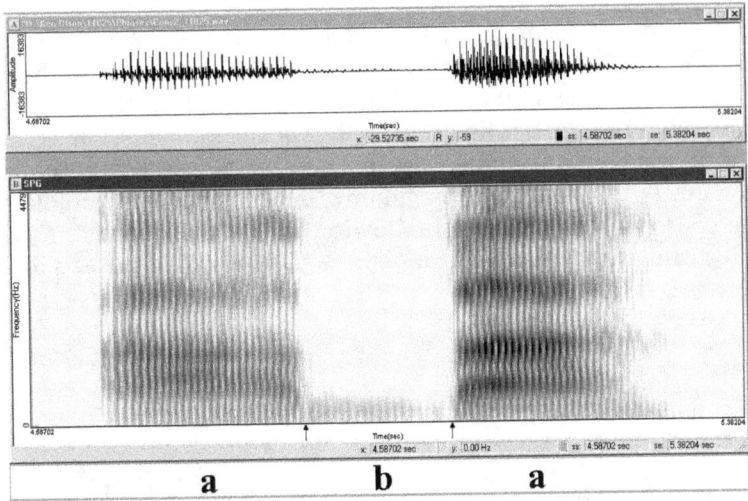

Figure 8.37. Waveform and spectrogram of the possible word *aba* (Speaker K).

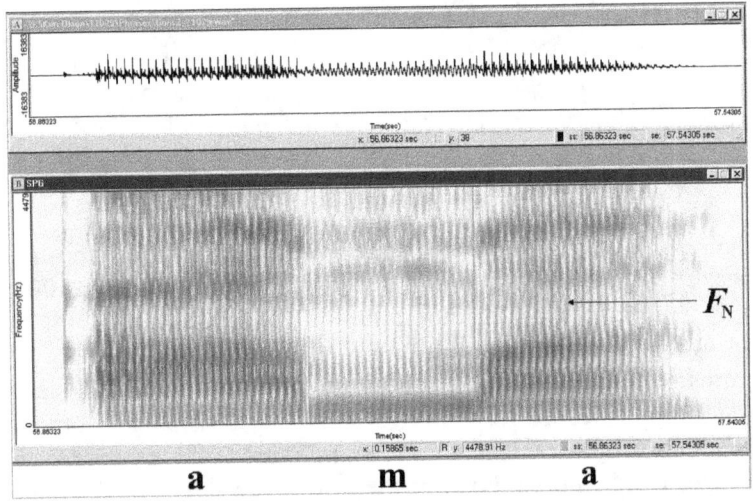

Figure 8.38. Waveform and spectrogram of the possible word *ama* (Speaker K). A nasal formant F_N is visible at approximately 2100 Hz.

There is an additional property in the speech of Speaker K providing further evidence for the presence of nasalization in the vowels adjacent to a nasal consonant. Examine again the spectrograms of the possible words *ama* and *ana* in figures 8.38 and 8.39. During the articulation of the nasal consonant in each case, there is a nasal formant F_N at a frequency of approximately 2100 Hz. It is lighter than the vocalic formants, but nevertheless it is visible. Also note that in the vowel preceding the nasal consonant, F_3 is visible at the beginning, but becomes less resolute close to the consonant. In the vowel following the nasal consonant, F_3 is not clearly distinguishable, but the nasal formant at 2100 Hz projects into the vowel area.

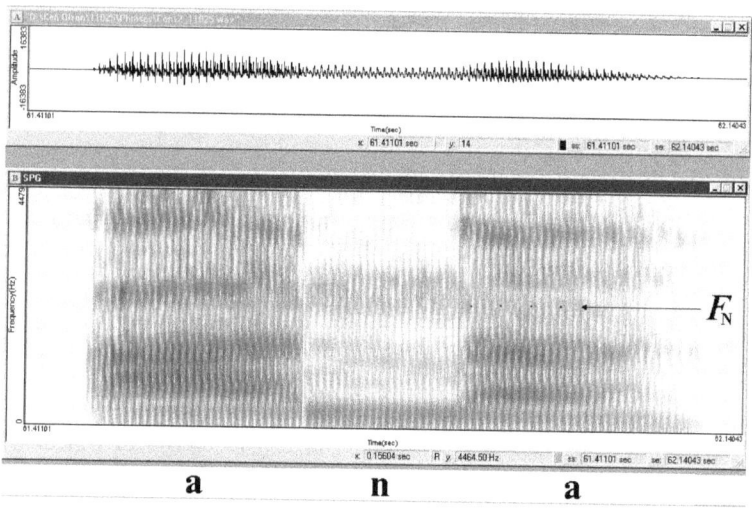

Figure 8.39. Waveform and spectrogram of the possible word *ana* (Speaker K). A nasal formant F_N is visible at approximately 2100 Hz. Formant tracking marks show F_N in second vowel.

Figures 8.40 and 8.41 show spectrograms of the words *bɔlɔ* 'tobacco' and *kɔnɔ* 'hippo', respectively. In figure 8.40, F_3 is visible for both vowels at about 2400 Hz, its typical value for ɔ. In figure 8.41, however, a couple of changes can be noted. First, in the initial vowel, F_3 has dropped to a value of about 2250 Hz, perhaps due to the influence of the nasal formant. In the second vowel, F_3 is not distinguishable. Rather, the nasal formant at 2100 Hz is visible, continuing out from the consonant into the vowel.

8.2 Vowels

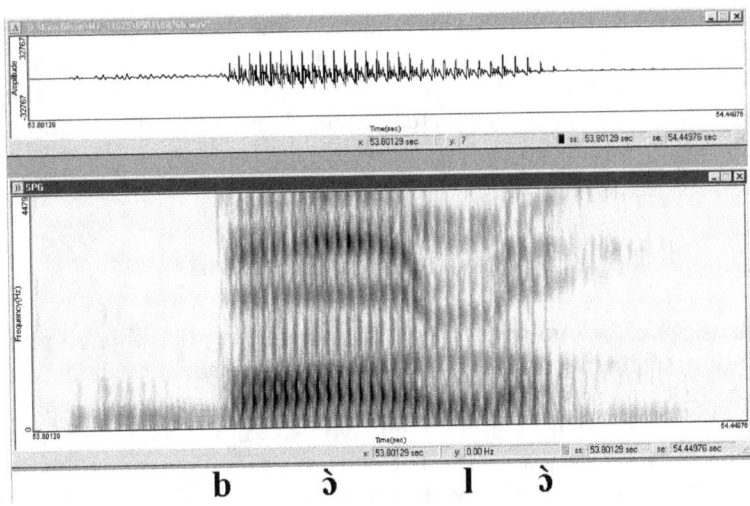

Figure 8.40. Waveform and spectrogram of the word *bɔ̀lɔ̀* 'tobacco' (Speaker K).

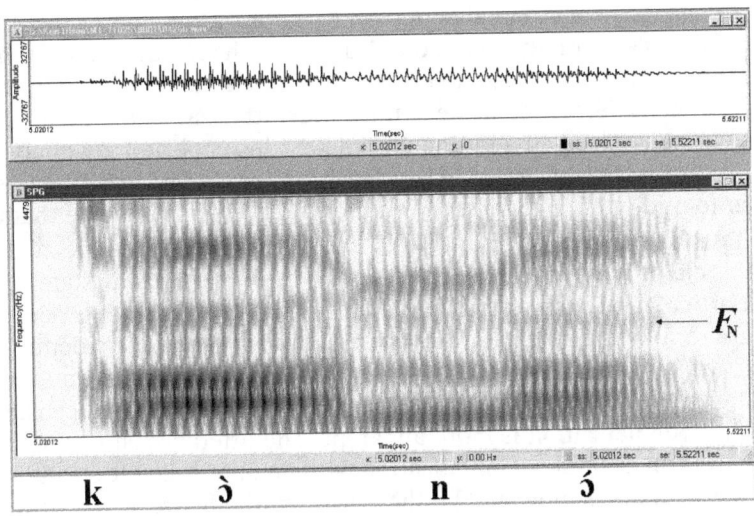

Figure 8.41. Waveform and spectrogram of the word *kɔ̀nɔ́* 'hippo' (Speaker K).

These findings confirm that a nasal consonant does induce nasalization on adjacent vowels. Both the vowel preceding the nasal consonant and the vowel following the nasal consonant are affected.

In section 2.2, I noted that nasalization sounds more pronounced on certain vowels than on others. When a nasal formant overlaps with an oral formant, the oral formant will be affected to a larger degree than in cases of non-overlap. The expected result, then, is that nasalization will sound more pronounced in cases of overlap.

8.3 Secondary Articulations

In this section, I examine two questions regarding the phonetic implementation of the secondary articulations of labialization and palatalization. In chapter 4, I claimed that labialization and palatalization in Mono are phonetically closer to mid vowels rather than high vowels. Since these two secondary articulations are generally assumed to correspond phonetically to high vowels, I need to bolster this claim. For example, Ladefoged and Maddieson (1996:363) note that palatalization concerns the "superimposition of a raising of the front of the tongue toward a position similar to that for *i* on a primary gesture."[5] Second, I argue in chapter 4 that labialization and palatalization do not bear tone. This claim is essentially a phonological claim, that is, the distribution of these segments with respect to tone argues for an interpretation in which they are considered not to bear tone. Nevertheless, phonetic evidence could be considered an additional argument in support of my analysis.

I first address the question of whether Mono secondary articulations are closer to mid or high vowels. My auditory impressions indicate that they are best transcribed as [e̞] and [o̞]. However, offering acoustic evidence for this claim is difficult. In normal speech there is no steady state during their articulation such as that found in vowels. As a result, it is necessary to turn to tokens spoken at a slow rate of speech in order to identify formant values. In my corpus, I was not able to identify a case of palatalization with steady-state formants. On the other hand, acoustic evidence for labialization is more apparent. The utterance shown in figure 8.42 gives an example of labialization with an unmistakable steady state. The steady state is indicated by the arrows in the figure.

---

[5]Smalley (1989) did not make this assumption. See especially pp. 176, 178, and 183.

8.3 Secondary Articulations

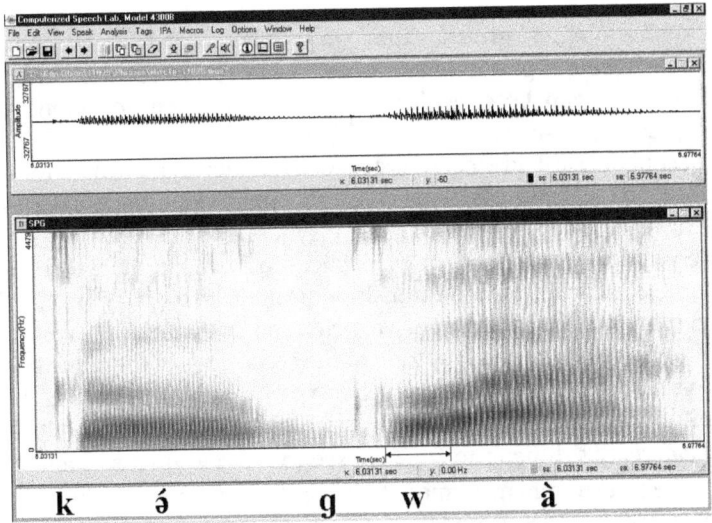

Figure 8.42. Spectrogram of the word *kɔ́-gwà* 'pack, wrap up' spoken at a slow speaking rate (Speaker K).

Table 8.7 compares the average values of F_1 and F_2 for *u* and *o* measured in section 8.2.1 with the values measured for the token in figure 8.42. The average value of F_2 is identical for the two vowels. However, we see that the value of F_1 of the secondary articulation in figure 8.42, 350 Hz, is much closer to the average value of F_1 for *o* (385 Hz) than the average value of F_1 for *u* (270 Hz). As a result, for this token, it is preferable to interpret labialization as corresponding to a mid vowel rather than a high vowel.

Table 8.7. Comparison of the values of F_1 and F_2 for the labialization in the token *kɔ́-gwà* 'pack, wrap up' spoken at a slow rate and the average values of F_1 and F_2 for *u* and *o*

	kɔ́-gwà	*u* (average)	*o* (average)
F_1	350	270	385
F_2	875	897	897

The second issue regarding secondary articulations concerns whether or not they bear tone. This is at its foundation a phonological question, depending on how the secondary articulations are interpreted to be distributed within the phonological system of the language. In section 4.1, I argue on phonological grounds that Mono secondary articulations do not bear tone. However, phonetic evidence which correlates with the phonological analysis can be considered to strengthen the argument for the phonological analysis.

The best phonetic evidence for arguing that a secondary articulation bears tone would come from cases in which a contour tone—analyzed as a sequence of level tones—occurs on a CGV syllable. If the secondary articulation does indeed bear tone, then we expect the change from the first tone to the second to coincide with the transition from the secondary articulation to the nuclear vowel. If the secondary articulation does not bear tone, then we expect the change from the first tone to the second to lag the transition from the secondary articulation to the nuclear vowel. This latter case is what we find in Mono. Figure 8.43 shows an F_0 trace and a spectrogram of the expression ə́ gjáà gjà 'it's difficult to stir'. We see that the formants F_1 and F_2 have reached their maximum movement towards the target vowel a by point A (at the time mark of 29.18 seconds). At this point in time, F_0 has only dropped slightly from its starting value of about 170 Hz. The major part of the transition from the High tone to the Low tone takes place after this point. The contour tone occurs almost exclusively on the vowel a rather than on the preceding secondary articulation.

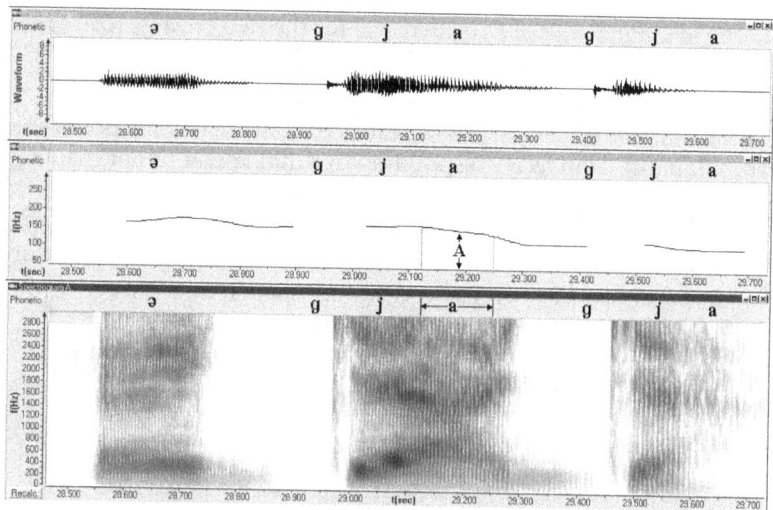

Figure 8.43. Waveform, F_0 trace, and spectrogram of the phrase ə́ gjáà gjà 'it's difficult to stir' (Speaker K).

8.4 Summary and Further Research

Figure 8.44 gives an example for labialization as well. Here we see an F_0 trace and spectrogram for the underlined portion of the phrase èndʒē sɔ́ kɔ́-kwáā-kwā ngɔ́ngɔ́ nə̀ ásɔ́ 'They will be returning now'. Here, the influence of the labialization has disappeared by point A (at the time mark of 0.825 sec). At this point on the pitch trace, the pitch is just beginning to drop from its high. Thus, the entire drop in pitch occurs after the articulation of labialization is completed. Once again, we see an offset between the transition between the secondary articulation and the nuclear vowel, on one hand, and the change from the first tone to the second on the other.

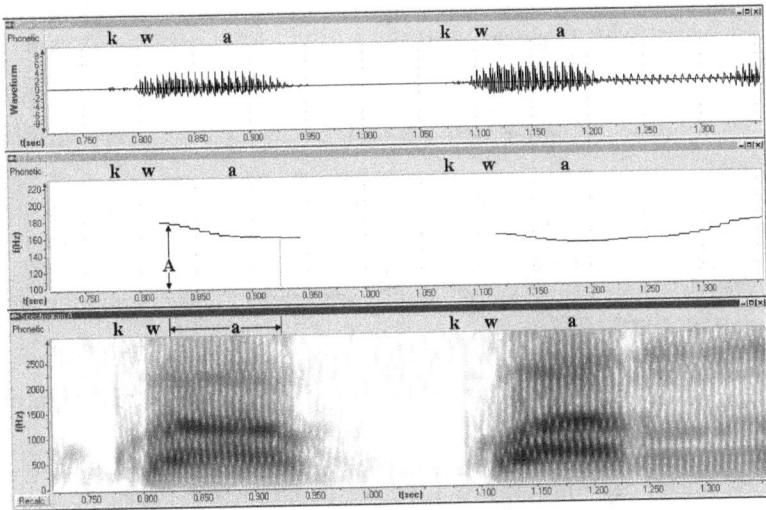

Figure 8.44. Waveform, F_0 trace, and spectrogram of the underlined portion of the phrase èndʒē sɔ́ kɔ́-kwáā-kwā ngɔ́ngɔ́ nə̀ ásɔ́ 'they will be returning now' (Speaker K).

8.4 Summary and Further Research

In this chapter, I have examined certain acoustic properties of Mono with the primary aim of supporting the transcription of the sound system I have proposed. In addition, I have also discussed how these properties compare to similar properties in other languages.

On this latter point, I have only scratched the surface. There is much more that could be looked at in considering how the phonetic properties of Mono relate to cross-linguistic universals and tendencies. Maddieson (1997), for example, sets forth a list of properties which occur in a significant number of the world's languages and are candidates for being considered universals. Some of the putative universal properties that Maddieson discusses which would be fruitful to examine in Mono include:

- Higher vowels have a higher F_0 than lower vowels (Ohala and Eukel 1987; Whalen and Levitt 1995).
- Higher vowels have a shorter duration than lower vowels (Lehiste 1970).
- Higher vowels have a greater tendency toward devoicing than lower vowels (Jaeger 1978).
- The vowel before a voiced consonant is longer than before its voiceless counterpart.
- F_0 tends to be higher after a voiceless consonant than after a voiced one.
- Bilabial stops have a longer closure duration than velar stops.
- The voice onset time (VOT) of velar consonants is longer than the VOT of coronal consonants, and the VOT of coronal consonants is longer than the VOT of labial consonants (Lisker and Abramson 1964, Byrd 1993).

There are other phonetic properties which would be worth examining as well. These include:

- My auditory impressions indicate that the Mono h has a greater amount of friction than the English h.
- Many Mono speakers are bilingual in Lingala, a Bantu language with two tones. According to Maddieson (per. comm.), for speakers who are fluent in two languages, one of which has three tones (high, mid, low) and one which has two tones (high and low), there are differing results as to what kind of correspondence there is between the tones of the two languages. For bilinguals in Hausa and Nupe, Hausa high corresponds to Nupe high, Hausa mid corresponds to Nupe low, and Hausa low corresponds to Nupe ∅. In other cases, the high of the two-tone language is between the high and mid of the three-tone language, and the low of the two-tone language is between the mid and low of the three-tone language.

Appendix A

Texts

This appendix contains a narrative text (section A.1), a procedural text (section A.2), and ten proverbs in Mono (section A.3) with a translation in English. The first line of each interlinearized sentence gives a phonemic transcription of the sentence. The second line parses words into their individual morphemes. The third line provides a gloss of each morpheme. The fourth line is a free translation of the clause.

In section A.4, I provide frequency counts for consonants, vowels, and tones in each of the three texts. In addition, frequency counts of these items were obtained for a larger corpus of texts not included in the present volume; these are given in the miscellaneous (Misc) columns of the tables.

A.1 The Elephant, the Turtle, and the Hippo (Narrative text)

1. ʔà   jí   ndɔ́   kɔ́dʒì   ndə́mà   tòrò ngɔ́ngɔ́ nə̀
   ʔà   ji-´   ndɔ́   kɔ́-dʒì   ɔ́ndɔ́-àmà   tòrò ngɔ́ngɔ́ nə̀
   1PL.INCL enter-NF   mark INF-hear   mark-mouth PN   time   DET

   ásə́kē.
   ásə́-kē
   this-DEIC
   'Let's hear a story now.'

2. ndə́mà   tòrò nə́ mbàlà,   bākòngō, ə́dō kɔ̀nɔ́.
    ə́ndə́-àmà   tòrò nə́ mbàlà   bākòngō   ə́dō kɔ̀nɔ́
    mark-mouth PN   of   elephant turtle   and   hippo
    'The story of the elephant, the turtle, and the hippo.'

3. mbàlà   kə̀də́ àgjà   á   tʃə̀   sə́   ɓálə́   gūsū.
    mbàlà   kə̀də́ àgjà   á   tʃə̀   sə-´   ɓá-lə́   gūsū
    elephant COP   animal   REL   3SG   be-NF   at-in   bush
    'The elephant is an animal that lives in the bush.'

4. tʃə̀   sə́   tə̀   égérə́   nə̀.
    tʃə̀   sə-´   tə̀   égérə́   nə̀
    3SG   be-NF   with big   DET
    'He is large.'

5. ùndù   jē   ró   pá   àgjà   tʃə́lə́   gūsū   kɔ́kɔ́   jé.
    ùndù   jē   ro-´   pá   àgjà   tʃə́-lə́   gūsū   kɔ́kɔ́   jé
    size   3SG   pass-NF above   animal   in-in   bush   entire EMPH
    'His size surpasses all the animals in the bush.'

6. bākòngō   kə̀də́ àgjà   á   tʃə̀   sə́   téāʃó,   ɓálə́   gūsū.
    bākòngō   kə̀də́ àgjà   á   tʃə̀   sə-´   téāʃó   ɓá-lə́   gūsū
    turtle   COP   animal   REL   3SG   be-NF   small   at-in   bush
    'The turtle is a small animal who lives in the bush.'

7. ángá   àbākòngō   sə́   ndʒē   ɓálàngú.
    ángá   à-bākòngō   sə-´   ndʒē   ɓá-àlà-úngú
    other   PL-turtle   be-NF   also   at-eye-water
    'Other turtles live in the water.'

8. kɔ̀nɔ́   kə̀də́   égérə́   àgjà,   á   tʃə̀   sə́   ɓálàngú.
    kɔ̀nɔ́   kə̀də́   égérə́   àgjà   á   tʃə̀   sə-´   ɓá-àlà-úngú
    hippo   COP   big   animal   rel   3SG   be-NF   at-eye-water
    'The hippo is a large animal who lives in the water.'

9. ɔ̀lɔ̀   bàlē,   bākòngō   ná   ɓándə́   mbàlà.
    ɔ̀lɔ̀   bàlē   bākòngō   na-´   ɓá-ndə́   mbàlà
    day   one   turtle   go-NF   at-home elephant
    'One day, the turtle went to see the elephant.'

10. ɔ́ pá fə̄ mbàlà àdə́kē,
    ɔ́ pa-ˊ fə̄ mbàlà àdə́kē
    SS say-NF BEN elephant that
    'He said to the elephant.'

11. "mbàlà, àzɔ́ də̀ mə̄, ʔà sɔ́ də̀ ʔo."
    mbàlà àzɔ́ də̀ mə̄ ʔà sə-ˊ də̀ ò ʔò
    elephant 1PL.INCL with 1SG 1PL.INCL be-NF with word
    'Elephant, you and me, we have a problem.'

12. mbàlà jú ʃè ɓàdə́kē mà,
    mbàlà ju-ˊ ʃè àdə́kē mà
    elephant ask-NF 3SG that DISC
    'The elephant asked him,'

13. "ò ʔò gàɗè dá à gbɔ́ də̀ mə̄ à jámē?"
    ò ʔò gàɗè dá ʔà gbɔ-ˊ də̀ mə̄ à ájá-mə̄
    word what CLEFT 1PL.INCL find-NF with 1SG QUEST brother-1SG
    'What's the problem between us, brother?'

14. tʃə̀ pá fə̄ mbàlà àdə́kē,
    tʃə̀ pa-ˊ fə̄ mbàlà àdə́kē
    3SG speak-NF BEN elephant that
    'He said to the elephant,'

15. "mə̄ dʒí tʃɔ́lɔ́ ūtū mə̄ àdə́kē,
    mə̄ dʒi-ˊ tʃɔ́-lɔ́ ūtū mə̄ àdə́kē
    1SG hear-NF in-in ear 1SG that
    'I heard that,'

    ɓə̀ sɔ́ kə́jì àngbà mə̄.
    ɓə̀ sə-ˊ kə́-jì àngbà mə̄
    2SG be-NF INF-enter hatred 1SG
    'You hate me.'

16. ɓə̀ sɔ́ kə́pà àdə́kē,
    ɓə̀ sə-ˊ kə́-pà àdə́kē
    2SG be-NF INF-speak that
    'You're saying that,'

āmā kàdá kōló àgjà, á mā sá kázɨ ɔʃɔ.
āmā kàdá kōló àgjà, á mā sə-´ ká-zɨ ɔʃɔ
1SG COP only animal REL 1SG be-NF INF-eat soil
'I'm only an animal, that I eat dirt.'

17. òʔò nə̀ kó   mā wáā,
    òʔò nə̀ ko-´ mā wáā
    word DET put-NF 1SG much
    'That really bothered me.'

    á mā nā   kájù   ɓə̀ ásā.
    á mā na-¯ ká-jù ɓə̀ ásā
    REL 1SG go-SUBJ INF-ask 2SG this
    'so I came to ask you about it.'

18. wù   sá   nə̀ àdákē àzá   də̀ mā, ʔàá
    wu-` ə́sá nə̀ àdákē àzá   də̀ mā   ʔà-´
    see-IMP place DET that 1PL.INCL with 1SG 1PL.INCL-FUT
    'Know that, you and me,'

    kò   tʃálá mà   kāná àzá   jékà,
    ko-` tʃá-lá àmà kāná àzá   jékà
    give-FUT in-in mouth hand 1PL.INCL then
    'we're going to fight'

    á òʔò nə̀ á kà."
    á òʔò nə̀ á ka-`
    REL word DET SS end-FUT
    'until this thing is settled.'

19. mbàlà   pá   fə̄ ʃè àdákē,
    mbàlà   pa-´ fə̄ ʃè àdákē
    elephant speak-NF BEN 3SG that
    'The elephant told him,'

20. "ékpé ājā zə̀ ásá à?!
    ékpé ājā zə̀ ásá à
    bad   small 2SG this QUEST
    'What kind of bad thing is this?'

21. mɔ́   zùrù   tʃɔ́lɔ́   zə̀   kə̀rə̀ná   ɔ́   kà   jé!"
    mə-´   zurù-`  tʃɔ́-lɔ́  zə̀   kə̀rə̀ná   ɔ́   ka-`   jé
    1SG-FUT tread-FUT in-in 2SG crushed SS end-FUT EMPH
    'I'll stomp on you ... until it's over!'

22. bākòngɔ̄   pá   àdə́kē,
    bākòngɔ̄   pa-´   àdə́kē
    turtle   speak-NF   that
    'The turtle said,'

23. "ɓɔ́   wù   mə̄   zə̀!"
    ɓə-´   wu-`   mə̄   zə̀
    2SG-FUT see-FUT   1SG there
    'You will see me!'

24. èndʒē pá   ʔò   nə̀   kpə́mə̀   ə́rːɔ́
    èndʒē pa-´   òʔò   nə̀   kpə́-mə̀   ə́rːɔ́
    3PL   speak-NF   word   DET just.in-DEIC until
    'They argued like that until'

    ɔ́   dɨ́   mbúlù   kōʃē.
    ɔ́   dɨ-´   mbúlù   kōʃē
    SS   count-NF   date   fight
    'they settled on a date for the fight.'

25. bākòngɔ̄   zá   āwā,   ɔ́   gú   dàá.
    bākòngɔ̄   za-´   āwā   ɔ́   gu-´   dà
    turtle   take-NF   road   SS   return-NF   away
    'The turtle left and returned home.'

26. ɔ́   tárà   ɓálàngú   ɓándɔ́   kɔ̀nɔ́.
    ɔ́   tarà-´   ɓá-àlà-úngú   ɓá-ndɔ́   kɔ̀nɔ́
    SS   descend-NF   at-eye-water   at-home   hippo
    'He descended into the water to the hippo's place.'

27. ɔ́   pá   fə̄   kɔ̀nɔ́   àdə́kē,
    ɔ́   pa-´   fə̄   kɔ̀nɔ́   àdə́kē
    SS   speak-NF   BEN hippo   that
    'He said to the hippo,'

28. "kɔ̀nɔ́,   àzɔ́   də̀   mā,   ʔà   sɔ́   də̀   ʔò."
     kɔ̀nɔ́   àzɔ́   də̀   mā   ʔà   sə-´   də̀   òʔò
     hippo   1PL.INCL   with   1SG   1PL.INCL be-NF   with   word
     'Hippo, you and me, we have a problem.'

29. kɔ̀nɔ́   pá   fə̄   ʃè   àdə́kē,
     kɔ̀nɔ́   pa-´   fə̄   tʃə̀   àdə́kē
     hippo   speak-NF   BEN   3SG   that
     'The hippo responded,'

30. "mā   sɔ́   ɓálàngú,   ɓə̀   sɔ́   ɓálɔ́   gūsū.
     mā   sə-´   ɓá-àlà-úngú   ɓə̀   sə-´   ɓá-lɔ́   gūsū
     1SG   be-NF   at-eye-water   2SG   be-NF   at-in   bush
     'I'm in the water, you're in the bush.'

31. òʔò   gàɗè   dá   à   gbɔ́   də̀   mā   à?"
     òʔò   gàɗè   dá   ʔà   gbɔ-´   də̀   mā   à
     word   what   CLEFT   1PL.INCL   find-NF   with   1SG   QUEST
     'What's the problem that you've found with me?'

32. tʃə̀   pá   fə̄   kɔ̀nɔ́   àdə́kē,
     tʃə̀   pa-´   fə̄   kɔ̀nɔ́   àdə́kē
     3SG   speak-NF   BEN   hippo   that
     'He said to the hippo,'

33. "mā   dʒí   tʃə́lɔ́   ūtū   mā
     mā   dʒı-´   tʃə́-lɔ́   ūtū   mā
     1SG   hear-NF   in-in   ear   1SG
     'I've been hearing that'

     ɓə̀   sɔ́   kə́jì   àngbà   mā.
     ɓə̀   sə-´   kə́-jì   àngbà   mā
     2SG   be-NF   INF-enter   hatred   1SG
     'you hate me.'

34. ʔàá   ngà   kōʃē   də̀   mā   jékà
     ʔà-´   nga-`   kōʃē   də̀   mā   jékà
     1PL.INCL-FUT   fight-FUT   fight   with   1SG   then
     'We will fight'

ɔ̀lɔ̀   nə̀   kə̀tɔ́,   ɓɔ́   wù   mɨ̄   tɔ́zə̀   zə̀.
ɔ̀lɔ̀   nə̀   kə̀-tɔ́   ɓə-ˊ   wu-ˋ   mɨ̄   tɔ́-zə̀   zə̀
day DET COND-pound 2SG-FUT see-FUT 1SG   REFL-2SG   EMPH
'When the day comes, you'll see me yourself.'

35. ʔàá   ngà   kōʃē   də̀   mɨ̄   tɔ́   kɔ́gbòtà   ír:í   mbímbí.
     ʔà-ˊ   nga-ˋ   kōʃē   də̀   mɨ̄   tɔ́   kɔ́-gbòtà   ír:í   mbímbí
     1PL.INCL-FUT fight-FUT fight with 1SG ??   INF-pull   taut   tired
     'We will fight the tug-of-war.'

36. ɔ̀lɔ̀   nə̀   kə̀lí,   ɓɔ́   sə̀   ɓálàngú,
     ɔ̀lɔ̀   nə̀   kə̀-lí   ɓə-ˊ   sə-ˋ   ɓá-àlà-úngú
     day DET COND-be.ready 2SG-FUT be-FUT   at-eye-water
     'When the day comes, you'll be in the water.'

     ə̄mə̄, mɔ́   sə̀   ɓálɔ́   gūsū."
     ə̄mə̄   mə-ˊ   sə-ˋ   ɓá-lɔ́   gūsū
     1SG   1SG-FUT be-FUT at-in   bush
     'And me, I'll be in the bush.'

37. ɔ̀lɔ̀   nə̀   lí   jé,   bākòngō   ná   də̀   úwú.
     ɔ̀lɔ̀   nə̀   li-ˊ   jé   bākòngō   na-ˊ   də̀   úwú
     day DET be.ready-NF   EMPH   turtle   go-NF   with   rope
     'When the day came, the turtle got some rope.'

38. ɔ́ zá   àmà   nə̀   fɔ̄   kɔ̀nɔ́   ɓálàngú,   ɔ́   wútà.
     ɔ́ za-ˊ   àmà   nə̀   fɔ̄   kɔ̀nɔ́   ɓá-àlà-úngú   ɔ́   wutà-ˊ
     SS take-NF mouth   DET   BEN   hippo   at-eye-water   SS   exit-NF
     'He gave one end of it to the hippo in the water, then he got out of the water.'

39. ɔ́ zá   dú   àmà   nə̀   fɔ̄   mbàlà   ɓálɔ́   gūsū.
     ɔ́ za-ˊ   údú   àmà   nə̀   fɔ̄   mbàlà   ɓá-lɔ́   gūsū
     SS take-NF end   mouth   DET   BEN   elephant   at-in   bush
     'He gave the other end to the elephant in the bush.'

40. tʃə̀   ká   kpúgúrú   nə̀.
     tʃə̀   ka-ˊ   kpɔ́-úgúrú   nə̀
     3SG   leave-NF   just.in-between   DET
     'He went in between.'

41. tʃə́ tá ráwá,
    tʃə́ ta-´ ráwá
    3SG cut-NF yell
    'He yelled,'

42. "gbòtà, gbòtà də́ ɔ́gbɔ́ nə̀,
    gbotà-` gbotà-` də́ ɔ́gbɔ́ nə̀
    pull-IMP pull-IMP with hard DET
    'Pull! Pull with all your might!'

    gbòtà, də́ ɔ́gbɔ́ nə̀."
    gbotà-` də́ ɔ́gbɔ́ nə̀
    pull-IMP with hard DET
    'Pull with all your might!'

43. èndʒē sə́ kə́gbòtà tə́nə̀.
    èndʒē sə-´ kə́-gbòtà tə́nə̀
    3PL be-NF INF-pull it
    'They were pulling.'

44. mbàlà sə́ kə́gbòtà tə́nə̀.
    mbàlà sə-´ kə́-gbòtà tə́nə̀
    elephant be-NF INF-pull it
    'The elephant was pulling.'

45. kɔ̀nɔ́ sə́ kə́gbòtà tə́nə̀ ɓálàngú.
    kɔ̀nɔ́ sə-´ kə́-gbòtà tə́nə̀ ɓá-àlà-úngú
    hippo be-NF INF-pull it at-eye-water
    'The hippo was pulling in the water.'

46. èndʒē gbótà tə́èndʒē ɔ́r:ɔ́ kpì fə̄ àkɨ́dàlà.
    èndʒē gbotà-´ tə́-èndʒē ɔ́r:ɔ́ kpì fə̄ àkɨ́dàlà
    3PL pull-NF REFL-3PL until all.day BEN dusk
    'They pulled against each other until the end of the day.'

47. ūzū   bàlē á   gbɔ̀gbɔ́ jē ró   pá   jāngá nɜ̀,
    ūzū   bàlē á   gbɔ̀gbɔ́ jē ro-ˊ pá   jāngá nɜ̀
    person one REL strength 3SG pass-NF above friend DET

   tʃɜ̀ gúgú   nēnē.
   tʃɜ̀ gú-gu-ˊ   nēnē
   3SG RED-be.NEG-NF NEG

   'The strength of one did not surpass the strength of the other.'

48. mbàlà   mɔ́   jé.
    mbàlà   mɔ-ˊ   jé
    elephant be.tired-NF EMPH
    'The elephant became tired.'

49. kɔ̀nɔ́   mɔ́   jé.
    kɔ̀nɔ́   mɔ-ˊ   jé
    hippo be.tired-NF EMPH
    'The hippo became tired.'

50. bākòngɔ̄ ná,   ɔ́   jú   àmà   mbàlà.
    bākòngɔ̄ na-ˊ   ɔ́   ju-ˊ   àmà   mbàlà
    turtle   go-NF SS ask-NF mouth elephant
    'The turtle went and asked the elephant.'

51. ɔ́   pá   àdɔ́kē,
    ɔ́   pa-ˊ   àdɔ́kē
    SS speak-NF that
    'He said,'

52. "ɓɜ̀ pá   límā   àdɔ́kē
    ɓɜ̀ pa-ˊ   límā   àdɔ́kē
    2SG speak-NF a.while.ago   that
    'You said before that'

    ɜ̀ɓɜ̀ kɜ̀dɔ́ égérɔ́ àgjà.
    ɜ̀ɓɜ̀ kɜ̀dɔ́ égérɔ́ àgjà
    2SG COP   large   animal
    'you're a large animal.'

53. ɓɔ́   zùrù   mā kə̀rə̀ná jé.
    ɓə-́   zurù-̀   mā kə̀rə̀ná jé
    2SG-FUT tread-FUT 1SG crushed EMPH
    'That you would tread on me.'

54. mbə̀rə̀ gàɗè kpə́ʃèkē á   gbɔ̀gbɔ́ mā rō   pá   zə̀ à?
    mbə̀rə̀ gàɗè kpə́ʃèkē á   gbɔ̀gbɔ́ mā ro-̄   pá   zə̀ à
    for   what today   REL strength 1SG pass-SUBJ above 2SG QUEST
    'How come today my strength surpassed yours?'

55. tʃè   ná   ɓándə́   kɔ̀nɔ́.
    tʃè   na-́   ɓá-ndə́   kɔ̀nɔ́
    3SG   go-NF at-home hippo
    'He went to the hippo.'

56. ɔ́   pá   fə̄ ʃè   àdə́kē,
    ɔ́   pa-́   fə̄ ʃè   àdə́kē
    SS speak-NF BEN 3SG that
    'He said to him,'

57. "ɓə̀ pá   límā   àdə́kē əmā kə̀də́ ājā   àgjà.
    ɓə̀ pa-́   límā   àdə́kē əmā kə̀də́ ājā   àgjà
    2SG speak-NF a.while.ago that 1SG COP small animal
    'You said before that I'm only a small animal.'

58. ɓɔ́   dɔ̀   tʃə́lɔ́ mā jé.
    ɓə-́   dɔ-̀   tʃə́-lɔ́ mā jé
    2SG-FUT kick-FUT in-in 1SG EMPH
    'That you'd kick me.'

59. mbə̀rə̀ gàɗè kpə́ʃèkē á   gbɔ̀gbɔ́ mā rō   pá   zə̀
    mbə̀rə̀ gàɗè kpə́ʃèkē á   gbɔ̀gbɔ́ mā ro-̄   pá   zə̀
    for   what today   REL strength 1SG pass-SUBJ above 1SG

         ásōkē   à?"
         ásō-kē   à
         this-DEIC QUEST
    'How come today my strength surpassed yours?'

60. gbòngɔ́gbɔ́ ndɔ́mà   tòrò.
    gbòngɔ́gbɔ́ ɔ́ndɔ́-àmà   tòrò
    conclusion mark-mouth PN
    'Now the conclusion of the story.'

61. àdà bùdú   nə̀ sɔ́   àtà.
    àdà bùdú   nə̀ sə-´ àtà
    foot bottom DET be-NF thus
    'This is the moral.'

62. àgbózū   pá   àdɔ́kē,
    à-gbózū   pa-´   àdɔ́kē
    PL-elder speak-NF that
    'The elders said,'

63. "kúwùsɔ́rə̀ ró   pá   gbɔ̀gbɔ́ jé."
    kɔ́wùsɔ́rə̀ ro-´   pá   gbɔ̀gbɔ́ jé
    wisdom   pass-NF above strength EMPH
    'Knowledge surpasses strength.'

64. ɓə̀ kə̀sɔ́   də̀   gbɔ̀gbɔ́, ɔ́ lí   àdɔ́kē,
    ɓə̀ kə̀-sɔ́ də̀   gbɔ̀gbɔ́   ɔ́ li-´   àdɔ́kē
    2SG COND-be with strength SS be.fitting-NF that
    'If you have strength, it is good that'

    ɓə̀ sə̀   də̀   kɔ́wùsɔ́rə̀ gàpá   nə̀.
    ɓə̀ sə-`   də̀   kɔ́wùsɔ́rə̀ gà-pá   nə̀
    2SG be-OB with wisdom   to-above DET
    'you have knowledge on top of it.'

A.2 Preparing the fields for planting (Procedural text)

1. ɓándɔ́   ʔā,   ntángò nɔ́ kɨndɨ kə̀lîi   jé,
    ɓá-ndɔ́   ʔā   ntángò nɔ́ kɨndɨ kə̀-li-^   jé
    at-home   1PL.EXCL time   of field COND-be.sufficient-STAT   EMPH
    'Where we come from, when planting time comes,'

    ɓə̀ ná   ɔ́   wú   àmà   kɨndɨ má   ɔ́ zúrù   jé.
    ɓə̀ na-´ ɔ́   wu-´   àmà   kɨndɨ má   ɔ́ zurù-´   jé
    2SG go-NF SS see-NF mouth field DISC SS step.on-NF EMPH
    'you go stake out your field.'

2. ɓə̀ kə̀zúrù   àmà   kɨ̄ndɨ́ á   kə̀ká   jé,
   ɓə̀ kə̀-zúrù   àmà   kɨ̄ndɨ́ á   kə̀-ká   jé
   2SG COND-step.on mouth field REL COND-finish EMPH
   'After staking out your field,'

   ɓə̀ gú   ə́ tɔ́   àmà   kàmbà.
   ɓə̀ gu-´   ə́ tɔ-´   àmà   kàmbà
   2SG return-NF SS pound-NF mouth knife
   'then you return and sharpen your knife.'

3. ɓə̀ kə̀tɔ́   àmà   kàmbà jé   óʃó kɔ́rə̀,
   ɓə̀ kə̀-tɔ́   àmà   kàmbà jé   óʃó kɔrə̀-´
   2SG COND-pound mouth knife EMPH place open-NF
   'After sharpening your knife, at daybreak,'

   ɓə̀ ná   ndə́ kə́gàrà kɨ̄ndɨ̄.
   ɓə̀ na-´   ndə́ kə́-gàrà kɨ̄ndɨ̄
   2SG go-NF for INF-cut field
   'you go clear the field.'

4. ɓə̀ gárà, ɓə̀ gárà.
   ɓə̀ garà-´ ɓə̀ garà-´
   2SG cut-NF 2SG cut-NF
   'You cut and you cut.'

5. ɓə̀ kə̀gárà   ángá   ɔ̀lɔ̀ vōtɔ̀ kɨ̄ndɨ̄ má ká   jé,
   ɓə̀ kə̀-gárà ángá   ɔ̀lɔ̀ vōtɔ̀ kɨ̄ndɨ̄ má ka-´   jé
   2SG COND-cut another day three field DISC finish-NF EMPH
   'After having cleared the field for three days,'

   ɓə̀ ká   tə́ nə̀ àtà.
   ɓə̀ ka-´   tə́ nə̀ àtà
   2SG leave-NF on DET thus
   'you leave it that way.'

6. ə́ kə̀mbə́rə̀ ndámbò ná ɔ̀lɔ̀,
   ə́ kə̀-mbə́rə̀ ndámbò ná ɔ̀lɔ̀
   SS COND-do some of day
   'After a few days,'

ɓə́ ná ə́ ʃó jé, kə́ʃò tə́nə̀.
ɓə́ na-´ ə́ ʃo-´ jé kə́-ʃò tə́nə̀
2SG go-NF SS burn-NF EMPH INF-burn it
'you set fire to it [the field].'

7. ē?ē bándà kə́dè tʃámāngbá nə̀,
ē?ē bandà-´ kə́-dè tʃá-māngbá nə̀
2PL begin-NF INF-chop towards-after DET
'You begin to chop what remains,'

mbə̀rə̀ kə́rò àmà ēʃē ɔ̄jɔ̄ nə̀ gàsə́ nə̀.
mbə̀rə̀ kə́-rò àmà ēʃē ɔ̄jɔ̄ nə̀ gà-ə́sə́ nə̀
in.order INF-gather mouth root tree DET to-place DET
'in order to gather the roots together.'

8. ē?ē kə̀ró àmà ēʃē ɔ̄jɔ̄ á kə̀ká jé,
ē?ē kə̀-ró àmà ēʃē ɔ̄jɔ̄ á kə̀-ká jé
2PL COND-gather mouth root tree REL COND-finish EMPH
'After having gathered the roots,'

jē sə́ kə́kàtə̀ jāvūrū.
jē sə-´ kə́-kàtə̀ jāvūrū
2PL be-NF INF-wait rain
'you wait for the rain.'

9. jāvūrū kə̀ɲí, ē?ē ná gàlə́ kɨndɨ,
jāvūrū kə̀-ɲí ē?ē na-´ gà-lə́ kɨndɨ
rain COND-rain 2PL go-NF to-in field
'When it rains, then you go to the field'

ə́ bándà kə́lù ngwàrə̀ gàlə́ kɨndɨ nə̀ gázə̀ àdə́kē
ə́ bandà-´ kə́-lù ngwàrə̀ gà-lə́ kɨndɨ nə̀ gá-zə̀ àdə́kē
SS begin-NF INF-plant seed to-in field DET to-there that
'and begin to sow seeds there so that'

ē?ē zɨ̀ də̀ àwō zə̀, də̀ àgbòlò.
ē?ē zɨ-` də̀ àwō zə̀ də̀ à-gbòlò
2PL eat-OB with wife 2SG with PL-child
'you, your wife, your kids will be able to eat.'

10. ɔ́ gá   wā.
    ɔ́ ga-´   wā
    ss be.good-NF much
    The end.

A.3 Proverbs

1. í   ví   īpī   lìāka jāngá zɜ̀   nēnē.
   ɔ́   vi-´   īpī   lìāka jāngá zɜ̀   nēnē
   ss dance-NF dance like friend 2SG NEG
   'If your friend is doing something, and you don't know why, don't follow him.'
   Lit.: 'Don't dance like your friend.'

2. mbàlà   wú   tɜ́jē   kpɔ̄rɔ́ jékà, á mèrɜ̀   élé ɔ̄kɔ̄lɔ̄.
   mbàlà   wu-´   tɜ́-jē   kpɔ̄rɔ́ jékà á merɜ̀-` élé ɔ̄kɔ̄lɔ̄
   elephant see-NF REFL-3SG ??   then REL swallow-FUT fruit coconut
   'Before doing something, make sure that you have the capability to do it.'
   Lit.: 'Elephant knows himself well before swallowing a coconut.'

3. kātʃā-kātʃā   wó   jàmízɨ̀.
   kātʃā-kātʃā   wo-´   jàmízɨ̀
   RED-quickly   kill-NF Yamizi
   'Don't speak too soon.'
   Lit.: 'Haste killed Yamizi.'

4. àjēngɔ̀ bākòngɔ̄ jī   ndɔ́ nɜ̀, jékà á èndʒé dè   ʃè.
   àjēngɔ̀ bākòngɔ̄ jɨ-´   ndɔ́ nɜ̀ jékà á èndʒe-´ de-´ ʃè
   owner turtle enter-SUBJ mark DET then REL 3PL-FUT cut-FUT 3SG
   'If the owner agrees, then you can use something of his.'
   Lit.: 'If the owner of the turtle agrees, then they can cut the turtle.'

5. kpɔ̀lɔ̀   sɔ́   kùtí jē, ɔ́ mbɜ́rɜ̀   tʃɔ́lɔ́   àmà   gbòlò nɔ́
   kpɔ̀lɔ̀   sə-´ kùtí jē   ɔ́ mbərɜ̀-´ tʃɔ́-lɔ́ àmà   gbòlò nɔ́
   nightjar be-NF only 3SG   SS do-NF   in-in mouth child of

   jē kpàhà
   jē kpàhà
   3SG wide.open
   Lit.: 'The nightjar is only himself. He made his child's mouth abnormally large.'

6. ɓə́ sə́   ɓàtà kàmbà mōnō.
   ɓə̀ sə-´ ɓàtà kàmbà mōnō
   2SG be-NF like knife Mono
   'You speak with a forked tongue.'
   Lit.: 'You are like a Mono knife.'

7. úngú kpā   də̀   kùtí jē, ə́ déngɔ̀.
   úngú kpa-¯ də̀   kùtí jē   ə́ dengɔ̀-´
   water run-SUBJ with ??   3SG SS bend-NF
   'If you do something by yourself, you'll get off-track.'
   Lit.: 'Water runs by itself, and thus it curves and bends.'

8. ɓə̀ kə̀dʒídʒí   àgbózū nēnē, ɓə́   ndʒò   úngú
   ɓə̀ kə̀-dʒí-dʒɪ-´   à-gbózū nēnē ɓə-´ ndʒo-`   úngú
   2SG COND-RED-hear-NF PL-elder NEG 2SG-FUT drink-FUT water

   àkɔ̀kɔ̀.
   à-kɔ̀kɔ̀
   PL-termite
   'If you don't listen to your elders, you'll wind up dead.'
   Lit.: 'If you don't listen to your elders, you'll drink termite water.'

9. gbòlò kə̀ngé   lēngā gbózū kə́vì   tə́jē   ndə́ nə̀,
   gbòlò kə̀-ngé   lēngā gbózū kə́-vì   tə́-jē ndə́ nə̀
   child COND-beat drum elder INF-dance REFL-3SG mark DET

   gbózū kə̀ngé   lēngā, gbòlò kə́vì   tə́jē   ndə́ nə̀.
   gbózū kə̀-ngé   lēngā gbòlò kə́-vì   tə́-jē ndə́ nə̀
   elder COND-beat drum child INF-dance REFL-3SG mark DET
   'You can listen to the wisdom of both adults and children.'
   Lit.: 'If a child beats a drum, then an elder will dance to it; if an elder beats a drum, then a child will dance to it.'

10. èndʒē zú   gbòlò tərālē   də̀ kə́nà ʃè nēnē.
    èndʒē zu-´   gbòlò tərālē   də̀ kə́-nà ʃè nēnē
    3PL   give.birth-NF child directly with INF-go 3SG NEG
    'It takes time to learn something.'
    Lit.: 'A child doesn't walk the day it is born.'

11. lèkpà   kpā   jékà   á   ɨ̀dɨ̀   jē   ɔ́   nɔ̀.
    lèkpà   kpa-¯   jékà   á   ɨ̀dɨ̀   jē   ɔ́   nɔ-`
    gazelle flee-SUBJ then   REL horn   3SG SS   turn-FUT
    'If you avoid danger, you will live long.'
    Lit.: 'If a gazelle flees, its horns will curve.'

A.4 Frequency counts

Table A.1. Frequency counts of consonants in texts

	Elephant	Fields	Proverbs	Misc	TOTAL	%
b	11	2	1	50	64	2.1%
ɓ	30	11	4	80	125	4.1%
d	44	4	5	109	162	5.3%
ɗ	3	0	0	4	7	0.2%
dʒ	3	0	2	10	15	0.5%
f	10	0	0	22	32	1.0%
g	24	10	0	104	138	4.5%
gb	24	1	7	25	57	1.9%
h	0	0	1	2	3	0.1%
j	27	13	14	84	138	4.5%
k	77	31	19	262	389	12.6%
kp	6	0	6	28	40	1.3%
l	43	7	14	124	188	6.1%
m	39	9	4	107	159	5.2%
mb	16	5	3	45	69	2.2%
n	42	13	13	257	325	10.6%
nd	8	12	3	60	83	2.7%
ndʒ	5	0	3	39	47	1.5%
ng	22	3	10	60	95	3.1%
ngb	2	1	0	3	6	0.2%
ɲ	0	1	0	1	2	0.06%
p	20	0	1	58	79	2.6%
r	25	14	4	110	153	5.0%
s	34	2	2	121	159	5.2%
ʃ	10	5	2	23	40	1.3%
t	26	7	7	103	143	4.6%

tʃ	16	1	3	49	69	2.2%
v	0	3	3	4	10	3.2%
w	10	4	2	51	67	2.2%
w̌	0	0	0	3	3	0.1%
z	19	5	5	96	125	4.1%
ʒ	0	0	1	1	2	0.06%
ʔ	11	5	0	72	88	2.9%
TOTAL					3080	

Table A.2. Frequency counts of vowels in texts

	Elephant	Fields	Proverbs	Misc	TOTAL	%
a	212	64	35	826	1137	30.9%
e	64	22	35	284	405	11.0%
ə	252	60	34	966	1312	35.6%
i	12	3	13	47	75	2.0%
ɨ	7	15	3	94	119	3.2%
o	45	13	16	198	272	7.4%
ɔ	66	11	12	83	172	4.7%
u	53	11	11	114	189	5.1%
TOTAL					3681	

Table A.3. Frequency counts of tones in texts

	Elephant	Fields	Proverbs	Misc	TOTAL	%
H	286	71	51	969	1377	37.5%
M	129	43	42	540	754	20.5%
L	296	85	66	1095	1542	42.0%
TOTAL					3673	

Appendix B

Wordlist

The items in this lexicon come from texts and from wordlists and elicited phrases, including words from a draft version of the SIL Comparative African Word List (CAWL) developed by Keith Snider and Jim Roberts.

Each entry includes the word transcribed phonemically, the part of speech (cf. list of abbreviations on p. xv), and the gloss; or the transcription may be followed by a cross reference. Additional information is included when pertinent. This includes variant forms, morphological analysis, and the reference numbers for the SIL CAWL.

— a —

à, *quest.* question marker for yes/no questions.

à, *pl.* plural prefix; attaches to animate nouns, descriptive adjectives, and ordinal numbers.

á, *conj.* subordinating conjunction which precedes a relative clause.

á, cf. **pá**.

àbá, *n.* father. 0329, 0333, 0345, 0353.

ābā, *n.* yam. 0624.

ábá, *n.* camp (for initiation rites). 0857.

àbá mbējā, *n.* father-in-law (wife's father), son-in-law. 0330, 0367.

ábálá, *n.* hello. 1299.

àbáládúwū, *pn.* June.

àbángà, *n.* molar tooth. 0066.

àbàngūlū, *n.* type of sugarcane. 0621.

àbórónà, *n.* Arabs.

àbūtʃɔ́, cf. **būtʃɔ́**.

àɓí, *n.* hammer. 1086.

àdà, *n.* leg, foot, footstep. 0041, 0061, 0109.

ádá, *n.* meaning, reason.

ádá bùdú, *n.* moral (of a story).

ádá òʔò, *n.* meaning. 1372.
àdà ɔ̄jɔ̄, *n.* base of tree trunk. 0626.
àdà ūkū, *n.* hip, back of thigh.
àdāngà, *n.* lake. 0685.
àdēngɔ̀, *n.* bend, crook, curve. 0654.
àdékē, *Variants:* àdɘ́kē, bàlékē *conj.* that.
àdílà, *cf.* àkídàlà.
àdɘ́nà, *conj.* that.
àdòlò, *n.* watch. *Morph:* àdà-ɔ̀lɔ̀.
àdú, *n.* knot. 0818.
àdʒà, *n.* type of grass (tall).
ádʒá, *adj.* real, true.
ádʒá ɨpɨ, *cf.* dʒápū.
àdʒùkùmá, *n.* ghost, ogre. 1170, 1175.
àfú, *n.* ant (reddish-brown biting). 0499.
āgā, *n.* horn (the musical instrument), two way radio, microphone.
āgārā ngbāɓī, *n.* skeleton. 0085.
àgārāwò, *n.* match. *Morph:* à-garà-òwò.
àgíngí, *n.* abscess (small). 0204.
àgjà, *n.* animal. 0394.
àgjà gūsū, *Variant:* àgjà tʃɘ́lɘ́ gūsū. *n.* wild animal. 0466.
àgjà tʃálàkpɨ́, *n.* domesticated animal. 0479.
àgjà tʃálàngú, *Variant:* àgjàngú. *n.* fish. *Morph:* àgjà-úngú. 0417.
āgwā, *n.* buffalo. 0402.
āgwā tʃálàkpɨ́, *n.* cow.
àgbà, *n.* tuft, bundle. 0122, 0798.
ágbá, *Variant:* āgbā. *adj.* useless, pointless.
ágbá, *n.* dugout canoe. 0801.
àgbàrà, *n.* bridge. 0656.
àgbárá, *n.* comb.
àgbīvī, *n.* pimple. 0223.
āhārā, *adj.* dry.
àjà, *n.* fish trap. 1035.

ājā, *adj.* small.
ájá, *n.* man's brother. 0318, 0361.
ājā hèrèlà, *n.* key.
ājā ngbúgú jāvūrū, *n.* rainy season (little). 0750.
ājā ɔ̄jɔ̄, *Variant:* ājājō. *n.* small tree, small stick.
ājā úngú, *n.* small river, creek.
àjābó, *Variant:* ájá ōgō. *n.* clan. *Morph:* à-jā-óbó. 0323.
àjēngɔ̀, *Variants:* àjīngɔ̀, àjī, àjē. *n.* person, owner.
àjēngɔ̀ ɘ̀rɘ̀, *n.* owner. 0297.
àjēngɔ̀ kɘ́zùmɘ̄, *n.* one who begets (parent). *Morph:* kɘ́-zu-mɘ̄. 0344.
àjī, *n.* mother. 0346, 0352, 0354.
àjī àgènè, *n.* host. *Morph:* à-gènè. 0287.
àjī àjāʃē bīʃà, *n.* polygamist. *Morph:* à-jāʃē. 1205.
àjī àkɨ́, *n.* person who performs a circumcision.
àjī àkwà, *Variant:* àjēngɔ̀ àkwà. *n.* servant, employee. 0301.
àjī āngbā, *Variant:* àjēngɔ̀ āngbā. *n.* thief. 0387.
àjī àwà, *n.* coward. 0277.
àjī àw̌á, *n.* messenger. 0381.
àjī bītū, *n.* deaf person.
àjī fùngà, *n.* hunchback. 0288.
àjī gūsū, *n.* bush dweller. 0275.
àjī íjí, *n.* madman (crazy person), lunatic.
àjī kāná, *n.* thumb. 0095.
àjī kɘ́ɓì lóbà, *n.* weaver. 0390.
àjī kɘ́gùmà òʔò, *n.* messenger. 0381.
àjī kɘ́gbàrà ʔò, *n.* prophet.
àjī kɘ́mbɘ̀rɘ̀ gbārɘ̀ ótó, *n.* potter. 0383.
àjī kɘ́ndʒò kɨndɨ, *n.* farmer. 0376.
àjī kɘ́wò àgjà gūsū, *n.* hunter. 0379.

àjī kɔ́wò àgjàngú, *n.* fisherman. 0378.
àjī kòɓà, *n.* patient, sick person. 0302.
àjī kōngwá, *n.* insect. 0512.
àjī kūmù, *n.* enemy, supporter. 0282.
àjī kúwùsɔ́ʔò, *n.* wise person. 1398.
àjī lèfà, *n.* midwife. 0382.
àjī mārā, *n.* sterile person. 0304.
àjī mbējā, *n.* mother-in-law (wife's mother). 0349.
àjī ndàwò, *n.* blacksmith. 0371.
àjī ngèndʒà, *n.* rich man. 0300.
àjī òjò, *n.* poor man. 0298.
àjī ókó, *n.* wicked person. 1397.
àjī òʔò, *n.* guilty. 1656.
àjī ɔ̄dɔ̄, *n.* careless, lazy person. 1636.
àjī ɔ̄jɔ̄, *n.* doctor, fetish priest, medicine man. 0374, 0377, 0380.
àjī ràwò, *n.* sorcerer, witch. 0386, 0391.
àjī wùtì, *n.* beggar. 0272.
àjībó, *n.* relative. Morph: **àjī-óbó**. 0359.
àjíngá, *n.* co-wife. 0334.
àjó, *n.* 1) family, kinship. 2) love. 1200, 1370.
àjōgō, *n.* inhabitant, person of. Morph: **àjī-ōgō**. 0290.
àjōndɔ̀, *n.* principal wife. 0358.
ākā, *n.* wound. 0231.
àkídʒì, *n.* bead (plastic). 1066.
àkí, *n.* razor, knife used in circumcision rite. 0832.
àkídàlà, Variants: **àdílà**, **àlàkídà**, **dàdílà**, **kídàlà**. *time.* dusk, afternoon, early evening. 0761.
àkjó, Variant: **ɔ̀kjó**. *n.* hoof. 0540.
àkɔ̄, *n.* husband. 0264, 0347.
ākɔ̄, *n.* male.
ākɔ̄, cf. **ɔ̄kɔ̄**.

ākɔ̄ jābùrù, *n.* he-goat. 0483.
àkwà, *n.* work. 1104.
àkwàrà, *n.* arrowhead.
ákwárá, *n.* chick-peas, garbanzo beans.
ákpá lóbà, *n.* loincloth, cloth worn by woman. 0823, 1068.
àkpàlà óʃó, *n.* platform. 0828.
àpùtù, *n.* herd (of cattle or sheep). 0553.
àlà, *n.* eye, surface (clear or reflective), point, blade. 0030.
àlàkídà, cf. **àkídàlà**.
àlà ūdū, *n.* spear head. 1040.
àlà wólé, *n.* arrowhead. 1040.
àlàwò, *n.* flame. Morph: **àlà-òwò**. 0671.
àlédʒōzó, *n.* hail. 0742.
àlí, *adj.* first thing. 1519.
àlívù, *n.* family, offspring. 0265, 0328.
àlúgù, *n.* mushroom. 0608.
àmà, *n.* mouth, language, edge, boundary, price. 0067, 0655, 1128.
àmà kōtā, *n.* seashore. 0711.
àmà lóbà, *n.* hem. 1071.
àmànə̀, *n.* price.
àmàzì, Variant: **dàmàzì**. *time.* morning, dawn. Morph: **à-àmà-ìzì**. 0764, 0772.
àméndè, *n.* glue.
āmbā, *adj.* plain, ordinary.
ámbálá, *n.* bait. 1029.
áná, Variant: **ɔ́nɔ́**. *n.* trip, journey, walk. 1763.
àndà, *n.* house. 0869.
àndà àbòbò, *n.* termite hill.
àndà màkòsà, *n.* cook house.
àndà òwò, *n.* kitchen. 0870.
àndíríɓì, *n.* uvula.
àndòrò, *n.* witchcraft. 1181.

ándʒá àmà, *n.* tip of something. 1777.
āngā, *n.* bottle, thermos, bowl, calabash. 0917, 0918, 0920.
ándʒòró, cf. ndʒòró.
ángá, *adj.* another, other. 1504.
ángá nə̀, *n.* some. 1507.
ángàlà, *n.* ladder, scaffolding. 1087, 1096.
ángándòrò, *n.* ancestral spirits. *Morph:* ángá-àndòrò.
àngándʒá, *pn.* August.
àngāngōlē, *n.* type of sugar cane. 0621.
àngàrà, *n.* single person, bachelor. 0270.
āngbɔ́, cf. ɔ́ngbɔ́.
àngérépè, *n.* star. 0718.
ángjá, *n.* 1) bamboo, raffia. 2) nail. 0571, 0583, 1090.
àngɔ́, *n.* rat.
àngɔ́rɔ́, *Variant:* àngóró. *n.* throat. 0094.
àngwà, *n.* seed.
ángwá, *n.* difficulty.
àngbà, *n.* hatred.
āngbā, *n.* theft. 1207.
ángbá, *adv.* after.
āngbā bùdú, *n.* adultery.
āngbā kānɔ́, *n.* theft (with the hand)
àngbɔ́lèngāndā, *n.* peg. 0826.
àngbó, *n.* festival.
àpá, *n.* tsetse fly. 0526.
àrùgū, *n.* biting midge.
ásɔ́, *Variant:* ásɔ̄. *deic.* this.
ásɔ́ ɓáʔē, *deic.* that. (there).
ásɔ́kē, *deic.* this. *Morph:* ásɔ́-kē.
ásɔ́mə̀, *deic.* that (anaphoric). *Morph:* ásɔ́-mə̀.
àsūngù, *n.* flood. 0740.
àʃōngbɔ̀, *n.* type of sugar cane. 0621.
àtà, *adv.* thus, also. 1509. *adj.* such.

átà, *n.* grandparent, grandchild. 0332, 0337, 0338, 0339, 0340, 0341, 0343.
àtàkē, *Variant:* nàtàkē. *adv.* like this. *Morph:* àtà-kē.
àtàmə̀, *adv.* like that, in that way. *Morph:* àtà-mə̀.
àtàrà, *n.* age-mate. 0314.
àtí, *loc.* down, below.
àtú, *n.* type of cat. 0407.
àtʃó, *n.* louse (lice). 0516.
àwà, *n.* fear. 1363, 1821.
āwā, *n.* path, way, road, track. 0706, 0723.
áwá, *n.* diarrhea.
āwā bàlē, *adv.* the same as.
āwā gūsū, *n.* path. 0696.
àwà ndʒàbā, *n.* awe, fear of God. 1164.
āwā úngú, *n.* course of river. 0662.
àwájà, *n.* baby. 0255.
àwákú, *n.* cable for a trap.
àwāzà, *pn.* October.
àwō, *n.* wife. 0369.
àwó, *n.* lung. 0065.
àwúá, *n.* mask. 1202.
áw̌árá, *n.* fierceness. 1615.
àw̌éngè, *n.* rainbow. 0702.
àw̌étòrò, *Variant:* àw̌étòtò. *n.* activator in an animal trap.
àw̌í, *n.* hyena.
àzɔ́, *pron.* first-person plural inclusive pronoun: citation, object, and possessive form. cf. ʔà.
àzū kɔ́, *n.* everybody. 1492.
àʔá, *n.* aunt (father's sister or wife of mother's brother). 0316.
āʔā, *pron.* first-person plural exclusive pronoun: citation form. cf. ʔā.
áʔjárá, *adj.* small (plural).
àʔú, *n.* uncle (brother of mother). 0350.

— b —

bādōrō, *n.* sweet potato. 0622.
bàdʒà, *n.* 1) stone, rock (big). 2) battery. 0697, 0707, 0719.
bádʒá, *n.* dried sand (where water usually lies), rocks of the water.
bàgá, *n.* cheek. 0023.
bágàrà, *n.* cow, ox. 0477, 0490.
bákjákjáà, *adv.* shallow. 1682.
bākòngɔ̄, *n.* tortoise (land turtle). 0461.
bākòngɔ̄ngú, *n.* turtle (water turtle). *Morph:* bākòngɔ̄-úngú. 0462.
balà, *Variant:* balà óʃó. *v.* greet. 1337.
bálángbá, *n.* shield. 0839.
bàlàngbà ngɔ̄tō, *n.* comb (on a rooster).
bàlē, *num.* one, first. 1523.
bàlékē, cf. **àdə́kē**.
bàlēlà, *n.* being one-eyed. *Morph:* bàlē-àlà. 0233.
bāmàrā, *n.* lion. 0436.
bambà, *v.* exaggerate.
bandà, *v.* begin (loan from Lingala *kobanda*).
Bàndà, *pn.* the Banda ethnic/language group.
bàngànà, *n.* zebra. 0468.
bàràkàngbà, *n.* bat (large). 0398.
bātīmā, *n.* rope (heavy).
be, *v.* swell, be big, become fat. 1605.
be àmà, *v.* stop up. 1750.
belègɔ̀, *Variant:* bələ̀gɔ̀. *v.* become bent (with age). 0128.
bərə̀, *v.* quarrel.
bərə̀ tə́ óʃó, *v.* argue. 1324.
bījā, *n.* ebony. 0576.
bījō, cf. **bīwā**.
bīkò, *Variant:* bīkwà. *time.* day of the week (loan from Ngbandi, cf. Kamanda 1998:653).

bīkò bàlē, *time.* Monday.
bīkò bīʃà, *time.* Tuesday.
bīkò mīndúù, *time.* Friday.
bīkò vànā, *time.* Thursday.
bīkò vōtɔ̀, *time.* Wednesday.
bìndī, *n.* locust. 0515.
bīngī, *n.* bracelet, ring, lip ring. 0797, 0803, 0833.
bìrùlú, *n.* porcupine. 0451.
bīʃà, *num.* two, second. 1524 (two).
bītū, *n.* deaf, deaf man. *Morph:* bī (?)-ūtū. 0236, 0279.
bīwā, *Variant:* bījō. *n.* nasal mucus.
bìlì ndə́mà tə́ zə̀, *v.* imitate. 1424.
bìlì ūzū, *v.* incite. 1244.
bíngí, *n.* compound, home. 0859, 0868.
bòā, *n.* priest, Catholic (loan from French *abbé*?).
bòbò, *n.* termite.
bóngjá, *n.* material inside bamboo. *Morph:* óbó-ángjá.
bówō, *n.* python. 0453.
bɔ̀lɔ̀, *n.* tobacco. 0850.
bu, *v.* make black. 1571.
Búbàndà, *pn.* the Mono-Bubanda dialect and people.
bùdú, *n.* buttocks, back, rear, bottom. *prep.* at the bottom. 0008, 0021.
būlà, *n.* blindness, blind man. *Morph:* ūbū-àlà. 0234, 0274.
būtʃɔ́, *Variants:* àbūtʃɔ́, dàbūtʃɔ́. *time.* darkness, night. *Morph:* ūbū-(?). 0763, 0774.

— ɓ —

ɓá-, *prep.* at (cf. Cloarec-Heiss 1986:272).
ɓáàtí, *loc.* low. *Morph:* ɓá-àtí. 1782.
ɓákē, *loc.* here. *Morph:* ɓá-kē.

ɓákèlé, *prep.* behind. *Morph:* ɓá-kèlé.
ɓálàngú, *loc.* in the water. *Morph:* ɓá-àlà-úngú.
ɓálɔ́, *prep.* in. *Morph:* ɓá-lɔ́.
ɓámbàtʃā, *time.* tomorrow. 0783.
ɓámbìjā, *time.* day after tomorrow. 0765.
ɓándɔ́, *prep.* place, at the home of. *Morph:* ɓá-ndɔ́.
ɓápá, *prep.* on (top). *Morph:* ɓá-pá. 1483.
ɓásə̀ndá, *loc.* inside. *Morph:* ɓá-ɔ́sɔ́-àndà.
ɓáʃú, *Variant:* ɓáúʃú. *loc.* outside. *Morph:* ɓá-úʃú. 1484.
ɓàtà, *Variants:* ɓātā, bàtà. *conj.* 1) since (as, because). 2) like. 1663, 1664.
ɓātā, *Variant:* ɓàtà, bàtà. *prep.* like. 1663, 1664, 1675.
ɓátà, *Variant:* bátà. *quest.* where. *Morph:* ɓá-táà. 1513.
ɓátʃákùdú, *prep.* in. *Morph:* ɓá-tʃá-kùdú.
ɓázà, *quest.* where. *Morph:* ɓá-zə̀-à.
ɓázə̀, *loc.* there. *Morph:* ɓá-zə̀.
ɓáʔé, *loc.* there (imprecise). *Morph:* ɓá-ʔé(?) 1776.
ɓə̀, *pron.* second-person singular pronoun: clitic form (subject, direct object, possessive for nominalized verbs). cf. ə̀ɓə̀.
ɓi, *Variant:* i. *v.* hit, thresh, sew, hit with a hammer, beat, hit with a stick/spear, strike (with hand). 0988, 1075, 1109, 1890, 1901, 1902.
ɓi ítʃī, *v.* sing. 1163.
ɓi kùtùrù-kùtùrù, *v.* smash, break. 1911.
ɓi lēngā, *v.* beat (drum). 1145, 1156.

ɓi tʃɔ́lɔ́ ōmbō, *v.* flap the wings. 0563.

— d —

da, *v.* slap, clap.
dà, *Variant:* dàá. *adv.* motion away from the listener.
dàbūtʃó, cf. būtʃɔ́.
dá, *cleft.* signals focus.
dàdídà, cf. àkídàlà.
da kānɔ́, *v.* clap (hands). 0158.
da lēngā, *v.* beat (drum). 1145, 1156.
dakà, *v.* borrow. 1218.
dakà ə̀rə̀, *v.* get into debt. 1135.
dakà fə̄, *v.* lend. 1252.
dàmbá, *n.* tail. 0544.
dāmbà, *adv.* still, yet.
dàndòrò, *n.* spider. 0523.
dàndú, cf. dɔ̀ndú.
dàrà ndɔ́ óʃó, *v.* curse. 1185.
dàrà pá kūmù, *v.* surpass (height or importance).
dàrà ūtū, *v.* attend to.
dàràmà, *Variant:* dàrà àmà. *v.* swear, make an oath. 1355.
dàràmbèʃà, *n.* slipperiness. 1621.
de, *v.* chop, cut down (a tree), cut firewood, burst. 0946, 0998, 1895, 1896.
de átá nə̀, *v.* shorten. 1608.
de də̀ àmà, *v.* peck. 0569.
de gbàrá-gbàrá, *v.* shiver, tremble. 0186, 1992.
de tʃɔ́lɔ́, *v.* chop into pieces, crush (with the feet), split. 0994, 1898, 1977.
də, *v.* be, copula employed for equation or proper inclusion.
də̀, *Variant:* dɔ̀, tə̀. *prep.* 1) with. 2) of. *conj.* and. 1517.
də̀ ótʃɔ́ nə̀, *adv.* good, well. 1510, 1654.

Wordlist

dә́mә̀, *deic.* that.
di, *v.* be tangled.
díngíní, *n.* elbow. 0029.
dɨ, *v.* 1) count. 2) read. 3) lean to the side, bend, bank. 1411.
dɨ mbētɨ, *v.* read. 1439.
dɨ tʃә́lә́mà, *v.* cackle. 0561.
dɨ tʃә́lә́mà fә̄, *v.* beseech, entreat, pray. 1327, 1347.
do, *v.* be foolish.
do pánә̀, *v.* abound. 1625.
dōlō, *n.* elephantiasis.
dòmótò, *n.* tomato (loan from French *tomate*). 0623.
dongɔ̀, dongà, cf. dɔngɔ̀.
dōrō, *n.* partridge. 0449.
dɔ, *v.* stomp, kick. 1874, 1903.
dɔ jí, *v.* escape, evade. 1055, 1056.
dɔ pá, *v.* avoid. 1790.
dɔ úngú, *v.* swim. 0194.
dә́kә́lә́ngbā, *n.* scorpion. 0521.
dɔ̀ndú, *Variant:* dàndú. *pn.* December.
dɔ̀ngә́, *n.* part of the meal that is not the starch (can be either greens or meat).
dɔngɔ̀, *Variants:* dongɔ̀, dongà. *v.* honor. 1243, 1622.
dә́ngә́, *n.* praise. 1307.
dɔngɔ̀ ītʃī, *v.* praise, sing. 1162.
du, *v.* punch, tether (sheep or goats), tie up, twist. 0987, 1022, 1884.
du mә́lә̄, *v.* play. 1259.
dulà, *v.* tie a knot. 1021.

— dʒ —

dʒa, *Variant:* dʒa kóté. *v.* mix, spot, speckle. 1749.
dʒà, *prep.* opposite.
dʒa àndà, *v.* daub. 0999.
dʒàgálàfó, *prep.* up, above. *Morph:* dʒà-gálàfó. 1487.

dʒàgàtʃátʃū, *n.* front. *prep.* towards. *Morph:* dʒà-gà-tʃátʃū. 1485, 1761.
dʒàgàpá, *prep.* above. *Morph:* dʒà-gàpá. 1475, 1483.
dʒàgáʃú, *prep.* outside. *Morph:* dʒà-gàùʃú. 1484.
dʒākātā, *Variant:* dʒāgātā. *adj.* true (superlative).
dʒangà, *v.* mix, tangle. 0950, 1990.
dʒápū, *Variant:* ádʒá ɨpɨ. *excl.* really. 1506.
dʒe, *v.* coil, wind. 1926, 1997.
dʒèlә́nә̀, *?.* some. 1507.
dʒèngétè, *n.* pepper. 0910.
dʒèpè, *n.* fishscale. 0537.
dʒerә̀, *Variant:* dʒerә̀ ndә́. *v.* 1) forget, be forgotten by. 2) stir a thin liquid. 0958, 1418.
dʒèzà, *adv.* everywhere.
dʒè?èrә̀ mīndū, *n.* coarse sand, gravel. 0753.
dʒi, *v.* 1) sense (hear, smell, taste...). 2) dig, harvest (tubers), hollow out. 0976, 1001, 1007, 1342.
dʒi òʔò, *v.* obey, listen. 1345.
dʒi ɔ́tʃә́ ә̀rә̀, *v.* taste. 0195.
dʒi tʃáfù, *v.* smell (something). 0189.
dʒígí, *adj2.* whole. 1705.
dʒìjū, *n.* great grandparent.
dʒìlíkírә́, *adj.* round.
dʒìndɨ, *n.* greens.
dʒingìlì, *v.* get lost. 1823.
dʒīngīlī, *n.* mistake. 1203.
dʒingíndɨ, *n.* bladder. *Morph:* dʒī-ngíndɨ. 0012.
dʒitɔ̀, *Variant:* dʒutɔ̀. *v.* bathe. 0145, 0146.
dʒitɔ̀ lóbà, *v.* wash clothes. 1024.
dʒo, *v.* 1) cultivate (something), hoe, crouch, squat. 2) cut (with an axe). 3) plait. 1013, 1814, 1873.

dʒo ərə, *n.* weave (a basket or mat). 1073.
dʒòjɔ̄, *n.* 1) stem of maize, millet, etc. 2) stake. *Morph:* (?)-ɔ̄jɔ̄. 0643, 1097.
dʒókòrò, *n.* rib. *Morph:* dʒó(?)-òkòrò. 0078.
dʒōrò, *n.* sorghum. 0620.
dʒùjū, *n.* ancestor, greatgrandparent. 0315.

— e —

èbè, *n.* liver. 0063.
ēbē, *n.* type of grass (small), thatch. 1098.
ébé, *adj.* big, fat.
ēdʒē, *n.* clitoris. 0026.
èɗè, *quest.* who. 1515.
égérɔ́, *adj.* big. *n.* height. 1575, 1577, 1582.
égérɔ́ ágbá, *n.* boat. 0795.
égérɔ́ kūmù, *n.* pride.
égérɔ́ lēngā, *n.* big drum. 1146.
égérɔ́ ògò, *n.* famine. 1196.
égérɔ́ ōgō, *n.* district, province, country. 0862.
égérɔ́ tʃɔ́lɔ́ mīndū, *n.* desert. 0664.
égérɔ́ ūzū, *n.* important person, king, master. 0289, 0291, 0293.
éhérɔ́, *n.* wax. 0854.
éhérɔ́ àwátèrə̀, *n.* beeswax, beebread. 0550.
éhérɔ́ ōpōrō, *n.* eggshell. 0532.
éjà, *n.* firstborn. 0335.
éjà jāwūrù, *n.* elder sister. 0364.
éjè, *pron.* somebody, someone (unknown, unspecified).
éjérɔ́, *adj.* yellow, brown. 1563.
éjérɔ́ kūmù, *n.* gray hair. 0111.
ékpé, *adj.* bad, evil. 1168, 1630.
ékpé gūsū, *n.* weeds. 0591.
ékpé tʃáfù, *n.* bad smell (of fish). 1611.

ēlē, *n.* kidney. 0057.
élé, *n.* fruit, grain, bean. 0593.
élé ndʒōpōrō, *n.* testicle. *Morph:* ndʒō(?)-ōpōrō. 0092.
élé ngímá, *n.* palm nut. 0613.
élé òwò, *n.* shot gun shell.
élé ōwō, *Variant:* **éléwō**. *n.* rice. 0618.
élé ɔ̄jɔ̄, *Variant:* **léjɔ̄**. *n.* 1) fruit of a tree, grain (usually for eating). 2) pill. 0893.
ènē, *pron.* third-person plural logophoric pronoun. cf. **ə̀nɔ̄**.
èndʒē, *Variant:* **ə̀ndʒē**. *pron.* third-person plural pronoun.
ēngē, *n.* needle. 1072.
èʃè, *pron.* third-person singular pronoun: citation form. cf. **tʃə̀**, **ʃè**. 1453, 1454, 1455.
ēʃē, *n.* root.
ēʃē ɔ̄jɔ̄, *Variant:* **ʃējō**. *n.* tree root. 0639.
ēvērɔ̄, *n.* type of bamboo. 0571.
ēʒē, *n.* caterpillar. 0503.
ēʔē, *pron.* second-person plural pronoun: citation form. cf. **ʔē**.
éʔélé, *n.* grudge holding.

— ə —

ɔ́, *pron.* same subject pronoun, inanimate subject pronoun.
ə̀bə́rɔ́, *n.* quarrel. 1264.
ə̀ɓə̀, *pron.* second-person singular pronoun: citation form. cf. **ɓə̀**, **zə̀**.
ɔ́də̀, *conj.* if. 1497.
ɔ́dɔ́, *Variant:* **gàndɔ́**. *conj.* and, noun phrase coordination. 1490.
ɔ́də̀ ɔ́tē, *?.* perhaps. 1505.
ɔ́də̀ndʒē, *?.* same. 1681.
ɔ́gɔ́rɔ́, *n.* waist. 0103.
ɔ̄mɔ̄, *pron.* first-person singular pronoun: citation form. cf. **mɔ̄**.

ə̄nēkē, Variant: ʃə̄nēkē, tʃə̄nēkē. *deic.* that, which. *Morph:* tʃə̀-nēkē.
ə̀nɔ̄, *pron.* third-person singular logophoric pronoun. cf. ènē.
ə̀nɔ́, cf. nɔ́.
ɔ́nɔ́, cf. áná.
ə̀nɔ̄tà, *quest.* which. *Morph:* ə̀nɔ́-ta. 1514.
ɔ́ndɔ́, *n.* 1) mark, impression, print, track, imprint, drawing. 2) the impression that something or someone makes. 3) can also have a sense of "presence" for an animate object. 4) footprint. 5) point. (cf. Cloarec-Heiss 1986:28, 160, 401). 0552, 1770.
ɔ́ndɔ́ àdà, *Variant:* ndɔ́dà. *n.* footprint.
ə̀ndʒē, cf. èndʒē.
ə̀ràdà, cf. ràdà.
ə̀rə̀, *n.* thing. 1466.
ɔ́rɔ́, *conj.* until.
ə̀rə̀ ɓándá kòbà, *n.* bride price.
ə̀rə̀ kɔ́gbɔ̀tà də̀ òfòrò, *n.* rake.
ə̀rə̀ kɔ́-kɔ́, *n.* everything. 1493.
ə̀rə̀ nɔ́ ūzū, *n.* belongings. 1120.
ə̀rə̀ ògò, *Variant:* ròɡò. *n.* food.
ə̀rə̀ tʃángbá, *n.* inheritance. 1124.
ɔ́sɔ́, *n.* place, point (cf. Cloarec-Heiss 1986:28, 160). 0699, 1770.
ɔ́sɔ́ kɔ́lì ɔ̀lɔ̀, *n.* west. 1779.
ɔ́sɔ́ kɔ́wùtà ɔ̀lɔ̀, *loc.* east. 1758.
ɔ́sɔ́ ōlō, *n.* sleeping place. 0878.
ɔ́tɔ́, *n.* being, entity, physical person, body (cf. Cloarec-Heiss 1986:28, 160).
ɔ́tɔ́ nə̀, *pron.* that (subject).

— f —

fa, *v.* become, cook, prepare, translate, change, alter, turn round. 1706, 1707, 1710, 1883.
fa dʒì, *v.* go round. 1831.
fa ndʒēngènè, *v.* spread (as disease or fire). 1979.
fa ódóró nə̀, *v.* make red. 1573.
fa ōndō nə̀, *v.* become short. 1609.
fa ò?ò, *v.* contradict. 1331.
fa tɔ́, *v.* become.
fa tìndìwírí, *v.* become round. 1607.
fa tʃápá gbɔ̀, *v.* abandon. 1209.
fa tʃɔ́lɔ́, *v.* translate.
fàngú, *n.* gruel, pap. 0897, 0909.
farà ūzū, *v.* deceive. 1333.
fe gbàgà, *v.* shell (groundnuts). 0983.
félò, *n.* iron (for ironing clothes) (loan from French *fer*).
fɔ̄, *ben.* to (a person or animal), indicates the beneficiary of an action.
fó, *loc.* up.
fōòtʃē, *n.* fever.
fōwò, *n.* hot. *Morph:* (?)-òwò. 1658.
fu, *v.* be rotten, smell (bad). 1678, 1744.
fùfú, *n.* red ant.
fúmù, *n.* Protestant.
fùngà, *n.* hunch (of hunchback), bump (on back). 0052, 1614.
fūrūtʃā, *n.* soap, foam. 0673.

— g —

ga, *v.* be good, be beautiful, be pleasant, be sweet. 1632, 1673.
gà-, *Variant:* gá- *prep.* towards, to (cf. Cloarec-Heiss 1986:272).
ga tɔ́, *v.* please, satisfy. 1260.
gàdɛ̀, *quest.* what. 1511.
gàfūrū, *n.* mortar. 1089.
gàlá, *n.* market (loan from Sango?). 0871.
gálàfó, *loc.* up. *Morph:* gà-àlà-fó.
gálàngú, *loc.* to the water. *Morph:* gà-àlà-úngú.
gàlɔ́, *prep.* into. *Morph:* gà-lɔ́.

gámāngbá, *prep.* behind. *Morph:* **gà-māngbá.**
gámə̄, *loc.* here. *Morph:* **gà-mə̄.**
gambà, *v.* honor, admire. 1243, 1401, 1622.
gànjá, *n.* branch. 0628.
gàndə́, *prep.* place. *Morph:* **gà-ndə́.**
gándìrì, *prep.* side. *Morph:* **gà-ndìrì.** 1772.
gàngā, *n.* calf. 0470.
gàpá, *prep.* on. *Morph:* **gà-pá.**
garà, *v.* cut (grass/hay, with a knife/coupe-coupe), mow, weed (with a machete). 0991.
Gārābà-Mòléngè, *pn.* the Mono-Garaba dialect and people.
gàràndʒà, *n.* type of traditional dance.
gàràngà, *n.* manioc, cassava. 0594.
gàsə́, *prep.* in. *Morph:* **gà-ə́sə́.**
gásə̀ndá, *loc.* in the house. *Morph:* **gà-ə́sə́-àndà.**
gátà, *quest.* where. *Morph:* **gà-táà.**
gàtə́, *prep.* place. *Morph:* **gà-tə́.**
gàtí, *loc.* down. *Morph:* **gà-tí**(?)
gàtʃá, *prep.* bottom of. *Morph:* **gà-tʃá.**
gàtʃákùdú, *prep.* under. *Morph:* **gà-tʃá-kùdú.**
gàúʃú, *loc.* outside. *Morph:* **gà-úʃú.**
gáūtʃū, *prep.* in front of. *Morph:* **gà-ūtʃū.**
gàvà, *n.* panther.
gàzá, *n.* 1) circumcision. 2) one who has completed the circumcision rite.
gàzá āgā, *n.* type of circumcision dance (lit., horn circumcision).
gàzá jāʃē, *n.* female circumcision.
gàzá mbàlà, *n.* type of circumcision dance (lit., elephant circumcision).
gàzá tʃálàkpí, *n.* medical circumcision (non-ceremonial, done by a nurse).

gázə̀, *loc.* there. *Morph:* **gà-zə̀.**
gàʔé, *loc.* there [imprecise]. *Morph:* **gà-ʔé**(?).
gèlè, *adj.* left. 1764.
gènè, *n.* stranger, guest. 0285.
gerə̀, *v.* grow, grow up, sprout. 0650, 1240, 1729.
gerə̀ ngwàrə̀, *v.* grow (of plants). 0649.
getà, *v.* chase away, knock down, blow down. 1805, 1904, 1924.
gi, *v.* 1) push. 2) return (something). 1267.
gi jāʃē, *v.* annul a marriage.
gi kūɗā, *v.* pay (debt). 1139.
gi ə́tʃə́ ə̀rə̀, *v.* thank. 1358.
gi ūzū gáūtʃū nə̀, *v.* help. 1242.
gi ʔò, *v.* answer (a call). 1322.
gi ʔò fə̄, *v.* answer, reply. 1323.
gɨ, *v.* 1) sow, scatter seeds. 2) cause to defecate. 3) carve, file. 1106.
gɨ ɔ̄jɔ̄, *v.* work wood. 1119.
gɨ tìndìwǐrí, *v.* make round, cut. 1110.
gɨ tʃápá, *v.* plane off. 1115.
gɨ tʃə́lə́, *v.* hollow out. 1115.
gɨ úkú, *v.* set (trap), trap (animal), build a trap. 1061, 1065.
gíríʃì, *n.* bile, gall bladder. 0011, 0044, 0110.
gja, *v.* stir (with difficulty), do something repeatedly (with perseverance).
go, *v.* sprinkle (e.g., dust). 1980.
Gōbú, *pn.* The Gobu language and people.
gòjó, *Variant:* **gòjé.** *n.* goiter, crop (bird). 0211, 0531.
gòndá, *n.* axe. 1028.
gorò, *v.* touch.
gōrōkpā, *n.* cave. *Morph:* **ōgōrō-ākpā**(?). 0659.
gōrōmàmú, *n.* vagina. *Variant:* **ōgōrō-màmú.** 0101.

gōrūjū, *Variant:* **ōgōrō ūjū.** *n.* anus. *Morph:* **ōgōrō-ūjū.** 0003.
gósá, *n.* type of green, traditional Mono food.
gotè, *Variant:* **gotè də̀ kódà.** *v.* kneel. 1835.
gɔ, *v.* bend down. 1794.
gɔ gàpá, *v.* lean (become leaning). 1736.
gɔ gàtí, *v.* become bent. 1709.
gɔ gàtʃákūdú, *v.* bow, bend. 1796.
gɔrɔ̀, *v.* drive away, send away, chase. 1228, 1270, 1804.
gɔrɔ̀ ékpé íʃírí, *v.* exorcise, drive out a devil. 1187.
gu, *v.* 1) be (existential, used in the negative). 2) return (back to where you started). 3) curse. 4) thatch. 1829.
gu dàá, *v.* say goodbye, take leave of. 1239.
gu ɔ́sɔ́, *v.* despise. 1413.
gu ōgō, *v.* move away, migrate. 1847.
gu óʃó, *v.* insult. 1343.
gūgàtí, *n.* prostitute. *Morph:* **gu-gàtí.** 0384.
gumà, *v.* prepare, repair, fix.
gumà ə̀rə̀, *v.* arrange. 1404.
gumà sɔ́ àjàrə̀, *v.* tend animals. 0986.
gumà sɔ́ ə̀rə̀, *v.* store. 1016.
gumà tʃándɔ́, *v.* fix, mend. 1108, 1112.
gumà zɨ́ɨ́, *v.* flatten. 1937.
gurù, *v.* fade. 1932.
gúrúdàmbá, *n.* type of cat. 0467.
gūsū, *n.* grass (in general, all types), grassland, bush country. 0579, 0658, 0679.
gūsū ngālābò, *n.* pipe-stem. 0827.
gūzà, *n.* mouse. 0443.
gwa, *v.* pack (a package), wrap up. 1011, 1999.

— gb —

gba, *v.* 1) moisten, be wet, rot, wet, immerse. 2) push down on ground (like grass). 1703, 1996.
gbá, *n.* perfect. 1672.
gba də̀ úngú, *v.* become wet. 1756.
gbáāmbā nə̀, *adv.* purposeless, worthless, empty. *Morph:* **ágbá-āmbā.** 1502, 1645.
gbābù, *n.* giddiness. 1365.
gbádà, *n.* crippled (in the feet), lame. *Morph:* **ágbá-àdà.** 0235, 0239.
gbādāvū, *n.* fatness. *Morph:* **gbādā-ɨ̄vɨ̄.** 1576.
gbàdò, *n.* grub.
gbàdʒà ngùbí, *pn.* May.
gbàdʒàdʒà, *n.* parcel of land, fence. 0807.
gbàdʒéè, *n.* pineapple. 0615.
gbàgà, *n.* ground nut, peanut. 0602.
gbàgò, *n.* tobacco pipe. 0851.
gbàgūrū, *n.* proverb. 1309.
gbāgbā, *n.* camp (for travelers), cattle pen, courtyard, enclosure, farm (loan from Sango?). 0857, 0858, 0860, 0863, 0865.
gbàjà, *n.* type of traditional dance.
gbákānɔ́, *n.* crippled (in the arms). *Morph:* **ágbá-kānɔ́.**
gbākíndɨ, *n.* cripple. 0278. *Morph:* **āgbā-kɨndɨ(?).**
gbākòtò, *n.* anthill. 0548. *Morph:* **āgbā-kòtò.**
gbákòtò, *n.* latrine, outhouse.
gbàlákà, *n.* drying rack.
gbālóbà, *n.* rag. 0831. *Morph:* **āgbā-lóbà.**
gbāndà, *n.* temporary shelter in field or forest, hut. *Morph:* **ágbá-àndà.** 0816.
gbándà, *n.* net. 1043, 1045.

gbándà àgjàngú, *n.* fishing net. 1038.
gbándá dàndòrò, *n.* spider's web. 0557.
gbāndà vūrū, *n.* whirlwind.
gbàngàwò, *n.* gum disease.
gbāngbālé, *adv.* baldness. 0106, 0127.
gbarà, *v.* announce, preach.
gbarà òʔò, *v.* prophesy. 1348.
gbàràgà, *n.* falling trap. 1051.
gbārə̀, *n.* utensil, dish, furniture. 0939.
gbārə̀ ōlō, *n.* bed.
gbázə̀, *time.* day after day after tomorrow.
gbe, *v.* think, believe.
gbe də̀, *v.* look after, believe, need, remember, think. 1253, 1406, 1433, 1441, 1446.
gbe də̀ kə́mbə̀rə̀, *v.* plan. 1436.
gbe tə́, *v.* want, desire. 1449.
gbe tʃə́lə́, *v.* hope.
gbètʃə́lə́, *n.* hope, oath, idea, thought. *Morph:* **gbe-tʃə́-lə́.** 1306, 1366.
gbō, *adv.* the sound that a drum makes when it is hit.
gbògbò, *n.* mat. 0824.
gbókū, *adj.* dried.
gbōlò, *n.* child. 0257, 0368.
gbōlò jākōʃē, *n.* boy, young man, son. 0256, 0312, 0366.
gbōlò jāʃē, *n.* girl, young woman. 0263, 0313.
gbòngó, *n.* zombie.
gborò, *v.* grow (plural).
gbóró, *adj.* holy.
gbotà, *Variant:* **gbotɔ̀.** *v.* 1) pull. 2) drag. 3) record. 1818, 1854.
gbotà àwátèrə̀, *v.* take out (honey from hive). 0985.
gbotà ə̀rə̀, *v.* take away. 1286.
gbotà lə́, *v.* pull out. 1855.
gbotà tʃə́lə́ úwú, *v.* lengthen. 1606.
gbotà úngú, *v.* take out of water. 0961.
gbɔ, *v.* 1) receive, find, get, succeed. 2) be difficult, be hard (physically). 3) become old, grow, be fully developed, become mature, become ripe. 0131, 1122, 1236, 1282, 1417, 1642, 1738, 1739, 1740.
gbɔ àlà, *v.* pay attention, take care. 1435.
gbɔ ə̀rə̀, *v.* receive. 1265.
gbɔ ndə́, *v.* protect, guard, domesticate, tame, keep, put away, bless. 0971, 1248, 1959.
gbɔ ndə́ àgjà, *v.* herd (cattle or sheep). 0977.
gbɔ ndə́ gbòlò, *v.* bring up (a child). 1219.
gbɔ tə́, *v.* meet.
gbɔ ùkù, *v.* hurt oneself. 0247.
gbɔ̀gbɔ́, *n.* force, strength. 1623, 1694.
gbɔgbɔ̀ tə́ʃó, *v.* hasten, hurry. 1833.
gbə́kóté, *n.* fierceness. *Morph:* **gbɔ-(?).** 1615.
gbə́kū ə̀ʃɔ̀, *n.* clod. 0660.
gbə́kūmù, *adj.* difficult. 1642.
gbə́kwákwá, *adj.* hard. 1657.
gbɔlɔ̄, *n.* road.
gbɔ̀ngə́gbə́, *n.* conclusion.
gbə̀ʃɔ̀, *n.* bedroom, room. 0856, 0877.
gbotə́ ə̀rə̀, *v.* sieze (by force, e.g., military). 1060.
gbə́zū, *Variant:* **gbózū.** *n.* elder, parent, old, adult. *Morph:* **ə́gbə́-ūzū.** 0135, 0253, 0293, 0375, 1655.
gbə́zū ōgō, *n.* chief, headman. 0373.
gbúrúwā, *adv.* lasting.

Wordlist

— h —

háàō, *adv.* in vain, without success.
hàgà, *adv.* hard, wide. 1604.
hàò, *adv.* brightly.
háò, *adv.* very fast, without reflecting on what you are doing.
hàrá, *adv.* giant, high. 0284, 1590.
héré, *adv.* sharp. 1683.
hérélá, *n.* gourd rattle.
hérélá màndà, *n.* lock.
herə̀ ōpōrō, *v.* hatch. 0566.
hójá ò?ò, *n.* whisper. 1316.
hɔ̀rɔ̀gɔ̀, *adv.* hidden, safe, well-protected.
hwìjà, *adv.* hot.

— i —

i, cf. **ɓi.**
íjā, *n.* mother. cf. **àjī.** 0348.
íjí, *n.* fool, madness, mad. 1371, 1388.
íjí wólé, *n.* shaft (of arrow). 1047.
īkī, *adj.* sharp.
íkpí, *adj.* tart.
ílí, *adj.* deep.
īmī, *adj.* thick.
ímbí, *adj.* white, off-white, silver.
ímbí ɔ́kɔ́, *n.* color of white man's skin, pink. 1564.
ímbí ɔ̀ʃɔ̀, *n.* whitewash.
īndʒī, *n.* blood. 0013.
índʒí, *n.* seed, grain (for sowing).
índʒí àlà, *n.* pupil of eye. 0077.
índʒí kɔ́sō, *n.* pumpkin pip. 0638.
índʒí léjō, *n.* kernel. 0632.
īngbī, *n.* fish trap.
īpī, *n.* dance. 1144.
ípí, *n.* alcoholic beverage.
īpī āgā, *n.* "horn" male circumcision dance.
īpī àmbàlà, *n.* a traditional dance.
īpī gàzá, *n.* circumcision dance.
īpī mbàlà, *n.* "elephant" male circumcision dance.
ípí mbùndʒú, *n.* beer, mead. 0882, 0902.
iʃi, *n.* thorn, splinter. 0645, 0844.
íʃírí, *n.* shadow, image, spirit, drawing, photograph. 0712, 1179.
íʃírí jápū, *n.* moonlight. 0747.
íʃírí ūzū, *n.* soul. 1178.
ītʃī, *n.* song. 1155.
īʒī, *n.* tooth, tusk (of warthog). 0098, 0545.
īʒī mbàlà, *n.* elephant's tusk. 0534.

— ɨ —

ɨ̀dɨ̀, *Variant:* **ɨ̀dɨ̀.** *n.* horn, antler. 0541.
ɨgɨ, *n.* neck. 0071.
ɨkɨ, *n.* crying, groaning, request, sound. 1298, 1310, 1311.
ɨkɨ jāvóró, *n.* dog bark.
ɨkɨrɨ, *n.* plant stalk.
ɨlɨ, *n.* sweat.
ímí, *n.* thick. 1600.
ɨmbɨlɨ, *n.* needle. 1072.
ɨ̀ndɨ̀, *n.* stupidity. 1376, 1395.
ɨ̀ngɨ̀, *n.* younger sibling. 0370.
ɨ̀ngɨ̀ àbá, *n.* father's brother. 0331, 0359.
ɨ̀ngɨ̀ àjī, *n.* aunt (mother's sister). 0351, 0359.
ɨ̀ngɨ̀ júngɔ́, *n.* younger sister. 0365.
ɨngɨrɨ, *adj.* long, tall. *n.* noise. 1305, 1595.
ɨngɨrɨ jāvūrū, *n.* thunder. 0758.
ɨngɨrɨ kàmbà, *n.* sword, machete. 1048.
ɨngɨrɨ nə̀, *n.* length. 1578.
ɨngbɨ, *n.* metal rattle with wooden handle, bell. 0794.
ɨngbɨrɨ, *Variant:* **ɨngbɨrɨ.** *n.* salt. 0911, 0956.

íngbíʃó, *n.* light. 0688. *Morph:* íngbí-óʃó.
ípɨ, *Variant:* **ūpū**. *n.* matter, affair, truth. 1192.
írɨ, *adv.* hard.
ívɨ, *Variant:* **ūvū**. *n.* abdomen, stomach, belly. 0001, 0010.
ìzì, *n.* 1) cold. 2) air (breathed). 0651, 0734, 1638.
íʔìrì, *n.* name. 1303.

— j —

ja, *v.* singe. 1974.
ja ndá, *v.* hesitate. 1421.
ja tɔ́, *v.* spend time, lie down, rest. 1276, 1666.
ja tɔ́ óʃó, *v.* rest. 0182.
jābó, *n.* member. *Morph:* ājā-óbó.
jābùrù, *n.* goat. 0482.
jābùrù tàbà, *Variant:* **jābùrù tàɓà**. *n.* sheep. 0481, 0492, 0494.
jāgbɔ́zū, *n.* old man. *Morph:* jā(?)-gbɔ́zū. 0294.
jājō, *n.* baby sitter.
jàká, *n.* marsh, pool. 0690, 0701.
jākɨndɨ, *n.* garden. *Morph:* ājā-kɨndɨ. 0894.
jākóró, *n.* snake. 0457.
jākōʃē, *n.* male.
jākōʃē kàngà, *n.* male slave. 0292.
jākōʃē kùzū, *n.* dead man. 0260.
jākótʃā jābùrù, *n.* lamb. 0488.
jākɔ̄nɔ́, *Variant:* **jākānɛ́, jɔ̄kɔ̄nɔ́**. *n.* finger. *Morph:* ājā-kānɔ́. 0037.
Jākpà, *pn.* the Yakpa language and people.
jālāwū, *Variant:* **jālàwū**. *n.* grinding stone. 0928, 0938.
jambà, *v.* learn. 1428. *v.* try, test. 1447.

jāmbùrù, *n.* 1) cooking stones (usually three, on top of which the pot is put), fireplace, brazier (*bambola*). 2) family, clan. 0923, 0926.
jānū, *Variant:* **jɔ̄nū**. *n.* bird, fowl. 0401, 0418.
jāngā, *n.* joy.
jāngá, *n.* friend. 0262.
jāngàngú, *n.* brook, stream. 0657.
jāngōpé, *n.* fingernail, claw. 0530.
jāngɔ̄tō, *n.* chick. *Morph:* ājā-ngɔ̄tō. 0475.
jāngbā, *n.* type of traditional dance.
japà, *v.* alter (clothes). 1707.
jápū, *Variant:* **jépū**. *n.* moon, month. 0692, 0771.
jápū ɓándɔ́ zìjénā, *n.* full moon. 0677.
jārākō, *n.* iron.
jārɛ̀, *n.* livestock, e.g., cattle, domesticated animal. 0473.
jāsā, *n.* spring. 0717.
jásù, *n.* rat. 0455.
jāsūrū, *n.* orphan. 0296.
jāʃē, *n.* woman, female. 0268.
jāʃē kàngà, *n.* female slave. 0283.
jāʃē kōjà, *n.* widow. 0311.
jāʃē mārā, *n.* barren woman. 0271.
jāʃí, *n.* cup, bowl.
jāvóró, *n.* dog. 0478.
jāvūrū, *n.* rain, flash of lightning (thunderbolt). 0739, 0748, 0751.
jāwāzà, *n.* old woman. 0295.
jāwè, *pn.* January.
jāwò, *n.* firewood. *Morph:* (?)-òwò. 0927.
jāwūrù, *n.* girl.
jāwɛ̌lè, *n.* catfish.
jáʔɔ̀ngɔ̀, *n.* eel. 0415.
jē, *pron.* third-person singular possessive pronoun.
jē, *conj.* 1) but. 2) and.
jé, *emph.* affirmative, already.

je kóté, *v.* polish, make smooth. 1014, 1745.
jéka, *conj.* 1) then. 2) still. 0780.
jekè, *v.* sieve. 0957.
jèngà, *n.* celebration (loan from Lingala *eyenga*).
jerə̀, *v.* have ringworm. 0226.
jèròwá, *num.* hundred. 1555.
jèròwá bīʃà, *num.* two hundred. 1556.
Jésù, *pn.* Jesus (loan from Lingala *Yesu*).
ji, *v.* enter something into something
ji àngbà, *v.* hate. 1420.
ji gálà, *v.* dip, soak. 1929, 1976.
ji ndə́, *v.* like (something), love, want, desire, accept, agree, admit (to a wrong), wish. 1402, 1449, 1451.
ji ndə́ òʔò, *v.* accept, receive, take, agree. 1212.
ji sə́, *Variant:* **ji sə́rə̀.** *v.* teach, guide, lead, show. 1241, 1251, 1274, 1287.
ji tə́, *v.* get used to.
ji tə̀ àgə́gə̀rə̀, *v.* exchange. 1233.
ji úwú, *v.* thread (beads). 1076.
jìmà, *adv.* slowly. 1784.
jìní, *n.* husband's mother, daughter-in-law. 0326.
jiwà, *v.* lose, be lost, disappear. 1930, 1950.
jiwà tə́nə̀, *v.* hide. 1422.
jìwú, *Variant:* **jùwú.** *n.* children of mother's brothers, nephew, niece. 0324, 0356, 0357.
jo, *v.* abstain.
jo bīwā, *v.* blow nose. 0151.
jo ngūʃī, *v.* spit. 0191.
jòmbá, *n.* type of cat. 0407, 0467.
jòngómbè, *n.* vulture. 0463.
jɔ, *v.* buy. 1134.
jɔ kə́zìrì, *v.* purchase food. 1142.
jɔ ndə́, *v.* ask, need something. 1325.

jɔ̄gbɔ̄dɔ̄ lóbà, *n.* robe (man's gown). 0834.
jɔ̄kɔ̄dɔ̀, *Variant:* **jɔ̄kɔ̄dɔ̀.** *n.* toe. 0096.
jɔrò tʃə́lə́, *v.* stretch. 1987.
jɔ̄rɔ̄ngɔ̄, *n.* globe shaped. 1587.
jɔ̄ʔɔ́, *n.* cricket. 0506.
ju, *v.* 1) ask. 2) become cooked. 1718.
ju ə̀rə̀, *v.* boil. 0941.
ju ípí, *v.* ferment (alcohol). 1725.
jùgú, *n.* wind. 0731, 0759.
júngɔ́, *n.* man's sister, woman's sibling. 0319, 0361, 0362.
jurù, *v.* stretch out.
jutɔ̀, *v.* wash. 1995.
jutɔ̀ lóbà, *v.* wash clothes. 1024.

— k —

ka, *v.* be finished, finish, used up, cease, pull up, come to a halt, wait, take heed. 1701, 1716, 1726, 1727, 1856.
ka, *v.* hurt, sell.
ká, *conj.* so.
ka gàpá, *v.* decide. 1412.
ka làfó, *v.* stand. 1278.
ka ndʒí, *v.* become straight. 1752.
ka pá ūzū, *v.* order (someone to do something). 1346.
ka tə́, *v.* leave, finish. 1838, 1839.
kàbá ngímá, *n.* palm-wine. 0908.
kádá, *n.* oil, grease. 0906.
kàdà ājā nə̀, *n.* animal fetus.
kàdá gbòlò, *n.* human fetus. 0036.
kádá ngímá, *n.* palm oil. 0907.
kàdángérē, *n.* gecko. 0421.
káɗàwú, *n.* hiccough. 0214.
kàféè, *n.* coffee (loan from French *café*). 0596.
Kàgà, *pn.* the Mono-Kaga dialect and people.
kàgà, *n.* mountain, hill. 0694.

kakàrà, *v.* dig up (yams), snatch. 0970, 1869.
kàkílí, *n.* basket. 0810.
kākó, *n.* leaf. 0633.
kākó dɔ̀ngɔ́, *n.* vegetable. 0913.
kākó gbàngwà, *n.* notebook, paper.
kākó màngé, *n.* leaf of corn plant. 0634.
kākó ngímá, *n.* leaf of palm. 0635.
kākó ɔ̄jɔ̄, *n.* leaf.
kàlábí, *n.* head pad. 0813.
kàlàkpà, *n.* flat. 1586.
kàlángò, *n.* plate. 0934.
kālāwō, *Variant:* **kàlàwò.** *n.* machete, bush-knife. 1033.
kama, *num.* hundred (loan from Lingala *kámá*).
kàmàjū, *n.* dung beetle. 0507.
kàmbà, *n.* knife. 0929.
kānɔ́, *Variant:* **kāné.** *n.* arm, hand. 0004, 0047, 0811.
kānɔ́ bàlē, *n.* fist (lit., one hand). 0039.
kānɔ́ gèlè, *n.* left hand. 0060.
kānɔ́ jākōʃē, *Variant:* **kāné jākōʃē.** *adj.* right.
kānɔ́ jāʃē, *adj.* left.
kàngà, *n.* slave, captive, prisoner, deacon. 0276, 0299, 0303.
kāngā, *Variant:* **tʃápá kāngā.** *n.* shoulder, upper arm. 0082, 0100.
kārā, *n.* stranger. 0305.
kàràvā, *n.* charm, fetish. 1165.
kásō, *n.* gourd, squash.
katɔ̀, *Variant:* **katè.** *v.* wait (for). 1291, 1448.
kātʃā, *adv.* quickly, early, fast. 0769, 1649.
kātʃātʃā, *time.* long ago.
kátʃū ɔ̄jɔ̄, *n.* bark.
kawà, *v.* snap, break. 1912.
kàwǎ, *n.* gruel. 0897.
káʔjà, *n.* weaver-bird. 0465.

káʔjá, *n.* paddle. 0825.
kē, *deic.* this.
kekà ōpōrō, *v.* hatch. 0566.
kèlèkpā, *n.* bed, village bed made out of bamboo. 0792.
kéngbā, *n.* alone. 1628.
kèrèdʒà, *n.* type of broom (for outside).
kewě, *v.* fold. 1940.
kewě àmà lóbà, *v.* hem. 1074.
kewě gàpá, *v.* bend back. 1793.
kèwětò, *n.* weak. 1702.
kə̀-, *cond.* prefix for marking a conditional phrase.
kə́-, *inf.* 1) prefix indicating infinitive form of the verb. 2) nominalizer that turns a verb into a noun.
kə́dà ə̀rə̀, *n.* mold. 0581.
kə́dɨ ə̀rə̀, *n.* number. 1521.
kə́dòngà, *n.* honor. *Morph:* **kə́-dongà.**
kə́dʒà tʃápá àndà, *Variant:* **kə́dʒà tʃápá nə̀.** *n.* plaster, roughcasting. 1092.
kə́gā, *n.* beauty.
kə́gbɔ̀ kōwō, *n.* payment. 1126.
kə́jìndə́rə̀, *n.* kindness. 1199.
kə́jìndə́ʔò, *n.* agreement. 1295.
kə́kàrà, *n.* cease (of rains). 0732.
kə́kò tə́ àzū, *n.* marriage. 1201.
kə̀léngɔ̀ngɔ̀, *n.* chameleon. 0406.
kə̀lɔ́, *Variant:* **kèlɔ́.** *n.* spoon. 0937.
kə́lì ɔ̀lɔ̀, *n.* sunset. 0779.
kə́mɔ̀, *n.* fatigue. 0209.
kə́nà, *n.* going.
kə́ndʒà, *n.* vomiting.
kə́ngáàngà, *n.* acidity. 1610.
kə́pè ɨzɨ̀, *n.* wind (weak). 0731.
kə̀rə̀ná, *adv.* broken, crushed.
kə́tò ɨʔɨrɨ, *n.* splendor. 1622.
kə́tò lɔ́ ɨʔɨrɨ, *n.* namesake (lit., originate from name). 0355.
kə́tòrə̀, *n.* gift.

kə́tɔ̀ ndàwò, *n.* blacksmithing. 1206.
kə́tùrù tə́nə̀, *n.* movement. 1768.
kə̀vū, *Variant:* kə̀vɨ́, kùvū. *n.* stomach (organ). *Morph:* ə̀kə̀(?)-ɨ̀vɨ̀. 0090.
kə́wò ófó, *n.* hot weather. 0745, 1616.
kə́wò tʃə́lə́ ɔ́kɔ́, *n.* fever (not malaria). 0210.
kə́wū, *Variant:* kə́wù fà. *n.* breath. 0107.
kə́wùrə̀, *n.* vision (supernatural apparition). *Morph:* kə́-wu-ə̀rə̀. 1180.
kə́wùsə́rə̀, *n.* knowledge. *Morph:* kə́-wu-ə́sə́-ə̀rə̀. 1368.
kə́wùtà ɔ̀lɔ̀, *time.* sunrise. 0778.
kə́zɨ̀rɨ̀, *n.* food. *Morph:* kə́-zɨ-ə̀rə̀. 0892.
kə́zɨ̀rɨ̀ àdɨ̀là, *n.* evening meal. 1194.
kə́zō gàràngà, *Variant:* kə́zō də̀ gàràngà. *n.* bread. 0883.
kə́ʔòmà lɔ̀sù, *n.* nausea. 0221.
ki, *v.* be sharp.
ki àmà, *v.* sharpen (as a knife). 1018.
kɨ́dàlà, *cf.* àkɨ́dàlà.
kìngì, *n.* hamper, basket. 0810, 0916.
kìngìw̌ɨ́rɨ́, *n.* round. 1597.
kìtì, *n.* squirrel. 0459.
kɨ, *v.* cry, weep. 0167.
kɨ fə̄, *v.* pray. 1347.
kɨ ɨ́kɨ, *v.* groan. 1338.
kɨ jāvóró, *v.* bark (as dog). 0560.
kɨ ɔ́kɔ̄ ngɔ̄tō, *v.* crow (as a rooster). 0562.
kɨ tɔ́ ə́sə́, *v.* suffer. 1445.
kɨkɨ̀lɨ̀, *adj.* heavy, serious, dull. 1589.
kɨkɨ̀lɨ̀ ə̀rə̀, *n.* load. 0822.
kɨndɨ, *n.* garden, field, agriculture. 0669, 0963

kɨrɨngbādē, *n.* 1) wasp. 2) quiver. 0527, 1046.
kjākjā, *adj.* small.
ko, *v.* 1) take, get (more than one thing). 2) give, put (more than one thing). 3) sprout. 4) fight. 5) bother.
ko àlà tə́, *v.* watch. 1450.
ko də̀ ɔ́gbɔ́, *v.* plunder (a town). 1261.
ko ə̀rə̀ jāʃē, *v.* give bridewealth. 1136.
ko gàúʃú, *v.* take out. 1989.
ko gálà kógbà, *v.* store up. 1281.
ko gàlə́, *v.* load. 1844.
ko gápá, *v.* add. 1400.
ko gàtɨ́, *v.* lower, unload. 1845, 1885.
ko kōwō, *v.* pay (for goods or services). 1140.
ko ngèndʒà, *v.* pay (wages or fine). 1141.
ko ngwàrə̀, *v.* germinate. 0648.
ko tɔ̀ gándɨ̀rɨ̀, *v.* put side by side. 1438.
kòɓà, *Variant:* kòɓà. *n.* illness, sickness, malady, evil spirit. 0216, 0242.
kòɓà ɨ̀zɨ̀, *n.* malaria (fever). 0220.
kòɓà kōtā, *n.* leprosy. 0219.
kòɓà lòsù, *n.* heartburn.
kòɓà mbàlà, *n.* elephantiasis. 0208.
kōdà, *n.* knee. 0058.
kògwà, *n.* box. 0796.
kógbà, *n.* granary. 0896.
kójā, *n.* penis. 0075.
kòkò, *n.* quiet, silent. 1674, 1685.
kōló, *Variant:* kə̄ló, kōtə́, kə̄tə́. *func.* only.
kómá, *n.* nest. 0555.
kómádɨ̄rɨ̀, *n.* hawk. 0427.
kōmē, *n.* iguana. 0431.
kòmbá, *n.* guinea fowl. 0424.
kómbēlē, *n.* butterfly. 0502.

kòné, *Variant:* kònɔ́. *n.* vein. 0102.
kòndāngà, *n.* trouble. 1377.
kondʒà, *v.* rule over. 1268.
kòndʒà, *n.* woven mat. 0824.
kōngō, *n.* crab. 0409.
kōpū, *pn.* September.
kórógbà, *n.* pangolin (scaly anteater). 0447.
kōʃē, *Variant:* kōsē. *n.* war. 1208.
kōtā, *n.* 1) large river, sea. 2) pearl. 0704, 0710, 1066.
kótɔ́, *n.* body. *Morph:* ɔ́kɔ́-ɔ́tɔ́.
kòtò, *n.* small hill. 0682.
kòtóó, *quest.* how many, how much, how. 1495, 1496.
kówà, *n.* baby sling. 0790.
kōwō, *n.* iron, metal, gold, iron ore, lead, money, large scale war. 0678, 0683, 0820.
kōwō àméndè, *n.* tin. 0849.
kōʔjà, *n.* fruit bat. 0399.
kɔ, *v.* harvest, reap, gather, weave (tissue). 0976, 1058, 1077.
kɔ́, *Variant:* kɔ́kɔ́. *func.* all. 1489. cf. Kamanda (1998:326).
kɔ àlà, *v.* wink at. 0203.
kɔ léjɔ̄, *v.* gather (fruit). 0973.
kɔ tʃɔ́lɔ́ óʃó, *v.* settle dispute. 1273.
kɔ́dò, *n.* type of caterpillar.
kɔ̄dʒɔ́, *n.* lizard. 0437.
kɔ́ɗɔ̀, *n.* monkey. 0442.
kɔ̀kɔ́, *n.* termite. 0524.
kɔkɔ̀rɔ̀ tɔ́, *v.* jam. 1734.
kɔ̀nɔ́, *n.* hippopotamus, rhinoceros. 0429, 0456.
kɔ̄ngɔ̄dùrù, *n.* mantis, wasp. 0518, 0527.
kɔ̄ngɔ̄tō, *n.* rooster (cock). *Morph:* kɔ̄(?)-ngɔ̄tō. 0493.
kɔ́ngbɔ́ ndàwò, *n.* bellows. *Morph:* kɔ́-ngbɔ ndàwò. 1081.
kɔ̀pù, *n.* silk cotton tree, kapok. 0586.

kɔrɔ̀, *v.* open. 1671, 1849.
kɔrɔ̀ àmà, *v.* open the mouth. 0179.
kɔrɔ̀ màndà, *v.* open (set ajar) (as a door). 1010.
kɔ̄rɔ̄jɔ̄ òvòrò, *n.* backbone. *Morph:* ɔ́kɔ̄rɔ̄-ɔ́jɔ̄ òvòrò. 0007.
kɔrɔ̀nɔ̀, *v.* rub between the fingers, rub hands, rub body (e.g., when washing yourself), crush (with the hands). 0183, 1898, 1964.
kɔ̀sò, *n.* pig, hog (loan from French *cochon*?). 0486, 0491.
kɔ́sō, *n.* squash.
kɔ́tʃū, *n.* bark (of tree). 0625.
ku, *v.* press, push, squeeze. 1857, 1981, 1983.
kùdú, *n.* hole, pit. 0554, 0698.
kùdú òvòrò, *n.* small of back. 0088.
kùdú úngú, *n.* well. 0855.
kūdā, *n.* debt. 1121.
kūkū, *n.* bedbug, flea. 0400, 0508.
kùlù, *adj.* big.
kùlúngūrū, *Variant:* kùlíngūrū. *n.* centipede, millipede. 0504, 0519.
kūmù, *Variant:* kūmà. *n.* head, top. 0048, 1778.
kūmù àndà, *n.* roof. 1095.
kūmù àndà ēbē, *n.* thatched roof. 1099.
kūnì, *adj.* right (direction). *n.* right hand. 0079, 1771.
kùndī, *n.* harp.
kùndú, *prep.* in front of.
kurù, *v.* give out, share, divide, grow thin, grow lean. 1224, 1591.
kurù tʃɔ́lɔ́, *v.* separate, become separated, spread everywhere. 1742, 1872, 1970.
kūrūdʒá, *n.* thin (not fat). 1601, 1603.
kùsɔ́nɛ̀, *n.* barrier.
kùtú, *func.* only. 1670.
kùtùrù jāwò, *n.* log. 0689.
kútʃá, *n.* mosquito. 0520.

kūvū, cf. kə̀vū.
kúwùsɔ́ʔò, *n.* wisdom. *Morph:* kɔ́-wu-ɔ́sɔ́-òʔò. 1379.
kùzū, cf. òkò ūzū.
kúzū, *n.* semen. 0117.
kwa, *v.* go back to, return. 1827.
kwákwá, *n.* grasshopper. 0511.

— kp —

kpa, *v.* run, flee, run away. 1863, 1864.
kpá-, *rep.* again. 1488.
kpa dʒì, *v.* surround. 1785.
kpa ndàjì, *v.* slide on water. 1824.
kpàhà, *adv.* wide open.
kpálá, *adv.* something done regularly.
kpalàkà, *v.* spill (liquid). 1870.
kpàràkà, *pn.* July.
kpārāmēnā, *n.* brain. 0017.
kpàsùrù, *n.* slipperiness. 1621.
kpàtà, *n.* mud. 0695.
kpēkpérɔ́, *n.* joint. 0056.
kpēkpérɔ́ kānɔ́, *n.* wrist. 0105.
kpɔ́-, *prep.* just in (cf. Cloarec-Heiss 1986:272).
kpɔ́ə̀dòrò, *adv.* naked. 0134.
kpɔ́kē, *time.* a few days ago. *loc.* here. 1762.
kpɔ̄līndūvū, *n.* kidney.
kpɔ́mə̀, *loc.* there (refers back to a previously mentioned place). *Morph:* kpɔ́-mə̀.
kpɔ́pá, *prep.* in the presence of. *Morph:* kpɔ́-pá.
kpɔ́sɔ́, *prep.* in. *Morph:* kpɔ́-ɔ́sɔ́.
kpɔ́ʃèkē, *Variant:* kpɔ́ʃè, kpɔ́səkɔ̄. *time.* today, day, daytime. 0767, 0782.
kpɔ́tà, *quest.* where. *Morph:* kpɔ́-táà. 1513.
kpɔ́tə̀, *time.* just happened (within the past few minutes). *Morph:* kpɔ́-tə̀.
kpɔ́tɔ́ àzū bīʃà, *Variant:* zàzū bīʃà. *num.* forty.
kpɔ́tɔ́ àzū bīʃà də̀ ndʒòkpá, *num.* fifty. 1550.
kpɔ́tɔ́ àzū mīndúù, *num.* one hundred. 1555.
kpɔ́tɔ́ àzū vànā, *num.* eighty.
kpɔ́tɔ́ àzū vànā də̀ ndʒòkpá, *num.* ninety. 1554.
kpɔ́tɔ́ àzū vōtɔ̀, *num.* sixty.
kpɔ́tɔ́ àzū vōtɔ̀ də̀ ndʒòkpá, *num.* seventy. 1552.
kpɔ́tɔ́ ūzū bàlē, *Variant:* zāzū bīʃà. *num.* twenty. 1542.
kpɔ́tɔ́ ūzū bàlē də̀ ndʒòkpá, *num.* thirty. 1548.
kpi, *v.* be tart, be sour, spoil (food). 1691, 1748.
kpì, *n.* whole day.
kpíkpí, *adv.* different. 1641.
kpìkpì, *n.* eagle, vulture. 0414, 0463.
kpīngbīlī, *n.* plank. 1091.
kpīngbīlī màndà, *n.* wooden door. 0805.
kpōkɔ̀, *n.* big hoe. 0965.
kpòndòrò òwò, *n.* burn (slight). 0206.
kpòó, *adv.* close together, adjacent, tight, side by side. 1697, 1783.
kpòròkòtò, *adj.* black (for things). 1561.
kpòtò, *n.* hat. 0812.
kpɔ, *v.* coagulate. 0162.
kpɔ̀lɔ̄, *n.* nightjar.
kpu, *v.* heap up. 1006.
kpu ɔ́kɔ́, *v.* become wrinkled. 0125.
kpu tɔ́ àzɔ́, *v.* assemble, meet. 1215.
kpúgúrú, *adj.* half. 1522.
kpùrú, *adv.* extra, exceedingly.
kpùrùkùtù, *n.* owl. 0446.

— l —

la, *v.* lick. 0250.
làɓàwò, *n.* flame. 0671.
làɓòtò, *n.* millet-beer. 0905.
làfó, *loc.* above. *Morph:* **àlà(?)-fó**.
lagà, *v.* be disorderly.
lágā, *n.* disorderliness.
làkɨ̀rɨ̀, *n.* threshing-floor. 0879.
làkpàngbà, *n.* level. 1662.
làkpòtò, *n.* millet-beer. 0905.
làmàlá, *pn.* March.
làmbó, *n.* abscess (large).
làngà, *n.* calf (animal). 0470.
Làngbàsī, *Variant:* **Làngbàʃī**. *pn.* the Langbasi language and people.
làpá, *n.* gift. 0809.
làpàrà, *n.* 1) shoulder blade. 2) airplane. 0083.
le, *v.* bear fruit. 0647.
le ə̀rə̀, *v.* babble. 1326.
léjɔ̄, cf. **élé ɔ̄jɔ̄**.
lēlē, *n.* horse. 0487, 0495.
lēngā, *n.* talking drum.
lerà, *v.* smear.
lérā, *n.* squash.
lə, *v.* be (existential, plural).
lɔ́, *prep.* in, inside, by.
lə̀tɔ̀rɔ̀, *n.* toad. 0460.
li, *v.* 1) enter, lead to, go in. 2) be sufficient, be fitting, become equal. 1651, 1724, 1830.
li àlà, *v.* harmonize. 1160.
li də̀, *v.* befit, suit. 1405.
li gàlɔ́, *v.* jam. 1734.
li kūdā, *v.* borrow. 1218.
li lɔ́ indʒɨ̀, *v.* be accustomed. 1627.
li lɔ́ ɔ́kɔ́, *v.* be accustomed. 1627.
líbī, *time.* yesterday. 0785.
líjā, *time.* olden times, earlier. 0777, 0788.
límā, *time.* a long time ago.
límā kātʃātʃā, *time.* olden times (very old). 0777.
lìndə́nə̀, *n.* enough. 1646.
lingbì, *v.* weigh, measure. 1025, 1432.
lìwà, *n.* pigeon (wild). 0450.
lɨ, *v.* cut, shave. 2) be heavy. 3) sweat. 1588, 1972.
lɨ sùkūmù, *v.* cut hair. 0168.
lo, *v.* 1) lie down, sleep, remain. 2) bite. 1841, 1891.
lo də̀, *v.* copulate, lit., sleep with. 0165.
lo də̀ ɨʒɨ̀, *v.* crunch. 0166.
lo gàtí, *v.* lie down.
lo kóté, *v.* gnaw. 0175.
lo ōlō, *v.* sleep, lie down. 0188, 1666.
lo wɨ̌rɨ̀má, *v.* gnaw around.
lóbà, *Variant:* **lɔ́bà**. *n.* clothes, garment, cloth. 0808, 1067, 1069.
lòsù, *n.* heart (figurative).
lōsú, *Variant:* **lēsú**. *n.* clay pot, also for metal pot.
lɔ̀gbɔ̀dɔ̀ lóbà, *n.* trousers. 0853.
lɔ̀kākpí, *time.* noon. *Morph:* **ɔ̀lɔ̀-ka-kpí**. 0775.
lɔ̄sú úngú, *n.* pot (for water). 0935.
lɔ̀ʃɔ̀, cf. **ɔ̀ʃɔ̀**.
lɔ̀ʔɔ́rɔ̀, *Variant:* **làʔɔ́rɔ̀**. *n.* class (in school). *Morph:* **àlà-ʔɔrɔ̀**.
lu, *v.* 1) plant (to make a hole and put the seed in), cultivate, sow (for rice, corn, peanuts, etc.). 2) cook/prepare greens or meat (the part of the meal that is not starch). 3) curve, bend. 0944, 0969, 0981, 0984, 1815.
lu ūlū, *v.* dream. 1414.
lùbà, *n.* flute. 1151.
lūngbù, *pn.* April.
lùú, *adv.* anew.

— m —

ma, *v.* show. 1274.

Wordlist

má, *time.* this morning.
má, *deic.* that.
màgjà, *n.* sickle. 0966.
màkātò, *n.* boundary, frontier. 0655, 0676, 0676.
màlégò, *n.* breastbone, sternum. 0019.
málègbāngā, *n.* ladle. 0930.
málēngɔ́rɔ́, *n.* intestinal worm. 0217.
màlūlū, *n.* cold weather. 0735.
màmú, *n.* female genitals, clitoris. *Morph:* àmà-mú(?).
màndà, *n.* door, doorway. *Morph:* àmà-àndà. 0805, 0806.
māndá, *prep.* after.
màndà gbāgbā, *n.* entrance hut. 0864.
màndɨrɨ, *n.* law.
màngé, *n.* corn (maize). 0605.
màngɨ, *n.* stick/wood used for animal trap.
māngbá, *Variant:* tʃámāngbá. *prep.* after. *Morph:* tʃá-māngbá.
mápòrò, *n.* motorcycle.
Màrā, *pn.* god of the trap.
màrā, *n.* 1) tribe. 2) type, sort. 0267.
mārā, *n.* barren, sterile, impotent. 0232, 0238.
màʃèngà, *n.* neighbor.
màwūtɔ̄, *n.* hip. 0051.
méjā, *n.* twin (male or female). 0307, 0308, 0309.
merə̀, *v.* 1) swell. 2) swallow. 0193.
mə̀, *deic.* that.
mə̄, *pron.* first-person singular pronoun: clitic form (subject, object, possessive). 1457, 1458. cf. ə̄mə̄.
mi, *v.* 1) bother, irritate. 2) grow, increase, become large, be fat, be thick. 1584.
mīndū, *n.* sand. 0708.
mīndúù, *num.* five, fifth. 1527.
mīndúù dàmà nə̀ bàlē, *num.* six, sixth. *Morph:* də̀-àmà.
mīndúù dàmà nə̀ bíʃà, *num.* seven, seventh.
mīndúù dàmà nə̀ vànā, *num.* nine, ninth.
mīndúù dàmà nə̀ vōtɔ̀, *num.* eight, eighth.
mɨ, *v.* counsel.
mɨ ɨpɨ, *v.* advise. 1319.
mja, *Variant:* mea. *v.* shake. 1971.
mja kānɔ́, *v.* wave (hand as a greeting). 1889.
m̀m̀, *excl.* yes. 1518.
mòdó, *n.* pride.
Mōnō, *pn.* the Mono language and people.
móròpágō, *n.* traveler. 0389.
mōwā, *Variant:* mūwā. *n.* mourning, grief. 1204.
mɔ, *v.* 1) be tired, be weak, ripen, become cooked. 2) build. 0141, 1105, 1123, 1677, 1702, 1718, 1740, 1755.
mɔ ɔ́mɔ́, *v.* laugh. 1369, 1427.
mɔ ɔ́mɔ́ mbà, *v.* smile. 1443.
mɔ tʃátʃū, *v.* become cheerful. 1408.
mɔ̀kɔ́, *n.* cola nut. 0597.
mɔ́lɔ̄, *n.* playing.
múrú, *n.* leopard. 0435.

— mb —

mbàlà, *n.* elephant. 0416.
mbàmbà, *n.* mollusk (fresh-water). 0439.
mbárátá, *n.* horse. 0487, 0489.
mbātā, *n.* stool. 0845.
mbāzā, *n.* xylophone.
mbējā, *n.* the man's in-laws, i.e., the family of the wife (parents and brother), brother-in-law. 0320, 0321, 0360.
mbēlē, *n.* blue duiker, gazelle. 0420.

mbēlēngā, *Variant:* mbélēngá. *n.* crocodile.

mbēngē, *n.* forest pig, wild boar.

mbèpà, *n.* dove (domestic pigeon). 0412.

mbētī, *n.* paper, book, letter (loan from Sango?). 0821.

mbərə̀, *v.* do, act, create, make. 1918, 1928, 1951.

mbə̀rə̀, *conj.* because, for, in order to, ago. 1491.

mbərə̀ àkwà, *v.* work. 1293.

mbərə̀ àkwà ɓātà àjī kə́mɔ̀ndà, *v.* work as a mason. 1117.

mbərə̀ àkwà fɔ̄, *v.* serve. 1272.

mbərə̀ àngwà, *v.* beget. 0148.

mbərə̀ ɓàtà, *v.* pretend. 1437.

mbərə̀ ékpé ə̀rə̀, *Variant:* mbərə̀ ékpé ìpì. *v.* err, make a mistake. 1415.

mbərə ə́ndə́, *v.* draw. 1226.

mbərə̀ ə̀rə̀ fɔ̄, *v.* help, aid, assist.

mbə̀rə̀ gàɗè, *quest.* why. 1516.

mbərə̀ lìndə́nə̀, *v.* satisfy. 1442.

mbərə̀ lōsú, *v.* make a clay pot.

mbərə̀ mbùrù-mbùrù, *v.* become dark. 1572.

mbərə̀ óʃó, *v.* be drunk. 0130.

mbərə̀ tə́, *v.* abuse. 1211.

mbərə̀ ūzū, *v.* poison (a person). 1189.

mbə́rə́jē ɔ̀lɔ̀, *n.* sunshine. 0757.

mbíkpà, *adj.* whitish. *Morph:* ímbí-(?).

mbìrìlù, *adj.* pale color.

mbíù, *adj.* albino.

mbíwà, *adj.* white. *Morph:* ímbí-(?). 1569.

mbɨmbɨ̀ sə́, *v.* spy. 1277.

mbombò, *v.* faint. 0172.

mbòwó, *n.* coco yam, taro. 0595.

mbɔ̀kɔ̀ ngímá, *n.* palm branch. 0637.

mbɔ̀kɔ̀lɔ̀, *n.* sunrise. 0778.

mbúgú, *n.* 1) dry season. 2) year.

mbúlù, *n.* date, promise. 1308.

mbùndʒú, *n.* white person (loan from French *bonjour*?). 0310.

mbūrūsù, *n.* white hair. *Morph:* mbūrū(?)-ùsù. 0104.

— n —

na, *v.* go, come, walk. 1825, 1887.

na áná, *v.* voyage, travel. 1879.

na átá ə́nə́, *v.* take a walk. 1285.

na də̀, *v.* accompany (lit., go with). 1786.

na dʒèzə̀, *v.* wander. 1888.

na gàtə́ʃó, *v.* go away. 1826.

na kātʃā-kātʃā, *v.* be in a hurry. 1732.

na māngbá, *Variant:* na māndá. *v.* follow. 1822.

na mbējā, *v.* negotiate for a wife.

na óró àgjà, *v.* hunt. 1059.

na pá jāʃē, *v.* cohabit. 1222.

nàtàkē, cf. àtàkē.

Ndʒàbā, *Variant:* Ndʒàpā. *pn.* God (loan from Sango *Nzàpa*). 1171.

nēnē, *Variant:* nə̄nē, nē, ʔḿʔm̀. *func.* no, not. 1500, 1503.

nə̀, *art.* definite article.

nə̀, *pron.* inanimate object pronoun.

nə́, *Variant:* ə̀nə́. *conj.* of, used to indicate possession for inanimate and animate nouns; for, to.

nə̄kpɔ̄rɔ̄, *n.* dwarf, pygmy. 0281.

ni, *Variants:* nu, nju, nji, ny. *v.* 1) defecate. 2) rain.

ni ūjū, *v.* defecate. 0169.

nìkpɨ̀, *n.* puff adder, poisonous snake. 0452, 0458.

nja lə́, *v.* have patience with.

njáō, *n.* cat (loan from Lingala *niao*).

nkoto, *num.* thousand (loan from Lingala *nkoto*).

nɔ, *v.* 1) pluck, play (instrument). 2) shoot. 1161, 1909.
nɔnɔ̀, *v.* wring out. 2000.
ntángò, *time.* time (loan from Lingala *ntángo*).
Nzámbè, *pn.* God (loan from Lingala *Nzámbe*).

— nd —

ndábà, *n.* table.
ndangà, *v.* annoy, disturb, bother. 1403.
ndàwò, *n.* forge. *Morph:* **àndà-òwò**. 1085.
ndévé, *n.* mane. 0543.
ndɔ́, *prep.* at the home of, for, in order to; this preposition is from the word **ɔ́ndɔ́** 'mark'. cf. Cloarec-Heiss (1986:28, 160, 401).
ndɔ́ gàɗè, *quest.* why. 1516.
ndɔ́bùdú ò?ò, *n.* meaning. *Morph:* **ɔ́ndɔ́-bùdú**. 1372.
ndɔ́dà, cf. **ɔ́ndɔ́ àdà**.
ndɔ́mà, *n.* story, tale, sting of insects, some. *Morph:* **ɔ́ndɔ́-àmà**. 0558.
ndɔ́mà jāwò, *n.* log. 0689.
ndɔ́mà lóbà, *n.* strap. 0847.
ndɔ́mà ūzū, *n.* speech. 1312.
ndɔ́màtòrò, *n.* story, tale. *Morph:* **ɔ́ndɔ́-àmà-tòrò**. 1313.
ndɔ́mà?ò, *n.* account (report), announcement, news. *Morph:* **ɔ́ndɔ́-àmà-ò?ò**. 1294, 1296, 1304.
ndímù, *n.* orange (loan from Lingala *ndímo*). 0612.
ndìw̌á, *n.* rubber. 0836.
ndɨ, *v.* spoil, go bad, break down, be ruined. 1680, 1893, 1894.
ndɨ ə̀rə̀, *v.* destroy, spoil. 1899.
ndíbùdú, *n.* last, end. *Morph:* (?)-**bùdú**. 1660, 1760.
ndíkɨdʒí, *n.* curse. 1166.

ndíndɨ ɔ̄jɔ̄, *n.* stump. 0644.
ndɨ̀rɨ̀, *prep.* around, outside of, next to.
ndívɨdà, *Variant:* **ndíbɨdà**, **ndúvūdà**. *n.* heel. *Morph:* (?)-**àdà**. 0050.
ndɨw̌ɨrɨ̀, *v.* swarm.
ndíw̌írí, *n.* crowd, herd, swarm. 0259, 0474, 0559.
ndo, *v.* approach. 1787.
ndō, *func.* near. 1482.
ndógòlējā, *Variant:* **ndógòlēā**. *time.* day before yesterday. 0766.
ndoròmbà, *v.* drown. 1900.
ndɔ̄kɔ̄, *n.* flower. 0578.
ndɔ̄kɔ̄lí, *n.* ant (soldier). 0500.
ndóngóló, *n.* boundary, last (final), end. 0655, 1660, 1760.
ndu, *v.* be sweet. 1695.
ndùɓúrùɓú, *n.* blunt. 1634.
ndúkú, *n.* vine or pole.
ndurù, *v.* drown. 1900.
ndùrùgòjó, *n.* heron. 0428.

— ndʒ —

ndʒa, *v.* vomit. 0252, 1975.
ndʒàpà, *n.* stick (for disciplining children).
ndʒàràpándà, *n.* ladder, scaffolding. 1087, 1096.
ndʒē, *adv.* also.
ndʒèkē, *n.* chicken pox, measles.
ndʒengèlè, *v.* infect. 0249.
ndʒi, *v.* be straight. 1693.
ndʒo, *v.* 1) drink (something). 2) open (a book). 0170.
ndʒo bòlò, *v.* smoke (tobacco). 1275.
ndʒo tɔ̀pánə̀ kpùrú, *v.* (become) drunk. 1229.
ndʒóbóró, *n.* bow. 1031.
ndʒoɓà úngú, *v.* drown. *Morph:* **ndʒo-**(?) **úngú**. 1721.
ndʒòkpā, *num.* ten, tenth. 1532.

ndʒorò, *v.* suck. 0192.
ndʒòró, *Variant:* **àndʒòró.** *adj2.* many, large number. 1520, 1667.
ndʒɔ, *v.* scratch, dig (the ground). 1969.
ndʒɔ tʃágúrú, *v.* divorce. 1225.
ndʒɔ tʃə́lə́, *v.* clear away, scatter. 0995, 1966.
ndʒɔ tʃə́lə́ tə́, *v.* scatter. 1965.

— ng —

nga, *v.* 1) bark. 2) fight, box. 3) get angry. 4) be bitter, be sharp. 1633.
ngà, *adv.* spread out.
nga àgjà, *v.* growl. 1339.
nga fɔ̄, *v.* grumble. 1340.
nga kōʃē, *v.* fight. 1234.
ngàɓà, *n.* snail. 0522.
ngàdà, *n.* hook, fishhook. 0815, 1036.
ngágō, *n.* eggplant. 0600.
ngalà àmà, *v.* sharpen (as an arrow) (bring to a point). 1019.
ngàndè, *Variant:* **ngàndē.** *n.* chair. 0802.
ngapà, *v.* defend. 1054.
ngápó, *n.* A short-handled hoe. 0964.
ngàrá, *n.* tendon. 0091.
ngáwò, *n.* smoke, fume. *Morph:* ángá(?)-òwò. 0715.
ngāwū, *n.* nose. 0072.
ngèndʒà, *n.* money, silver (loan from Sango or Ngbandi?). 0841, 1125.
ngesà, *v.* sneeze. 0251.
ngésā, *n.* rope, light.
ngézì jāvūrū, *n.* drizzle. 0752.
ngímá, *n.* palm tree, oil palm. 0582, 0609.
ngíndɨ, *n.* urine. 0123.
ngirì, *v.* snore. 0190.

ngírɨ́ʃì, *n.* gall bladder.
ngɨrɨwò, *Variant:* **ngɨrɨwù.** *n.* charcoal. *Morph:* ɨngɨrɨ-òwò. 0921.
ngjērə̄, *adv.* sound that a bell makes.
ngólà, *n.* tears. *Morph:* úngú-àlà. 0120.
ngòlòmànē, *n.* wardrobe, cupboard.
ngómē, *n.* dew. 0665.
ngòmbè, *n.* gun. 1039.
ngómbè, *n.* cow (loan from Lingala *ngómbe*).
ngōpē, cf. **sùngōpē.**
ngɔ ɨ̄pɨ̄, *v.* dance in a trance. 1158.
ngɔ̄hɔ́rɔ́, *adv.* narrow, hollow. 1596, 1617.
ngɔ́lɔ̄, *Variant:* **ngólō.** *n.* fish trap, hoop net. 1035.
ngɔ̄lɔ̄gbɔ̄, *n.* valley. 0724.
ngòndòrò, *n.* devil, god. 1167, 1172.
ngɔ́ngɔ́, *n.* of this time, now. 0776.
ngɔ́ngɔ́ nə̀ ásə́, *time.* now.
ngɔ̄tō, *n.* chicken. 0476, 0485.
ngòzū, *n.* jigger, maggot. 0513, 0517.
ngurù, *v.* scrape, rake, weed (with a hoe). 0991.
ngurù kótə́, *v.* scratch. 0184.
ngúʃi, *n.* saliva, spittle. *Morph:* úngú-ɨʃi(?). 0080.
ngūzù, *n.* pregnancy. *Morph:* úngú-zu. 0224.
ngwángwà, *n.* gizzard. 0539.
ngwàrə̀, *n.* seed (in general, what is planted). *Morph:* àngwà-ə̀rə̀. 0640, 0895.

— ngb —

ngba, *v.* be many.
ngbáàkóró, *n.* funeral. 1197.
ngbāɓɨ̄, *Variant:* **ngbāɓɨ.** *n.* bone. 0015, 0536.

Wordlist

ngbāɓī ngāwū, *n.* bridge of the nose. 0020.
ngbādē, *n.* bag, pocket. 0791, 0829.
ngbákò, *n.* wine (alcohol). 0914.
ngbālābò, *n.* tobacco pipe. 0851.
ngbàljāljā, *pn.* November.
ngbánjá, *n.* echo. 1311.
ngbàndò, *n.* length. 1578.
ngbándʒì, *n.* rust. 1620.
ngbāngēwò, *n.* type of cat. 0407.
ngbángírí ītʃī, *n.* humming of a tune. 1153.
ngbāngú, *n.* medium drum. 1147.
ngbàngbò, *num.* thousand. 1558.
ngbèjà, *n.* white clay, lime, whitewash. 0728, 1088.
ngbālēkō, *n.* iron. 0817.
ngbɔ́réné, *n.* copper. 0804.
ngbī, *Variant:* **ngbì**. *adv.* deep. 1640.
ngbí, *adv.* clear, open.
ngbíkɨrɨ, *n.* temporary waterhole.
ngbɨndɨ, *adj.* bad, wrong, false.
ngbìngí, *n.* warthog. 0464.
ngbōbōlō, *n.* hyena. cf. **àwí**.
ngbōndʒō kèlèkpā, *n.* bedstead, bed frame. 0793.
ngbɔ, *v.* light, sweep. 1009, 1020.
ngbɔ tɔ́ òʔò, *v.* agree. 1320.
ngbɔɓà, *v.* join, mix with, assemble, cleave, make love, accumulate, gather up. 1917, 1919, 1941.
ngbɔɓà tɔ́ àzɔ́, *v.* assemble, meet. 1215, 1246.
ngbɔ́jū, *n.* fresh. 1652.
ngbɔ́lɔ́, *n.* grass (a tall type of *esóbé* with which you can make a whistle).
ngbɔ̀ndɔ̀, *n.* beam, rafter. 1080.
ngbōngɔ́, *n.* shin. 0081.
ngbúgú, *n.* dry season, hot season, season. 0736, 0737, 0738, 0744, 0754.
ngbúgú jāvūrū, *n.* rainy season. 0749.

— o —

óbó, *n.* flesh.
ōdō, *n.* foolishness.
ódóró, *adj.* red, ripe, purple, pink, dark orange. 1568.
ódóró òʃɔ, *n.* red soil. 0703.
òfòrò, *Variant:* **òfōrò**. *n.* grass (lawn).
ògò, *n.* hunger, desire, need. 0112, 0133.
ōgō, *n.* village. 0881.
ògò úngú, *n.* thirst. 0121, 0140.
ōgōrō, *n.* small hole (e.g., hole in the wall).
ōgōrō-màmú, cf. **gōrōmàmú**.
ōgbōrō, *adj.* large (plural).
òjò, *n.* sadness, poverty, pity, sorrow. 1127, 1131, 1373, 1375, 1392.
ókó, *n.* badness. 1612.
òkò ūzū, *Variant:* **kùzū**. *n.* corpse, death. *Morph:* **òkò-ūzū**. 0258, 0129.
òkòrò, *n.* chest, torso. 0024.
ókóró, *n.* small talking drum.
òkpòrò, *adj.* true.
òkpòrò ʔò, *n.* truth. 1378.
ōlō, *n.* sleep, slumber, day. 0118, 0138.
ōlō gàdè, *quest.* when. 1512.
ōmbō, *n.* wing. 0547.
ōndō, *adj.* short. 1598.
ōndō nà, *n.* wideness. 1581.
ōndōrō, *n.* dew, mist, fog, cloud. 0733, 0741.
ōngbō, *n.* town. 0880.
ōpōrō, *n.* egg. 0889.
óró, *n.* 1) hunt, gathering of food. 2) alive (for animals and plants). 1042.
óʃó, *n.* place, message. 0699.
óʃó kɔ́, *n.* everywhere. 1494.
ótó, *n.* clay (for making pots), potter's clay. 1083, 1093.

òvòrò, *n.* back. 0006.
ōvōrō, *n.* young, youth. 0143, 0269.
òwò, *n.* fire, lamp, flashlight, running engine. 0670.
òwò, *adj.* hot.
ózó, *n.* root.
ōʒōrō, *n.* fat. 0890.
óʒóró àwátèrə̀, *Variant:* ōʒōrō. *n.* honey. 0899.
òʔò, *n.* 1) word, news, message. 2) language, speech. 3) affair, problem. 1317.
óʔó, *n.* wailing, ululation (at funeral). 1315.
òʔò àkwà ōgō, *n.* command. 1297.
òʔò àmà ōgō, *n.* language. 1300.
òʔò nēnē, *n.* innocent. 1659.
òʔò ōgō, *n.* law. 1301.
òʔò ūzū, *n.* speech. 1312.

— ɔ —

ɔ̄dɔ̄, *n.* laziness. 1661.
ɔ̀gɔ̀, *n.* breastbone.
ɔ́gbɔ́, *adj.* hard, difficult, rough. *n.* elder brother. 0322, 1679.
ɔ́gbɔ́ úngú, *n.* medium sized river.
ɔ́gbɔ́wè, *pn.* February.
ɔ̄jɔ̄, *n.* 1) tree, wood, club, cudgel, fetish. 2) medicine. 0590, 0729, 1034, 1169.
ɔ̄jɔ̄ gàfūrū, *n.* pestle.
ɔ̄jɔ̄ iʃì, *n.* thorn-tree. 0589.
ɔ́jɔ́ kùzū, *n.* poison. 0830.
ɔ̄kɔ̄, *Variant:* ākɔ̄. *n.* epilepsy, malice.
ɔ́kɔ́, *n.* 1) skin (of man), shell, hide (of animal), body. 2) health, male, color. 0014, 0086, 0556, 0842, 1041, 1559.
ɔ́kɔ́ àlà, *n.* eyelid. 0033.
ɔ́kɔ́ àmà, *n.* lip. 0062.
ɔ́kɔ́ àmà jɔ̄nū, *n.* beak, bill. 0529.
ɔ́kɔ́ àmbùndʒú, *n.* color of white man's skin, pink. 1564.

ɔ́kɔ́ bágàrà, *n.* bull. 0469.
ɔ́kɔ́ gbàgà, *n.* shell of groundnut. 0641.
ɔ́kɔ́ léjɔ́, *n.* skin (fruit). 0642.
ɔ̄kɔ̄ lēngā, *n.* small drum. 1148.
ɔ́kɔ́ màngé, *n.* corn husk. 0631.
ɔ́kɔ́ tʃálàfó, *adj.* blue. 1562.
ɔ́kɔ́lɔ́ mbùndʒú, *n.* coconut palm. 0575.
ɔ̄kɔ̄rɔ̄, *n.* skull. 0087.
ɔ̀lɔ̀, *n.* 1) sun. 2) time, hour. 0721, 0768, 0781.
ɔ̀lɔ̀ jèngà, *time.* Sunday.
ɔ̀lɔ̀ pósò, *time.* Saturday.
ɔ̀lɔ̀ kpì, *time.* all day. 0762.
ɔ̄mɔ̄, *adj.* soft, easy. 1690.
ɔ́mɔ́, *n.* laughter.
ɔ̀ndɔ̀, *n.* pasture. 0873.
ɔ̀ngɔ̀, *n.* breast, udder. 0018, 0546.
ɔ̄ngɔ̄, *n.* beehive. 0549.
ɔ́ngbɔ́, *Variant:* ángbɔ́. *n.* banana, plantain. 0592, 0616.
ɔ́ngbɔ́ būwèlè, *n.* type of plantain.
ɔ̀ngbɔ̀ làzā, *n.* small, sweet banana.
ɔ̄rɔ̄, *n.* speed. 1774, 1821.
ɔ́rɔ́, *adj.* tough (food).
ɔ̀sɔ̀, *n.* elephant trunk. 0533.
ɔ̄sɔ̄, *n.* pus. 0225.
ɔ̀ʃɔ̀, *Variant:* lɔ̀ʃɔ̀. *n.* soil, earth, ground, land, floor, mud. 0680, 0686, 1084.
ɔ̀ʃɔ̀ àdʒūngbūngbū, *n.* slime. 0714.
ɔ̀ʃɔ̀ àndà, *n.* wall, brick.
ɔ̀ʃɔ̀ kìndi̱, *n.* fertile soil. 0668.
ɔ̄tʃɔ̄, *n.* character. *ADJ.* delicious.
ɔ́tʃɔ́, *adj.* good.
ɔ́tʃɔ́ lɔ̀sù, *n.* generosity. 1364.
ɔ́ʔrɔ́, *adj.* dry. *n.* crust. 0924, 1644, 1688.
ɔ́ʔrɔ́ kākó, *n.* piece of paper, book (lit., dry leaf).

— p —

pa, *v.* say, speak.
pá, *Variant:* **á.** *prep.* on, above, over.
pa dùrú, *v.* chat. 1330.
pa fɔ̄, *v.* tell someone. 1357.
pa ndɔ́ ʔò, *v.* announce. 1321.
pa ndɔ́mà, *v.* tell.
pa ndɔ́màʔò, *v.* explain, teach. *Morph:* **pa ɔ́ndɔ́-àmà-òʔo.** 1335.
pa ɔ̀gɔ̄ngɔ̀, *v.* stutter. 1354.
pa pàrɜ̀, *v.* gossip. 1336.
pa wālā, *v.* lie (tell lies). 1344.
pa zūngbāʔò, *v.* divine. *Morph:* **zūngbā-òʔò.** 1186.
pa ʔò, *v.* say, speak, talk. 1350, 1353, 1356.
pagàtà, *Variant:* **pakàtà.** *v.* forbid, prevent, prohibit. 1235, 1262.
Pákè, *pn.* Easter (loan from French *Pâques*).
pákūlú, *n.* parrot. 0448.
palà, *v.* interlace. 1008.
pálà, *n.* forehead. *Morph:* **pá-àlà.** 0043.
pāngā, *n.* 1) house corner. 2) hip.
pàpájì, *n.* papaya (loan from French *papaye*). 0614.
parà, *v.* look for. 1430.
pārá, *adj2.* every, entire.
parà jāwò, *v.* fetch firewood. 0998.
pārá kɔ́kɔ́, *adv.* everything, all, altogether. 1629, 1667.
parà tʃɔ́lɔ́, *Variant:* **parà tʃágúrú.** *v.* choose. 1409.
párángò, *n.* cockroach. 0505.
pe, *v.* winnow, blow, fan. 0992, 1922, 1934.
pe òwò, *v.* work the bellows. 1118.
pējà, *n.* navel (normal). 0070.
pélɔ́mà, *n.* 1) bud. 2) stopper. 0629, 0846.
pélézū, *n.* bat. 0397.
pètè, *adv.* full. 1653.
pewò, *v.* wither. 1757.
pi, *v.* stick. 1985.
píngíw̌í, *adv.* suddenly.
pōdʒódʒō, *n.* narrow. 1596.
pōrōngōtō àdà, *n.* ankle. *Morph:* **ōpōrō-ngɔ̄tō.** 0002.
pósò, *n.* week (loan from Lingala *póso*).
pɔ gàtɔ́ nɜ̀, *v.* press. 1908.
pɜ̀tú, *adv.* sharp. 1683.
pu, *v.* 1) shake hands. 2) squeeze out. 1982.

— r —

ràdà, *Variant:* **ɜ̄ràdà.** *n.* shoe. *Morph:* **ɜ̀rɜ̀-àdà.** 0840.
ráwá, *n.* yell.
ràwò, *n.* bad spirit, witchcraft. 1181.
rɜná, *v.* crush.
ri, *v.* jump.
ro, *v.* 1) pass, go, overtake. 2) gather. 1850, 1851.
ro gáūtʃū nɜ̀, *v.* continue, resume. 1717.
ro ndʒì, *v.* go straight, steer. 1832.
ro pá, *v.* surpass, dominate, overcome. 1258, 1877.
ro pá nɜ̀, *v.* abound. 1625.
ròdóngà, *n.* last child.
rògò, *n.* food. *cf:* **ɜ̀rɜ̀-ògò.**
rógó, *adv.* shriveled, wrinkled. 1684.
ru, *v.* 1) go out, be extinguished. 2) put out, extinguish, quench. 3) fly. 0564, 1960.
ru ɜ̀rɜ̀, *v.* be patient, take courage.
ru òwò, *v.* be extinguished. 1647.
ru tálā-tálā, *v.* float. 1938.

— s —

sa, *v.* leak, filter, drip, trickle. 0947, 1931, 1947, 1993.
sakà, *v.* spread out to dry, sprawl. 1871, 1978.

sanduku, *n.* trunk (loan from Lingala *sandúku*, originally from Arabic).
sàngápé, *Variant:* **sɔ̀ngápé.** *n.* worm (earthworm). 0528.
sarà kūmù, *v.* comb. 0163.
sárábà, *n.* wild duck. 0413.
sàràkòpèjà ə̀rə̀, *Variant:* **sàràkòpjà ə̀rə̀.** *n.* slipperiness. 1621.
sə, *v.* be (existential), dwell. 1230.
sə ɓá, *v.* be at. 1792.
sə ɓātà àgjà, *v.* be fierce. 1650.
sə də̀, *v.* have. 1731.
sə də̀ àwà, *v.* be afraid, be startled. 1380, 1394.
sə də̀ áwá, *v.* have diarrhea. 0246.
sə də̀ ékpé gbètʃə́lə́, *v.* slander. 1352.
sə də̀ ékpé lɔ̀sù, *v.* slander. 1352.
sə də̀ gbètʃə́lə́, *v.* be restless, unsettled. 1391.
sə də̀ gbɔ̀gbɔ́, *v.* be courageous, be able. 1384, 1624.
sə də̀ ɪndʒī, *v.* conceive, become pregnant (when the fetus is small). 0164.
sə də̀ jāngā, *v.* be joyful, be happy, be pleased, rejoice. 1386, 1389, 1440.
sə də̀ kòɓà, *v.* be ill. 0248.
sə də̀ kúwùsə́rə̀, *v.* be intelligent. 1387.
sə də̀ mòdó, *v.* be proud. 1390.
sə də̀ ngūzù, *v.* be pregnant, conceive (when you see that the woman's stomach is enlarged). 0164, 0241.
sə də̀ ókó, *v.* be angry. 1381.
sə də̀ tʃūlà, *v.* be ashamed. 1382.
sə dígó, *v.* stoop. 1875.
sə dòpá nə̀, *v.* be abundant. 1626.
sə gàtí, *v.* sit, sit down, be seated. 0137, 1867.
sə hàgà, *v.* be broad (e.g., large stomach).
sə ɪ̀ndìrɪ̀ òwò, *v.* warm oneself (by a fire). 0200.
sə kə́tʃì òwò, *v.* become lit. 1737.
sə kòkò, *v.* remain silent, calm oneself. 1349, 1407.
sə kùlə́, *v.* lie across. 1840.
sə kpàwù, *v.* be broad (e.g., river). 1583.
sə kpàzìtì, *v.* be shy. 1393.
sə ōndō nə̀, *v.* become short. 1609.
sə pá àzū, *v.* rule over. 1268.
sə pá ōpōrō, *v.* incubate. 0567.
sə ròpá nə̀, *v.* be abundant. 1626.
sə téāʃó, *v.* be little. 1594.
sə tə̀ gbɔ̀kwákwá, *v.* become hard. 1730.
sə tə̀ héré-héré, *v.* become sharp. 1743.
sə tə̀ ōmɔ̄ nə̀, *v.* become soft. 1746.
sə tə̀ pɔ̀tú-pɔ̀tú, *v.* become sharp. 1743.
sə tìndìwǐrí, *v.* become round. 1607.
səpè, *Variant:* **sepè.** *v.* stay, remain. 1861.
səpè būtʃó, *v.* stop for the night. 1280.
so ókó, *v.* be angry. 1381.
so ūjū, *v.* break wind. 0124, 0153.
sóngbā, *n.* meat, flesh, muscle. 0040, 0068, 0903.
sorò, *v.* contract, tighten. 1927.
sòró, *n.* soul, life, alive (for humans). *Morph:* (?)-**óró.** 0126, 0687.
sɔ, *v.* harvest (corn) (the act of breaking it off the stalk), break off. 0968, 0976.
sɔ də̀ ndʒàpà, *v.* whip. 1026.
sɔ kótó, *v.* have an itch, tickle. 0218, 1289.
sɔ màngé, *v.* harvest (maize). 0974.
sɔ ɔ́kɔ́, *v.* skin, take off skin, strip off. 1062, 1988.
sɔ ɔ́kɔ́ màngé, *v.* husk (corn). 0978.
sɔ tʃə́lə́, *v.* cross. 1812.

su, *v.* 1) draw (water), pour, fill up. 2) uproot, pull up, weed (by hand). 3) pierce, stab, sew. 4) write. 5) be full. 0991, 1002, 1075, 1905, 1913.

su gbàdʒà, *v.* fence in. 1003.

su gbàgà, *v.* harvest peanuts.

sù kūmù, *n.* hair.

su mbētī, *v.* write. 1452.

su sɔ́, *v.* patch. 1114.

sukù tɔ́, *v.* swell. 1753.

sùkūmù, *n.* hair (of head). *Morph:* ùsù-kūmù. 0046.

sùmà, *n.* beard. *Morph:* ùsù-àmà. 0009.

sùngōpē, *Variant:* **ngōpē.** *n.* nail (fingernail or toenail), claw. *Morph:* ùsù-ngōpē. 0038.

sùngúlà, *n.* eyelash, eyebrow. *Morph:* ùsù-úngú-àlà. 0031, 0032.

sùrà, *n.* broom. 0919.

surù, *v.* tear (cloth). 1698, 1991.

sùtʃápáʃé, *Variant:* **ùsù tʃápáʃé.** *n.* pubic hair. *Morph:* ùsù-tʃá-pá-ʃé(?). 0115.

— ʃ —

ʃarà, *v.* give doubt.

ʃe, *v.* 1) heal, save, cure. 2) get well, be cured. 1184, 1728.

ʃè, *pron.* third-person singular object pronoun: clitic form. cf. èʃè.

ʃe gàtɔ́ nə̀, *v.* construct, put together (assemble to make something). 1107.

ʃédòrò, *n.* lemon (loan from French *citron*). 0604.

ʃējō, cf. ēʃē ɔ̄jɔ̄.

ʃekè, *v.* pluck (chicken). 0952.

ʃékpé, *n.* hamper. 0810.

ʃèngà, *n.* falling trap. 1051.

ʃerə̀, *v.* split (wood), cut with an axe (after the tree is already felled), peel bark.

ʃə̀nēkē, cf. ə̀nēkē.

ʃɔ́tá, *Variant:* **ʃétá.** *n.* intestines. 0053.

ʃi, *v.* 1) plant (a shoot or a stem), thrust into the ground, plant. 2) bury. 0989, 0993.

ʃi ābā, *v.* plant, harvest (yams). 0982.

ʃi tʃɔ́lɔ́, *v.* transplant. 0990.

ʃĭkù, *Variant:* **ʃĭkù.** *n.* scar. *Morph:* ĭʃĭrĭ-ùkù. 0116.

ʃo, *v.* burn. 1714, 1715.

ʃu, *v.* be bitter.

— t —

ta, *v.* 1) cut (palm nuts). 2) light.

ta àdà, *v.* be mutilated. 0240.

ta àmbàrà, *v.* decorate, be multicolored. 1000, 1567.

ta ímbí ə̀rə̀, *v.* make white. 1574.

ta òwò, *v.* blaze. 1712.

ta ráwá, *Variant:* **ta rāwā.** *v.* yell, cry out, shout. 1332, 1351.

ta úngú, *v.* bale out (canoe). 1791.

ta ùvù, *v.* be multicolored. 1567.

táà, *quest.* where. *Morph:* tɔ́-à.

tàdʒà, *n.* lamp, torch. 0819, 0852.

tāfò, *adj.* new. 1668.

tāfò jápū, *n.* new moon. 0773.

táhárá, *adj.* light (not heavy). 1593.

tàkàwàrà, *n.* crooked. 1639.

tāmè, *n.* rock, flat rock, pebble. 0672, 0697, 0707.

tāndù, *n.* deaf mute. 0280.

tarà, *v.* descend (to water), sink, flow. 1866, 1939.

tàwóngé, *n.* spark, lightning bug, lightning. 0716, 0746.

tà?wá, *n.* large basin (used for fetching water), cooking pot (earthenware), metal pot. 0922, 0932.
te, *v.* fall, drop. 1820.
te àjĭ ngèndʒà, *v.* be rich. 1132.
te bùdú, *v.* start.
te də̀, *v.* fail. 1933.
te də̀ ókó, *v.* become fierce. 1416.
te də̀ ò?ò, *v.* be wrong. 1399.
te mbèrə̀-mbèrə̀, *v.* appease, decrease. 1214, 1720.
te ɔ̄jɔ̄, *v.* protect by charm. 1190.
te pá ūzū, *v.* seize (someone). 1060.
te ūzū də̀ ɔ̄jɔ̄, *v.* sacrifice. 1191.
téāʃó, *Variant:* táāʃó, téēʃó. *adj2.* small, few. 1585, 1599.
tekə̀, *v.* cough. 0243.
tékɔ̄, *n.* cough, phlegm. 0114, 0207.
tepá, *v.* grasp, hold in arm. 0176.
tèrə̄, *Variant:* tə̀rē. *n.* magic. 1173.
tèw̌é, *n.* ant (big, black). 0498.
tə̀, cf. də̀.
tə́, *prep.* on. *func.* reflexive marker, passive marker.
tə́àzə́, *pron.* ourselves (inclusive). *Morph:* tə́-àzə́.
tə́èndʒē, *pron.* themselves. *Morph:* tə́-èndʒē.
tə́jē, *pron.* himself, herself. *Morph:* tə́-jē.
tə́kə́kà, *n.* pain. 0222.
tə́mə̄, *pron.* myself. *Morph:* tə́-mə̄.
tə́nə̀, *pron.* third-person inanimate object pronoun. *Morph:* tə́-nə̀.
tə̀ràlē, *adv.* directly.
tə́rə́jè, *n.* umbilical cord, bud. 0099, 0629.
tə́zə̀, *pron.* yourself. *Morph:* tə́-zə̀.
tə́?ā, *pron.* ourselves (exclusive). *Morph:* tə́-?ā.
tə́?ē, *pron.* yourselves. *Morph:* tə́-?ē.
ti, *v.* look.

tīmà, *n.* tongue. 0097.
tìndìw̌írí, *n.* circle, ring, round. 0803, 1597.
tɨ, *v.* pick up.
tĭ, *adv.* just there.
tɨ gálàfó, *v.* lift. 1842.
tɨrĭndʒĭ, *n.* leech. 0514.
to, *v.* 1) give (as present), get for, take out (from container). 2) marry. 3) leave. 4) be sticky. 0962, 1238, 1254, 1692.
to ɓá, *v.* come from. 1809.
to ìrì, *v.* cause to swell. 1754.
to ìzì, *v.* blow up, inflate. 1925.
to kānə́ gàpá, *v.* bless. 1217.
to kānə́ tə́, *v.* help. 1242.
to kə́zìrì, *v.* feed (animals). 0972.
to ókóró fə̄ àngɔ̀ndòrò, *v.* make offerings to the dead. 1188.
togbà, *v.* border on. 1795.
Tògbò, *pn.* the Togbo language and people.
togbɔ̀, *Variant:* togbà. *v.* meet, join, put together. 1256, 1946.
tolà, *v.* begin.
tòmbèlè, *n.* morning-star (Venus). 0693.
to ndə́, *v.* look at. 0178, 1429.
to ndə́ tʃándìrì, *v.* look round. 1431.
tóò, *adv.* clean. 1637.
torò, *v.* make a hole (in order to plant corn/maize).
Tòrò, *pn.* the hero of Banda folk stories, a trickster.
tóróʃɔ̀, *n.* old (not new). 1669.
tɔ, *Variant:* tɔ ndàwò. *v.* 1) pound, forge, grind. 2) give pain, hurt, be bitter, sharp, sting. 0174, 0953, 1004, 1005, 1986.
tɔ àgjà, *v.* lead (out) cattle. 0979.
tɔ ìndʒĭ, *v.* bleed. 0150.
tɔ ìlɨ, *v.* perspire. 0181.
tɔ kɔ́ngbɔ́, *v.* work the bellows. 1118.

tɔ lɔ́, v. revive. 1962.
tɔ lɔ̀sù, v. palpitate. 0180.
tɔ ōgōrō, v. bore a hole. 1892.
tɔ ɔ̄kɔ̄, v. grunt with effort. 1341.
tɔ pá, v. uncover. 1994.
tɔ̄ndù, n. dumb (voice). 0237.
tɔpè, v. stick. 1984.
tɔrɔ̀, v. poke. 1906.
tu, v. throw (a liquid substance).
tu ngúʃī, v. spit (lit., throw spittle). 0191.
tu pá nə̀, v. spill (a solid). 1870.
tùjū, n. fresh. 1652.
tùkíà, Variant: tùkjà. n. cotton, cotton plant (loan from Lingala tukía). 0598, 1070.
túkpá, n. whiteness. 1560.
tùndúmàné, n. blunt. 1634.
tùngbɔ́jù, adj. fresh.
turù, v. budge, move, wipe. 1846, 1998.
turù tɔ́ ɔ́ʃɔ́, v. touch. 0196.
turù tʃɔ́lɔ́ bùdú, v. wipe off (excreta). 1292.
tùrúgù, n. soldier. 0385.
túrúgù, n. large navel that sticks out.
turùmà, v. scrape, pick off (with a scraper). 1968.
tùrùʃà, Variant: tùrùʃɔ̀. n. dust, ash. 0667.

— tʃ —

tʃá, prep. place (cf. Cloarec-Heiss 1986:161).
tʃá làkòrò, n. chest.
tʃáāgāmà, n. jaw. Morph: tʃá-āgā-àmà. 0054.
tʃáàgūʒàrà, n. shade, shelter. 0838.
tʃáàkpà, adv. all.
tʃàálà, n. jackal. 0432.
tʃáàndóɓò, n. chin. Morph: tʃá-àndóɓò(?). 0025.

tʃáàngbēndè, n. calf.
tʃáàtʃí, n. bank, shore (hollow). 0652.
tʃáàtʃí kōtā, n. river bank. 0705.
tʃábàgá, n. jaw (bone). Morph: tʃá-bàgá. 0055.
tʃábùdú, prep. under. Morph: tʃá-bùdú.
tʃábùdú ïvï, n. lower abdomen. 0064.
tʃádà, Variant: tʃáàdà. n. sole (of foot). Morph: tʃá-àdà. 0089.
tʃádà ngɔ́rɔ́, n. 1) throat. 2) voice.
tʃàdʒà, n. pen.
tʃádɔ̀ngɔ́rɔ́, Variant: tʃádɔ̀ngɔ́rɔ́. n. voice Morph: tʃá-dɔ̀(?)-àngɔ́rɔ́. 1314.
tʃáfù, n. smell. Morph: tʃá-fu. 0119.
tʃágúrú, n. middle. 1767.
tʃágbòlò, n. smallness. 1579.
tʃágbúrú kūmù, n. crown of the head. Morph: tʃá-gbúrú(?). 0027.
tʃákàlá, adj. side, part. Morph: tʃá-kàlá(?).
tʃákàlá kótɔ́, n. side of body. 0084.
tʃákānɔ́, n. palm of hand. Morph: tʃá-kānɔ́. 0074.
tʃákāngā, n. armpit. Morph: tʃá-kāngā. 0005.
tʃákòrò, n. height, length. 1576, 1577.
tʃákùdú, prep. under, below. Morph: tʃá-kùdú. 1486.
tʃákūmù, n. highest point, utmost, level. 0681, 1765.
tʃálàfó, loc. above, sky, heaven. Morph: tʃá-àlà-fó. 0713.
tʃálàkpí, loc. in the village. Morph: tʃá-àlà-kpí(?).
tʃálàngú, loc. in the water. Morph: tʃá-àlà-úngú.
tʃálàsù wówò, n. heartburn. 0212.
tʃálɔ̀ndɔ̀ ïpï, n. ritual place. 0876.

tʃámāngbá, cf. māngbá.
tʃámbélé òwò, *n.* burnt grass. 0573.
tʃándɔ́, *prep.* in. *Morph:* tʃá-ɔ́ndɔ́.
tʃándɪ̀rɪ̀, *n.* edge. 1759.
tʃándú, *n.* country. 0661.
tʃàndʒà, *n.* thumb piano, hand piano. 1152.
tʃangà, *v.* melt. 1952.
tʃángbá, *prep.* behind. *Morph:* tʃá-ángbá. 1478.
tʃángbángélé, *adj.* green. 1566.
tʃàngbédà, *n.* fork (in road). 0866.
tʃápá bádʒá, *n.* ford. 0674.
tʃápá kāngā, cf. kāngā.
tʃápá mīndū, *n.* beach. 0653.
tʃápádú, *n.* grave, cemetery. 0867, 0874.
tʃápándíkɔ́, *n.* rubbish. 0837.
tʃápáʃé, *n.* pubes. *Morph:* tʃá-páʃé(?). 0076.
tʃápáʃɔ̀, *n.* world. *Morph:* tʃá-pá-ɔ̀ʃɔ̀. 0730.
tʃátɔ́ àmà, *n.* edge. 1759.
tʃátùrúgù, *n.* army. *Morph:* tʃá-tùrúgù. 0254.
tʃátʃū, *n.* face. *prep.* in front of. *Morph:* tʃá-ūtʃū. 0034, 1477.
tʃébàlē, *n.* alone. *Morph:* (?)-bàlē. 1628.
tʃèjɔ̄, *n.* handle. *Morph:* (?)-ɔ̄jɔ̄.
tʃèjɔ̄ gàfūrū, *Variant:* tʃèɔ̄ gàfūrū. *n.* pestle. 0933.
tʃéné, *n.* midrib of palm-frond, type of broom. 0636.
tʃétʃé, *n.* full. 1653.
tʃētʃērə, *n.* insect, tick. 0512, 0525.
tʃə̀, *pron.* third-person singular subject pronoun: clitic form. cf. èʃè. 1453, 1454, 1455.
tʃɔ́-, *prep.* within.
tʃɔ́lɔ́, *prep.* inside. *Morph:* tʃɔ́-lɔ́.
tʃɔ́lɔ́mà, *Variant:* tʃélɔ́mà. *n.* palate. *Morph:* tʃɔ́-lɔ́-àmà. 0073.

tʃɔ́lɔ́wāpē, *n.* crevice. 0663.
tʃə̀nēkē, cf. ə̀nēkē.
tʃi, *v.* shine, be bright, give light. 1635, 1942, 1973.
tʃi ɔ̀lɔ̀, *v.* be light (of day). 0789.
tʃìkí, *n.* island. 0684.
tʃìkɪrɪ, *n.* winnow. 0967.
tʃɔ, *v.* taste good, be tasty. 1696.
tʃɔ tʃápá ə̀rə̀, *v.* peel. 0951.
tʃɔ̀ngbɔ́lɔ́, *n.* stick for sowing seeds (corn, peanuts, rice), walking stick, cane, thin pole. 0628, 0799, 1100.
tʃu, *v.* 1) die. 2) close, shut. 0244, 1807, 1865.
tʃu ògò, *v.* be starved. 0139.
tʃūlà, *n.* shame. 1374.
tʃwa, *Variant:* tʃowà. *v.* scrape, scratch, dig. 1967, 1969.

— u —

ūbū, *adj.* black (for beings). 1561.
ùbù óʃó, *n.* darkness. 0763.
ūbū ūzū, *n.* black person. 0273.
ūbūrū, *n.* filth, dirt. 0666, 1643.
ūbūrū, *n.* swollen stomach.
ūdū, *n.* spear, lance. 1044.
údú, *adj.* the rest of.
údú dòngɔ́, *n.* leftovers (food). 0900.
ùdʒùrù, *n.* waterfall. 0726.
ūfū, *adj.* rotten. 1619.
úgú, *adj.* far.
úgúrú, *prep.* in between, amongst.
ūjū, *n.* excrement. 0108.
újú, *n.* female, unmarried girl, female animal. 0261.
ùkù, *n.* wound, hurt (a sore). 0215, 0228.
ūkū, *n.* thigh (the part of the leg above the knee, front and back). 0093.

Wordlist

úkú, *n.* 1) trap, animal trap, bird line (adhesive to catch birds). 2) jealousy. 1030, 1050, 1367.
ùkù gbàdʒà, *n.* ulcer. 0230.
ūkūrū, *n.* lean, meager. 1592.
úkpúlú, *n.* heap. 0814.
ùlù, *n.* heart (the organ). 0049.
ūlū, *n.* dream. 1361.
ūmbūrū, *n.* soot. 0936.
úmbúrú, *n.* gunpowder.
ùmbùrù óʃó, *time.* nightfall. 0787.
únú, *n.* sesame. 0619.
ùndù, *n.* size.
ūndū, *n.* body.
úndú, *adj.* sweet. *n.* hernia, swelling, hump (of cow). 0213, 0229, 0542, 1614.
ùndù ɔ̄jɔ̄, *n.* trunk (of tree). 0646.
úngú, *n.* 1) water. 2) river. 3) year, season. 0725, 0754, 0784.
úngú dɔ̀ngɔ́, *n.* broth, sauce, soup. 0885, 0912.
úngú jāvūrū, *n.* rainy season.
úngú kākó gàràngà, *adj.* green. 1566.
úngú òwò, *n.* coffee, kerosene, diesel.
úngú ɔ̀ngɔ̀, *n.* milk. 0904.
ūngūrū, *adj.* small, thin (not thick). 1602.
ūngūrū lēngā, *n.* medium drum. 1147.
úngbúrú, *adj.* old.
ūpū, cf. īpī.
ùrù īdī, *v.* whistle. 1360.
ùsù, *n.* fur, human body hair, feather. 0535, 0538.
ùsù jānū, *n.* feathers.
ùsù tʃápáʃé, cf. sùtʃápáʃé.
ūʃū, *adj.* bitter, bitterness. 1613, 1711.
úʃú, *loc.* outside.
ūtū, *n.* ear. 0028.
ùtùrù mīndū, *n.* fine sand. 0709.

ūtʃū, *prep.* before, in front of. 1477.
ūtʃū nə̀, *func.* first. 1519.
ūvū, cf. ívī.
ūvū àndà, *n.* wall. 1101.
ūvūrū, *,n.* weight. 1580.
ūwū, *adj.* empty. 1645.
úwú, *n.* string, rope, cord, wire, line. 0835, 0848, 1103.
úwú àngɔ́rɔ́, *n.* larynx. 0059.
úwú ə̀rə̀, *n.* line of objects. 1766.
úwú ndʒóbóró, *n.* bowstring. 1032.
úwú ngàdà, *n.* fishing line. 1037.
ūzū, *n.* person. 0266, 0336.
ūzū nēnē, *n.* nobody.

— v —

va, *v.* 1) pour (a granular substance). 2) scoop (a granular substance).
va ɔ̀tɔ̀ ūzū, *v.* accuse. 1318.
vānā, *num.* four, fourth. 1526.
vaʔé, *v.* throw out.
vàʔè, *adv.* throw out (plural form).
ve, *v.* 1) hit. 2) stone.
vèdʒà, *n.* forest. 0675.
vèjā, *n.* thicket. 0722.
vèkè, *n.* okra. 0610.
verə̀, *v.* 1) wear (clothes), undress. 2) strip off a stem. 0201, 1290.
verə̀ élé ōwō, *Variant:* verə̀ éléwō. *v.* harvest (rice). 0975.
verə̀ lóbà, *v.* dress (someone). 1227.
vi, *v.* dance.
vi īpī, *v.* dance. 1159.
vɨ kānɔ́ zə̀, *v.* close the fist.
vɨvɨ, *n.* ant. 0497.
vōkā, *n.* nape of neck. 0069.
vōmā, *n.* fly (insect). 0509.
vòngbá, *n.* warthog. 0464.
vorò, *v.* roast, fry. 0948.
vóró, *adv.* good health. 0142, 0286.
vōrōwò, *Variant:* vòròwò. *n.* ash, cinders. 0915.
vōtɔ̀, *num.* three, third. 1525.

vu àlà, *v.* close the eyes. 0161.
vu àmà, *v.* close the mouth. 0160.
vu kānɔ́, *v.* close fist. 0159.
vu sɔ́ ò?ò, *v.* deny. 1334.
vúdà, *n.* cultivated ground. 0861.
vūvù, *n.* sugar ant.

— w —

wa, *v.* cut, slice (with a knife), whittle, mark out, peg out (ground). 0946, 1111.
wā, *Variant:* **wáā.** *func.* very, much, many, forever, always. 0786.
wa átá nə̀, *v.* shorten. 1608.
wa àtí, *v.* make (facial) incisions, tattoo, slash. 0177, 1910.
wa gàzá, *v.* circumcise. 0157.
wa īndʒī, *v.* cause to bleed.
wa ndɔ́, *v.* obstruct. 1848.
wa ò?ò, *v.* judge. 1247.
wa tʃɔ́lɔ́ ?járá-?járá, *v.* cut up, flay, slaughter. 1053.
wàí, *excl.* yes, okay.
wájà, *n.* baby.
wàjóò, *excl.* That's right!.
wālā, *n.* lie (falsehood). 1302.
wārə̀, *n.* manioc paste.
wátèrə̀, *n.* bee. 0501.
wélé, *Variant:* **wólé.** *n.* arrow. 1027.
wo, *v.* 1) kill, slaughter. 2) be hot. 1063, 1249.
wo ófó, *v.* be hot (of person). 0132.
wo òwò, *v.* have a fever.
wògà, *n.* antelope. 0395.
wòlā, *adj.* yellow. 1570.
wòmbá, *n.* sister-in-law. 0321, 0363.
wu, *v.* 1) see (something). 2) breathe. 3) press (with your hand). 0154, 0178, 0185.
wu də̀ àlà, *v.* allow. 1213.
wu ə̀rə̀, *v.* notice. 1434.
wù íʃírɔ́, *n.* mirror.
wu òjò, *v.* forgive.
wu òjò ūzū, *v.* forgive. 1217.
wu sɔ́, *v.* know. 1426.
wu sɔ́ kə́mbə̀rə̀, *v.* know how to. 1425.
wu tʃɔ́lɔ́ ɔ́kɔ́, *v.* feel. 0173.
wūljā, *n.* giraffe. 0423.
wùsə́tə́wú, *n.* stupid person. *Morph:* **wu-ə́sɔ́-(?).** 0306.
wutà, *v.* leave, exit, arrive, pass by, come (or go) out. 1788, 1810.
wutà gàpá ɔ̀ʃɔ̀, *v.* be born. 0152.

— w̌ —

w̌a, *v.* send (someone or something). 1269.
w̌a ìʃì, *v.* extract a thorn. 0245.
w̌a óʃó ndɔ́, *v.* invite, assemble (people). 1246.
w̌a ɔ̄jɔ̄, *v.* cut down. 0996.
w̌a ūzū ndɔ́, *v.* send (someone to do something). 1271.
w̌adù, *v.* take out.
w̌àlà, *n.* bone marrow. 0016.
w̌angà, *v.* cut across.
w̌arà, *v.* 1) be fast. 2) open.
w̌arà tɔ́, *v.* refuse, reject. 1266.
w̌arà tɔ́ óʃó tɔ́, *v.* abstain. 1210.
w̌arà tʃɔ́lɔ́ ə̀rə̀, *v.* untie. 1023.
w̌égē, *adv.* hot.
w̌i, *v.* throw, sprinkle (water). 1914, 1980.
w̌i gbàgòndà, *v.* swing. 1878.
w̌i ngàdà, *v.* fish. 1057.
w̌ì?í, *adv.* throw out (singular form).
w̌ílí, *n.* lower leg, calf, shin.
w̌ítí, *n.* calf of leg. 0022.
w̌ùrùjū, *n.* dung beetle. 0507.

Wordlist

— z —

za, *v.* take, get (one thing); give, put (one thing); place, set; catch (person or animal); hold; pick up. 1237, 1052, 1284, 1860, 1944, 1956.
za àngɔ́rɔ́, *v.* choke. 1897.
za àwà, *Variant:* **za àwà fɔ̄**. *v.* frighten, startle. 1419, 1444.
za də̄ ājō, *v.* carry on a pole. 1800.
za dì, *v.* hang up. 1943.
za ə̀rə̀, *v.* catch (object). 1803.
za fɔ̄, *v.* offer, bring. 1257, 1797.
za gálàfó, *v.* raise.
za gàlɔ́ āwā nə̀, *v.* apply (ointment), besmear. 0144.
za gàlɔ́ kānɔ́, *v.* carry in arms. 1799.
za gàlɔ́ kūmù, *v.* carry on head. 1801.
za gándìrì nə̀, *v.* put away. 1016.
za gàpá, *v.* increase. 1945.
za gàpá òvòrò, *v.* carry (child) on back. 1802.
za gàtí, *v.* put down. 1858.
za gàtí lɔ́ kūmù, *v.* unload from head. 1886.
za gbòlò, *v.* carry a child. 1221.
za ìvìrì, *v.* come on suddenly, take in the act. 1410.
za jāʃē, *v.* marry a wife. 1255.
za jītúmbù, *v.* punish (loan from Lingala *etumbu*). 1263.
za jìwà tɔ́nə̀, *v.* hide (tr.). 1423.
za jɔ̀rə̀, *v.* sell. 1143.
za kópé, *v.* stalk. 1064.
za kùlɔ́, *v.* bar (door). 1920.
za kùtə̄nə̀ɔ́kù, *v.* place crosswise. 1853.
za mì, *v.* lean. 1837.
za mìʃó, *v.* support. 1283.
za ngbándʒì, *v.* rust. 1741.
za ōgō, *v.* conquer, defeat. 1223.

za pòtɔ́, *Variant:* **za pòòtɔ́**. *v.* carry away. 1798.
za tàwó, *v.* take from cooking fire. 0960.
za tàʔwá gátàwó, *v.* put a pot on the fire. 0954.
za tɔ́, *v.* boast, brag, praise oneself. 1328.
za tɔ́ gápá nə̀, *v.* increase. 1733.
za tɔ́ ndɔ́, *v.* be eager. 1362.
za tɔ̀ndʒì, *v.* straighten. 1751.
za tɔ̀ʃɔ́, *v.* stumble. 1876.
za tʃɔ́lɔ́, *v.* knead, mould pottery. 0949, 1113.
za ūzū àkwà, *v.* hire. 1137.
za wìʔí, *v.* throw away. 1915.
zàjā, *n.* anvil. 1079.
zàrà, *n.* far. 1780.
zarà ɔ̀ʃɔ̀, *v.* be barren (of land). 1631.
zarà sɔ́, *v.* spy. 1277.
zatʃù gàpá, *v.* cover. 0945.
zāwá, *n.* bitter herbs.
zàzū bīʃà, cf. **kpɔ́tɔ́ àzū bīʃà**.
zāzū bīʃà, cf. **kpɔ́tɔ́ ūzū bàlē**.
zə̀, *pron.* second-person singular object pronoun. cf. **ə̀bə̀**.
zə̀, *emph.* indeed. (Kamanda 1998:521, 720 defines this word as *là-bas*, following Cloarec-Heiss 1972:58, 128).
zi, *v.* eat. 0171.
zi àkwándɔ́ ngwàrə̀, *v.* eat first of new crops. 1231.
zi āngbā, *v.* steal. 1279.
zi də̄ àndòrò, *v.* bewitch. 1183.
zi də̄ ràwò, *v.* bewitch. 1183.
zi tʃɔ́lɔ́ ə̀rə̀, *v.* chew. *Morph:* zi-tʃɔ́-lɔ́-ə̀rə̀. 0156.
zìí, *adv.* smooth, flat. 1689.
zìngì, *n.* monitor lizard. 0441.
zìtì, *v.* cool off, become cold, decrease, pacify. 1719, 1720, 1954.

zìtì, *adj.* cold, peaceful.
zo, *v.* grill, roast, bake. 0955.
zomà tɔ́, *v.* embrace. 1232.
zomàpò, *v.* blow away. 1923.
zu, *Variant:* **zu páʃɔ̀**. *v.* give birth to, loosen. *Morph:* zu-pá-ɔ̀ʃɔ̀. 0147, 1949.
zu àgjà, *v.* give birth (animals). 0565.
zu ōpōrō, *v.* lay (eggs). 0568.
zu tɔ́ndà, *v.* be loose. 1665.
zu tʃɔ́lɔ́ ɔ̀rɔ̀, *v.* untie. 1023.
zu úngú, *v.* cross river. 1813.
zu w̌ɛrɔ̀-w̌ɛrɔ̀, *v.* be loose. 1665.
zūngbā, *adj.* hidden.
zurù, *v.* 1) delimit, stake out (a field), divide up. 2) step on, tread. 3) be slippery, be sticky. 1687, 1692, 1880.
zurù dàràmbèʃà, *v.* glide, slip. 1824, 1868.
zùrú ɔ̀rɔ̀, *n.* slipperiness. 1621.
zúwū, *Variant:* **zúwā**. *n.* flour. 0891.
zúwū gàràngà, *n.* manioc flour.

— ʒ —

ʒe, *v.* grovel.
ʒe wùtù, *v.* beg (for money). 1216.
ʒerɔ̀, *v.* descend, go down. 1816.
ʒi, *v.* belch. 0149.
ʒingbà, *v.* grumble, roar. 1340, 1963.
ʒīwù, *n.* embers. 0925.
ʒo, *v.* wake up. 0198, 0199.
ʒu, *v.* burn. 1713.
ʒūgwā, *n.* evil forest spirit.

— ʔ —

ʔa, *v.* suck.
ʔà, *pron.* first-person plural inclusive pronoun: clitic form. cf. **àzɔ́**.
ʔā, *pron.* first-person plural exclusive pronoun: clitic and possessive form. cf. **āʔā**.
ʔa ɔ̀ngɔ̀, *v.* nurse, breastfeed.
ʔalà fó, *Variant:* **ʔa fó**. *v.* stand up, stand, rise up. 1862.
ʔarà, *v.* dig up, fill in.
ʔe, *v.* call.
ʔē, *pron.* second-person plural pronoun: clitic and possessive form. cf. **ēʔē**.
ʔe iʒi, *v.* show teeth. 0187.
ʔe óʃó, *v.* call. 1329.
ʔi, *v.* 1) attach, tie, bind, pack (e.g., a truck), stop. 2) jump, dive. 1011, 1817, 1834, 1921.
ʔi gbóndʒùrù, *v.* be astonished, be surprised. 1383, 1396.
ʔi ivìrì gárá, *v.* be depressed (emotional state). 1385.
ʔi jākōʃē, *v.* marry a husband.
ʔi káʔjá, *v.* paddle. 1012.
ʔi ngíndi, *v.* urinate. 0197.
ʔi pò, *v.* fasten. 1935.
ʔi tɔ́, *v.* go to the bathroom (lit., to tie oneself), urinate.
ʔi úngú sù gàtɔ́, *v.* become wet. 1756.
ʔimà, *v.* yawn.
ʔiri òwò, *v.* rub (fire) with fire stick. 1017.
ʔḿʔm̀, cf. **nēnē**.
ʔo dʒó, *v.* wail, ululate (at funeral).
ʔomà, *v.* boil over. 0942.
ʔorò, *v.* split, cut open, saw (wood). 0997, 1116.
ʔorò élé dʒōpōrō, *v.* castrate. *Morph:* ʔorò-élé-dʒō(?)-ōpōrō. 0155.
ʔorò óʃó, *v.* look at. 1429.
ʔorò óʃó dʒìndìrì, *v.* look round. 1431.
ʔɔ, *v.* climb, go up, ascend, mount. 1789, 1806, 1953.
ʔɔ gálàfó, *v.* be elevated, rise. 1781.

ʔɔrɔ̀, *v.* 1) dry. 2) crawl. 1722, 1723, 1811.
ʔɔ̄rɔ̄ngɔ̄, *n.* frog. 0419.
ʔu, *v.* caress, flatter. 1220.
ʔu ūzū, *v.* incite. 1244.

ʔurù, *v.* blow. 1157, 1922.
ʔurù ɨ̀dɨ̀, *v.* whistle. 1704.
ʔurù òwò, *v.* blow on a fire.
ʔurù tʃɨ́lɨ́ ūtū, *v.* kiss. 1250.
ʔwàrà, *adv.* (until) the morning.

Appendix C

Recordings

Labial flap

(1) Files
   labfl1.wav (Speaker A)
   labfl2.wav (Speaker A)
   labfl3.wav (Speaker A)
   labfl4.wav (Speaker K)
   labfl5.wav (Speaker K)

(2) jāw̌èlè   'catfish'
    àw̌étòrò   'activator in an animal trap'
    àw̌í   'hyena (or some similar animal)'
    w̌ílí   'thigh'
    w̌ítí   'calf'
    w̌àlà   'bone marrow'
    kə́w̌à   'to send'
    kə́w̌àrà   'to untie'
    kə́w̌ì   'to throw'
    ndíw̌írí àzū   'crowd'
    áw̌árá   'brave, proud, haughty'
    w̌égē   'hot'
    tèw̌é   'ant (big, black)'   (0498)

wǔrùjū	'dung beetle'	(0507)
àw̌éngè	'rainbow'	
tìndìw̌írí	'circle, ring'	(0803)
ndìw̌á	'rubber'	(0836)
kɔ́w̌àrà tɔ́	'refuse'	(1266)
kɔ́kàw̌à	'to snap'	
kɔ́kèw̌è	'to fold'	
kèw̌ètò	'be weak'	(1702)
tàkàw̌àrà	'be crooked'	(1639)
wǐʔí	'throw out'	
ɔ̀lɔ̀ tó w̌égē-w̌égē	'It's hot out.'	
mɔ̄ sɔ́ kɔ́zà wǐʔí	'I'm throwing out something (*one* thing, e.g., a piece of paper).'	
àw̌ūrūngù	'vehicle'	
kàw̌àngòndā	'place near Bili'	
w̌átò	'termite (sp.)'	

Flap sentence

(3) File
labfl5.wav (Speaker K)

(4) *ájá dɔ̀ àmà w̌á mɔ̄, mə nà ɔ́ w̌àrà àwákú nɔ́ jē mɔ̄ ná w̌àrà dɔ̀ àw̌étòtò nà kɔ́ ɔ́ gú zá wǐʔí tī tɔ́ āwā*
'My friend Ama sent me to disable his animal trap cable. I went and disabled it—including the activator. But as I was coming back, I threw it all away along the way.'

Labial-velar stops

(5) Files
lvstp1.wav (Speaker A)
lvstp2.wav (Speaker A)
lvstp3.wav (Speaker A)
lvstp4.wav (Speaker K)
lvstp5.wav (Speaker K)

(6)
sóngbā	'flesh'
ngbāɓī	'bone'
tʃágbúrú kūmù	'top of head'
gbòlò	'child'

ngbōngɔ́	'shin'	
gbāngbālé	'baldness'	
àgbà	'tuft'	
kə́gbɔ̀	'to harden'	
gbɔ́zū	'elder'	
àgbīvī̀	'pimple'	
gbādà	'be crippled'	
jāgbɔ́zū	'old person'	
ōngbórō	'old person'	
nɨ̀kpɨ̀	'puff adder'	
kpɨ̀kpɨ̀	'vulture'	
ngbìngɨ́	'warthog'	
dɔ́kɔ́lɔ́ngbā	'scorpion'	(0521)
gbākòtò	'anthill'	(0548)
ɔ́ngbɔ́	'banana'	(0592)
gbàgà	'groundnut'	
àgbàrà	'bridge'	(0655)
gōrōkpā	'cave'	(0659)
ɔ̀ʃɔ̀ àdʒūngbūngbū	'erosion'	(0714)
ngbúgú	'dry season'	
jùgú kpɨ̀kpɨ̀kpɨ̀	'hard wind'	(0743)
úkpúlú	'heap'	(0814)
ngbādē	'pocket'	(0829)
gbāgbā	'camp, pen, compound'	(0857)
gbārə̀	'utensil'	(0939)
āngbā	'theft'	

Implosives and labialization

(7) Files
    implo1.wav (Speaker A)
    implo2.wav (Speaker A)
    implo3.wav (Speaker A)
    implo4.wav (Speaker K)
    implo5.wav (Speaker K)

(8)
kə́ɓì	'to hit'	
kɔ́ɗɔ̀	'monkey'	
ngàɓà	'snail'	
làɓàwò	'flame'	(0671)
ɓámbìjā	'day after tomorrow'	(0765)

ɓámbàtʃá	'tomorrow'	
gàɗè	'what'	
àɓí	'hammer'	(1086)
kə́gì kūɗā	'pay (debt)'	(1139)
əɗè	'who'	
ɓàtà	'where'	
ɓálə́	'inside'	(1481)
ɓáʃú	'outside'	(1484)
ndùɓúrùɓú	'be blunt'	(1634)
ɓáɗɔngɔ́rɔ́	'throat'	
àkwà	'work'	
kwákwá	'grasshopper'	
ngwàrə̀	'seed'	
kə́gwà	'pack'	(1011)
gbɔ́kwákwá	'be hard'	(1657)
àngwà	'seed'	
ákwárá	'type of bean'	

Miscellaneous phrases (a)

(9) File
 misc1a.wav (Speaker K)

(10) Labial flap
 ɔ̀lɔ̀ tó w̌égē-w̌égē   'It's hot out.'
 mə̄ sə́ kə́zà w̌ì?í   'I'm throwing out something'
              (*one* thing, e.g., a piece of paper).

(11) Enya
 jāvūrū sə́ kə́nì tə́nə̀   'It's raining.'
 mə̄ ɲá lə́ mə̄   'I'm having patience.'

(12) *a → e* in *jānū*
 jānū sə́ kə́dè gàràngà   'The bird is pecking manioc.'

(13) High front rounded vowel [tʃy]
 tʃə̀ tʃú líbī   'He died yesterday.'

(14) Vowel nasalization
 mə̄ sə́ kə́mɔ̀ ɔ́mɔ́   'I am laughing.' (orig. ɔ̄mɔ̄)
 ʔā sə́ kə́dù mɔ́lɔ̄   'We are playing.'

Miscellaneous phrases (b)

(15) File
 misc1b.wav (Speaker K)

(16) tʃə̀ wú sə́ kə́pà Mōnō   'He knows how to speak Mono.'
 kūmù mə̄ ká mə̄ wáā   'I have a headache.'
 ...vōtɔ̄, vànā, mīndúù...   '...three, four, five...'
 mə̄ sə́ kə́nà áná   'I'm going on a trip.' (orig. *ānā*)
 mə̄ wú-wú sə́ nə̀ nə̄nē   'I don't know.'

Miscellaneous phrases (c)

(17) File
 misc1c.wav (Speaker K)

(18) Does ɔ̄lɔ̄ become ōlō in the plural?
 mə̄ ná áná mbə̀rə̀ ɔ̄lɔ̄ bàlē   'I went on a trip for one day.'
 mə̄ ná áná mbə̀rə̀ ɔ̄lɔ̄ bīʃà   'I went on a trip for two days.'
 mə̄ ná áná mbə̀rə̀ ɔ̄lɔ̄ vōtɔ̄   'I went on a trip for three days.'

(19) Tone
 káā-kā téāʃó   'Wait a minute.'
 ɓə̀ nā gàlə́ kɨndɨ də̀ ɔ̄lɔ̄ gàɗē 'When do you (habitually) go to the field?'

Miscellaneous phrases (d)

(20) File
 misc1d.wav (Speaker K)

(21) əndʒē sə́ kə́kwáā-kwā ngɔ́ngɔ́ nə̀ ásə́ 'They will come back here now.'
 ə́ ʃúù-ʃù   'It is bitter.'
 ə́ kpíì-kpì   'It is tart.'
 ə́ gjáà-gjà   'It is hard.'
 zà úngú fə̄ mə̄, mə̄ ndʒō   'Give me water to drink.'

Miscellaneous phrases (e)

(22) File
 misc1e.wav (Speaker K)

(23) Secondary articulations
    mā sɔ́ kɔ́gwà àgjà   'I'm packaging some meat.'
                                    (orig. *àgjà*)
    mā sɔ́ kɔ́gwáā-gwā mpōndū   '*Nalingi kosala mpondu ya liboke.*'
    tʃɔ́ lòsù jē sɔ́ tə̀ hàò nə̀   'He gets mad easily.' (orig. *tʃɔ́ lòsù*)

Liquids (CV₁LV₁)

(24) File
    liqui1_11025.wav (Speaker A)
    liqui2_11025.wav (Speaker K)

(25) CV₁LV₁ → CLV
íʃírí	'shadow'
wátèrə̀	'bee'
īngbīrī	'salt'
ɔ́bɔ́rɔ́	'quarrel'
àgbàrà	'bridge'
jābùrù	'goat'
jāvóró	'dog'
àngɔ́rɔ́	'throat'
āhārā	'dry'
ákwárá	'chick-peas'
áʔjárá	'small (PL)'
jārākō	'iron'
ōpōrō	'egg'
àw̃étòrò	'stick used for an animal trap'
bādōrō	'sweet potato'
ōndōrō	'dew'
óʒóró	'fat'
jākóró	'snake'
ōgōrō	'hole'
òkpòrò	'true'
ōgbōrō	'large (PL)'
kàkílí	'basket'
jāw̃èlè	'catfish'
kīkɨ̀lɨ̀	'heavy'
gbètʃɔ́lɔ́	'hope'
āmbālā	'type of dance'
àbángūlú	'sugarcane'
tʃɔ̀ngbɔ́lɔ́	'stick for sowing seeds'

mbàlà	'elephant'
gbòlò	'child'
gèlè	'left'
múrú	'leopard'

Leftward vowel spreading/vowel hiatus

(26) Files
  left1_11025.wav (Speaker A)
  left2_11025.wav (Speaker K)

(27) Leftward vowel spreading
mɨ̄ sɔ́ kɔ́vì ɨ̄pɨ̄	'I'm dancing.'
mɨ̄ sɔ́ kɔ́kɨ̀	'I'm crying.'
mɨ̄ sɔ́ kɔ́ʒù	'I'm burning.'
mɨ̄ sɔ́ kɔ́dè	'I'm chopping.'
mɨ̄ sɔ́ kɔ́kò và?è	'I'm gathering stuff to throw away.'
mɨ̄ sɔ́ kɔ́nà ánà	'I'm traveling.'
mɨ̄ sɔ́ kɔ́tɔ̀ ndàwò	'I'm forging.'
mɨ̄ sɔ́ kɔ́wà	'I'm cutting.'
mɨ̄ sɔ́ kɔ́jà tɔ́-mɨ̄	'I'm resting.'
mɨ̄ sɔ́ kɔ́kwà	'I'm returning.'
mɨ̄ sɔ́ kɔ́gjà wārə̀	'I'm stirring manioc.'
ɓɔ́ rò ɓátà	'Where are you going?'
mɨ̄ sɔ́ kɔ́wùsɔ́nə̀	'I'm understanding.'

(28) Vowel hiatus
nà də̀ ɔ́tʃɔ́ nə̀	'Go well.'
mɨ̄ gú jé	'I've returned.'
mɨ̄ bálà ɓə̀ àtà	'I greet you, also.'
mɨ̄ kpá-lú ángá nə̀	'I planted more again.'

Proverbs

(29) Files
  prov1_11025.wav (Speaker A)
  prov2_11025.wav (Speaker K)

(30) See appendix A

Mono vowels in isolation

(31) File
vowel1.wav (Speakers A & K)

(32) i a o ɔ u ɨ e ə

Mono consonants in aCa frame

(33) Files
cons1.wav (Speaker A)
cons2.wav (Speaker K)

(34) apa aba amba ata ada anda aka aga anga akpa agba angba
ama ana afa ava ala ara awa aja aʔa atʃa adʒa andʒa aɓa
aɗa asa aza aʃa aʒa aw̌a aha

Labial contrasts

(35) File
labcont1.wav (Speakers A and K)

(36)
w̌à	'send'
ɓátà	'where'
bàlà	'later'
mbàlà	'elephant'
fà	'cook'
và	'pour'
mà	'show'
ɓàtà	'as, like'

The Elephant, the Turtle, and the Hippo

(37) Files
mbkown1_11025.wav
mbkown2_11025.wav
mbkrd1_11025.wav
mbkrd2_11025.wav
mbkrd3_11025.wav
random1a_11025.wav
random1b_11025.wav

Recordings

      random1c_11025.wav
      random1d_11025.wav
      random2a_11025.wav
      random2b_11025.wav
      random2c_11025.wav
      random2d_11025.wav

(38) See appendix A
    a. Own words. Speakers A and K told story in their own words.
    b. Paragraph format. Speakers A and K read story.
    c. Sentence by sentence format. Speakers A and K were presented these in a non-scientifically randomized order. The order was the same for each of them.

204-item wordlist (Speaker M)

(39) Files

001water.wav	*024ngiri.wav*	*042fa.wav*
002ikpi.wav	*025owo.wav*	*043uku.wav*
003ombo.wav	*025wo.wav*	*044budu.wav*
004na.wav	*026awa.wav*	*045jo.wav*
005shu.wav	*027yabur.wav*	*046vi.wav*
006agya.wav	*028yavor.wav*	*047alafo.wav*
007ungu.wav	*029oeroe.wav*	*048izhi.wav*
008_e.wav	*030mindu.wav*	*049bisha.wav*
009oyo.wav	*031losu.wav*	*050pa.wav*
010_i.wav	*031ulu.wav*	*051za.wav*
011imbi.wav	*032kaga.wav*	*052loolo.wav*
012njo.wav	*032koto.wav*	*053kaney.wav*
013ga.wav	*033di.wav*	*053kuni.wav*
013oco.wav	*034wusoe.wav*	*054ungu.wav*
014ama.wav	*035uwu.wav*	*055kacuo.wav*
015kane.wav	*036idi.wav*	*056mbala.wav*
016ondor.wav	*037angor.wav*	*057gbolo.wav*
017zhu.wav	*037igi.wav*	*058zu.wav*
018sho.wav	*038gara.wav*	*059be.wav*
018showo.wav	*039de.wav*	*059meroe.wav*
020asoeb.wav	*039jo.wav*	*060ji.wav*
021asoe.wav	*039shere.wav*	*061vwa.wav*
022vorow.wav	*040tungu.wav*	*062ishi.wav*
023kindi.wav	*041ji.wav*	*063anger.wav*

064gene.wav
065uyu.wav
066mboer.wav
067yawo.wav
068ogo.wav
069zuwa.wav
070yashe.wav
071kowo.wav
071yarak.wav
072owo.wav
074gband.wav
075ka.wav
076akwar.wav
076wele.wav
077ulu.wav
078tonda.wav
079da.wav
080izi.wav
081le.wav
082ngawo.wav
083gele.wav
083kaney.wav
084koda.wav
085kada.wav
085ozhor.wav
086egere.wav
087nguru.wav
088voro.wav
088zo.wav
089koshe.wav
089kowo.wav
090gusu.wav
091yakos.wav
092avwi.wav
093eshe.wav
094enje.wav
095sheta.wav
096oemoe.wav
097ameya.wav
098vwi.wav
099tima.wav

100yuto.wav
101ingir.wav
102li.wav
103yapu.wav
104anda.wav
105zi.wav
106naana.wav
107ekpe.wav
108ayi.wav
108iya.wav
109kaga.wav
110lo.wav
111gafur.wav
112voma.wav
113cu.wav
114nene.wav
115tafo.wav
116ngawu.wav
117ubu.wav
118i_iri.wav
119ngba.wav
120peya.wav
120turug.wav
121a_a.wav
121azoe.wav
122abuco.wav
123ala.wav
123cacu.wav
124oporo.wav
125yanu.wav
126_a_u.wav
127sungu.wav
128utu.wav
129ngbab.wav
130gava.wav
130muru.wav
131oko.wav
132aba.wav
133uzu.wav
134aya.wav
134teash.wav

135awa.wav
136ada.wav
137baja.wav
138uku.wav
139lu.wav
139shi.wav
140su.wav
141ki.wav
142yavur.wav
143usu.wav
143usuya.wav
144agyac.wav
145aco.wav
146ngato.wav
147fu.wav
147ufu.wav
148za.wav
149ili.wav
150su.wav
151vana.wav
152damba.wav
153ede.wav
154gade.wav
155eshe.wav
155esheo.wav
156wu.wav
157soega.wav
158moomo.wav
159ngome.wav
159ondor.wav
160odoro.wav
161mindu.wav
162udu.wav
163unguy.wav
164ngbug.wav
165ngush.wav
166inji.wav
167o_oro.wav
168ango.wav
169ingbi.wav
170eleoy.wav

Recordings

170inji.wav	*182bakon.wav*	*194na.wav*
171fu.wav	*183ko.wav*	*195yugu.wav*
171ufu.wav	*184teko.wav*	*196uvu.wav*
172yakor.wav	*185ki.wav*	*197dongo.wav*
173olo.wav	*186su.wav*	*197songb.wav*
174_uruo.wav	*187akwa.wav*	*198ogo.wav*
175_a.wav	*188voto.wav*	*199wu.wav*
176ndu.wav	*189kudu.wav*	*200ru.wav*
177andaa.wav	*189ogoro.wav*	*201ziang.wav*
177bobo.wav	*190oeboe.wav*	*202nja.wav*
178osho.wav	*191wo.wav*	*203yindo.wav*
179kumu.wav	*192bale.wav*	*204_e.wav*
180_aang.wav	*193ngind.wav*	
181te.wav	*194gu.wav*	

(40) See appendix in Olson (1996)

Phrases (Speaker M)

(41) Files
  ph01.wav
  ph26.wav

(42)
ājā, mā́ bálà ɓə̀	'I greet you, brother.'
ə̄ə̄, mā́ bàlà ɓə̀ àtà ājā	'I greet you, also, brother.'
kōtóò	'How are you?'
ə̀rə̀ gú-gú nēnē	'I'm fine (lit., there are no issues).'
ɓə̀ sə́ zə̀ à	'lit., You are?'
ə̄ə̄, mā́ sə́ zə̀	'lit., Yes, I am.'
ɓə̀ tó ɓátà á gù ā	'Where are you coming from?'
mā́ tó ɓálə́ kɨ̄ndɨ̄ á gù ásə́-mə̀	'I'm coming from the field and going home.'
mā́ tó ɓándə́ àkèlò	'I'm coming from Kelo.'
ɓə̀ sə́ kə́nà ɓátà	'Where are you going?'
mā́ sə́ kə́nà gàlə́ àndà ɔ̄jɔ̄	'I'm going to the hospital.'
ɓə̀ sə́ kə́mbə̀rə̀ gàɗè	'What are you doing?'
mā́ sə́ gbáàmbà nə̀	'I'm doing nothing'
mā́ gú dà jé	'I'm going home.'
gù də̀ ɔ́tʃɔ́ nə̀	'lit., Go well.'
ɓə́ gù də̀ ɔ́tʃɔ́ nə̀	'lit., You go well.'
kúgù ɓə̀ dá à	'Are you going home?'

ɛ̃ɛ̃, kúgù mə̄ dɔ́-mə̀	'Yes, I'm going home.'
mə̄ gú jé	'I've returned.'
ājā mə̄ jí ndɔ́ kújù ɓə̀	'Brother, I'd like to ask you something.'
wù jù mə̄	'Forgive me.'
ʔà lī gásə̀ndá	'Let's go inside.'
sə̀ gàtɨ́	'Have a seat.'
ɨ́ʔɨ̄rɨ̄ mə̄ kə̀dɔ́ mbàkúwùsè	'My name is Mbakuwuse.'
mə̄ ná líbī gàndɔ́ àgàràbà	'I went to Garaba yesterday.'
mɔ́ nà bámbàtʃá gàndɔ́ àgàràbà	'I'm going to Garaba tomorrow.'
mə̄ wǎ óʃó fə̄ àwō mə̄ gàndɔ́ àgàràbà	'I sent a message to my wife in Garaba.'
tʃɔ́lɔ́ mà jē kpàhà	'He has a wide mouth.'
hérélá màndà	'lock'
ngbàljāljā	'November'
ɓə̀ kə̀gú ɓə̀ bālə̀ àwō zə̀ fə̄ mə̄	'If you go home, greet your wife for me.'
ndʒòkpā də̀ mīndúù də̀ àmànə̀ bàlē	'16'
úngú kɔ́ndʒò tɔ́nə̀ sɔ́pè téāʃó	'There's a bit of drinking water left.'
fūrūtʃā ká jé	'We're out of soap.'
mə̄ jí ndɔ́ kɔ́jùtò kótɔ́ mə̄	'I want to take a bath.'
kūmù mə̄ ká mə̄ wáā	'I've got a headache.'
ásɔ́ kə̀dɔ́ gàɗè	'What is that?'
gàɗè dá à	'What is that?'
á tʃə̀ sɔ́ kə̀dɔ́ èɗè	'Who is that?'
mə̄ dʒí-dʒí nə̄nē	'I didn't hear.'
mə̄ wú sɔ́ nə̀ nēnē	'I don't know.'
ʔà wūtà gàúʃú	'Let's go outside.'
ɔ́tɔ́ nə̀ dɔ́-mə̀	'That's right.'
óʃó kɔ́rɔ̀ jé à	'Good morning.'
ádʒá ūpū à	'Isn't that so true?'
ɔ́ gá wā	'It's good.'
úngú àsɔ́ tʃɔ́ wā	'This is good water.'

Preparing the fields for planting (Speaker M)

(43) File
field.wav

(44) See appendix A

Appendix D

Additional Examples

D.1 Consonant-vowel co-occurrences (cf. chapter 2)

D.1.1 Labial consonants

D.1.1.1 Contrasts between labial consonants in word-initial position.
a. Labial consonants before i:

ɓ	ɓi	'hit'
p	pi	'stick'
b	bīʃà	'two'
mb	mbíkpà	'whitish'
f	-	
v	vi	'dance'
m	mi	'bother'
w̌	w̌i	'throw'

b. Labial consonants before e:

ɓ	-	
p	pe	'winnow'
b	be	'swell'
mb	mbēpā	'dove'
f	fe	'shell'
v	ve	'hit'

m	merə̀	'swell'
w̌	w̌égē	'hot'

c. Labial consonants before ɨ:

ɓ	-	
p	pɨ́ngɨ́w̌ɨ́	'suddenly'
b	bɨlɨ̀	'incite'
mb	mbɨmbɨ̀	'spy'
f	-	
v	vɨ̀vɨ̀	'ant (sp.)'
m	mɨ	'counsel'
w̌	w̌ɨ́lɨ́	'calf'

d. Labial consonants before ə:

ɓ	ɓə̀	'2SG'
p	-	
b	-	
mb	mbərə̀	'do'
f	fə̄	'for'
v	-	
m	mə̄	'1SG'
w̌	w̌ərə̀	'roll' (Kamanda 1998:141)

e. Labial consonants before a:

ɓ	ɓá-lə́	'at'
p	pa	'say'
b	bàdʒà	'rock'
mb	mbātā	'stool'
f	fa	'become'
v	va	'pour'
m	ma	'show'
w̌	w̌a	'send'

f. Labial consonants before u:

ɓ	-	
p	pu	'shake hands'
b	bu	'make black'
mb	mbúgú	'year'
f	fu	'be rotten'
v	vu	'close'
m	múrú	'leopard'
w̌	w̌ùrùjū	'dung beetle'

D.1 Consonant-vowel co-occurrences (cf. chapter 2)

   g. Labial consonants before o:
ɓ	-	
p	pōdʒódʒō	'narrow'
b	-	
mb	-	
f	fó	'up'
v	vōkā	'nape'
m	móròpágò	'traveler'
w̌	-	

   h. Labial consonants before ɔ:
ɓ	-	
p	pɔ̀tú	'sharp'
b	bɔ̀lɔ̀	'tobacco'
mb	-	
f	-	
v	-	
m	mɔ	'be tired'
w̌	-	

D.1.1.2 Contrasts between labial consonants in word-medial position

   a. Labial consonants before i:
ɓ	ngbāɓī	'bone'
p	īpī	'dance'
b	kàlábí	'head pad'
mb	ɓámbìjā	'day after tomorrow'
f	-	
v	kə́-vì	'to dance'
m	kə́-mì	'to bother, to grow'
w̌	ángbɔ́ būw̌ìlɨ̀	'banana (sp.)'

   b. Labial consonants before e:
ɓ	-	
p	dʒèpè	'fish scale'
b	èbè	'liver'
mb	ngòmbè	'gun'
f	kàféè	'coffee' (loanword from French)
v	ndévé	'mane'
m	àméndè	'glue'
w̌	kew̌è	'fold'

c. Labial consonants before ɨ:

ɓ	-	
p	ɨpɨ ~ ūpū	'matter'
b	ndɨ́bɨdà	'heel'
mb	ɨmbɨlɨ	'needle'
f	-	
v	àgbɨ̄vɨ̄	'pimple'
m	ɨ́mɨ́	'thick'
w̌	àw̌ɨ́	'hyena'

d. Labial consonants before ə:

ɓ	ə̀ɓə̀	'2SG'
p	púpə̀lə̀	'kapok' (Kamanda 1998:133)
b	ə́bə́rə́	'quarrel'
mb	kə́-mbə̀rə̀	'to do'
f	-	
v	-	
m	gámə̄	'here'
w̌	-	

e. Labial consonants before a:

ɓ	kòɓà	'illness'
p	àpá	'tsetse fly'
b	lóbà	'clothes'
mb	kàmbà	'knife'
f	àjī lèfà	'midwife'
v	gàvà	'panther'
m	gumà	'prepare'
w̌	kàw̌á	'gruel'

f. Labial consonants before u:

ɓ	ndùɓúrùɓú	'blunt'
p	jápū	'moon, month'
b	jābùrù	'goat'
mb	jāmbùrù	'cooking stones'
f	tʃáfù	'smell, odor'
v	gbādāvū	'fatness'
m	kūmù	'head'
w̌	àw̌ūrūngù	'vehicle'

g. Labial consonants before o:

ɓ	làɓòtò	'millet beer'

D.1 Consonant-vowel co-occurrences (cf. chapter 2)

p	ngápó	'hoe'
b	bòbò	'termite'
mb	làmbó	'abscess'
f	tāfò	'new'
v	jāvóró	'dog'
m	dòmótò	'tomato' (loanword from French)
w̌	-	

h. Labial consonants before ɔ:

ɓ	-	
p	kə́-pɔ̀	'press'
b	-	
mb	-	
f	-	
v	-	
m	kə́mɔ̀	'fatigue'
w̌	-	

D.1.2 Alveolar consonants

D.1.2.1 *Contrasts between alveolar consonants in word-initial position*

a. Alveolar consonants before i:

ɗ	-	
t	tīmà	'tongue'
d	di	'be tangled'
nd	ndìw̌á	'rubber'
s	-	
z	-	
n	ni ~ ɲi	'defecate'
r	ri	'jump'
l	li	'enter'

b. Alveolar consonants before e:

ɗ	-	
t	te	'fall, drop'
d	de	'chop'
nd	ndévé	'mane'
s	sepè ~ səpè	'stay'
z	-	
n	nēnē ~ nə̄nē	'not'

r　　　-
　　　l　　　le　　　'bear fruit'
　c. Alveolar consonants before ɨ:
　　　ɗ　　　-
　　　t　　　tɨ　　　'pick up'
　　　d　　　dɨ　　　'count'
　　　nd　　ndɨ　　'spoil'
　　　s　　　-
　　　z　　　zɨ　　　'eat'
　　　n　　　nɨ̀kpɨ̀　'puff adder'
　　　r　　　-
　　　l　　　lɨ　　　'cut, share'
　d. Alveolar consonants before ə:
　　　ɗ　　　-
　　　t　　　tə́　　　'REFL'
　　　d　　　də　　　'be (equative)'
　　　nd　　ndə́　　'at the home of'
　　　s　　　sə　　　'be (existential)'
　　　z　　　zə̀　　　'2SG'
　　　n　　　nə̀　　　'DET'
　　　r　　　rə ná　　'crush'
　　　l　　　lə　　　'be (existential plural)'
　e. Alveolar consonants before a:
　　　ɗ　　　-
　　　t　　　ta　　　'cut'
　　　d　　　da　　　'slap'
　　　nd　　ndábà　　'table'
　　　s　　　sa　　　'leak'
　　　z　　　za　　　'give, take'
　　　n　　　na　　　'go, come'
　　　r　　　ráwá　　'yell'
　　　l　　　la　　　'lick'
　f. Alveolar consonants before u:
　　　ɗ　　　-
　　　t　　　tu　　　'throw'
　　　d　　　du　　　'tether'
　　　nd　　ndu　　'be sweet'
　　　s　　　su　　　'draw (water)'

D.1 Consonant-vowel co-occurrences (cf. chapter 2)

z	zu	'give birth'
n	-	
r	ru	'go out'
l	lu	'plant'

g. Alveolar consonants before o:

ɗ	-	
t	to	'give'
d	do	'become a fool'
nd	ndo	'approach'
s	sòró	'life'
z	zo	'grill, roast'
n	-	
r	ro	'pass'
l	lo	'lie down'

h. Alveolar consonants before ɔ:

ɗ	-	
t	tɔ	'forge'
d	dɔ	'stomp'
nd	ndɔ́kɔ̄	'flower'
s	sɔ	'harvest'
z	-	
n	nɔ	'pluck'
r	-	
l	lɔ̀gbɔ̀dɔ̀	'trousers'

D.1.2.2 Contrasts between alveolar consonants in word-medial position

a. Alveolar consonants before i:

ɗ	-	
t	kìtì	'squirrel'
d	kómádīrī	'hawk'
nd	kùndī	'harp'
s	-	
z	-	
n	kūnì	'right'
r	kə́-rì	'to jump'
l	àlí	'first thing'

b. Alveolar consonants before e:
ɗ	èɗè	'who'
t	dʒèngétè	'pepper'
d	àdēngɔ̀	'bend'
nd	àméndè	'glue'
s	kɔ́-sèpè ~ kɔ́-sɔ̀pè	'stay'
z	-	
n	gènè	'guest, stranger'
r	àngérépè	'star'
l	bàlē	'one'

c. Alveolar consonants before ɨ:
ɗ	-	
t	àjī wùtɨ̀	'beggar'
d	ɨdɨ̀	'horn, antler'
nd	kɨ̄ndɨ̄	'field'
s	-	
z	ɨ̀zɨ́	'cold'
n	jìní	'husband's mother; daughter-in-law'
r	gɨ́rɨ́ʃì	'bile, gall bladder'
l	ɨ̄mbɨ̄lɨ̄	'needle'

d. Alveolar consonants before ə:
ɗ	-	
t	kótɔ́	'body'
d	ɔ́dā	'and'
nd	ɔ́ndɔ́	'mark'
s	ɔ́sɔ́	'place, point'
z	àzɔ́	'1PL.INCL'
n	ɘnɔ́	'of'
r	ɘ̀rɘ̀	'thing'
l	kɘ̀lɔ́ ~ kèlɔ́	'spoon'

e. Alveolar consonants before a:
ɗ	kūɗā	'debt'
t	kōtā	'large river, sea'
d	kádá	'oil, grease'
nd	màndà	'door'
s	gósá	'green vegetable (sp.)'
z	mbāzā	'xylophone'
n	vànā	'four'

D.1 Consonant-vowel co-occurrences (cf. chapter 2)

r	bāmàrā	'lion'
l	ámbálá	'bait'

f. Alveolar consonants before u:

ɗ	-	
t	bītū	'deaf'
d	bùdú	'bottom'
nd	mīndū	'sand'
s	gūsū	'grass, bushland'
z	kùzū	'death'
n	únú	'sesame'
r	bìrùlú	'porcupine'
l	bìrùlú	'porcupine'

g. Alveolar consonants before o:

ɗ	àngbòɗō	'louse' (Kamanda 1998:134)
t	ótó	'clay'
d	gbàdò	'grub'
nd	ōndō	'short'
s	kásō ~ kɔ́sō	'squash'
z	ózó	'root'
n	mōnō	'Mono'
r	dʒórò	'sorghum'
l	gbòlò	'child'

h. Alveolar consonants before ɔ:

ɗ	kɔ́ɗɔ̀	'monkey'
t	dʒitɔ̀ ~ dʒutɔ̀	'wash'
d	ɔ̄dɔ̄	'laziness'
nd	àjōndɔ̀	'first wife'
s	ɔ̀sɔ̀	'elephant trunk'
z	àlédʒōzɔ́	'hail'
n	kɔ̀nɔ́	'hippopotamus'
r	àngɔ́rɔ́	'throat'
l	mɔ́lɔ̄	'playing'

D.1.3 Palatal consonants

D.1.3.1 Contrasts between palatal consonants in word-initial position

a. Palatal consonants before i:

tʃ	tʃi	'shine'

dʒ	dʒi	'sense'
ndʒ	ndʒi	'be straight'
ʃ	ʃi	'plant'
ʒ	ʒi	'belch'
ɲ	ɲi ~ nì	'rain'
j	ji	'enter'

b. Palatal consonants before e:

tʃ	tʃētʃērə̄	'tick'
dʒ	dʒe	'coil'
ndʒ	ndʒē	'also'
ʃ	ʃe	'heal'
ʒ	ʒe	'grovel'
ɲ	-	
j	je	'EMPH'

c. Palatal consonants before ɨ:

tʃ	-	
dʒ	-	
ndʒ	-	
ʃ	ʃɨkù ~ ʃīkù	'scar'
ʒ	-	
ɲ	-	
j	-	

d. Palatal consonants before ə:

tʃ	tʃə̀	'3SG'
dʒ	-	
ndʒ	-	
ʃ	ʃə́tá ~ ʃétá	'intestines'
ʒ	-	
ɲ	-	
j	-	

e. Palatal consonants before a:

tʃ	tʃáfù	'smell'
dʒ	dʒa	'spot'
ndʒ	ndʒa	'vomit'
ʃ	ʃarà	'give doubt'
ʒ	-	
ɲ	ɲa	'have patience'
j	ja	'rest'

D.1 Consonant-vowel co-occurrences (cf. chapter 2)

f. Palatal consonants before u:
tʃ	tʃu	'die'
dʒ	-	
ndʒ	-	
ʃ	ʃu	'be bitter'
ʒ	ʒu	'burn'
ɲ	-	
j	ju	'ask'

g. Palatal consonants before o:
tʃ	-	
dʒ	dʒo	'cultivate'
ndʒ	ndʒo	'drink'
ʃ	ʃo	'burn'
ʒ	ʒo	'wake up'
ɲ	-	
j	jo	'abstain'

h. Palatal consonants before ɔ:
tʃ	tʃɔ	'taste good'
dʒ	-	
ndʒ	ndʒɔ	'scratch'
ʃ	-	
ʒ	-	
ɲ	-	
j	jɔ	'buy'

D.1.3.2 Contrasts between palatal consonants in word-medial position

a. Palatal consonants before i:
tʃ	ītʃī	'song'
dʒ	àkídʒì	'bead'
ndʒ	ngbándʒì	'rust'
ʃ	ngúʃī	'saliva'
ʒ	īʒī	'tooth, tusk'
ɲ	kə́-ɲì ~ kə́-nì	'to rain'
j	àjī	'mother'

b. Palatal consonants before e:
tʃ	-	
dʒ	gbàdʒéè	'pineapple'

ndʒ	əndʒē	'3PL'
ʃ	kōʃē	'war'
ʒ	ēʒē	'caterpillar'
ɲ	-	
j	àjēngɔ̀	'person'

c. Palatal consonants before i:

tʃ	-
dʒ	-
ndʒ	-
ʃ	-
ʒ	-
ɲ	-
j	-

d. Palatal consonants before ə:

tʃ	gbè-tʃə́-lə́	'hope, thought'
dʒ	-	
ndʒ	-	
ʃ	-	
ʒ	-	
ɲ	-	
j	-	

e. Palatal consonants before a:

tʃ	fūrūtʃā	'soap'
dʒ	bàdʒà	'stone, rock'
ndʒ	ngèndʒà	'money, silver'
ʃ	bīʃà	'two'
ʒ	gūʒà	'house rat' (Kamanda 1998:140)
ɲ	gàɲá	'branch'
j	mbējā	'in-law'

f. Palatal consonants before u:

tʃ	tʃátʃū	'face'
dʒ	àdʒùkùmá	'ghost, ogre'
ndʒ	mbùndʒú	'foreigner'
ʃ	ūʃū	'bitterness'
ʒ	kə́-ʒù	'to burn'
ɲ	-	
j	dʒùjū	'ancestor'

D.1 Consonant-vowel co-occurrences (cf. chapter 2)

g. Palatal consonants before o:
tʃ	àtʃó	'louse'
dʒ	pōdʒódʒō	'narrow'
ndʒ	ngbōndʒō	'frame'
ʃ	téāʃó	'small'
ʒ	ōʒōrō	'fat'
ɲ	-	
j	gòjó	'goiter, crop'

h. Palatal consonants before ɔ:
tʃ	būtʃɔ́	'darkness, night'
dʒ	kɔ̄dʒɔ́	'lizard'
ndʒ	-	
ʃ	gbɔ̀ʃɔ̀	'bedroom'
ʒ	-	
ɲ	-	
j	ɔ̄jɔ̄	'tree'

D.1.4 Velar and glottal consonants

D.1.4.1 Contrasts between velar and glottal consonants in word-initial position

a. Velar/glottal consonants before i:
ʔ	ʔi	'attach'
k	ki	'be sharp'
g	gi	'push, return'
ng	ngímá	'palm tree'
h	-	

b. Velar/glottal consonants before e:
ʔ	ʔe	'call'
k	kekà	'hatch'
g	gerɛ̀	'grow'
ng	ngésā	'rope'
h	héré	'sharp'

c. Velar/glottal consonants before ɨ:
ʔ	ʔɨrɨ̀	'rub'
k	kɨ	'cry'
g	gɨ	'sow'
ng	ngɨrɨ̀	'snore'
h	-	

d. Velar/glottal consonants before ə:
- ʔ   -
- k   kəlɔ́   'spoon'
- g   -
- ng   -
- h   -

e. Velar/glottal consonants before a:
- ʔ   ʔa   'suck'
- k   ka   'be finished'
- g   ga   'be good'
- ng   nga   'bark'
- h   hàgà   'hard'

f. Velar/glottal consonants before u:
- ʔ   ʔu   'caress'
- k   ku   'press'
- g   gu   'return'
- ng   ngūzù   'pregnancy'
- h   -

g. Velar/glottal consonants before o:
- ʔ   ʔorò   'split'
- k   ko   'put'
- g   go   'sprinkle'
- ng   ngólà   'tears'
- h   hójá òʔò   'whisper'

h. Velar/glottal consonants before ɔ:
- ʔ   ʔɔ   'climb'
- k   kɔ   'harvest'
- g   gɔ   'bend down'
- ng   ngɔ̀zū   'jigger'
- h   hɔ̀rɔ̀gɔ̀   'hidden'

D.1.4.2 Contrasts between velar and glottal consonants in word-medial position

a. Velar/glottal consonants before i:
- ʔ   wǐʔí   'throw out'
- k   àkídʒì   'bead'
- g   dʒígí   'whole'
- ng   bīngī   'bracelet, ring'

D.1 Consonant-vowel co-occurrences (cf. chapter 2)

    h   -

b. Velar/glottal consonants before e:
- ʔ   và?è   'throw out (PL)'
- k   vèkè   'okra'
- g   égérɔ́   'big'
- ng   màngé   'corn, maize'
- h   éhérɔ́   'wax'

c. Velar/glottal consonants before ɨ:
- ʔ   ɨ?ɨrɨ   'name'
- k   àkɨ́   'razor'
- g   àgɨ́ngɨ́   'abscess'
- ng   bɨ́ngɨ́   'compound, home'
- h   -

d. Velar/glottal consonants before ə:
- ʔ   -
- k   -
- g   -
- ng   -
- h   -

e. Velar/glottal consonants before a:
- ʔ   ā?á   'aunt'
- k   dakà   'borrow'
- g   bàgá   'cheek'
- ng   lēngā   'slit drum'
- h   kpàhà   'wide open'

f. Velar/glottal consonants before u:
- ʔ   à?ú   'uncle'
- k   ndúkú   'vine, pole'
- g   àlúgù   'mushroom'
- ng   fàngú   'gruel, pap'
- h   ngòhūrū   'frog' (Kamanda 1998:141)

g. Velar/glottal consonants before o:
- ʔ   ò?ò   'word, language'
- k   bākòngɔ̄   'turtle'
- g   ōgō   'village'
- ng   kōngō   'crab'
- h   -

h. Velar/glottal consonants before ɔ:
ʔ	jɔ̄ʔɔ́	'cricket'
k	kɔ̀kɔ̀	'termite'
g	belègɔ̀	'become bent with age'
ng	bākòngɔ̄	'turtle'
h	ngɔ̄hɔ́rɔ́	'narrow, hollow'

D.1.5 Labial-velar consonants

D.1.5.1 Contrasts between labial-velar consonants in word-initial position

a. Labial-velar consonants before i:
kp	kpi	'be tart'
gb	-	
ngb	ngbī	'deep'
w	-	

b. Labial-velar consonants before e:
kp	kpèkpérə́	'joint'
gb	gbe	'think, believe'
ngb	ngbèjà	'white clay'
w	wélé ~ wólé	'arrow'

c. Labial-velar consonants before ɨ:
kp	kpɨ̀kpɨ̀	'eagle, vulture'
gb	-	
ngb	ngbɨ́	'clear, open'
w	-	

d. Labial-velar consonants before ə:
kp	kpə́tə̀	'just happened'
gb	gbə̀də́rə́	'clumsy' (Kamanda 1998:136)
ngb	ngbə̄lēkō	'iron'
w	-	

e. Labial-velar consonants before a:
kp	kpa	'flee'
gb	gba	'moisten'
ngb	ngba	'be many'
w	wa	'cut'

f. Labial-velar consonants before u:
kp	kpu	'heap up'
gb	-	

D.1 Consonant-vowel co-occurrences (cf. chapter 2)

    ngb   ngbúgú   'dry season'
    w   wu   'see'
g. Labial-velar consonants before o:
    kp   kpòtò   'hat'
    gb   gbo   'sound of drum'
    ngb   ngbōndʒō   'frame'
    w   wo   'kill'
h. Labial-velar consonants before ɔ:
    kp   kpɔ   'coagulate'
    gb   gbɔ   'receive'
    ngb   ngbɔ   'light, amass'
    w   -

D.1.5.2 Contrasts between labial-velar consonants in word-medial position

a. Labial-velar consonants before i:
    kp   kpíkpí   'different'
    gb   -
    ngb   lingbì   'weigh, measure'
    w   -
b. Labial-velar consonants before e:
    kp   ʃékpé   'hamper'
    gb   kɔ́-gbè   'think, believe'
    ngb   tʃàngbédà   'fork in road'
    w   jāwè   'January'
c. Labial-velar consonants before ɨ:
    kp   nɨ̀kpɨ̀   'puff adder'
    gb   àgbɨvɨ   'pimple'
    ngb   kpɨngbɨlɨ   'plank'
    w   -
d. Labial-velar consonants before ə:
    kp   -
    gb   -
    ngb   àngbɔ́lèngāndā   'peg'
    w   -
e. Labial-velar consonants before a:
    kp   ndʒòkpā   'ten'
    gb   kógbà   'granary'

ngb	kéngbā	'alone'
w	bīwā	'nasal mucus'

f. Labial-velar consonants before u:

kp	úkpúlú	'heap'
gb	tʃágbúrú kūmù	'crown of the head'
ngb	lūngbù	'April'
w	káɗàwú	'hiccough'

g. Labial-velar consonants before o:

kp	làkpòtò	'millet beer'
gb	gbògbò	'mat'
ngb	àngbó	'festival'
w	ndàwò	'forge'

h. Labial-velar consonants before ɔ:

kp	nə̄kpɔ̄rɔ̄	'dwarf'
gb	gbɔ̀ngɔ́gbɔ́	'conclusion'
ngb	ángbɔ́	'banana'
w	-	

D.2. Vowel-vowel (CV₁CV₂) co-occurrences (cf. chapter 2)

i - i	dʒígí	'whole'
i - e	——	
i - ɨ	dʒìndɨ	'greens'
i - ə	kɔ́-jì-ndɔ́-rə̀	'kindness'
i - a	ngímá	'palm tree'
i - u	dʒìjū	'great grandparent'
i - o	àjī-bó	'relative'
i - ɔ	sə dígɔ́	'stoop'
e - i	ngéʒì jāvūrū	'drizzle'
e - e	dʒèpè	'fish-scale'
e - ɨ	——	
e - ə	dʒerə̀	'forget'
e - a	lēngā	'talking drum'
e - u	pélézū	'bat'
e - o	pewò	'wither'
e - ɔ	tékɔ̄	'cough'

D.2. Vowel-vowel (CV₁CV₂) co-occurrences (cf. chapter 2)

i - i	tīrīndʒī	'leech'
i - e	jápū ɓándɔ́ zìjéna	'full moon'
i - ɨ	bíngɨ	'compound'
i - ə	——	
i - a	ʔɨmà	'yawn'
i - u	àlɨ́vù	'family'
i - o	za mɨʃó	'support'
i - ɔ	——	
ə - i	kpɔ̄līndūvū	'kidney'
ə - e	kəléngɔ̀ngɔ̀	'chameleon'
ə - ɨ	kɔ́-dɨ̀ ərə̀	'number'
ə - ə	mbərə̀	'do'
ə - a	təràlē	'directly'
ə - u	kəvū ~ kùvū	'stomach'
ə - o	kpɔ́ə̀ndɔ̀rɔ̀	'naked'
ə - ɔ	lətɔ̀rɔ̀	'toad'
a - i	ngbāɓī	'bone'
a - e	bàlē	'one'
a - ɨ	màngɨ̄	'stick used for animal trap'
a - ə	gbārə̀	'utensil'
a - a	bàdʒà	'rock'
a - u	gbābù	'giddiness'
a - o	gbàdò	'grub'
a - ɔ	àlɔ̀ ~ ɔ̀lɔ̀	'sun'
u - i	kùndī	'harp'
u - e	buwĕlè	'type of banana'
u - ɨ	àjī wùtɨ̀	'beggar'
u - ə	màwūtə̄	'hip'
u - a	kútʃá	'mosquito'
u - u	bùdú	'buttocks'
u - o	ndùrùgòjó	'heron'
u - ɔ	júngɔ́	'sister'
o - i	——	
o - e	ngómē	'dew'
o - ɨ	——	

o - ə	kó-tə́	'body'
o - a	kōtā	'large river'
o - u	kōpū	'September'
o - o	bòbò	'termite'
o - ɔ	vōtɔ̀	'three'
ɔ - i	za tɔ̀ndʒì	'straighten'
ɔ - e	tɔpè	'stick'
ɔ - ɨ	——	
ɔ - ə	jākɔ̄nə́ ~ jākāné	'finger'
ɔ - a	ngbɔɓà	'join'
ɔ - u	kɔ̀pù	'silk cotton tree'
ɔ - o	ngɔ̄tō	'chicken'
ɔ - ɔ	bɔ̀lɔ̀	'tobacco'

D.3 Consonant-tone co-occurrences (cf. chapter 3)

D.3.1 Consonants before H

a. Labial consonants before H:

ɓ	àɓí	'hammer'
p	pákūlú	'parrot'
b	àbá	'father'
mb	dàmbá	'tail'
f	āfú	'ant (sp.)'
v	vúdà	'cultivated ground'
m	àméndè	'glue'
w̌	àw̌í	'hyena'
w	àwájà	'baby'

b. Alveolar consonants before H:

ɗ	-	
t	àtú	'cat (sp.)'
d	àdú	'knot'
nd	dɔ̀ndú	'December'
s	gósá	'type of green'
z	àzɔ́	'1PL.INCL'
n	kānɔ́ ~ kāné	'arm, hand'
r	hàrá	'giant'
l	lóbà	'clothes'

D.3 Consonant-tone co-occurrences (cf. chapter 3)

    c. Palatal consonants before H:
tʃ	àtʃó	'louse'
dʒ	dʒórò	'sorghum'
ndʒ	mbùndʒú	'foreigner'
ʃ	āʃóngbà	'type of sugarcane'
ʒ	-	
ɲ	gàɲá	'branch'
j	gòjó	'goiter, crop'

    d. Velar/glottal consonants before H:
ʔ	āʔá	'aunt'
k	káɗàwú	'hiccough'
g	bàgá	'cheek'
ng	ngágō	'eggplant'
h	héré	'sharp'

    e. Labial-velar consonants before H:
kp	íkpí	'tart'
gb	gbándà	'net'
ngb	ngbákò	'wine'

D.3.2 Consonants before M

    a. Labial consonants before M:
ɓ	ngbāɓī	'bone'
p	pāngā	'hip'
b	ābā	'yam'
mb	mbāzā	'xylophone'
f	òfōrò	'grass, lawn'
v	vūvù	'sugar ant'
m	límā	'a long time ago'
w̌	lo w̌ɨrɨmá	'gnaw around'
w	àwō	'wife'

    b. Alveolar consonants before M:
ɗ	kūɗā	'debt'
t	bītū	'deaf person'
d	àdāngà	'lake'
nd	bìndī	'locust'
s	àsūngù	'flood'
z	kùzū	'death'
n	ə̀nə̄	'3SG.LOG'

r	bāmàrā	'lion'
l	bàlē	'one'

c. Palatal consonants before M:

tʃ	tʃūlà	'shame'
dʒ	dʒīngīlī	'mistake'
ndʒ	əndʒē	'3PL'
ʃ	kōʃē	'war'
ʒ	ēʒē	'caterpillar'
ɲ	-	
j	àjī	'mother'

d. Velar/glottal consonants before M:

ʔ	āʔā	'1PL.EXCL'
k	kākó	'leaf'
g	àrùgū	'biting midge'
ng	ngāwū	'nose'
h	āhārā	'dry'

e. Labial-velar consonants before M:

kp	kpōkɔ̀	'big hoe'
gb	gbāndà	'temporary shelter'
ngb	ngbāngú	'type of drum'

D.3.3 Consonants before L

a. Labial consonants before L:

ɓ	kòɓà	'illness'
p	ndʒàpà	'type of stick'
b	bàdʒà	'stone, rock'
mb	mbòwó	'cocoyam, taro'
f	fàngú	'gruel, pap'
v	vūvù	'sugar ant'
m	kūmù	'head'
w̌	w̌ìʔí	'throw out'
w	kówà	'baby sling'

b. Alveolar consonants before L:

ɗ	kɔ́ɗɔ̀	'monkey'
t	átà	'grandparent, grandchild'
d	dàmbá	'tail'
nd	ndìw̌á	'rubber'
s	sùrà	'broom'

D.3. Consonant-tone co-occurrences (cf. chapter 3)

z	gūzà	'mouse'
n	kūnì	'right'
r	àrùgū	'biting midge'
l	būlà	'blind person'

c. Palatal consonants before L:

tʃ	tʃìkɨ́	'island'
dʒ	dʒìndɨ̄	'type of green'
ndʒ	ndʒòkpā	'ten'
ʃ	bīʃà	'two'
ʒ	ngéʒì jāvūrū	'drizzle'
ɲ	kɔ́-ɲì	'rain'
j	éjà	'firstborn'

d. Velar/glottal consonants before L:

ʔ	dʒèʔèrə̀ mīndū	'gravel'
k	kàkílí	'basket'
g	gàngā	'calf'
ng	ngàrá	'tendon'
h	hàrá	'giant'

e. Labial-velar consonants before L:

kp	kpɔ̀lɔ̄	'nightjar'
gb	gbàgūrū	'proverb'
ngb	ngbìngɨ́	'warthog'

D.4 Formant and bandwidth values for Mono vowels (Speaker K) (cf. chapter 8)

a

		F_1	F_2	F_3	F_4	BW_1	BW_2	BW_3	BW_4
bàgá (1) 'cheek'	Spec.	777.69	1440.16	2433.88	3441.99				
	LPC	701.67	1325.45	2322.83	3646.43	52.72	125.21	121.98	127.36
	FFT	700	1325	2325	3350				
bàgá (2)	Spec.	734.48	1425.76	2361.87	3787.63				
	LPC	702.35	1360.21	2433.79	3607.58	56.23	95.92	111.88	281.61
	FFT	700	1375	2375	3700				
bā̱kòngɔ̄ (1) 'turtle'	Spec	595.56	1148.59	2325.53	3431.58				
	LPC	598.31	1115.17	2292.36	3425.14	60.87	72.87	80.29	141.78
	FFT	625	1075	2325	3425				
bā̱kòngɔ̄ (2)	Spec	609.74	1205.31	2282.99	3488.3				
	LPC	622.15	1217.25	2296.55	3518.41	58.23	75.92	81.53	92.02
	FFT	625	1150	2275	3525				
bàle̱ (1) 'one'	Spec	763.29	1468.97	2491.48	3773.23				
	LPC	714.58	1462.72	2463.3	3628.64	68.10	46.99	122.22	108.90
	FFT	725	1450	2450	3550				
bàle̱ (2)	Spec	705.68	1569.78	2534.69	3701.22				
	LPC	761.17	1537.48	2521.28	3693.25	96.38	75.16	69.88	81.11
	FFT	775	1475	2475	3725				

D.4 Formant and bandwidth values for Mono vowels (Speaker K) (cf. chapter 8)

tàʔwá (1) 'basin'	Spec LPC FFT	638.1 639.26 650	1262.03 1248.22 1250	2254.63 2268.56 2225	3601.74 3394.72 3175	48.68	151.76	93.82	247.98

Note: The actual value of F_4 given by the LPC algorithm is 3500.61 Hz with a bandwidth of 1353.64 Hz. The values of F_4 and BW_4 given above are actually F_5 and BW_5, respectively, as calculated by the LPC algorithm.

tàʔwá (2)	Spec LPC FFT	623.92 630.15 625	1205.31 1183.66 1150	2240.45 2230.68 2100	3459.94 3521.84 3450	30.07	160.12	108.22	315.41

Note: The actual value of F_4 given by the LPC algorithm is 3497.40 Hz with a bandwidth of 224.91 Hz. The values of F_4 and BW_4 given above are actually F_5 and BW_5, respectively, as calculated by the LPC algorithm.

tāfō (1) 'new'	Spec LPC FFT	734.48 706.12 700	1454.56 1397.92 1350	2433.88 2394.98 2400	3758.82 3859.26 3725	25.63	62.04	61.99	132.3

tāfō (2)	Spec LPC FFT	705.68 681.73 700	1440.16 1332.22 1325	2462.68 2393.21 2400	3758.82 3845.7 3725	33.92	74.74	88.08	94.91

Note: The actual value of F_4 given by the LPC algorithm is 3429.16 Hz with a bandwidth of 286.48 Hz. The values of F_4 and BW_4 given above are actually F_5 and BW_5, respectively, as calculated by the LPC algorithm.

e

word	method								
mbḗjā (1) 'in-laws'	Spec	411.22	1885.95	2680.03	3516.66			109.15	63.23
	LPC	418.56	1888.25	2691.79	3535.34	22.5	47.32	109.15	63.23
	FFT	375	1900	2675	3500				
mbḗjā (2)	Spec	425.4	1758.33	2651.67	3502.48			74.04	49.77
	LPC	419.89	1771.03	2668.51	3519.55	25.67	91.97	74.04	49.77
	FFT	400	1775	2625	3500				
pètè (1) 'full'	Spec.	417.65	2001.83	2707.51	3557.2			102.55	69.57
	LPC	378.04	2015.92	2723.37	3523.04	12.92	56.00	102.55	69.57
	FFT	350	2050	2725	3525				
pètè (2)	Spec.	417.65	1973.02	2707.51	3514			101.26	51.8
	LPC	365.78	1897.79	2736.35	3490.68	14.26	56.79	101.26	51.8
	FFT	325	1925	2750	3450				
pḗjà (1) 'navel'	Spec	368.68	1942.67	2651.67	3516.66			146.27	94.18
	LPC	370.26	1971.16	2708.1	3527.19	30.44	33.18	146.27	94.18
	FFT	350	1950	2650	3475				
pḗjà (2)	Spec	382.86	1999.39	2736.75	3516.66			140.47	85.58
	LPC	386.97	2004.91	2738.68	3534.73	29.64	36.08	140.47	85.58
	FFT	350	2000	2700	3950				

Note: The actual value of F_4 given by the LPC algorithm is 3231.68 Hz with a bandwidth of 480.30 Hz. The values of F_4 and BW_4 given above are actually F_5 and BW_5, respectively, as calculated by the LPC algorithm.

D.4 Formant and bandwidth values for Mono vowels (Speaker K) (cf. chapter 8)

		F_1	F_2	F_3	F_4	BW_1	BW_2	BW_3	BW_4
tẽwẽ (1) 'ant (sp.)'	Spec	368.68	1843.41	2580.77	3403.22	37.42	44.58	96.65	61.48
	LPC	369.81	1846.96	2606.07	3416.74				
	FFT	325	1875	2575	3400				
tẽwẽ (2)	Spec	340.32	1956.85	2609.13	3459.94	23.18	68.08	100.6	47.44
	LPC	356.89	1957	2632.78	3443.3				
	FFT	325	1975	2625	3400				

Note: The actual value of F_4 given by the LPC algorithm is 2902.10 Hz with a bandwidth of 1913.07 Hz. The values of F_4 and BW_4 given above are actually F_5 and BW_5, respectively, as calculated by the LPC algorithm.

		F_1	F_2	F_3	F_4	BW_1	BW_2	BW_3	BW_4
vẽdʒà (1) 'forest'	Spec	340.32	1843.41	2779.29	3488.3	17.82	62.79	76.4	80.15
	LPC	353.98	1853.9	2789.33	3499.49				
	FFT	325	1850	2800	3475				
vẽdʒà (2)	Spec	368.68	1871.77	2736.75	3502.48	21.52	69.48	87.31	100.14
	LPC	353.16	1877.84	2747.88	3495.56				
	FFT	325	1900	2750	3450				

ə

		F_1	F_2	F_3	F_4	BW_1	BW_2	BW_3	BW_4
də (1) 'be'	Spec	368.68	1432.19	2325.53	3389.04	40.73	101.72	54.93	66.29
	LPC	371.23	1439.86	2329.88	3365.97				
	FFT	300	1400	2325	3350				
də (2)	Spec	354.5	1389.65	2268.81	3431.81	47.55	100.82	33.72	37.41
	LPC	377.58	1436.71	2299.65	3429.06				
	FFT	300	1375	2275	3450				

ɛ́bárɛ́ (1) 'quarrel'	Spec LPC FFT	453.76 472.18 425	1290.39 1298.02 1275	2410.61 2419.97 2450	3403.22 3442.25 3375	44.68	45.2	152.9	97.12

Note: The actual value of F_4 given by the LPC algorithm is 3341.60 Hz with a bandwidth of 315.12 Hz. The values of F_4 and BW_4 given above are actually F_5 and BW_5, respectively, as calculated by the LPC algorithm.

ɛ́bárɛ́ (2)	Spec LPC FFT	496.3 500.71 450	1276.21 1312.67 1275	2424.79 2464.13 2400	3502.48 3519.59 3500	31.18	59.17	136.6	24.56
ɛ́dɛ̀ (1) 'if'	Spec LPC FFT	467.94 463.37 425	1503.09 1481.8 1475	2410.61 2435.96 2450	3516.66 3562.12 3450	31.49	43.27	98.27	142.71

Note: The actual value of F_4 given by the LPC algorithm is 3425.03 Hz with a bandwidth of 420.08 Hz. The values of F_4 and BW_4 given above are actually F_5 and BW_5, respectively, as calculated by the LPC algorithm.

ɛ́dɛ̀ (2)	Spec LPC FFT	425.4 425.6 375	1503.09 1506.4 1475	2368.07 2410.37 2400	3630.1 3655.9 3650	45.78	72.23	83.33	44
ɛ́ndɛ́ (1) 'mark'	Spec LPC FFT	368.68 391.21 375	1418.01 1447.32 1400	2382.25 2389.11 2375	3360.68 3393.01 3375	47.17	95.4	37.6	24.66

D.4 Formant and bandwidth values for Mono vowels (Speaker K) (cf. chapter 8) 261

		F_1	F_2	F_3	F_4	BW_1	BW_2	BW_3	BW_4
éndé (2)	Spec	340.32	1418.01	2382.25	3389.04				
	LPC	355.4	1435.4	2385.69	3382.38	23.06	104.98	61.1	22.51
	FFT	325	1375	2350	3375				
tə̄kə̀kà (1) 'pain'	Spec	411.22	1559.81	2368.07	3431.58				
	LPC	414.01	1578.71	2402.32	3433.2	42.89	125.66	159.58	48.12
	FFT	350	1575	2375	3425				
tə̄kə̀kà (2)	Spec	397.04	1474.73	2339.71	3545.71				
	LPC	407.17	1511.15	2394.33	3555.79	46.93	81.19	95.38	29.24
	FFT	350	1475	2350	3525				

i

		F_1	F_2	F_3	F_4	BW_1	BW_2	BW_3	BW_4
bī̄jà (1) 'two'	Spec.	388.84	1987.42	2880.33	3499.6				
	LPC	312.45	1950.73	2874.22	3456.34	9.84	78.29	73.06	60.44
	FFT	250	1975	2875	3375				

Note: The actual value of F_4 given by the LPC algorithm is 3391.82 Hz with a bandwidth of 392.77 Hz. The values of F_4 and BW_4 given above are actually F_5 and BW_5, respectively, as calculated by the LPC algorithm.

		F_1	F_2	F_3	F_4	BW_1	BW_2	BW_3	BW_4
bī̄jà (2)	Spec.	388.84	2045.03	2808.32	3514				
	LPC	303.03	1954.43	2825.82	3531.35	9.04	53.82	76.49	100.12
	FFT	275	1975	2850	3425				

Note: The actual value of F_4 given by the LPC algorithm is 3366.12 Hz with a bandwidth of 184.12 Hz. The values of F_4 and BW_4 given above are actually F_5 and BW_5, respectively, as calculated by the LPC algorithm.

bīṭū (1) 'deaf'	Spec LPC FFT	360.04 296.33 250	1929.82 1936.86 1925	2577.89 2697.19 2650	3355.58 3292.09 3250	11.41	37.81	72.08	18.81
bīṭū (2)	Spec LPC FFT	374.44 289.62 250	1973.02 1925.2 1925	2693.1 2732.5 2775	3369.98 3282.43 3250	9.62	48.42	94.37	46.57
bijā (1) 'ebony'	Spec LPC FFT	297.78 295.42 275	1942.67 1944.73 1925	2892.73 2903.13 2925	3459.94 3483.92 3350	5.78	40.71	41.91	127.85
bijā (2)	Spec LPC FFT	283.6 282.68 275	1956.85 1979.28 1975	2963.63 2972.26 2975	3502.48 3463.73 3425	10.99	17.18	49.25	158.73
kìtî (1) 'squirrel'	Spec LPC FFT	269.42 278.27 250	1914.31 1930.95 1925	2878.55 2933.98 2950	3431.58 3364.07 3250	8.21	29.69	36.18	112.38
kìtî (2)	Spec LPC FFT	241.06 269.12 250	1857.59 1874.91 1875	2765.11 2793.56 2800	3346.5 3325.78 3300	11.83	57.41	30.66	33.22
līḅī (1) 'yesterday'	Spec LPC FFT	326.14 336.29 325	1999.39 1956.55 1975	2836.01 2849.76 2850	3417.4 3418.91 3425	12.11	100.26	64.13	35.19

D.4 Formant and bandwidth values for Mono vowels (Speaker K) (cf. chapter 8) 263

		F1	F2	F3	F4	B1	B2	B3	B4
líbì (2)	Spec	326.14	1914.31	2807.65	3403.22	8.51	71.77	80.24	36.25
	LPC	336.3	1905.6	2814.18	3389.04				
	FFT	325	1925	2800	3350				
ị									
àdílà (1) 'dusk'	Spec	269.42	1644.89	2282.99	3332.32	35.88	63	33.34	29.52
	LPC	294.48	1689.77	2305.55	3341.4				
	FFT	275	1675	2250	3350				
àdílà (2)	Spec	283.6	1715.79	2297.17	3417.4	39.29	91.99	61.34	21.41
	LPC	299.11	1773.83	2291.38	3419.99				
	FFT	250	1750	2250	3425				
àkí (1) 'razor'	Spec	311.96	1503.09	2268.81	3360.68	11.3	171.95	27.95	22.89
	LPC	312.02	1478.75	2275.99	3349.54				
	FFT	300	1500	2250	3325				
àkí (2)	Spec	297.78	1559.81	2467.33	3374.86	12.48	101.37	75.63	25.42
	LPC	315.28	1539.65	2428.79	3367.33				
	FFT	300	1525	2375	3325				
dì (1) 'count'	Spec	255.24	1630.71	2183.73	3346.5	33.92	190.53	76.99	16.16
	LPC	290.22	1600.38	2170.79	3369.16				
	FFT	250	1450	2150	3350				

Word	Method								
dì (2)	Spec	283.6	1744.15	2169.55	3346.5	41.04	201.91	105.74	36.33
	LPC	296.68	1702.52	2173.63	3376.53				
	FFT	250	1800	2175	3375				
kìndī (1) 'field'	Spec	297.78	1687.43	2325.53	3360.68	25.55	130.59	96.46	9.36
	LPC	302.09	1708.78	2341.72	3357.51				
	FFT	275	1700	2275	3325				
kìndī (2)	Spec	297.78	1673.25	2311.35	3318.14	16.11	99.16	58.88	36.62
	LPC	308.14	1680.74	2330.14	3346.65				
	FFT	275	1700	2325	3325				
kpìkpì (1) 'eagle'	Spec	283.6	1347.11	2183.73	3218.87	38.46	172.82	228.7	24.32
	LPC	295.68	1490.38	2428.49	3199.92				
	FFT	275	1325	2100	3200				
kpìkpì (2)	Spec	269.42	1247.85	2141.19	3204.69	55.04	137.22	118.27	14.45
	LPC	294.18	1288.39	2159.36	3214.47				
	FFT	250	1225	2075	3175				
o̩									
bó̩wō̩ (1) 'python'	Spec	388.84	950.51	2491.48	3269.17	109.08	144.34	184.77	123.23
	LPC	413.88	874.67	2375.46	3264.07				
	FFT	350	775	2475	3225				

D.4 Formant and bandwidth values for Mono vowels (Speaker K) (cf. chapter 8)

		F_1	F_2	F_3	F_4	BW_1	BW_2	BW_3	BW_4
bówō (2)	Spec	446.45	907.3	2520.28	3254.77	189.79	96.28	185.4	108.79
	LPC	402.57	837.72	2147.66	3530.69				
	FFT	375	825	?	3525				

Note: The actual value of F_4 given by the LPC algorithm is 3002.06 Hz with a bandwidth of 432.69 Hz. The values of F_4 and BW_4 given above are actually F_5 and BW_5, respectively, as calculated by the LPC algorithm.

		F_1	F_2	F_3	F_4	BW_1	BW_2	BW_3	BW_4
dōrō (1) 'partridge'	Spec	397.04	921.7	2467.33	3275.59	51.96	94.8	98.64	77.06
	LPC	409.36	911.2	2489.36	3337.98				
	FFT	375	850	2400	3200				
dōrō (2)	Spec	382.86	964.24	2481.51	3289.77	37.69	97.53	102.15	66.74
	LPC	407.25	968.4	2466.4	3288.42				
	FFT	350	950	2400	3225				
sòró (1) 'life'	Spec	411.22	950.06	2538.23	3346.5	65.04	41.94	66.49	53.71
	LPC	411.18	957.65	2544.32	3332.58				
	FFT	350	975	2475	3350				
sòró (2)	Spec	397.04	1020.96	2467.33	3417.4	48.05	103.56	69.86	36.78
	LPC	420.96	1011.21	2521.81	3416.09				
	FFT	350	1025	2450	3425				
vōkā (1) 'nape'	Spec	467.94	893.34	2495.69	3417.4	74.36	72.86	56.24	34.37
	LPC	458.02	911.36	2519.4	3430.44				
	FFT	400	850	2500	3425				

vōkā (2)	Spec LPC FFT	439.58 451.83 400	893.34 913.5 850	2495.69 2501.37 2500	3431.58 3439.67 3425	45.39	64.52	54.01	51.91
vōtò (1) 'three'	Spec LPC FFT	425.4 474.87 450	978.42 1001.67 875	2623.31 2639.35 2650	3374.86 3430.48 3400	42.49	95.17	71.23	162.37
vōtò (2)	Spec LPC FFT	496.3 494.26 450	1020.96 1014.76 1000	2580.77 2590.25 2600	3403.22 3430.17 3400	59.18	39.62	43.15	65.05
bɔ̄lɔ̀ (1) 'tobacco'	Spec LPC FFT	576.07 656.7 550	1036.92 935.47 975	2520.28 2515.09 2525	3485.19 3513.41 3500	137.86	311.92	122.23	33.13
bɔ̄lɔ̀ (2)	Spec LPC FFT	532.86 595.05 550	1036.92 967.11 925	2534.69 2543.61 2525	3499.6 3477.23 3475	141.42	150.76	134.6	27.88
kɔ̄kɔ̀ (1) 'termite'	Spec LPC FFT	524.66 564.05 550	935.88 961.72 900	2041.93 2077.07 2100	3247.23 3232.1 3250	85.26	80.54	51.71	35.72

D.4 Formant and bandwidth values for Mono vowels (Speaker K) (cf. chapter 8) 267

kɔ̀kɔ̀ (2)	Spec LPC FFT		510.48 542.03 550	992.6 990.03 950	2169.55 2169.03 2150	3374.86 3388.99 3375	98.5	112.12	98.72	19.16
mbɔ̀kɔ̀lɔ̀ (1) 'sunrise'	Spec LPC FFT		510.48 539.35 550	935.88 925.67 900	2453.15 2494.6 2450	3403.22 3477.86 3475	82.41	48.5	107.91	15.5

Note: The actual value of F_3 given by the LPC algorithm is 1891.11 Hz with a bandwidth of 257.38 Hz. The values of F_3 and BW_3 given above are actually F_4 and BW_4, respectively, as calculated by the LPC algorithm. The number of poles employed in the LPC algorithm was 14.

mbɔ̀kɔ̀lɔ̀ (2)	Spec LPC FFT		538.84 553.83 550	935.88 942.17 875	2552.41 2627.22 2600	3431.58 3450.62 3425	111.85	69.26	81.02	24.71

Note: The actual value of F_3 given by the LPC algorithm is 1958.99 Hz with a bandwidth of 1008.73 Hz. The values of F_3 and BW_3 given above are actually F_4 and BW_4, respectively, as calculated by the LPC algorithm. The number of poles employed in the LPC algorithm was 14.

ndɔ̄kō (1) 'flower'	Spec LPC FFT		510.48 535.85 550	1020.96 1023.9 975	2382.25 2421.93 2425	3459.94 3483.49 3450	77.33	70.06	121.08	34.04
ndɔ̄kō (2)	Spec LPC FFT		482.12 506.99 500	1020.96 1014.9 1000	2396.43 2389.88 2400	3488.3 3474.11 3450	44.59	38.33	112.5	51.33

ngólō (1) 'fish trap'	Spec	652.28	1162.77	2339.71	3530.84		
	LPC	586.86	919.95	2412.94	3558.12	80.4	134.21 66.18 35.89
	FFT	600	1075	2400	3550		

Note: The actual value of F_3 given by the LPC algorithm is 1786.87 Hz with a bandwidth of 296.84 Hz. The values of F_3 and BW_3 given above are actually F_4 and BW_4, respectively, as calculated by the LPC algorithm. The number of poles employed in the LPC algorithm was 14.

ngólō (2)	Spec	581.38	1106.05	2467.33	3445.76		
	LPC	549.31	981.81	2533.5	3470.05	66.11	124.49 91.26 49.85
	FFT	525	1075	2500	3475		

Note: The actual value of F_3 given by the LPC algorithm is 1762.21 Hz with a bandwidth of 374.07 Hz. The values of F_3 and BW_3 given above are actually F_4 and BW_4, respectively, as calculated by the LPC algorithm. The number of poles employed in the LPC algorithm was 14.

u

bùdú (1) 'bottom'	Spec	374.44	964.91	2261.06	3225.96		
	LPC	267.25	929.3	2260.57	3149.34	44.24	26.33 64.31 16.89
	FFT	250	900	2200	3150		
bùdú (2)	Spec	?	?	?	?		
	LPC	286.09	900.21	2281.03	3099.11	58.94	99.79 90.95 34.98
	FFT	250	800	2275	3100		
būlà (1) 'blind'	Spec	331.24	936.11	2390.67	3355.58		
	LPC	309.95	934.64	2463.52	3268.4	43.92	62.33 148.11 18.12
	FFT	250	875	2350	3250		

D.4 Formant and bandwidth values for Mono vowels (Speaker K) (cf. chapter 8)

Word		F1	F2	F3	B1	B2	B3
bu̱là (2)	Spec LPC FFT	345.64 310.84 275	921.7 892.48 825	2462.68 2477 2400	3355.58 3289.05 3250	53.1	56.73	72.24	8.22
bu̱tʃɔ́ (1) 'night'	Spec LPC FFT	269.42 277.3 250	935.88 913.61 875	2297.17 2400.08 2325	3204.69 3187.13 3175	43.48	44.61	94.38	19.47
bu̱tʃɔ́ (2)	Spec LPC FFT	283.6 293.07 250	964.24 911.92 925	2282.99 2391.41 2275	3233.05 3161.97 3225	57.88	172.93	217.03	132.58
tu̱kpá (1) 'white'	Spec LPC FFT	326.14 347.26 325	907.52 931.14 900	2410.61 2361.51 2300	3417.4 3426.68 3450	19.4	32.27	213.77	46.94
tu̱kpá (2)	Spec LPC FFT	340.32 360.52 350	907.52 941.8 925	3438.97 2474.08 2450	3431.58 3450.86 3425	13.93	72.69	59.04	11.78
tu̱jū (1) 'fresh'	Spec LPC FFT	269.42 281.07 250	1063.5 1098.51 950	2197.91 2199.78 2200	3289.77 3310.62 3300	25.82	155.91	48.9	21.23
tu̱jū (2)	Spec LPC FFT	255.24 277.16 250	1063.5 1049.09 1000	2226.27 2231.21 2250	3318.14 3323.53 3300	32.08	84.7	37.16	16.84

a ~ ʌ									
bı̄jā́ (1) 'two'	Spec	590	1526	2563	3571				
	LPC	556.68	1551.42	2565.91	3552.06	85.06	44.70	92.52	127.66
	FFT	550	1525	2550	3550				
bı̄jā́ (2)	Spec	619	1497	2606	3485				
	LPC	561.33	1483.32	2642.19	3494.94	60.47	41.00	222.13	49.06
	FFT	550	1500	2625	3475				
biwā̄ (1) 'mucus'	Spec	662	1310	2448	3528				
	LPC	627.45	1313.76	2420.50	3511.53	36.97	122.94	39.53	102.33
	FFT	600	1250	2400	3500				
biwā̄ (2)	Spec	662	1324	2405	3614				
	LPC	601.76	1301.93	2397.12	3600.14	77.88	197.64	67.93	55.92
	FFT	600	1300	2375	3600				
jā́vūrū̄ (1) 'rain'	Spec	518	1325	2261	3370				
	LPC	437.59	1284.71	2195.86	3352.22	29.07	56.72	82.87	8.28
	FFT	425	1300	2175	3325				
jā́vūrū̄ (2)	Spec	561	1397	2505	3542				
	LPC	516.55	1422.84	2467.12	3478.37	57.19	48.28	167.27	49.50
	FFT	475	1400	2275	3500				

Note: The actual value of F_4 given by the LPC algorithm is 3289.89 Hz with a bandwidth of 1430.50 Hz. The values of F_4 and BW_4 given above are actually F_5 and BW_5, respectively, as calculated by the LPC algorithm.

D.4 Formant and bandwidth values for Mono vowels (Speaker K) (cf. chapter 8)

word	method	F1	F2	F3	B1	B2	B3
ngbā̰ɓī (1) 'bone'	Spec	662	1425	2563	3557			
	LPC	629.21	1430.65	2455.06	3340.62	33.04	107.57	258.65	433.94
	FFT	600	1400	2200	3500			
ngbā̰ɓī (2)	Spec	576	1382	2491	3672			
	LPC	554.53	1413.54	2424.14	3594.75	75.59	97.66	146.03	29.13
	FFT	550	1375	2400	3625			
tʃá̰fʊ̄ (1) 'smell'	Spec	619	1454	2592	3643			
	LPC	613.24	1453.68	2619.09	3559.13	70.18	77.38	222.82	50.06
	FFT	550	1350	2575	3575			
tʃá̰fʊ̄ (2)	Spec	676	1425	2390	3557			
	LPC	634.92	1399.56	2461.79	3555.68	52.58	62.58	92.55	146.56
	FFT	625	1325	2400	3525			

D.5 Time location of vowel measurements (cf. chapter 8)

a		File	Time (sec.)
bàgá	'cheek'	0001	60.20850
		0001	61.52409
bākòngɔ̄	'turtle'	0451	20.53139
		0451	21.68133
bàlē	'one'	1501	72.83401
		1501	73.92792
tàʔwá	'basin'	0926	11.19753
		0926	11.95242
tāfò	'new'	1651	60.32950
		1651	61.39326

e			
mbējā	'in-laws'	0326	31.70049
		0326	32.84316
pètè	'full'	1651	8.07443
		1651	9.10484
pējà	'navel'	0051	53.64934
		0051	54.73717
tèwé	'ant (sp.)'	0476	50.25043
		0476	51.11576
vèdʒà	'forest'	0651	62.55095
		0651	63.70443

ə			
də	'be'	1501	53.22492
		1501	54.15351
ə́bə́rə́	'quarrel'	1251	43.61172
		1251	44.56395
ə́də̀	'if'	1476	67.01524
		1476	68.07800
ə́ndə́	'mark'	0551	0.51714
		0551	1.55409
tə́kə̀kà	'pain'	0201	42.88952
		0201	43.95130

D.5 Time location of vowel measurements (cf. chapter 8)

i

bīʃà	'two'	1501	75.14698
		1501	76.30464
bītū	'deaf'	0226	22.67357
		0226	23.67860
bījā	'ebony'	0576	0.34895
		0576	1.46995
kìtì	'squirrel'	0451	16.26414
		0451	17.14638
líbī	'yesterday'	0776	28.05782
		0776	29.02946

i̠

àdí̠là	'dusk'	0751	19.14772
		0751	20.05177
àkí̠	'razor'	0826	15.47033
		0826	16.39397
di̠	'count'	1401	26.74641
		1401	27.75384
kɨndi̠	'field'	0651	45.07321
		0651	46.17254
kpi̠kpi̠	'eagle'	0401	31.43022
		0401	32.35103

o

bówō	'python'	0451	4.62375
		0451	5.64240
dōrō	'partridge'	0426	28.27758
		0426	29.15557
sòró	'life'	0126	0.47931
		0126	1.61788
vōkā	'nape'	0051	51.09028
		0051	52.42393
vōtɔ̀	'three'	1501	77.57327
		1501	78.70772

ɔ

bɔ̠lɔ̀	'tobacco'	0826	54.05710
		0826	54.97960
kɔ̠kɔ̀	'termite'	0501	54.10045
		0501	55.10429
mbɔ̠kɔ̀lɔ̀	'sunrise'	0776	12.45498
		0776	13.62437
ndɔ̠kɔ̄	'flower'	0576	2.55956
		0576	3.60214
ngɔ̠́lɔ̄	'fish trap'	1026	20.96721
		1026	21.99769

u

bṳdú	'bottom'	0001	20.61422
		0001	19.14403
bṳ̄là	'blind'	0226	18.55569
		0226	19.59868
bṳ̄tʃɔ́	'night'	0751	53.81038
		0751	54.98348
tṳ́kpá	'white'	1551	33.56279
		1551	34.64122
tṳ̀jū	'fresh'	1651	4.58648
		1651	5.67622

a ~ ʌ

bīʃà̠	'two'	1501	75.47042
		1501	76.64570
bīwā̠	'mucus'	0101	28.65645
		0101	29.74978
jā̠vūrū	'rain'	0726	50.60369
		0726	32.16762
ngbā̠ɓī	'bone'	0001	37.64331
		0526	30.38840
tʃá̠fù	'smell'	0101	43.25629
		0101	44.44000

References

Arom, Simha, and France Cloarec-Heiss. 1976. Le langage tambouriné des Banda-Linda (R.C.A.). In Luc Bouquiaux (ed.), *Théories et méthods en linguistique Africaine,* 113–169. Bibliothèque de la SELAF 54–55. Paris: SELAF.

Bassole, Jean. 1982. *Phonologie du Lyele.* M.A. thesis. Université d'Abidjan.

Bendor-Samuel, Pamela M. 1962. Phonemic interpretation problems in some West African languages. *Sierra Leone Language Review* 4:85–90.

Bennett, Patrick R. 1983. Adamawa-Eastern: Problems and prospects. In I. R. Dihoff (ed.), *Current approaches to African linguistics* 1, 23–48. Dordrecht: Foris.

Bennett, Patrick R., and Jan P. Sterk. 1977. South Central Niger-Congo: A reclassification. *Studies in African Linguistics* 8:241–273.

Blevins, Juliette. 1995. The syllable in phonological theory. In John A. Goldsmith (ed.), *The handbook of phonological theory,* 206–244. Cambridge, Mass.: Blackwell.

Blühberger, Jutta. 1996. Rapport d'enquête sociolinguistique: Première évaluation parmi les Linda. Bangui: SIL. ms.

Bouquiaux, Luc, and Jacqueline M. C. Thomas. 1980. In Luc Bouquiaux (ed.), *Le peuplement oubanguien. L'expansion bantoue* 2, 807–824. Actes de Colloque International du CNRS, Viviers, 4–16 avril 1977. Paris: SELAF.

Boyd, Raymond. 1978. À propos des resemblances lexicales entre langues Niger-Congo et Nilo-Sahariennes. *Études comparatives,* 43–94. Bibliothèque de la SELAF 65. Paris: SELAF.

Boyd, Raymond. 1989. Adamawa-Ubangi. In John Bendor-Samuel and Rhonda L. Hartell (eds.), *The Niger-Congo languages*, 178–215. Lanham, Md.: University Press of America.

Boyd, Raymond. 1995. Introduction. In Raymond Boyd (ed.), *Le système verbal dans les langues oubangiennes*, 9–24. LINCOM Studies in African Linguistics 7. München/Newcastle: LINCOM EUROPA.

Breen, Gavin, and Rob Pensalfini. 1999. Arrernte: A language with no syllable onsets. *Linguistic Inquiry* 30(1):1–25.

Buchanan, Michael. 1996. *Rapport d'enquête sociolinguistique: Première évaluation parmi les Togbo*. Bangui: SIL. ms.

Burquest, Donald A. 2001. *Phonological analysis: A functional approach*, second revised edition. Dallas: SIL International.

Byrd, D. 1993. 54,000 stops. *UCLA Working Papers in Phonetics* 83:97–115.

Casad, Eugene H. 1974. *Dialect intelligibility testing*. SIL Publications in Linguistics and Related Fields 38. Norman: University of Oklahoma.

Catford, J. C. 1977. *Fundamental problems in phonetics*. Edinburgh: Edinburgh University Press. [Reprinted in 1982 by Indiana University Press, Bloomington.]

Chao, Yuen-Ren. 1934. The non-uniqueness of phonemic solutions of phonetic systems. Bulletin of the Institute of History and Philology. *Academia Sinica* 4(4):363–397.

Childs, G. Tucker. 1994. African ideophones. In Leanne Hinton, Johanna Nichols, and John J. Ohala (eds.), *Sound symbolism*, 178–204. Cambridge: Cambridge University Press.

Chomsky, Noam, and Morris Halle. 1968. *The sound pattern of English*. New York: Harper & Row.

Clements, G. N. 1990. The role of the sonority cycle in core syllabification. In J. Kingston and M. Beckman (eds.), *Between the grammar and physics of speech*, 283–333. Papers in laboratory phonology 1. Cambridge: Cambridge University Press.

Cloarec-Heiss, France. 1967. *Essai de phonologie du parler banda-linda de Ippy*. Bulletin de la SELAF 3. Paris: SELAF.

Cloarec-Heiss, France. 1969. *Banda-linda de Ippy: Phonologie - Dérivation et composition*. Bibliothèque de la SELAF 14. Paris: SELAF.

Cloarec-Heiss, France. 1972. *Le verbe banda: Études du syntagme verbal dans une langue oubanguienne de République Centrafricaine*. Langues et civilisations à tradition orale 3. Paris: SELAF.

Cloarec-Heiss, France. 1978. Étude préliminaire à une dialectologie banda. *Études comparatives*, 11–42. Bibliothèque de la SELAF 65. Paris: SELAF.

Cloarec-Heiss, France. 1986. *Dynamique et équilibre d'une syntaxe: Le banda-linda de Centrafrique*. Descriptions de langues et monographies ethnolinguistiques 2. Paris-London: SELAF and Cambridge University Press.

Cloarec-Heiss, France. 1988. Le Banda. In Yves Moñino (ed.), *Lexique comparatif des langues oubangiennes*, 59–61. Paris: Geuthner.

Cloarec-Heiss, France. 1995a. Emprunts ou substrat? In Robert Nicolaï and Franz Rottland (eds.), *Analyse des convergences entre le groupe banda et les langues du Soudan central. Proceedings of the Fifth Nilo-Saharan Linguistics Colloquium, Nice, 24–29 August 1992*, 321–355. Köln: Köppe Verlag.

Cloarec-Heiss, France. 1995b. Le banda-linda. In Raymond Boyd (ed.), *Le système verbal dans les langues oubangiennes*, 81–112. LINCOM Studies in African Linguistics 7. München/Newcastle: LINCOM EUROPA.

Cloarec-Heiss, France. 2000. Mesures dialectales en 3 dimensions: Application à une aire dialectale hétérogène, l'aire banda. In H. Ekkehard Wolff and Orin D. Gensler (eds.), *Proceedings of the 2nd World Congress of African Linguistics, Leipzig, 1997*, 175–195. Köln: Rüdiger Köppe.

Comrie, Bernard. 1976. *Aspect*. Cambridge: Cambridge University Press.

Comrie, Bernard. 1989. *Language universals and linguistic typology*, second edition. Chicago: University of Chicago Press.

Connell, Bruce. 1994. The structure of labial-velar stops. *Journal of Phonetics* 22:441–446.

Cordell, Dennis. 1983. The savanna belt of North-Central Africa. In David Birmingham and Phyllis M. Martin (eds.), *History of Central Africa* 1, 30–74. London and New York: Longman.

Cotel, Pierre. 1907. *Dictionnaire français-banda et banda-français précédé d'un essai de grammaire banda*. Brazzaville: Mission Catholique.

Crothers, John. 1978. Typology and universals of vowel systems. In Joseph H. Greenberg (ed.), *Universals of human language*, 2: Phonology, 93–152. Stanford, Cal.: Stanford University Press.

de Jong, Kenneth, and Samuel Gyasi Obeng. 2000. Labio-palatalization in Twi: Contrastive, quantal, and organizational factors producing an uncommon sound. *Language* 76(3):682–703.

Demolin, Didier. 1992. *Le mangbetu: Étude phonétique et phonologique*. Brussels: Université Libre de Bruxelles dissertation.

Demolin, Didier, and Bernard Teston. 1996. Labiodental flaps in Mangbetu. *Journal of the International Phonetic Association* 26(2):103–111.

Diffloth, Gérard. 1994. *i*: big, *a*: small. In Leanne Hinton, Johanna Nichols, and John J. Ohala (eds.), *Sound symbolism*, 107–114. Cambridge: Cambridge University Press.

Diki-Kidiri, Marcel, and France Cloarec-Heiss. 1985. Précis d'orthographe banda. Colloque sur la création de systèmes orthographiques en Afrique centrale, Université de Bangui, April 16, 1985. ms.

Doke, Clement Martyn. 1935. *Bantu linguistics terminology*. London: Longmans, Green.

Eboué, Felix. 1918. *Langues sango, banda, baya, mandjia*. Paris: Larose.

Eboué, Felix. 1933. *Les peuples de l'Oubangui-Chari*. Paris: Société d'Ethnographie de Paris.

Elders, Stefan. 2000. *Grammaire mundang*. Ph.D. dissertation. University of Leiden.

Fant, Gunnar. 1973. *Speech sounds and features*. Cambridge, Mass.: MIT Press.

Fultz, Jim, and David Morgan. 1986. *Les langues banda, ngbaka mabo, et furu dans les zones de Bosobolo et de Libenge*. Enquête dialectale de l'Ubangi et de la Mongala, région de l'Équateur, République du Zaïre 2. Gemena, D. R. Congo: Association Wycliffe pour la Traduction de la Bible. ms.

Giraud. 1908. *Vocabulaire sango, mandjia, banda, bakongo et azande*. Revue Coloniale. Paris.

Givón, Talmy. 1984. *Syntax: A functional-typological approach*, 1. Amsterdam/Philadelphia: John Benjamins.

Goldsmith, John A. 1990. *Autosegmental and metrical phonology*. Cambridge, Mass.: Blackwell.

Goldsmith, John A. 1995. Phonological theory. In John A. Goldsmith (ed.), *The handbook of phonological theory*, 1–23. Cambridge, Mass.: Blackwell.

Greenberg, Joseph H. 1970 [1963]. *The languages of Africa*, third edition. Bloomington, Ind.: Indiana University.

Grimes, Barbara F., ed. 2000. *Ethnologue: Languages of the world*, fourteenth edition. Dallas: SIL International.

Guthrie, Malcolm, and John F. Carrington. 1988. *Lingala: Grammar and dictionary*. London: Baptist Missionary Society.

Hartell, Rhonda L., ed. 1993. *Alphabets de langues africaines*. Dakar: UNESCO and Summer Institute of Linguistics.

Hockett, Charles F. 1958. *A course in modern linguistics*. New York: Macmillan.

Hubbard, Kathleen. 1995. 'Prenasalized consonants' and syllable timing: Evidence from Runyambo and Luganda. *Phonology* 12:235–256.

References

Hyman, Larry M. 1975. *Phonology: Theory and analysis.* New York: Holt, Rinehart, and Winston.

Ingozo, Totala. 1990. *Organisation socio-politique traditionnelle chez les Mono de la collectivité de Bili (zone de Bosobolo).* Mbandaka: Institut Supérieur Pédagogique.

International Phonetic Association. 1989. Report on the 1989 Kiel convention. *Journal of the International Phonetic Association* 19:67–80.

International Phonetic Association. 1999. *Handbook of the International Phonetic Association: A guide to the use of the International Phonetic Alphabet.* Cambridge: Cambridge University Press.

Jaeger, Jeri J. 1978. Speech aerodynamics and phonological universals. In Jeri J. Jaeger, Anthony C. Woodbury, Farrell Ackerman, Christine Chiarello, Orin D. Gensler, John Kingston, Eve E. Sweetser, Henry Thompson, and Kenneth W. Whistler (eds.), *Proceedings of the Fourth Annual Meeting of the Berkeley Linguistics Society,* 311–329. Berkeley: Berkeley Linguistics Society.

Kamanda Kola. 1985. *Éléments de phonologie et de morphologie du mɔnɔ.* Travail de fin d'études. Mbandaka: Institut Supérieur Pédagogique.

Kamanda Kola. 1998. *Étude descriptive du mono: Langue oubanguienne du Congo (ex-Zaïre). Phonologie et morphosyntaxe.* Ph.D. dissertation. Université Libre de Bruxelles.

Kenstowicz, Michael. 1994. *Phonology in generative grammar.* Cambridge, Mass.: Blackwell.

Kieschke, Regine. 1993. *Enquête sociolinguistique sur le ngbugu.* Bangui: SIL. ms.

Ladefoged, Peter. 1968 [1964]. *A phonetic study of West African languages,* second edition. London: Cambridge University Press.

Ladefoged, Peter. 1982. *A course in phonetics,* second edition. New York: Harcourt Brace Jovanovich.

Ladefoged, Peter. 1996. *Elements of acoustic phonetics,* second edition. Chicago: University of Chicago Press.

Ladefoged, Peter. 1997. Instrumental techniques for linguistic phonetic fieldwork. In William J. Hardcastle and John Laver (eds.), *The handbook of phonetic sciences,* 137–166. Malden, Mass.: Blackwell.

Ladefoged, Peter, and Ian Maddieson. 1986. (Some of) the sounds of the world's languages. UCLA Working Papers in Phonetics 64.

Ladefoged, Peter, and Ian Maddieson. 1996. *The sounds of the world's languages.* Cambridge, Mass.: Blackwell.

Lehiste, Ilse. 1970. *Suprasegmentals.* Cambridge, Mass.: MIT Press.

Levin, Beth. 1993. *English verb classes and alternations: A preliminary investigation.* Chicago: University of Chicago Press.

Lieberman, Philip, and Sheila E. Blumstein. 1988. *Speech physiology, speech perception, and acoustic phonetics.* Cambridge Studies in Speech Science and Communication. Cambridge: Cambridge University Press.

Liljencrants, Johan, and Björn Lindblom. 1972. Numerical simulation of vowel quality systems: The role of perceptual contrast. *Language* 48:839–862.

Lindau, Mona. 1984. Phonetic differences in glottalic consonants. *Journal of Phonetics* 12:147–155.

Lisker, Leigh, and Arthur S. Abramson. 1964. A cross-language study of voicing in initial stops: Acoustic measurements. *Word* 20:384–422.

Maddieson, Ian. 1984. *Patterns of sounds.* Cambridge: Cambridge University Press.

Maddieson, Ian. 1989. Prenasalized stops and speech timing. *Journal of the International Phonetic Association* 19(2):57–66.

Maddieson, Ian. 1993. Investigating Ewe articulations with electromagnetic articulography. *Forschungsberichte des Instituts für Phonetik und Sprachliche Kommunikation der Universität München* 31:181–214.

Maddieson, Ian. 1997. Phonetic universals. In William J. Hardcastle and John Laver (eds.), *The handbook of phonetic sciences*, 619–639. Cambridge, Mass.: Blackwell.

Maddieson, Ian, and Victoria Anderson. 1994. Phonetic structures of Iaai. UCLA Working Papers in Phonetics 87:163–182.

Maes, Vedast. 1983. *Les peuples de l'Ubangi: Notes ethno-historiques.* Antwerp: Pères O. F. M. Capucins.

McCarthy, John J., and Alan S. Prince. 1995. Prosodic morphology. In John A. Goldsmith (ed.), *The handbook of phonological theory*, 318–366. Cambridge, Mass.: Blackwell.

Moehama, Elisée. 1994. *Rapport d'enquête sociolinguistique: Première évaluation parmi les yakpa.* Bangui: SIL. ms.

Moehama, Elisée. 1995. *Rapport d'enquête sociolinguistique: Première évaluation parmi les yangere.* Bangui: SIL. ms.

Moñino, Yves, ed. 1988. *Lexique comparatif des langues oubangiennes.* Paris: Geuthner.

Newman, James L. 1995. *The peopling of Africa: A geographic interpretation.* New Haven, Conn.: Yale University Press.

Ohala, John J., and Brian W. Eukel. 1987. Explaining the intrinsic pitch of vowels. In Robert Channan and Linda Shockey (eds.), *In honor of Ilse Lehiste (Ilse Lehiste Pühendusteos)*, 207–215. Netherlands Phonetic Archives 6. Dordrecht: Foris.

Ohala, John J., and Haruko Kawasaki. 1984. Prosodic phonology and phonetics. *Phonology Yearbook* 1:113–127.

Olson, Kenneth S. 1996. On the comparison and classification of Banda dialects. In Lise M. Dobrin, Kora Singer, and Lisa McNair (eds.), *CLS 32: Papers from the Main Session*, 267–283. Chicago: Chicago Linguistic Society.

Olson, Kenneth S. 2001. *The phonology and morphology of Mono*. Ph. D. dissertation. University of Chicago.

Olson, Kenneth S. 2004. An evaluation of Niger-Congo classification. SIL Electronic Working Papers 2004. Dallas: SIL. Online. URL: http://www.sil.org/silewp/abstraact.asp?ref=2004-005. October 2004.

Olson, Kenneth S., and John Hajek. 1999. The phonetic status of the labial flap. *Journal of the International Phonetic Association* 29(2):101–114.

Olson, Kenneth S., and John Hajek. 2003. Crosslinguistic insights on the labial flap. *Linguistic Typology* 7(2):157–186.

Olson, Kenneth S., and John Hajek. 2004. A crosslinguistic lexicon of the labial flap. *Linguistic Discovery* 2(2):21–57. Online URL: http://linguistic-discovery.dartmouth.edu. April 2004.

Olson, Kenneth S., and Brian E. Schrag. 2000. An overview of Mono phonology. In H. Ekkehard Wolff and Orin D. Gensler (eds.), *Proceedings of the 2nd World Congress of African Linguistics, Leipzig, 1997*, 393–409, Köln: Rüdiger Köppe.

Payne, Thomas E. 1997. *Describing morphosyntax: A guide for field linguists*. Cambridge: Cambridge University Press.

Perrin, Mona, and Margaret V. Hill. 1969. *Mambila (parler d'Atta): Description phonologique*. Yaoundé: Université Fédérale du Cameroun, Section de Linguistique Appliquée.

Peterson, Gordon E., and Harold L. Barney. 1952. Control methods used in a study of the vowels. *Journal of the Acoustical Society of America* 24:175–184.

Peterson, Gordon E., and Ilse Lehiste. 1960. Duration of syllable nuclei in English. *Journal of the Acoustical Society of America* 32:693–703.

Pike, Eunice V. 1954. Phonetic rank and subordination in consonant patterning and historical change. *Miscellanea Phonetica* 2:25–41.

Pike, Kenneth L. 1947. *Phonemics: A technique for reducing languages to writing*. Ann Arbor: University of Michigan Press.

Pike, Kenneth L., and Eunice V. Pike. 1947. Immediate constituents of Mazateco syllables. *International Journal of American Linguistics* 13:78–91.

Robbins, Camille. 1984. *Mbanza phonology*. ms.

Robins, R. H. 1970 [1957]. Aspects of prosodic analysis. In F. R. Palmer (ed.), *Prosodic analysis*, 188–200. London: Oxford University Press.

Russell, Jann M. 1985. *Moba phonology*. M.A. thesis, Macquarie University.
Sampson, Douglas. 1985. A preliminary phonological overview of Banda-Tangbago. *Occasional Papers in the Study of Sudanese Languages* 4:133–152. Juba, Sudan: Summer Institute of Linguistics, Institute of Regional Languages, and University of Juba College of Education.
Santandrea, Stefano. 1965. *Languages of the Banda and Zande groups: A contribution to a comparative study*. Naples: Istituto Universitario Orientale.
Sapir, Edward. 1921. *Language: An introduction to the study of speech*. New York: Harcourt, Brace, and Company.
Smalley, William A. 1989. *Manual of articulatory phonetics*, revised edition. Lanham, Md.: University Press of America.
Stallcup, Kenneth Lyell. 1978. *A comparative perspective on the phonology and noun classification of three Cameroon grassfields Bantu languages: Moghamo, Ngie, and Oshie*. Ph.D. dissertation, Stanford University.
Stetson, R. H. 1951. *Motor phonetics: A study of speech movement in action*, second edition. Amsterdam: North-Holland Publishing Co.
Tabu, Sunguyase. 1989. *L'éducation traditionnelle de la femme mono et sa participation à l'effort de développement*. Mbandaka: Institut Supérieur de Développement Rural.
Thelwall, Robin. 1980. Trills and flaps. Linguistic studies in honour of Paul Christophersen. *Occasional Papers in Linguistics and Language Learning 7, November 1980*, 79–84. Coleraine, Northern Ireland: The New University of Ulster.
Thomas, Jacqueline M.-C. 1963. *Le parler ngbaka de Bokanga. Phonologie, morphologie, syntaxe*. The Hague: Mouton.
Tingbo-nyi-Zonga. 1978. *Étude grammaticale de la langue mbandza (dialecte de balawo)*. Lubumbashi: Centre de Linguistique Théorique et Appliquée.
Tisserant, R. P. Charles. 1930. *Essai sur la grammaire banda*. Travaux et mémoires de l'Institut d'Ethnologie 13. Paris: Institut d'Ethnologie.
Tisserant, R. P. Charles. 1931. *Dictionnaire banda-français*. Travaux et mémoires de l'Institut d'Ethnologie 14. Paris: Institut d'Ethnologie.
Tisserant, R. P. Charles. 1950. *Catalogue de la flore de l'Oubangui-Chari*. Mémoires de l'Institut d'Etudes Centrafricaines 2. Brazzaville.
Toqué, G. 1906. *Essai sur le peuple et la langue banda*. Paris: J. André.
Toronzoni, Ngama. 1989. *Description du ngbandi. Langue oubanguienne du nord-ouest du Zaïre*. Ph.D. dissertation, Université Libre de Bruxelles.
Trubetzkoy, N. S. 1969. *Principles of phonology*. Translated by Cristiane A. M. Baltaxe. Berkeley: University of California Press.

Tucker, A. N., and M. A. Bryan. 1956. *The non-Bantu languages of North-Eastern Africa.* Handbook of African Languages 3. London: Oxford University Press for the International African Institute.

Van Bulck, G., and P. Hackett. 1956. *Report of the Eastern team (Oubangui to Great Lakes).* Linguistic Survey of the Northern Bantu Borderland 1 (part II). London: Oxford University Press (for the International African Institute).

Van Everbroeck, René. n.d. *Dictionnaire lingala-français (Maloba ma lokóta lingála-français).* Kinshasa: Éditions l'Épiphanie.

Vergiat, A. M. 1981 [1936]. *Les rites secrets des primitifs de l'Oubangui.* Paris: L'Harmattan.

Welmers, William E. 1973. *African language structures.* Berkeley: University of California Press.

Whalen, D., and A. Levitt. 1995. The intrinsic pitch of vowels. *Journal of Phonetics* 24:349–366.

Williamson, Kay. 1989. Niger-Congo overview. In John Bendor-Samuel and Rhonda L. Hartell (eds.), *The Niger-Congo languages*, 3–45. Lanham, Md.: University Press of America.

Woods, Anthony, Paul Fletcher, and Arthur Hughes. 1986. *Statistics in language studies.* Cambridge: Cambridge University Press.

Yasikuzu, Inangawa. 1987. *Analyse sémantique de quelques chants liés à la danse traditionnelle yāngbā de mɔ̄nɔ̄.* Mbandaka: Institut Supérieur Pédagogique.

Zwicker, E., and E. Terhardt. 1980. Analytical expressions for critical-band rate and critical bandwidth as a function of frequency. *Journal of the Acoustical Society of America* 68(5):1523–1525.

Author Index

Abramson, Arthur S., 164
Anderson, Victoria, 148
Arom, Simha, 43
Barney, Harold L., 145
Bassole, Jean, 35
Bendor-Samuel, Pamela M., 58, 61–62, 67
Bennett, Patrick R., 5
Blevins, Juliette, 61, 67
Blühberger, Jutta, 8
Blumstein, Sheila, 124, 127, 156
Bouquiaux, Luc, 11
Boyd, Raymond, 5, 24, 31, 35, 49, 67, 89, 97, 99, 104
Breen, Gavin, 66
Bryan, M. A., 1, 4
Buchanan, Michael, 8
Burquest, Donald A., 24, 66–67
Byrd, D., 164
Carrington, John F., 1
Casad, Eugene H., 8
Casali, Roderic, 35
Catford, J. C., 53, 123
Chao, Yuen-Ren, 58, 62
Childs, G. Tucker, 83
Chomsky, Noam, 34
Clements, G. N., 67

Cloarec-Heiss, France, 2, 4–8, 16, 35, 38, 43, 46, 60, 75, 77, 88, 90, 94, 96–102, 104, 113, 187, 191, 201, 205, 213, 217
Comrie, Bernard, 87, 104
Connell, Bruce, 137–140
Cordell, Dennis, 11–12
Cotel, Pierre, 16
Crothers, John, 18, 35–36, 149
Darden, Bill, 54
de Jong, Kenneth, 127
Demolin, Didier, 123
Diffloth, Gérard, 83
Diki-Kidiri, Marcel, 60
Doke, Clement Martyn, 83
Eboué, Felix, 10, 16
Elders, Stefan, 83
Eukel, Brian W., 164
Fant, Gunnar, 145
Fletcher, Paul, 144
Fultz, Jim, 2–4, 8, 13–14
Giraud, 16
Givón, Talmy, 89
Goldsmith, John A., 22, 67, 71, 73, 99
Greenberg, Joseph H., 4–5, 89
Grimes, Barbara F., 2, 4–5
Guthrie, Malcolm, 1

Hackett, P., 2
Hajek, John, xiii, 24, 26
Halle, Morris, 34
Hartell, Rhonda L., 35
Hill, Margaret V., 35
Hockett, Charles F., 59, 73–75
Hubbard, Kathleen, 24, 142, 144
Hughes, Arthur, 144
Hyman, Larry M., 49
Ingozo, Totala, 15
International Phonetic Association, 25, 45
Jaeger, Jeri J., 164
Kamanda Kola, 1, 15, 24–25, 34–35, 39, 55, 77, 79, 85, 88–90, 92–93, 97–98, 100, 102, 104, 113, 136, 187, 200, 217, 234, 236, 241, 244, 247–248
Kawasaki, Haruko, 66
Kenstowicz, Michael, 50, 67, 73
Kieschke, Regine, 8
Ladefoged, Peter, 25, 53–56, 58, 62, 65, 67, 123, 128, 134, 136–137, 142, 145, 148, 150–151, 160
Lehiste, Ilse, 142, 155, 164
Levin, Beth, 99
Levitt, A., 164
Lieberman, Philip, 124, 127, 156
Liljencrants, Johan, 145
Lindblom, Björn, 145
Lindau, Mona, 127–128, 133, 135
Lisker, Leigh, 164
Maddieson, Ian, 24, 30, 36, 53–56, 58, 65, 128, 134, 137, 139, 142, 144, 148, 160, 164
Maes, Vedast, 2, 12
McCarthy, John J., 73
Moehama, Elisée, 8
Moñino, Yves, 7, 16, 77
Morgan, David, 2–4, 8, 13–14
Newman, James L., 11
Obeng, Samuel Gyasi, 127
Ohala, John J., 66, 164

Olson, Kenneth S., xiii, 7–8, 15, 24, 26, 34–35, 39, 61–62, 102, 121, 231
Payne, Thomas E., 1, 83, 88, 105
Pensalfini, Rob, 66
Perrin, Mona, 35
Peterson, Gordon E., 142, 145, 155
Pike, Eunice V., 45, 61
Pike, Kenneth L., 21, 45, 53, 61, 65, 67
Prince, Alan S., 73
Robbins, Camille, 16, 61, 63
Robins, R. H., 61
Russell, Jann M., 35
Sampson, Douglas, 16, 38, 43, 59
Santandrea, Stefano, 16
Sapir, Edward, 21
Schrag, Barbara, 87
Schrag, Brian E., 15, 34–35, 39, 61–62, 102
Smalley, William A., 160
Stallcup, Kenneth Lyell, 35
Sterk, Jan P., 5
Stetson, R. H., 65
Tabu, Sunguyase, 15
Terhardt, E., 148
Teston, Bernard, 123
Thelwall, Robin, 123–124
Thomas, Jacqueline M. C., 11, 41
Tingbo-nyi-Zonga, 16, 93, 100
Tisserant, R. P. Charles, 4, 6, 12, 15–16, 90, 100
Toqué, G., 16
Toronzoni, Ngama, 93
Trubetzkoy, N. S., 22
Tucker, A. N., 1, 4
Van Bulck, G., 2
Van Everbroeck, René, 30
Vergiat, A. M., 10
Welmers, William E., 70, 83
Whalen, D., 164
Williamson, Kay, 5
Woods, Anthony, 144
Yasikuzu, Inangawa, 15
Zwicker, E., 148

Subject Index*

ACATBA, 8
acoustic, 15, 17–18, 37, 54, 121–164
acoustic correlate (see correlate)
Adamawa, Adamawan, 2, 5, 35
Adamawa-Ubangi, 4–5, 16, 35, 104
adjective, 32, 43, 68, 73–74, 77–79, 83, 90–91, 95, 97–98, 109, 111, 183
   descriptive adjective, 79, 90, 97–98, 183
   predicate adjective, 109, 111
adverb, 18, 31–32, 43, 50, 73, 77, 83–85, 92–93, 103, 113–115
   locative adverb, 18, 50, 83, 113–114
   manner adverb, 83, 115
   temporal adverb, 103
adverbial word shape (see word pattern)
affricate, 25, 66
agentive, **96–97**
agglutinative, 19, **88**
airstream, 23, 135–137
allophone, allophonic, 22, 120, 152
alveolar, 23, 28–30, 38–39, 69, 124, 237–241, 252–254

alveopalatal, 29, 66
amplitude, 17, 123, 127–128, 132–136
anaptyxis, 18
animal name, 22, 31, 45, 79
animate, 1, 19, 88–93, **89**, 101, 183, 191, 204
animistic, 10
aperiodic, 125, 128, 133, 152
appositional, 80
approximant, 53–54
Arab, 12, 183
Arabic, 74, 210
Arrernte, 58, 66
articulation, 17, 25–27, 53–54, 62, 124, 128, 136–137, 140–141, 158, 160, 163
arytenoid, 128
assimilation, 75, 116
associative noun phrase, 80, 94–95, 97
aspect (see tense, aspect, and mood)
   consecutive aspect, 46
   progressive aspect, 104, 109
   repetitive aspect, 101, 105
   stative aspect, 45, 49, 97–99, 105

---

*Page numbers in **bold** indicate pages where terms are defined.

audio, 17, 122
auditory impression, 37, 136–137, 139, 160, 164
Azande, 12, 41
[back] (see feature)
backing of the tongue, 17, 27, 54, 127
Banda, 1–13, 16, 35, 38, 43, 59, 61, 93, 97, 102, 187, 212
  Central Banda, 7, 9
  Peripheral Banda, 7, 9
bandwidth (BW), 146 7 8 9 156 256–271
Bantu, 1–2, 12–13, 24, 35, 83, 89, 142, 144, 164
Bark scale, 148
Bida, 13
Bili, 1–4, 7, 10, 12–17, 89, 121, 222
bilabial, 17, 25, 27, 164
bilabial flap (see flap)
biphasic, 17, 128, 134–135
bisyllabic, 18, 41, 51, 77–80, 82, 89, 94, 97, 145
body part, 57, 75, 79, 89
Bosobolo, 2, 3
Bubanda, 2–3, 7, 10, 14–15, 187
burst, 125, 139–140, 143, 152
Cameroon, 2, 11, 16, 122
canonical form, **73**
Central African Republic (CAR), 1, 2, 5–6, 8–12, 14
Central Banda (see Banda)
Central Sudanic, 2, 5, 11, 35
certainty mood (see mood)
Chadic, 127
chest pulse, 65
Choctaw, 74
circumcision, 10, 184–185, 192, 195
citation form, 21, 48, **74**, 77, 80–82, 109, 186, 190
classification, 4–9
cleft, 80–81, 86, 167, 170, 188
clitic, 31, 76–77, 102–103, 116–117, 188, 203, 211, 214, 218
closure, 17, 53, 123–124, 126–128, 131, 133–137, 139, 141–144, 164

co-articulation, 53
co-occurrence, 22, 38–39, 41, 50, 59–62, 84, 233–255
coda, 61
code-switching, 14
cognate, 4, 6, 7, 77
cognate object construction, 19, **99**
comparative, 4, 7, 16, 70, 92, 183
compensatory lengthening, 24, 142
complementary distribution, 22, 55
compound, 74, 78, 93–97, 101
Computerized Speech Lab (CSL), 122
conditional mood (see mood)
consecutive aspect (see aspect)
consonant, 1, 7, 17–18, 22–34, 37–41, 49–50, 54–62, 65–68, 82, 116, 119, 122–145, 155–156, 158–159, 164–165, 180–181, 228, 233–250, 252–255
consonant system, 24–25, 58
constriction, 127
contour tone (see tone)
contrast, contrastive, 18, 21, 24, 27–31, 33–34, 37–39, 43–44, 47, 51, 54–55, 61, 68, 80, 82, 121, 142, 228, 233–250
Cool Edit 2000, 122
copula, 109, 188
coronal, 24, 67, 145, 164
corpus, 24–25, 28–29, 32, 39, 45, 57, 59, 62–63, 74, 85, 90–91, 99–100, 104, 106, 118–119, 145, 160, 165
correlate (acoustic), 17, 123–124, 127, 135, 141, 156
creaky voice (see laryngealization)
cross-linguistic, 17, 36, 55, 56, 61, 66, 142, 164
declarative, 84
Degema, 127
delayed release, 18, 53, 61
deletion, 94, 97, 145
Democratic Republic of the Congo (DRC), 1–4, 6, 9, 11–12, 14, 16–17
demography, 2–4
demonstrative, 115

Subject Index

depressor consonant, **49**
derivation, 46, 73, 77, 97, 99–100
descriptive adjective (see adjective)
deverbalization, 98
diachronic, 16, 70
dialect, 1–4, 6–9, 14–15, 187, 192, 197
diphthong, 59
discourse, 22, 25, 28–33, 36, 39, 45, 80, 84
distribution, distributional, 11, 17, 22, 24, 38–41, 49–52, 55–56, 59, 62–63, 66–67, 76, 88, 142, 148, 160
dorsum, 136
duration, 17, 84, 122–124, 142–144, 152–156, 164
echo vowel epenthesis (see vowel epenthesis)
economy, 24, 59
egressive, 17, 136–137
electromagnetic articulography, 137
elision, 18, 68, 70, 82, 118, 152–155
ellipse, 148
English, 31, 36, 54, 67, 74, 97, 99, 107, 150–151, 164–165
epenthesis (see vowel epenthesis)
equation, equative, 36, 38, 80, 109, 188, 238
Estonian, 74
ethnology, 9–12
Ewe, 70, 137, 139
excision, 10
existential, 36, 98, 109, 110, 193, 202, 210, 238
falling tone (see tone)
fast speech (see speaking rate)
feature (phonological), 17–19, 34, 75–76, 116
  [back], 18–19, 35, 76
  [high], 18–19, 35, 75–76
  [low], 35, 76, 116
  [round], 18–19, 35, 76
FFT (Fast Fourier Transform), 146, 256–271
Fijian, 74–75, 142, 144

flap, 23, 25, 124
  bilabial flap, labial flap, 17, 24–25, 27, 84, 122–127, 221–222, 224
  labiodental flap, 25
folktale, folk story, 10, 17, 122, 212
foot binarity, 73
formal reduction, **94**, 97
formant, 17, 37, 122–124, 128, 137, 141, 143, 145–147, 156–158, 160, 162, 256–271
frequency count, 22, 165, 180–181
frequency of occurrence, 22
French, 1, 1–4, 36, 44, 187, 189, 191, 197, 200, 204, 209, 211, 235, 237
fricative, 23–25, 38–39, 53, 125, 152
fundamental frequency (F_0), 134, 162–164
Furu, 2–4
fusional, **88**
future tense (see tense)
Galaba, 2–3, 7, 10, 15
Gbanziri, 2
Gbaya, 5, 97
generative, 16, 23, 65
geography, 2–4
Gilima, 3
glide (see semi-vowel)
glide formation, 88, 116, 119–120
glottal, 23, 30–33, 39, 56–57, 67, 70, 128, 136–137, 140, 245–248, 253–255
glottal stop, 31–32, 45, 81–82, 116, 119
Gobu, 2–4, 6–7, 12–13, 192
grammatical category, 73–74, 80, 83
grammatical function, 18, 43, 46–49
grammatical function word, 14, 43, **73**, 80, 85–86, 115
grammatical function word shape (see word pattern)
grammatical tone (see tone)
grammaticalization, 78, 97
Greenberg, 4–5, 89
Gur, 5, 35

Hausa, 127–128, 135, 164
heavenly bodies, 93
hiatus, hiatus resolution, 44, 68, 88, 97, 116, 118–120, 227
hierarchical, hierarchy, 12, 67, 73
[high] (see feature)
history, 9–12
Ibibio, 139–140
iconic lengthening, 83
ideophone, 22, 25, 31–32, 45, 57, 60, 66, 68, **83**–84
Ijo, 127
imperative mood (see mood)
implicational, 18, 62, 76
implosive, 17, 23–25, 28, 49, 122, 127–128, 132–136, 141, 223
inanimate, **89**–93, 190, 204, 212
index of fusion, 87–**88**
index of synthesis, **87**
infinitive, 21, 55, 82, 88, 96, 99–101, 104, 116, 198
inflect, inflection, 31–32, 73, 104–105
intelligibility, 8–9, 13–14
interdiction mood (see mood)
International Phonetic Alphabet (IPA), 23, 25, 32, 34, 45
interpretation, 18, 21, 31, 56, 58–62, 65, 82, 98–99, 102, 142, 160
isolating, **87**
isolation, 73–74, 79–80, 82, 113, 122, 152, 228
Japanese, 74
Kaga, 2–4, 197
kinship term, 31, 79–80, 89–90, 92
Kotto River, 11–12
Kouango, 2
Kpagua, 2, 6, 14, 35
Kpala, 2, 4
labial, 17, 23–27, 33–34, 39, 55, 60, 67–68, 76, 84, 122–127, 135–139, 141, 145, 164, 221–222, 224, 228, 233–237, 252–254
labial flap (see flap)
labialization, 18, 21, 53–63, **54**, 67, 70, 74, 160–163, 223

labial-velar, 23–25, 33–34, 57, 69, 122, 135–141, 222, 248–250, 253–255
labiodental, 17, 25
labiodental flap (see flap)
Langbasi, 2–7, 12–13, 35, 59, 77, 202
Lardil, 74
laryngealization, 18, 128, 133–135
lateral, 23
leftward tone spreading, 18
leftward vowel spreading, 18, 21, 55, 75–76, 116–118, 120, 145, 227
length, 28, 45, 49, 68, 123, 142
level tone (see tone)
lexical exceptions, 118–120
lexical function, 18, 43–46
lexical rule (see rule)
lexical tone (see tone)
lexical word, 18, 70, **73**
lexicostatistic, 5, 7–8
Libenge, 2–4
Linda, 6–9, 16, 35, 38–39, 43, 46, 59–60, 77, 88, 90–91, 96, 99, 101, 104
Lingala, 1, 12–15, 30, 39, 60, 75, 164, 187, 197–198, 204–206, 209–210, 213, 217
lip, 27, 53–54, 127
liquid, 61, 67–68, 82, 142, 152, 226–227
literacy, 17
loan, loanword, 22, 30, 45, 60, 66, 68, 75, 187, 189, 191, 193, 197–198, 200, 204–206, 209–211, 213, 217, 235, 237
locative adverb (see adverb)
locative question word, 115
logophoric pronoun (see pronoun)
[low] (see feature)
LPC (Linear Predictive Coding), 146, 256–271
Luganda, 24, 142
Mangbetu, 123
manner adverb (see adverb)
manner of articulation, 25

Subject Index

Margi, 50, 123
marginal, 22–23, 25, 28, 30, 32, 39, 50, 56, 66, 68, 75
Mba, 89
Mbandja, 2–7, 9, 12, 16, 59, 61, 93, 100
minimal pair, 44–45
minimality condition, minimal word constraint, 18, 70, **73**, 78, 85, 154
mirror image, 71
Mobayi, 3–4
modal, 128, 134
Modiri, 3
   mood (see tense, aspect, and mood)
   certainty mood, 45, 49, 56, 108–109
   conditional mood, 87, 101, 106, 198
   imperative mood, 48, 106–107
   interdiction mood, 48, 107
   obligation mood, 48, 107
   subjunctive mood, 48, 107
mora, moraic, 45, 73, 75, 142
morphology, 1, 7, 15–16, 19, 46, 87–120
   nominal morphology, 88–101
   prepositional morphology, 18–19, 51, 88, 113–115
   verbal morphology, 46–51, 56, 87–88, 101–113
Mpaka, 2–3, 10
narrative text (see text)
nasal, 1, 23–25, 30, 37, 68, 141–145, 156–160
nasalization, nasalized, 1, 23, 34, 37, 120, 122, 145, 156–160, 224
Ndogo, 123
negation, negative, 87–88, 102, 106, 109–112, 193
Ngbaka-Ma'bo, 3–4, 15, 41
Ngbaka-Minagende, 3, 12, 14, 100
Ngbaka-Sere, 11
Ngbandi, 3–4, 11–12, 93, 97, 100, 187, 206
Ngbundu, 3–4, 6

Ngbugbu, 93
Ngbugu, 3–4, 6, 8–9, 35
Ngbulu, 4
Ngombe, 2–3, 13
Ngundu, 4, 35
Niger-Congo, 4–5, 10–11, 16, 62, 89, 127–128, 133
Nilo-Saharan, 5, 11
nominal, 18–19, 74–81, 95–99
nominal morphology (see morphology)
nominal word shape (see word pattern)
nominalization, nominalize, 98–100, 198
non-future tense (see tense)
normal speech (see speaking rate)
normalizing, 150
North Volta-Congo, 5
noun, 1, 5, 19, 25, 31–32, 43, 59, 68, 73–83, 85, 88–90, 92–101, 103, 111, 117, 183, 190, 198, 204
noun class, 5, 89
noun phrase, 80, 90, 94–95, 97, 111, 190
nucleus, 59, 61, 67, 116
Nupe, 164
obligation mood (see mood)
obstruent, 49, 56, 61, 68, 141
off-glide, 54, 56–57, 59–61
on-glide, 59
onomatopoeia, onomatopoetic, 83, 85
onset (syllable), 21–22, 61, 66–67, 74
opacity, 18
optional rule (see rule)
oral, 17, 27, 123, 127, 135–136, 143, 156, 160
ordinal number, 90–91, 183
overapplication, overapply, 18, 78
palatal, 23, 25, 29–30, 38–39, 54–56, 69, 241–245, 253–255
palatalization, 18, 21, 53–63, **54**, 67, 70, 74, 160
Pandu, 3–4
Peripheral Banda (see Banda)

phonation, 128, 133
phoneme, phonemic, 6–7, 18, 21–41, 50, 54–56, 58–62, 65–67, 84, 118, 120–121, 149, 165, 183
phonestheme, 83
phonetic evidence, 36, 122, 142, 160, 162
phonological modification, **94**, 97
phonological processes, 21, 88, 116–120
phonological word, 71
phonotactic, 84, 119
place of articulation, 24–25, 76, 143
plant name, 22, 45, 79, 89, 93
plosive, 24, 28, 127–128
Plot Formants Hypercard, 147
plural, 1, 44, 88–93, 110, 183, 186, 190, 194, 202, 207, 215, 218, 225, 238
Pohnpeian, 54
polysynthetic, **87**
population, 2–4, 13–14
positive, 109
possession, possessive, 109, 111, 186, 188, 196, 203–204, 218
possible word, 123–124, 128–131, 133–134, 143, 156–158
postlexical rule (see rule)
predicate adjective (see adjective)
predicate locative, 109, 112
predicate nominal, 80, 109
prefixation, prefixing, 19, 88, 101–102
prenasalized, prenasalization, 24, 30, 37, 61, 122, 141–144
preposition, 18–19, 43, 51, 73, 77, 88, 111–113, 117
prepositional morphology (see morphology)
primary articulation, 18, 53–54
procedural text (see text)
progressive aspect (see aspect)
pronoun, 31, 46–48, 73–74, 77, 80–81, 86, 101–103, 109, 115, 117, 186, 188, 190–191, 196, 203–204, 211–212, 214, 217–218

logophoric pronoun (3SG.LOG), 107–108, 190–191, 253
same subject pronoun (SS), 36, 47–49, 56, 86, 91, 103, 107–108, 110–112, 117–118, 167–180, 190
proper inclusion, 80, 109, 188
prosodic hierarchy, 73
prothetic augmentation, 18
Proto-Banda, 5, 7
prototype, 84
proverb, 17, 165, 178–181, 193, 227
quantifier, 91–92
raising, 36, 54, 116, 120, 145–146, 152, 160
rapid appraisal, 8
rapid speech (see speaking rate)
Recorded Text Test (RTT), 8
reduplicant, reduplication, 7, 19, 45, 49, 56, 59, 63, 76–77, 79, 84, 87–88, 98–99, 101–102, 105–106, 108, 111–112
reflexive, 115, 212
release, 17–18, 53, 61, 66, 70, 123–124, 132, 135–137, 139–141
repetitive aspect (see aspect)
rising tone (see tone)
root, 18, 21, 46, 49, 55–56, 59, 75–77, 79, 81–82, 87, 89, 94, 98, 100–103, 105–108, 116–117, 120
[round] (see feature)
rule
   lexical rule, 118
   optional rule, 18, 21, 36, 44, 68, 76, 78, 82, 116, 118–120, 127, 145, 152
   postlexical rule, 118
rule-based, 78
Runyambo, 24, 142
Russian, 54
same subject pronoun (see pronoun)
sampling rate, 122
Sango, 12, 14, 97, 191, 193, 204, 206
Sara, Sara-Mbay, 12, 35
schwa, 55, 116–118

Subject Index

secondary articulation, 18, 21, 30, 53–63, 76, 84, 116, 119, 122, 160–163, 226
secret society, 10
Selayarese, 71
semantic restriction, **94**, 97
semi-vowel, 23, 54–55, 59–60, 62, 65, 67–68, 88, 116, 119–120, 124
Senoufo, 67
sequence, 18, 24–25, 30, 43–46, 56, 58–61, 65–68, 70, 84, 116, 141–144, 152–155, 162
shortened, shortening, 18, 68, 82, 109, 119–120, 145, 152–155
SIL, 8, 16, 122, 183
slave trade, 12, 196, 198
slow speech (see speaking rate)
sociolinguistic, 12–14, 22
song, 17
sonorant, 49, 61
sonority, 61, 67
Sonority Dispersion Principle, 67
Sonority Sequencing Principle, 61
sound symbolism, 83
SoundDesigner, 122
speaking rate
    fast, rapid, 18, 122, 152–155
    normal, 44, 122, 152–155, 160
    slow, 122, 160–161
spectrogram, 123–128, 131, 137–141, 143, 146, 152, 154–155, 157–159, 161–163
Speech Analyzer, 122
speech surrogate, 43
spread, spreading, 18–19, 21, 34, 37, 55, 75–76, 116, 118, 120, 145, 227
standard deviation (SD), 123–124, 140–141, 144, 147–149, 153, 156
stative aspect (see aspect)
steady state, 146, 160–161
stem, 90, 105–106
stop, 23–24, 30–32, 45, 53, 61, 67, 81–82, 116, 119, 122–125, 135–137, 139–145, 152, 156, 164, 222

striation, 143
stricture, 53, 61
structural, structualism, structuralist, 16, 21, 61, 65, 88
structural description, 97
structure preserving, 118–120
subjunctive mood (see mood)
subminimal root augmentation, 18, 59, **75**–77, 80, 89, 94, 97, 116, 120
suction, 136–137
Sudan, 2, 5–6, 10–11
Sukuma, 142
suprasegmental modification, 19, 88
syllable, 6–7, 18, 21, 24, 38–39, 46–47, 49, 51, 53–63, 65–71, 74–75, 77, 82, 84, 90, 98, 101–103, 105–107, 113, 116, 118, 142, 145, 154–156, 162
syllable boundary, 54
syllable-final, 67
syllable-initial, 55
syllable pattern, 21, 24, 58–62, 65–68, 70, 84, 90
synchronic, 16, 70
synesthesia, 83
synthetic, 19, 87
t-test, 144, 155
talking drums, 43, 115, 202, 207
Tangbago, 6, 16, 38–39, 43, 59
tap, 25, 123–124
teeth, 27
temporal adverb (see adverb)
tendency, 24, 61, 164
tense
    future tense, 47–48, 103–104, 106, 109
    non-future tense, 47, 87, 103–104, 106, 109
tense, aspect, and mood (TAM), 18, 21, 46, 50–51, 88, 102, 105, 108–109
text
    narrative text, 165–175
    procedural text, 165, 175–178
Togbo, 3–4, 6–9, 12–14, 95, 212

token, 17, 122–123, 127–128, 133–136, 139–140, 143–147, 153, 155–156, 160–161
tonal melody, 18, **50**–51, 100, 103
tonal polarity, 18, **51**, 113
tone
  contour tone, 43–46, 60, 68, 84, 152, 155, 162
  falling tone, 18, 32, 43–45, 105, 108
  grammatical tone, 46–49
  level tone, 18, 43–46, 51–52, 68, 90, 99, 102, 119, 155, 162
  lexical tone, 43–46, 103
  rising tone, 18, 43–44, 47, 84, 90, 103
tongue, 17, 27, 37, 54, 127, 160
Toro, 10
transcription, 1, 23, 46, 55, 121, 163, 165, 183
transition (formant), 17, 123–124, 137–139, 141, 162–163
trill, 23, 28
Twi, 62
typology, typological, 4–6, 15, 24, 35, 55, 62, 66, 73, 87–88, 121, 136, 145
Ubangi, Ubangian, 2–5, 10–12, 24, 31, 41, 49, 67, 89, 93, 97, 99–100
underlying, 18, 23, 43, 50, 70–71, 75–76, 78, 81, 94, 99, 114
universal, 18, 35–36, 62, 66, 164
utterance, 61, 132, 160
Vara, 6–9
variation, 14–15, 21–22, 25, 37, 41, **94**, 96, 128, 141
velar, 23–25, 27, 30–33, 39, 56–57, 67, 69, 135–137, 139, 141, 164, 245–248, 253–255
velarization, 28
verb, 19, 21, 25, 31–32, 43, 46–51, 55–56, 68, 73, 77–85, 87–88, 91, 95–112, 116–117, 188, 198
verbal morphology (see morphology)
verbal word shape (see word pattern)
video, 17, 27
vocal cord, 128

voice onset time (VOT), 136, 139–141, 164
voiced, voicing, 17, 23–24, 27, 49, 128, 136, 142–144, 164
voiceless, 23–24, 128, 134–135, 141–142, 164
vowel, 1, 18, 21–23, 25, 27, 34–41, 43–49, 54–62, 65, 67–68, 70–71, 75–78, 80, 82–85, 88, 90, 92, 94, 97–98, 116–120, 122, 124, 127, 145–165, 181, 224, 227–228, 233–252, 256–274
vowel duration (see duration)
vowel epenthesis (V-epenthesis), 18, **70**, 76, 78, 120
vowel nasalization (V-nasalization), 23, 27, 37, 120, 156–160, 224
vowel shortening (V-shortening), 18, 68, 82, 120, 145, 152–155
vowel space, 36, 55, 60, 145–152
vowel system, 18, 35–36, 58, 145
waveform, 133–134, 136
whistle-talk, 43
word minimality condition (see minimality condition)
word pattern, word shape, 18, 32, 60, 68, 73–86
  adverbial word shape, 83–85
  grammatical function word shape, 85–86
  nominal word shape, 74–81
  verbal word shape, 82–83
word-initial, 21–22, 25, 28, 30–31, 33, 37–39, 56, 58, 66, 74, 90, 126, 132, 139, 141, 156, 233–250
word-medial, 22, 25, 27, 29–31, 33–34, 38–39, 56, 233–250
wordlist, 6–7, 10, 17, 85, 121–122, 183–219, 229–231
xylophone, 43, 203
Yakpa, 2, 4, 6, 8–9, 35, 196
Yangere, 6–9, 12
Yaoundé, 16–17, 122
Yidin^y, 74
Zaire, 1
Zande (see Azande)
Zongo, 2, 4

SIL International and
The University of Texas at Arlington
Publications in Linguistics

Recent Publications

139. Language and life: Essays in memory of Kenneth L. Pike, ed. by Mary Ruth Wise, Thomas N. Headland, and Ruth M. Brend. 2003.
138. Case and agreement in Abaza, by Brian O'Herin. 2002.
137. Pragmatics of persuasive discourse of Spanish television advertising, by Karol J. Hardin. 2001.
136. Quiegolani Zapotec syntax: A Principles and Parameters account, by Cheryl A. Black. 2000.
135. A grammar of Sochiapan Chinantec: Studies in Chinantec languages 6, by David Paul Foris. 2000.
134. A reference grammar of Northern Embera languages: Studies in the languages of Colombia 7, by Charles Arthur Mortensen. 1999.
133. The geometry and features of tone, by Keith Snider. 1999.
132. Desano grammar: Studies in the languages of Colombia 6, by Marion Miller. 1999.
131. The structure of evidential categories in Wanka Quechua, by Rick Floyd. 1999.
130. Cubeo grammar: Studies in the languages of Colombia 5, by Nancy L. Morse and Michael B. Maxwell. 1999.
129. Aspects of Zaiwa prosody: An autosegmental account, by Mark W. Wannemacher. 1998.
128. Tense and aspect in Obolo grammar and discourse, by Uche Aaron. 1998.
127. Case Grammar applied, by Walter A. Cook, S. J. 1998.
126. The Dong language in Guizhou Province, China, by Long Yaohong and Zheng Guoqiao, translated from Chinese by D. Norman Geary. 1998.
125. Vietnamese classifiers in narrative texts, by Karen Ann Daley. 1998.
124. Comparative Kadai: The Tai branch, ed. by Jerold A. Edmondson and David B. Solnit. 1997.
123. Why there are no clitics: An alternative perspective on pronominal allomorphy, by Daniel L. Everett. 1996.

For further information or a full listing of SIL publications contact:

International Academic Bookstore
SIL International
7500 W. Camp Wisdom Road
Dallas, TX 75236-5699

Voice: 972-708-7404
Fax: 972-708-7363
Email: academic_books@sil.org
Internet: http://www.ethnologue.com

www.ingramcontent.com/pod-product-compliance
Lightning Source LLC
Chambersburg PA
CBHW052151300426
44115CB00011B/1617